INTERNATIONAL LAW IMMUNITIES AND EMPLOYMENT CLAIMS

This book provides the first comprehensive analysis of the international law regime of jurisdictional immunities in employment matters. Three main arguments lie at its heart. Firstly, this study challenges the widely held belief that international immunity law requires staff disputes to be subject to blanket or quasi-absolute immunity from jurisdiction. Secondly, it argues that it is possible to identify well-defined standards of limited immunity to be applied in the context of employment litigation against foreign states, international organisations and diplomatic and consular agents. Thirdly, it maintains that the interaction between the applicable immunity rules and international human rights law gives rise to a legal regime that can provide adequate protection to the rights of employees. This work is a much-needed study into an under-researched field of international and employment law.

International Law Immunities and Employment Claims

A Critical Appraisal

Pierfrancesco Rossi

• HART •

OXFORD • LONDON • NEW YORK • NEW DELHI • SYDNEY

HART PUBLISHING

Bloomsbury Publishing Plc

Kemp House, Chawley Park, Cumnor Hill, Oxford, OX2 9PH, UK

1385 Broadway, New York, NY 10018, USA

29 Earlsfort Terrace, Dublin 2, Ireland

HART PUBLISHING, the Hart/Stag logo, BLOOMSBURY and the Diana logo are trademarks of Bloomsbury Publishing Plc

First published in Great Britain 2021

A catalogue record for this book is available from the British Library.

Library of Congress Cataloging-in-Publication data

Names: Rossi, Pierfrancesco, author.

Title: International law immunities and employment claims : a critical appraisal / Pierfrancesco Rossi.

Description: Oxford ; New York : Hart, 2021. | Includes bibliographical references and index.

Identifiers: LCCN 2021032701 (print) | LCCN 2021032702 (ebook) | ISBN 9781509952977 (hardback) | ISBN 9781509953011 (paperback) | ISBN 9781509952991 (pdf) | ISBN 9781509952984 (Epub)

Subjects: LCSH: Administrative agencies—Officials and employees—Foreign countries. | International officials and employees—Legal status, laws, etc. | Labor laws and legislation. | International agencies—Privileges and immunities. | Immunities of foreign states.

Classification: LCC K3440 . R67 2021 (print) | LCC K3440 (ebook) | DDC 341.3/3—dc23

LC record available at https://lccn.loc.gov/2021032701

LC ebook record available at https://lccn.loc.gov/2021032702

ISBN: HB: 978-1-50995-297-7
ePDF: 978-1-50995-299-1
ePub: 978-1-50995-298-4

Typeset by Compuscript Ltd, Shannon

To find out more about our authors and books visit www.hartpublishing.co.uk. Here you will find extracts, author information, details of forthcoming events and the option to sign up for our newsletters.

Ai miei genitori

ACKNOWLEDGEMENTS

Writing this book would have been impossible without the guidance, encouragement and friendship of my mentors, Massimo Iovane and Fulvio M Palombino. I am also very much indebted to Pietro Pustorino and Guido Raimondi, for the trust they have shown in me, and to Daniele Amoroso, Riccardo Pavoni and Giovanni Zarra, for providing me with useful materials. Part of the research for this book was carried out at the Max Planck Institute for Comparative Public Law and International Law, where I benefited from a visiting fellowship funded by the Max Planck Society: thank you to the colleagues and friends I met in Heidelberg for stimulating discussions. Many thanks are due to the Hart Publishing team, notably Sinead Moloney, Sasha Jawed, Chris Myers and Tom Adams, for their professional, friendly and patient assistance. Finally, I would like to thank Caterina, my first reader and critic, and my parents, to whom this book is dedicated, for supporting me with love in innumerable ways.

Pierfrancesco Rossi
April 2021

TABLE OF CONTENTS

TABLE OF CASES

International

International Court of Justice

Anglo-Iranian Oil Co Case Judgment (Preliminary Objections) [1952] ICJ Rep 93 130
Application for Review of Judgement No 158 of the UNAT (Advisory Opinion) [1973] ICJ Rep 166 41
Application for Review of Judgement No 273 of the UNAT (Advisory Opinion) [1982] ICJ Rep 325 41
Application for Review of Judgement No 333 of the UNAT (Advisory Opinion) [1987] ICJ Rep 18 41
Armed Activities on the Territory of the Congo (Democratic Republic of the Congo v Uganda) Judgment [2005] ICJ Rep 168 142
Case Concerning the Arrest Warrant of 11 April 2000 Judgment [2002] ICJ Rep 3 .... 7–8, 11, 156
Effect of awards of compensation made by the UN Administrative Tribunal (Advisory Opinion) [1954] ICJ Rep 47 40
Fisheries Case (United Kingdom v Norway) Judgment [1951] ICJ Rep 116 142
Judgment No 2867 of the Administrative Tribunal of the International Labour Organization upon a Complaint Filed against the International Fund for Agricultural Development (Advisory Opinion) [2012] ICJ Rep 10 41
Judgments of the Administrative Tribunal of the ILO upon Complaints made against the UNESCO (Advisory Opinion) [1956] ICJ Rep 77 41
Jurisdictional Immunities of the State (Germany v Italy: Greece intervening) Judgment [2012] ICJ Rep 99 .... 8–9, 11–12, 15, 21, 144–45, 216–18
North Sea Continental Shelf (Federal Republic of Germany/Denmark; Federal Republic of Germany/Netherlands) Judgment [1969] ICJ Rep 3 143–44
Oil Platforms (Islamic Republic of Iran v United States of America) Judgment (Preliminary Objections) [1996] ICJ Rep 803 142
Oil Platforms (Islamic Republic of Iran v United States of America) Judgment [2003] ICJ Rep 161 174
Reparation for Injuries Suffered in the Service of the United Nations (Advisory Opinion) [1949] ICJ Rep 174 24
Territorial Dispute (Libyan Arab Jamahiriya/Chad) Judgment [1994] ICJ Reports 6 170

European Court of Human Rights

International Administrative Tribunals

Court of Justice of the European Union

European Commission of Human Rights

Human Rights Committee

Inter-American Court of Human Rights

Ad Hoc Arbitral Tribunals

National

Argentina

Bangladesh

Belgium

Greece

India

Ireland

Italy

Kenya

Lithuania

Mexico

Netherlands

New Zealand

Nigeria

Norway

Philippines

Poland

Portugal

Romania

Russia

Spain

Sri Lanka

Sweden

Switzerland

Ukraine

United Kingdom

United States of America

Uruguay

Venezuela

Zimbabwe

TABLE OF INSTRUMENTS

Treaties

Statutes of International Courts and Tribunals

UN General Assembly

International Law Commission

Human Rights Committee

Other United Nations documents

Council of Europe

European Union

North Atlantic Treaty Organization

Institut de droit international

International Law Association

National legislation

Argentina

Australia

Austria

Canada

France

Italy

Israel

Japan

Kenya

Malawi

Pakistan

Russia

Singapore

South Africa

Spain

Switzerland

United States of America

United Kingdom

1

Introduction

Large numbers of individuals find themselves in the employ of foreign states, international organisations (IOs) and diplomatic and consular agents, occupying positions ranging from the most menial of jobs to highly responsible administrative, technical or managerial roles.[1] Civil disputes arising from these employment relationships are frequently brought before the courts of the countries where the plaintiff employees perform their work.[2] Such legal actions are manifold. Most commonly, they concern wages and other entitlements (such as sick pay, holiday pay, maternity or paternity leave or retirement plans), unfair dismissal, discrimination based on sex, gender, religion, age, disability or other grounds, work accidents, workplace harassment and retaliation or trade union rights. In the most egregious cases, the employees may have been the victims of human trafficking, abuse or enslavement. When cases of this sort end up in court, the issue arises whether the respondent employer is entitled to immunity from jurisdiction under international law. The objective of this book, in a nutshell, is to answer this question.

The international legal regime of jurisdictional immunities in employment matters is fraught with a peculiar tension. On the one hand, states, IOs and diplomatic and consular agents would not be able to perform their functions without hiring and managing a workforce. The need to give these employers broad latitude to pursue their sovereign or institutional goals unimpeded may weigh the balance, on policy grounds, in favour of immunity from labour lawsuits. On the other hand, though, employment is a contract relationship whose parties should be expected to be able to obtain redress whenever their rights are infringed. Also, it is an anomalous contract relationship where one party is in a position of weaker bargaining power and structural subordination, which produces a particular need

[1] No universal legal definition of employment relationship exists. For a comparative overview, see N Countouris, *The Changing Law of the Employment Relationship. Comparative Analyses in the European Context* (London, Routledge, 2007). See also International Labour Conference Employment Relationship Recommendation No 198/2006. For the purposes of this study, employment can be broadly defined as any contractual arrangement whereby an employee undertakes to perform services for an employer under the employer's direction and control in exchange for remuneration.

[2] Notably, employment litigation makes up the largest share of domestic lawsuits filed against both foreign states and IOs: H Fox and P Webb, *The Law of State Immunity*, 3rd edn (Oxford, Oxford University Press, 2013) 440; C Ryngaert, 'The Immunity of International Organizations Before Domestic Courts: Recent Trends' (2010) 7 *International Organizations Law Review* 121, 122.

of legal protection for the human rights of the employee.[3] The tension between the public/institutional needs of the employers on the one hand and the contractual basis of the employment relationship and the safeguard of the workers' human rights on the other may be described as a 'duality' intrinsic to any relationship of employment between private individuals and persons entitled to immunities under international law.[4] This duality is a source of conceptual difficulties that make the state of international law in this field look largely unsettled and, to a degree, unsettling. More specifically, there appears to be still no generally accepted answer to the question of how to strike an appropriate balance between the needs of employers and those of employees in the ambit of immunity law. The ensuing uncertainties are problematic insofar as they undermine the consistency of the international immunity law regime and open the door to differential treatment and discrimination among workers.

Judicial and scholarly opinions have often treated the interests of employers as overriding, giving rise to a widespread belief that such persons are entitled to be totally immunised from domestic employment litigation. Notably, the majority view holds that IOs should enjoy blanket immunity from state jurisdiction concerning staff disputes, such claims being reserved to internal remedies set up by the organisation itself.[5] Municipal courts have refrained from adjudicating labour disputes with sitting diplomats, and the employees' entitlement to bring consuls or former diplomats before the receiving state's courts is contested.[6] As for foreign states, national courts have frequently treated any relationship of employment as an immune act in public law – particularly, but not exclusively, for work performed at embassies, consulates or other sovereign establishments.[7] The pervasiveness of the absolutist approach to employer immunities suggests that this tendency is not contingent solely on the specific rules of each of the three areas of immunity law analysed in this study. Rather, it may be seen as having its roots in the nature of the employment relationship itself – that is, in its structural proximity to the functions of persons enjoying immunities under international law. But this difficulty to depart from models of blanket immunity from jurisdiction is worrisome from the standpoint of the workers' rights protection. Webb has argued that the application

[3] On the protection of workers' rights in international law, see generally BJ Fick (ed), *International Labour Law* (Cheltenham, Edward Elgar, 2015).

[4] P Webb, 'The Immunity of States, Diplomats and International Organizations in Employment Disputes: The New Human Rights Dilemma?' (2016) 27 *European Journal of International Law* 745, 767.

[5] CH Brower, 'International Immunities: Some Dissident Views on the Role of Municipal Courts' (2001) 41 *Virginia Journal of International Law* 1, 69–70; F Seyersted, *Common Law of International Organizations* (Leiden, Nijhoff, 2008) 163. See also International Labour Organization Administrative Tribunal, Judgment No 2540, 12 July 2006, para 27: 'International civil servants – no matter how high their rank is – cannot protect their rights in national tribunals. Their only recourse is through the mechanisms established by the relevant Staff Rules.'

[6] In favour of absolute immunity of diplomatic and consular agents from staff disputes, see, eg *Tabion v Mufti and Mufti* 73 F.3d 535 (4th Cir 1996).

[7] On this trend, see H Fox, 'Employment Contracts as an Exception to State Immunity: Is All Public Service Immune?' (1995) 66 *British Year Book of International Law* 97.

of international law immunities in employment matters yields a 'human rights dilemma',[8] and concerns have been raised that, to the extent they leave workers without redress, immunities may be a free pass to abuses.[9]

In recent years, a vast movement of courts has attempted to curb this trend by challenging the immunities of employers from the standpoint of human rights law. The European Court of Human Rights (ECtHR), for instance, has consistently held that blanket grants of immunity to foreign states violate the employees' right to a fair trial under Article 6 of the European Convention of Human Rights (ECHR).[10] IO immunities too have come under increasing pressure, at least in cases when IO employees are left without effective redress from IO internal justice systems.[11] However, what amount of immunity constitutes a tolerable compression of an employee's right of access to justice remains highly controversial. No agreement seems to exist in case law as to what constitutes an adequate 'alternative remedy' for IO staff.[12] It is also unclear whether the employee's lack of access to an effective remedy may bear any relevance in matters of state or diplomatic immunity.[13] Most worryingly, courts in several non-European countries have remained extraneous to this trend, giving rise to fears that such challenges to employer immunities may be no more than a European anomaly.[14]

A further difficulty arising from the employment relationship's 'duality' is that, where courts and commentators have rejected a blanket approach to employer immunities, the development of limited standards of immunity from jurisdiction has proven contentious. State immunity law provides the prime example of such problems. The application to labour of the distinction between *acta jure imperii* and *acta jure gestionis* – the classic formulation of the restrictive state immunity doctrine – is problematic, because it is hard to classify employment with foreign states as a purely public or private act. Arguably, it has elements of both: it is a private law relationship which is essential in performing a state's public law activities,[15] so much so that the International Law Commission's (ILC) Special Rapporteur on state immunity, Sompong Sucharitkul, referred to employment as

[8] Webb (n 4).

[9] See, eg AM Castro, 'Abuse of Diplomatic Immunity in Family Courts: There's Nothing Diplomatic about Domestic Immunity' (2014) 47 *Suffolk University Law Review* 353.

[10] See, eg *Cudak v Lithuania* App No 15869/02, 23 March 2010. See also *Benkharbouche v Secretary of State for Foreign and Commonwealth Affairs and Secretary of State for Foreign and Commonwealth Affairs and Libya v Janah* [2017] UKSC 62.

[11] *Waite and Kennedy v Germany* App No 26083/94, 18 February 1999; *Beer and Regan v Germany* App No 28934/95, 18 February 1999.

[12] Ryngaert (n 2) 123.

[13] Against see *Ndayegamiye-Mporamazina v Switzerland* App No 16874/12, 5 February 2019, para 64.

[14] R Garnett, 'State and Diplomatic Immunity and Employment Rights: European Law to the Rescue?' (2015) 64 *ICLQ* 783.

[15] See, eg R van Alebeek and R Pavoni, 'Immunities of States and their Officials' in A Nollkaemper and A Reinisch (eds), *International Law in Domestic Courts: A Casebook* (Oxford, Oxford University Press, 2018) 100, 116; B Conforti and M Iovane, *Diritto internazionale*, 12th edn (Naples, Editoriale scientifica, 2021) 285, arguing that the distinction between acts *jure imperii* and *jure gestionis* is generally unhelpful in the field of employment claims.

the 'darkest area of the grey zones'.[16] Nor does an analysis of state practice provide easy solutions. According to the prevailing view in legal doctrine, not much seems to have changed since 1983, when the ILC grumbled about the 'startling number of inconsistencies and contradictions' among national judicial decisions on state immunity in labour matters.[17] Some 30 years later, it was still asserted in scholarship that the heterogeneity of practice 'ma[de] it impossible to deduce any uniform rules'.[18] The finalisation of the UN Convention on State Immunity (UNCSI)[19] – the outcome of 20-odd years of work by the ILC – does not appear to have settled the doubts pervading this area of the law of state immunity. Some courts, including the ECtHR, have turned to the UNCSI's provision on contracts of employment as codification of international custom,[20] but the accuracy of this sweeping assessment has been openly questioned in the subsequent literature and case law.[21]

Against this backdrop, this book intends to bring clarity to the state of the international law regime of jurisdictional immunities in employment matters.[22] Three main arguments lie at the heart of this study. First, the book challenges the widely held belief that international immunity law generally requires staff disputes to be subject to blanket or quasi-absolute immunity from jurisdiction. Secondly, it puts forward that it is possible to identify sufficiently well-defined standards of limited immunity to be applied in the context of employment litigation against states, IOs and diplomatic and consular agents. Thirdly, it argues that the interaction between the applicable immunity rules and the relevant rules of international human rights law gives rise to a legal regime which is able to provide adequate protection to the rights of employees.

[16] S Sucharitkul, 'Fifth Report on Jurisdictional Immunities of States and Their Property', ILC Yearbook 1983, vol II, Part 1, 38.

[17] ibid 34.

[18] X Yang, *State Immunity in International Law* (Cambridge, Cambridge University Press, 2012) 196.

[19] United Nations Convention on Jurisdictional Immunities of States and Their Property 2004, not yet entered into force.

[20] *Cudak* (n 10) para 67; Italy, Court of Cassation, *Embassy of Spain to the Holy See v De la Grana Gonzales*, 18 April 2014, No 9034.

[21] R Pavoni, 'The Myth of the Customary Nature of the United Nations Convention on State Immunity: Does the End Justify the Means?' in A van Aaken and I Motoc (eds), *European Convention on Human Rights and General International Law* (Oxford, Oxford University Press, 2018) 264; Opinion of Advocate General Mengozzi, Case No C-154/11 *Mahamdia v Algeria*, 24 May 2012, para 26.

[22] Two clarifications are in order as regards the scope of this work. First, this study is only concerned with immunities from civil claims. Criminal proceedings, which may perform an important role in preventing abuses by individual employers like diplomatic agents, are outside of its scope. Secondly, this book concerns only immunity from adjudicative jurisdiction and not from execution. This does not mean that the latter is not important in labour matters: if the respondent employer does not voluntarily comply with a judgment in favour of an employee, it is natural for the case to proceed to the stage of enforcement (see, eg Belgium, Court of Cassation, *General Secretariat of the ACP Group v BD*, 21 December 2009, ILDC 1576 (BE 2009)). However, because immunity from execution is regulated by different legal norms than immunity from adjudication (Yang (n 18) 361–62), the problems arising in the context of employment-related enforcement proceedings fall back into general issues of immunity law.

These arguments are developed over the course of five chapters.

Chapter two lays down a framework for the rest of the book by performing an overview of the immunities from civil jurisdiction to which foreign states, IOs and diplomatic and consular agents are entitled under international law. This chapter shows that, for all that the international law immunities make up a composite and diversified legal regime, in all three areas international law has developed non-absolute (ie limited) standards of immunity from civil jurisdiction. This suggests that, as a default rule, blanket approaches to immunity from civil jurisdiction are unwarranted, and that it is necessary to distinguish between admissible and non-admissible exercises of civil adjudicatory jurisdiction.

Chapter three turns to the problem of the persistence of absolute immunity in employment disputes. It shows that, in apparent contrast with the default rule of limited immunity in the context of civil litigation, both judicial decisions and scholarly writings manifest a substantial resistance to the application of non-absolute standards of immunity in employment matters. This chapter challenges the rationales for the persistence of absolute immunity in labour litigation and submits that none of the common justifications for absolute or quasi-absolute immunity holds up on closer examination, except for cases where absolute immunity results from unequivocal treaty provisions. The argument that this chapter puts forward is that any form of 'employment exceptionalism' in international immunity law is unwarranted. Just like any other form of civil litigation, it is necessary to devise limited immunity standards applicable to employment cases.

Chapter four examines how the doctrine of restrictive state immunity has been adapted to the peculiar context of employment litigation. The chapter's main claim is that this process of adaptation has taken place through the development of immunity standards that are peculiar to the area of labour and to a good extent are alternative to the classic formulation of restrictive state immunity, ie the distinction between *acta jure imperii* and *acta jure gestionis*. The discussion analyses the various employment-specific immunity criteria developed in international and domestic immunity instruments, as well as in domestic judicial decisions, and how such criteria have been applied to concrete cases. In light of a comprehensive analysis of existing state practice, the chapter concludes by bringing clarity to the much-debated issue of the status of the customary international law of state immunity in employment matters.

Chapter five aims to delineate non-absolute standards of immunity applicable to claims against employers other than the foreign state. Its key argument is that, despite the comparatively limited judicial practice available, it is possible to flesh out viable standards of limited immunity from staff claims brought against IOs and diplomatic and consular agents, both in post and after the end of posting. It further argues that, to this end, restrictive immunity standards developed in the context of employment disputes with states may, to some extent, provide relevant guidance *mutatis mutandis*.

Finally, chapter six investigates the interplay between the content of immunity law, as detailed in the previous chapters, and the employees' right of access to justice under international human rights law. After discussing the two main judicial approaches to the accommodation of such conflict, this chapter suggests that the adoption of a consistent approach is critical in order to avoid remedy gaps and differential treatment among workers. To this end, it submits that the rights of employees should be protected through a combination of limited immunity standards and of the principle of equivalent protection as developed in a growing body of human rights jurisprudence.

2

The International Law Immunities from Civil Jurisdiction – An Overview

I. Introduction

This chapter presents an overview of the immunities from civil jurisdiction arising from international law. Its main purpose is to identify the legal standards governing the scope of such immunities and the legal sources where these standards are set forth. The chapter also aims to lay down a broader conceptual framework for the rest of the book. To this end, it begins by clarifying the basic legal features of immunity rules at large, including their relationship to the concept of jurisdiction and to questions of substantive law (section II), and goes on to shed light on the rationale underpinning the international law immunities from civil jurisdiction (section III). The rest of the chapter then separately discusses the legal regime of the immunities enjoyed by foreign states (section IV), international organisations (IOs) (section V) and diplomatic and consular agents (section VI), assessing, for each type of immunity, the relevant legal sources and the applicable immunity standards. In the light of this analysis, the chapter submits that a common principle underlying this composite legal regime is that blanket grants of immunity from civil adjudicatory jurisdiction are unwarranted as a default rule. Save for express exceptions, international law lays down limited standards of immunity, ie it requires to draw a line between admissible and non-admissible exercises of jurisdiction (section VII).

II. Basic Concepts: Immunities, Jurisdiction and Substantive Law

In international law, immunities from legal process constitute restrictions on the power of national courts to exercise jurisdiction over certain proceedings. The assessment of jurisdiction logically precedes any discussion on immunity: if a court has no jurisdiction in the first place, no issue of immunity will arise.[1] As the International

[1] *Case Concerning the Arrest Warrant of 11 April 2000* Judgment [2002] ICJ Rep 3, Joint Separate Opinion of Judges Higgins, Kooijmans and Buergenthal, paras 3–4.

Court of Justice (ICJ) put it in *Arrest Warrant*, 'the rules governing the jurisdiction of national courts must be carefully distinguished from those governing jurisdictional immunities: jurisdiction does not imply absence of immunity, while absence of immunity does not imply jurisdiction'.[2]

Immunity rules impose obligations on the territorial state not to exercise jurisdiction, and confer a corresponding right not to be embroiled in judicial proceedings upon the subject that enjoys them.[3] Where the grant of immunity is not required – that is, where there is no prohibition under international law to exercise jurisdiction – a state is free to exercise its jurisdiction or not. Whether or not it chooses to do so is none of immunity law's concern. The idea that states may voluntarily refrain from exercising jurisdiction even where there is no obligation to do so is often expressed, in immunity law terminology, by saying that it is permissible to grant broader immunities than international law requires.[4] However, because international immunity law is only concerned with cases where the grant of immunity is *obligatory*, such unilateral grants of immunity are properly not a matter of international immunity law. They may instead raise issues of human rights law, namely whether the power of states to grant immunities on a unilateral basis should be limited by the right of individuals to have access to a court.[5]

Another basic property of immunity rules is their procedural character.[6] These norms are concerned with whether a court should exercise jurisdiction over a given claim and are normally applied *in limine litis* before addressing the merits.[7] An immediate effect of this feature is that immunity should be granted if provided for at the time of the proceedings, regardless of what the status of the law was when the underlying facts occurred or the dispute arose.[8] Furthermore, the procedural nature of the norms under scrutiny defines their interactions with questions of substantive law, ie the law applicable to the merits of the case. As a matter of principle, immunity law and substantive law operate on different levels.[9] While immunity bars the conduct of judicial proceedings, in no case does it entail an exemption from the law: whoever enjoys jurisdictional immunity under international law remains entirely subject to the substantive laws of the territorial state.[10]

[2] *Arrest Warrant* (n 1) Judgment, para 59.

[3] *Jurisdictional Immunities of the State (Germany v Italy: Greece intervening)* Judgment [2012] ICJ Rep 99, para 106.

[4] ibid para 55: 'States sometimes decide to accord an immunity more extensive than that required by international law'.

[5] See further ch 6.

[6] *Arrest Warrant* (n 1) para 60.

[7] On the distinction between procedural and substantive law, see S Talmon, 'Jus Cogens after Germany v Italy: Substantive and Procedural Rules Distinguished' (2012) 25 *Leiden Journal of International Law* 979, 982.

[8] *Jurisdictional Immunities* (n 3) para 58.

[9] ibid para 58: 'the law of immunity is essentially procedural in nature … and is thus entirely distinct from the substantive law which determines whether that conduct is lawful or unlawful'.

[10] See, eg Vienna Convention on Diplomatic Relations 1961 (VCDR), Art 41(1), setting forth a general duty upon diplomatic personnel to respect local laws.

And, indeed, where immunity is waived, national courts are fully entitled to adjudicate on the merits of a claim.[11] The applicability of domestic law may be excluded by other (substantive) norms of international or national law, but these so-called 'privileges' are unrelated to immunity norms.[12]

Just as the content of immunity rules does not affect substantive law, the reverse is also true: the reach of immunity is, in principle, not directly affected by the interaction with substantive international norms. This was restated in particularly categorical terms in *Jurisdictional Immunities*, where the ICJ refused to derive consequences in terms of immunity law from the fact that the proceedings concerned violations of *jus cogens*. The Court reasoned that, despite the higher status of *jus cogens* in the hierarchy of international legal sources, *jus cogens* could not override norms on state immunity because it had a purely substantive nature and therefore no direct conflict with state immunity could possibly arise.[13] This approach, as is well known, has not been immune from criticism, and one of the critiques it has received takes issue precisely with the categorisation of immunity as a purely procedural plea. In his dissent, Judge Cançado Trindade wrote that 'the separation between procedural and substantive law is not ontologically nor deontologically viable'.[14] This criticism, however, does not so much concern the conceptual categorisation of immunities as procedural norms as the effects that this qualification produces in the field of breaches of *jus cogens*.[15] It is a normative more than an analytical criticism.[16] Indeed, there is no evidence in legal literature of any tendency to dispose of the procedural character of immunity rules where it is not a matter of breaches of peremptory norms. None of the critics of the procedural–substantive divide, for example, suggests that a court should apply the rules of immunity as they were at the time when the facts of the dispute occurred, as would be the case if immunity were a substantive defence.[17]

Of course, to say that immunity rules have a procedural nature does not mean that there can be no tension between immunity and substantive norms. By preventing private parties from bringing their claims to court, immunity may limit

[11] H Fox and P Webb, *The Law of State Immunity*, 3rd edn (Oxford, Oxford University Press, 2013) 21.

[12] See, eg Arts 33–36 VCDR. On the distinction between privileges and immunities, see J Foakes and E Denza, 'Privileges and Immunities of Diplomatic Agents' in I Roberts (ed), *Satow's Diplomatic Practice*, 7th edn (Oxford, Oxford University Press, 2016) 246, 265 ff.

[13] *Jurisdictional Immunities* (n 3) paras 92–97. Similarly, see *Jones v Ministry of Interior Al-Mamlaka Al-Arabyia AS Saudiya (the Kingdom of Saudi Arabia)* [2006] UKHL 16.

[14] *Jurisdictional Immunities* (n 3) Dissenting Opinion of Judge Cançado Trindade, para 295. In the literature, see, eg A Orakhelashvili, 'State Immunity and Hierarchy of Norms: Why the House of Lords Got It Wrong' (2008) 18 *European Journal of International Law* 955.

[15] Talmon (n 7) 1002.

[16] Orakhelashvili, 'State Immunity' (n 14) 969, rejecting the distinction 'as necessarily leading to impunity'.

[17] In *Jurisdictional Immunities* (n 3) Germany contended that state immunity was a substantive rule of international law: see Memorial of the Federal Republic of Germany, 12 June 2009, para 92. This was strategically aimed at inducing the ICJ to apply the law of state immunity in force at the time of World War II.

or negate the enjoyment of substantive rights.[18] However, this does not affect the content of immunity law per se. As will be analysed more thoroughly in chapter six, this tension may instead be managed through coordination between immunity law and the human right of access to justice, ie the norm which entitles individuals to a procedure before a court or some other legal remedy. The right of access to justice is a procedural norm that operates on the same plane as immunity norms.[19] A direct normative conflict between the two sets of rules may therefore arise; indeed, many national and international courts – including the main protagonist, the European Court of Human Rights (ECtHR) – have developed an extensive jurisprudence on how such conflict should be resolved.

A final defining feature of immunity rules is that they set forth obligations of result.[20] Immunity does nothing other than requiring that jurisdiction not be exercised over certain claims, and is unconcerned with the means through which this outcome is achieved. The procedural details of how jurisdiction is to be denied are governed by domestic law. An international obligation to grant immunity is not breached if a national court reaches the required outcome by relying on doctrines other than immunity, eg the lack of subject-matter jurisdiction or the principle of *forum non conveniens*; what matters is for the court to decline to exercise jurisdiction on the merits.[21] It is also a matter of national law whether immunity should be recognised by a court *proprio motu* or the defendant should raise it during the proceedings.[22] National practice varies between states where the litigants have to raise a plea of immunity[23] and others, arguably the majority, where courts should decide on immunity on their own motion.[24] From the standpoint of international law, an assessment by the courts *proprio motu* is undoubtedly preferable: because a failure to appear before a court to claim immunity does not in itself signify a waiver,[25] not granting immunity when immunity is not pleaded may lead to a breach of international law. However, even

[18] E Cannizzaro, 'A Higher Law for Treaties?' in E Cannizzaro (ed), *The Law of Treaties Beyond the Vienna Convention* (Oxford, Oxford University Press, 2011) 425, 434.

[19] M Iovane, 'Conflicts between State-Centred and Human-Centred International Norms' in R Pisillo Mazzeschi and P De Sena (eds), *Global Justice, Human Rights and the Modernization of International Law* (Cham, Springer, 2018) 205, 218.

[20] A Reinisch, *International Organizations before National Courts* (Cambridge, Cambridge University Press, 2000) 138.

[21] M Karagiannakis, 'State Immunity and Fundamental Human Rights' (1998) 11 *Leiden Journal of International Law* 9, 15.

[22] E Denza, *Diplomatic Law: Commentary on the Vienna Convention on Diplomatic Relations*, 4th edn (Oxford, Oxford University Press, 2016) 255, noting that the VCDR does not prescribe when or how national courts should assess the entitlement to diplomatic immunity.

[23] See, eg Foreign States Immunity Law 2008 (Israel), s 12; *Gould Inc v Pechiney Ugine Kuhlmann* 853 F.2d 445 (6th Cir 1988).

[24] See, eg UK State Immunity Act 1978, s 1(2). See also United Nations Convention on Jurisdictional Immunities of States and Their Property 2004 (UNCSI), Art 6, not yet in force.

[25] C Amirfar, 'Waivers of Jurisdictional Immunity' in T Ruys and N Angelet (eds), *The Cambridge Handbook of Immunities and International Law* (Cambridge, Cambridge University Press, 2019) 167, 175.

the procedural details of a determination *proprio motu* may vary significantly, depending on national civil procedure.[26]

III. The Functional Rationale of the International Law Immunities from Civil Jurisdiction

The above theoretical rundown clarified the key structural features of immunity rules, but said little as to the reasons why such rules exist or the normative objectives that they pursue. Inquiring into the rationale of these norms is key to avoiding a purely mechanistic description of their functioning and to correctly construing their scope, particularly where the content of the law appears uncertain.[27]

Starting from state immunity, the most widely held view describes this rule as a direct derivation of a number of general principles, mainly including the sovereign equality of states, their independence or their dignity;[28] references to such concepts have been somewhat interchangeable in legal discourse.[29] Their gist is commonly encapsulated in the Latin phrase *par in parem non habet jurisdictionem*.[30] Restatements of this view in state practice are innumerable, with the earliest occurrences dating back to the era of absolute immunity.[31] When state practice transitioned to restrictive immunity, courts and commentators kept referring to sovereign equality (or one of its many other iterations) as the main rationale for state immunity.[32] Even the ICJ affirmed in *Jurisdictional Immunities* that state immunity 'derives from the principle of sovereign equality of States' enshrined in Article 2, paragraph 1 of the UN Charter.[33]

Despite the broad support that these justifications for immunity have drawn, the above views are not entirely conclusive. On the one hand, one may agree that reliance on such principles played a role in the early days of the law of state immunity as a justification of absolute immunity.[34] Under classic international law, at a time when states were conceived of as possessing unbound sovereignty, deriving

[26] T Grant, 'Article 6' in R O'Keefe and CJ Tams (eds), *The United Nations Convention on Jurisdictional Immunities of States and Their Property: A Commentary* (Oxford, Oxford University Press, 2013) 105, 108.

[27] Draft Articles on Diplomatic Intercourse and Immunities with commentaries, ILC Yearbook 1958, vol II, 95, re the rationale of diplomatic immunity.

[28] *Ex multis* EC Okeke, *Jurisdictional Immunities of States and International Organizations* (Oxford, Oxford University Press, 2018) 39.

[29] X Yang, *State Immunity in International Law* (Cambridge, Cambridge University Press, 2012) 48.

[30] See, eg Report of the Working Group on jurisdictional immunities of States and their property, ILC Yearbook 1978, vol II, Part 2, 153.

[31] See England, Court of Appeal, *The Parlement Belge* (1880) LR 5 PD 197; Tribunal of Antwerp, *Gouvernement ottoman v Société de Sclessin et Depp et Roef* PB 1877, III, 28.

[32] eg *Al-Adsani v United Kingdom* App No 35763/97, 21 November 2001, para 54; *Jones* (n 13) para 14.

[33] *Jurisdictional Immunities* (n 3) para 57.

[34] Indeed, the *par in parem* principle is rightly treated as a synonym for absolute immunity by Judges Higgins, Kooijmans and Buergenthal in *Arrest Warrant* (n 1) para 72.

absolute immunity from such a principle could appear to many as a simple logical deduction.[35] On the other hand, once it is admitted that international law allows for areas of non-immunity, the explanatory power of the principle of equality of states is limited.[36] Because 'Sovereign equality also means equal territorial sovereignty',[37] the *par in parem* principle is ultimately self-defeating: the state of the forum has as much reason for invoking its sovereignty as the basis for exercising jurisdiction as the impleaded state has for invoking its own sovereignty as the basis of immunity.[38] There is, in other words, no inherent reason why one sovereignty claim should prevail over the other.[39] Even less compelling is the 'dignity of the state' argument, a notion that Lauterpacht had termed 'an archaic survival' as long ago as 1951.[40] As argued by Jennings and Watts, 'There is no obvious impairment of the rights of equality, or independence, or dignity of a state if it is subjected to ordinary judicial processes within the territory of a foreign state'.[41]

A possible alternative might be to rationalise immunity as a manifestation of comity among nations, ie as a discretionary gesture of *courtoisie* aimed at maintaining good international relations. This view is particularly popular in the USA, where the Supreme Court has long considered sovereign immunity to be 'a matter of grace and comity on the part of the United States'.[42] But the same considerations may apply with respect to this view: while comity was arguably one of the factors contributing to the historical emergence of immunities in international law, it is unable in itself to account for the existence of international obligations to grant jurisdictional immunity. Actually, it does the opposite – it denies the immunities' legal character.[43] The ICJ rebuffed this conception in *Jurisdictional Immunities* in no uncertain terms.[44] The US practice itself is far from unambiguous in its adherence to the 'grace and comity' approach to state immunity: with the US Foreign Sovereign Immunities Act 1976 (US FSIA), Congress expressly acknowledged that state immunity is an obligation under international law.[45]

[35] TR Giuttari, *The American Law of Sovereign Immunity: An Analysis of Legal Interpretation* (New York, Praeger Publishers, 1970) 5.

[36] See already D Anzilotti, 'L'esenzione degli Stati stranieri dalla giurisdizione' (1910) 5 *Rivista di diritto internazionale* 471, 503.

[37] M Bothe, 'Remedies of Victims of War Crimes and Crimes against Humanities: Some Critical Remarks on the ICJ's Judgment on the Jurisdictional Immunity of States' in A Peters et al (eds), *Immunities in the Age of Global Constitutionalism* (Leiden, Brill, 2015) 99, 101.

[38] Z Douglas, 'State Immunity for the Acts of State Officials' (2012) 82 *British Year Book of International Law* 281, 316–18.

[39] GM Badr, *State Immunity: An Analytical and Prognostic View* (The Hague, Nijhoff, 1984) 88.

[40] H Lauterpacht, 'The Problem of Jurisdictional Immunities of Foreign States' (1951) 28 *British Year Book of International Law* 220, 231.

[41] R Jennings and A Watts, *Oppenheim's International Law*, 9th edn (Oxford, Oxford University Press, 1992) 341–42.

[42] *Verlinden BV v Central Bank of Nigeria* 461 US 480 (1983) 486. This idea is traditionally traced back to *The Schooner Exchange v McFaddon* 11 US 116 (1812).

[43] L Damrosch, 'Changing the International Law of Sovereign Immunity through National Decisions' (2011) 44 *Vanderbilt Journal of Transnational Law* 1185; *Compania Naviera Vascongado v The Cristina* (1938) AC 485, 502.

[44] *Jurisdictional Immunities* (n 3) para 53.

[45] US FSIA, s 1602.

Thus, there is need for a different theoretical basis for why international law establishes immunities from civil jurisdiction. The literature on diplomatic immunity provides some useful hints in this regard. It is noteworthy that, similarly to state immunity, diplomatic immunity was once dominantly conceived as deriving from certain general principles of international law, but such explanations have subsequently been refuted and discarded by the majority view. The two theories most commonly invoked used to be that of representative character and that of extraterritoriality.[46] The former treated the diplomat as a personification of the foreign state: so conceived, diplomatic immunity was itself rooted in the *par in parem* principle.[47] The latter theory relied on the fiction that the foreign diplomat never left the territory of the sending state and was thus not subject to the receiving state's jurisdiction.[48] While both theories had an influence on the historical development of diplomatic law,[49] they are both unable to account for its current state. The theory of representative character lends itself to the same criticism that can be addressed to the sovereign equality justification of state immunity: 'Il y a deux souverainetés en cause,' wrote Special Rapporteur Sandström, 'et il ne va pas de soi que l'une doit céder le pas à l'autre'.[50] Extraterritoriality, for its part, has long been considered an 'untenable fiction'.[51] Crucially, it is unable to account for the purely procedural character of jurisdictional immunities and for the general obligation of the diplomatic agent to comply with the receiving state's laws.[52]

By contrast, the current consensus is that the purpose of diplomatic and consular immunities is to ensure the unimpeded exercise of diplomatic or consular functions, a rationale condensed in the phrase *ne impediatur legatio*.[53] The underlying concept of functional necessity is also held by universal recognition to be the theoretical basis for granting immunity to IOs (*ne impediatur officia*).[54] That IO immunities should be understood as a means to safeguard the proper operation of IOs has always seemed self-evident, and not just because many instruments, including the UN Charter, proclaim that IOs 'shall enjoy … such privileges and immunities as are necessary for the fulfilment of [their] purposes'.[55] The parallel

[46] E Young, 'The Development of the Law of Diplomatic Relations' (1964) 40 *British Year Book of International Law* 141.

[47] *The Parlement Belge* (n 31) 220: 'an ambassador cannot be personally sued … because such a suit would be inconsistent with the independence and equality of the state which he represents'.

[48] See, eg J Lorimer, *The Institutes of the Law of Nations*, vol 1 (Edinburgh, Blackwood, 1883) 248.

[49] As acknowledged by Draft Articles on Diplomatic Intercourse (n 27) 94–95.

[50] AEF Sandström, 'Report on Diplomatic Intercourse and Immunities', ILC Yearbook 1955, vol II, 14, para 21 ('There are two sovereignties at issue and it is not self-evident that one must give way to the other').

[51] JL Kunz, 'Privileges and Immunities of International Organizations' (1947) 41 *American Journal of International Law* 828, 837.

[52] Denza (n 22) 111.

[53] See the VCDR and VCCR Preambles. *Ex multis* R van Alebeek, 'Immunity, Diplomatic' (2009) *Max Planck Encyclopedia of Public International Law*, para 3.

[54] Report of the ILC on the work of its forty-first session (2 May–21 July 1989), ILC Yearbook 1989, vol II, Part 2, 136, para 723.

[55] Art 105(1) UN Charter.

with diplomatic immunity always exercised an influence on the conceptualisation of IO immunity: as Adatci and de Visscher precociously wrote in 1924 with regard to the League of Nations, its immunities were essentially meant to satisfy 'un intérêt de fonction. C'est, du reste, la même considération qui, dans la conception moderne, se trouve à la base des immunités des agents diplomatiques' ('a functional interest. It is, after all, the same consideration that, according to the modern conception, lies at the basis of the immunities of diplomatic agents').[56]

In sum, it is established authority that the jurisdictional immunities of diplomats, consuls and IOs have a functional character. Against this backdrop, it is somewhat surprising that the rationale of state immunity continues to be explained in terms of logical derivation from arcane fundamental principles of international law.[57] A functional approach can provide a fully adequate explanation for all of the jurisdictional immunities from civil jurisdiction; in this light, state immunity should simply be understood as a rule to facilitate the performance of public functions by the foreign state.[58] There is little point in regressing any further and pondering why international law facilitates state functions (or, for that matter, diplomatic, consular and organisational functions). This rationale is an amalgam of the historical evolution of international immunity law and the multiple ideological inputs that have shaped its current form. It captures both the importance traditionally given to the safeguard of the independence of foreign states and IOs, and therefore the interest of the immunity's recipient to perform its functions undisturbed,[59] and the role played by considerations of comity, which capture the interest of the forum state and of the whole international community in smoothing the conduct of international relations.[60] Moreover, where it is not absolute, immunity also reflects a balance with the interest of private parties to enforce their rights in court.[61]

IV. Scope of State Immunity

The focus of the chapter now turns to the specific legal features of each category of immunity. The present section is concerned with assessing the scope of immunity owed to foreign states. The discussion starts by enumerating the legal sources

[56] M Adatci and C de Visscher, 'Rapport sur l'art. 7, al. 4: Privilèges et Immunités diplomatiques des Agents de la S.D.N.' (1924) *Annuaire de l'Institut de droit international* 1, 3.

[57] LM Caplan, 'State Immunity, Human Rights, and Jus Cogens: A Critique of the Normative Hierarchy Theory' (2003) 97 *American Journal of International Law* 741, 748.

[58] H Krieger, 'Between Evolution and Stagnation – Immunities in a Globalized World' (2014) 6 *Göttingen Journal of International Law* 177, 197–98.

[59] See R Quadri, *La giurisdizione sugli Stati stranieri* (Milan, Giuffrè, 1941) 96.

[60] CA Whytock, 'Foreign State Immunity and the Right to Court Access' (2013) 93 *Boston University Law Review* 2033, 2046–47.

[61] R Higgins, 'Certain Unresolved Aspects of the Law of State Immunity' (1982) 29 *Netherlands International Law Review* 265, 272.

relevant to this field (section IVA). It then expounds on the content of restrictive state immunity. In this regard, section IVB describes the complications arising from the canonical distinction between *acta jure imperii* and *acta jure gestionis*, and submits that these difficulties should be overcome by acknowledging that restrictive immunity is in fact not necessarily built around the public–private divide.

A. The Sources of the Law of State Immunity

Customary international law constitutes the primary source of the law of state immunity. This was expressly acknowledged by the ICJ in *Jurisdictional Immunities*, where it affirmed that state immunity has been 'adopted as a general rule of customary international law solidly rooted in the current practice of States'.[62] There is practical unanimity among municipal courts that a customary obligation to grant immunity to foreign states in certain circumstances does exist; the disagreements, however frequent, only concern the scope of this obligation.

Except for specific areas, such as in the regulation of the status of visiting military forces,[63] treaty law has traditionally performed a lesser role in matters of state immunity. There have, however, been two major attempts at compehensively regulating state immunity law in a binding text. The first such attempt was the 1972 European Convention on State Immunity (ECSI),[64] drafted by a committee of legal experts within the framework of the Council of Europe. This Convention reflects a complex compromise between the positions followed at the time by the participating states, and is characterised by a fair amount of experimentalism.[65] Most notably, due to the drafters' intention to ensure coordination with the 1968 Brussels Convention on the Jurisdiction and Enforcement of Judgments,[66] its provisions often combine immunity rules and jurisdictional links. Thus, somewhat unusually for an immunity instrument, the ECSI is also preoccupied with ensuring that the jurisdiction of the forum state's courts is properly established, in particular by limiting the exercise of jurisdiction to acts performed or located in the territory of the forum state.[67]

The UN Convention on State Immunity (UNCSI) is the second comprehensive multilateral instrument in the field of state immunity, and the only one with universal character. This Convention is the offspring of the works of the International Law Commission (ILC) on the topic of the jurisdictional immunities of states

[62] *Jurisdictional Immunities* (n 3) para 56, quoting from Report of the ILC on the work of its thirty-second session (5 May–25 July 1980), ILC Yearbook 1980, vol II, Part 2, 147, para 26. See also UNCSI Preamble, first recital: 'the jurisdictional immunities of States … are generally accepted as a principle of customary international law'.

[63] A Sari, 'The Immunities of Visiting Forces' in Ruys and Angelet (n 25) 559, 568–73.

[64] European Convention on State Immunity 1972 (ECSI).

[65] Fox and Webb (n 11) 118–25.

[66] Brussels Convention on jurisdiction and the enforcement of judgments in civil and commercial matters 1968.

[67] On the conceptual distinction between jurisdiction and immunity, see above s II.

and their property, conducted over the course of 13 years under the guidance of Special Rapporteurs Sompong Sucharitkul and Motoo Ogiso.[68] The Commission adopted a set of draft articles in 1991;[69] these were later substantially amended by two working groups established by the General Assembly Sixth Committee and the ILC itself with a view to solving a number of fundamental issues that remained outstanding.[70] The text of the UNCSI was eventually finalised by an Ad Hoc Committee created by the General Assembly.[71] Both the ECSI and the UNCSI resort to the same drafting technique to translate the doctrine of restrictive immunity into concrete provisions: they spell out a general rule of immunity and enumerate an exhaustive list of exceptions where immunity does not apply.[72]

Neither convention has so far received broad acceptance. The ECSI is only in force for eight European states,[73] while the UNCSI, which has been ratified by 22 states as of 2021, will enter into force upon its thirtieth ratification.[74] Until the prospective entry into force of the UNCSI, the role of treaty law as a source of state immunity obligations will continue to be marginal. It would, however, be erroneous to understate the importance of these two instruments for the law of state immunity at large. Indeed, the influence that both texts have exercised on state practice makes them fundamental stepping stones to the consolidation and development of customary international law.

The relevance of the two conventions can easily be perceived by looking at national legal systems. First, many domestic courts have turned to their provisions for assessing the content of customary international law.[75] Secondly, the vast majority of municipal legislation on state immunity has been drafted under the influence of one of the two state immunity conventions. The ECSI was the main inspiration for the text of the UK State Immunity Act 1978 (UK SIA), which was approved precisely in order to enable the UK to ratify the Convention.[76] The UK SIA, in turn, has influenced the drafting of state immunity legislation in other common law jurisdictions.[77] More recently, Japan and Spain adopted state immunity legislation that textually reproduces large swaths of the UNCSI,[78] and so did

[68] UN General Assembly Resolution 32/151 (19 December 1977) recommending to commence work on the topic.

[69] Draft Articles on Jurisdictional Immunities of States and Their Property, with commentaries, ILC Yearbook 1991, vol II, Part 2, 13.

[70] UN General Assembly Resolution 46/55 (9 December 1991) point 4; Report of the ILC on the work of its fifty-first session (3 May–23 July 1999), ILC Yearbook 1999, vol II, Part 2, paras 10 and 481–84.

[71] UN General Assembly Resolution 55/150 (12 January 2001).

[72] See Art 15 ECSI and Art 5 UNCSI for the residual rule of immunity, and Arts 1–14 ECSI and Arts 7–17 UNCSI for the list of exceptions.

[73] Austria, Belgium, Cyprus, Germany, Luxembourg, the Netherlands, Switzerland and the UK.

[74] Art 30 UNCSI.

[75] See Italy, Court of Cassation, *Embassy of Spain to the Holy See v De la Grana Gonzales* 18 April 2014, No 9034, ILDC 2436 (IT 2014); *Jones* (n 13) para 8. The same is true for the ECtHR: eg *Oleynikov v Russia* App No 36703/04, 14 March 2013, paras 66–68.

[76] Fox and Webb (n 11) 170–72.

[77] See, eg State Immunity Act 1979 (Singapore); State Immunity Ordinance 1981 (Pakistan); Foreign States Immunities Act 1981 (South Africa).

[78] Act on Civil Jurisdiction over Foreign States 2010 (Japan); Law No 16 (2015) (Spain).

Russia, which signed but did not ratify the Convention.[79] Only a handful of state immunity statutes – namely those of the USA, Canada and Argentina – are neither directly nor indirectly inspired by the ECSI or the UNCSI.[80] They do, nonetheless, follow the same structure, whereby immunity is the general rule and the exceptions are exhaustively enumerated.

B. The Problematic Distinction between *Acta Jure Imperii* and *Acta Jure Gestionis*

There is no question that the scope of state immunity under current international law is restrictive, so that it is necessary to distinguish between admissible and non-admissible exercises of jurisdiction. The near consensus is that this distinction hinges on the divide between *acta jure imperii* and *acta jure gestionis*: under this conception, jurisdiction may be lawfully exercised only over state acts that do not implicate sovereign functions.[81] The innumerable national courts that have professed their faith in this distinction have generally defined acts *jure gestionis* as those that may be performed by any private person.[82] Thus, the test would seem to go as follows: *jure gestionis* refers to what *also* a private party can perform; *jure imperii* refers to what *only* a state can do.[83] Yet, the consensus over the 'private person' test is in fact more apparent than real. It is often acknowledged that this standard is difficult to apply to concrete situations.[84] Drawing the line is 'much more easily stated than made', according to the Supreme Court of Victoria in *Reid*.[85] The German Bundesverfassungsgericht expressed similar doubts in *Empire of Iran*, but did not budge: 'The fact that it is difficult to draw the line … is no reason for abandoning the distinction.'[86] The problem, quite evidently, is that a test so worded leaves ample room for subjective evaluation. It cannot become workable in a courtroom unless it is somehow made less elusive.

[79] Law on Jurisdictional Immunity of a Foreign State and a Foreign State's Property 2015 (Russia).

[80] US FSIA; State Immunity Act 1985 (Canada); Law No 24.488 (1995) (Argentina).

[81] R van Alebeek and R Pavoni, 'Immunities of States and their Officials' in A Nollkaemper and A Reinisch (eds), *International Law in Domestic Courts: A Casebook* (Oxford, Oxford University Press, 2018) 100, 177, noting that this view enjoys 'virtually universal acceptance'.

[82] eg Belgium, Court of Cassation, *Société anonyme Compagnie des chemins de fer liégeois limbourgeois v État néerlandais* 11 June 1903, (1904) 31 *Journal de droit international privé* 417, 427; Italy, Court of Cassation, *Ditta Campione v Ditta Peti Nitrogenmuvek, Repubblica popolare d'Ungheria* 14 November 1972, No 3368, (1973) 96 *Foro italiano* 1139, 1150; *Kuwait Airways Corp v Iraqi Airways Corp and Others* [1995] 3 All ER 694, 706; *Saudi Arabia v Nelson* 507 US 349 (1993), 360.

[83] Higgins (n 61) 269, defining *acta jure gestionis* as acts that 'anyone could have made'.

[84] J Crawford, *Brownlie's Principles of International Law*, 9th edn (Oxford, Oxford University Press, 2019) 471; Fox and Webb (n 11) 415.

[85] Australia, Supreme Court of Victoria, *Reid v Republic of Nauru* 17 February 1992, 101 ILR 193, 194.

[86] *Claims against the Empire of Iran Case* 30 April 1963, 45 ILR 57, 79. See also *Holland v Lampen-Wolfe* [2000] UKHL 40: 'Difficult as the distinction may be at common law, we have to do the best we can to apply it' (Lord Clyde).

The attempts to concretise this test may be divided into two main camps. The first approach looks exclusively at the nature of the act at issue.[87] In a textbook manifestation of this approach, Lord Denning reasoned in *Trendtex* that a contract to buy boots for the army remained a non-immune commercial transaction: 'The seller is not concerned with the purpose to which the purchaser intends to put the goods.'[88] Other courts, by contrast, have given primary weight to whether the state act pursues a public purpose.[89] Between the two extremes, a variety of intermediates have also been proposed: in *I Congreso*, for example, Lord Wilberforce argued that purpose, although 'not decisive[,] may throw some light upon the nature of what was done'.[90] The two versions of the 'private person test' may lead to radically different outcomes. For instance, in *Weltover*, the US Supreme Court considered Argentina's failure to repay its debt to be an activity that was commercial in nature,[91] but the same activity was held to be *jure imperii* by the Italian Court of Cassation by reason of the 'eminently public purposes' underpinning a state's management of its finances.[92]

As this last example illuminates, the key criticism that can be levied against an approach based purely on purpose is that it is almost invariably conducive to immunity.[93] Schreuer persuasively wrote that 'Once we start inquiring into the underlying motives of a State partner to a transaction we will most probably end up with some political purpose somewhere'.[94] However, even though the nature of the act would appear prima facie to offer clearer guidance, the objectivity of this approach is to some extent illusory because the outcomes are predetermined by one's definition of private and public acts.[95] This definition, in turn, may vary significantly, depending on the 'ideological conceptions and policy preferences of the particular forum'.[96] The nature test too, in sum, is prone to subjective evaluation, especially in the vast number of cases at the borderline between public and private law.[97] As has been rightly argued, if the 'nature test' were to be applied to its

[87] A Weiss, 'Compétence et incompétence des tribunaux à l'égard des états étrangers' (1923) 1 *Recueil des cours* 521, 546; Higgins (n 61) 267.

[88] *Trendtex Trading Corporation v Central Bank of Nigeria* [1977] 2 WLR 356, 369. *cf* also *Empire of Iran* (n 86) 80; s 1603(d) US FSIA: 'The commercial character of an activity shall be determined by reference to the nature of the … act, rather than its purpose.'

[89] eg France, Court of Cassation, *Société nationale des pétroles iraniens (NIOC) v Pipe Line Service (PLS) et MX* 29 May 1990, No 87-16788.

[90] *I Congreso del Partido* 16 July 1981, 64 ILR 308, 323. See also *Littrell v United States of America (No 2)* [1995] 1 WLR 82, 91 (Rose LJ).

[91] *Republic of Argentina v Weltover Inc* 504 US 607 (1992).

[92] *Borri v Republic of Argentina* 27 May 2005, No 11225.

[93] Y Banifatemi, 'Jurisdictional Immunity of States – Commercial Transactions' in Ruys and Angelet (n 25) 125.

[94] CH Schreuer, *State Immunity: Some Recent Developments* (Cambridge, Grotius, 1988) 15.

[95] R van Alebeek, *The Immunity of States and Their Officials in International Criminal Law and International Human Rights Law* (Oxford, Oxford University Press, 2008) 54.

[96] I Brownlie, 'Contemporary Problems Concerning the Jurisdictional Immunity of States, Preliminary Report' (1987) 62 *Annuaire de l'Institut de droit international* 13, 27.

[97] L Ferrari Bravo, 'Le controversie in materia d'impiego presso enti internazionali e la giurisdizione italiana' (1956) 39 *Rivista di diritto internazionale* 550, 552.

extreme consequences, immunity may be ruled out in virtually all cases because most state activities – including those quintessentially sovereign, such as military activities – can be and in fact *are* also performed by private parties, including through contractual arrangements.[98] If the 'purpose test' may ultimately collapse into absolute immunity, the 'nature test' may very well collapse into the outright extinction of state immunity.

A variety of suggestions have been put forth to tackle these difficulties. Some have opined that the yardstick for distinguishing between public and private acts should be provided by the *lex fori*.[99] While this idea is rarely encountered in contemporary literature, the more popular view considering state immunity to be more of a flexible principle than a well-defined legal rule merely expresses the same concept in different terms:[100] to say that states retain discretion as to how to apply immunity is no different than saying that domestic law is controlling. Hence, these views lend themselves to the same criticism. If states were really free to do as they please in matters of state immunity, that would mean that no obligation to grant jurisdictional immunity existed.[101] If state immunity is a rule of international law, we must expect international law to draw the distinction between immune and non-immune claims.[102] Finally, the difficulties surrounding restrictive state immunity have also produced a strand of more radical views according to which the diversity of practice would demonstrate that no obligation to grant state immunity exists under international custom.[103] But clearly this viewpoint hardly reflects what national courts do in real life: they instead recognise that international law requires *some* immunity, and that such immunity is limited in scope.

The views analysed so far, however different as far as the conclusions that they reach, all share the premise that restrictive immunity must necessarily resort to the distinction between *acta jure imperii* and *acta jure gestionis*. If one accepts this assumption, it is probably inevitable to conclude that, insofar as the distinction between private and public acts is blurred, the content of the rule of state immunity is itself, by syllogism, also ill-defined. Yet there seem to be reasons for caution with regard to this approach.

[98] A Orakhelashvili, 'Jurisdictional Immunity of States and General International Law – Explaining the *Jus Gestionis* v. *Jus Imperii* Divide' in Ruys and Angelet (n 25) 105, 117: 'The range of acts that both individuals and States can perform … encompasses nearly every area of economic, social, political and military activity'.

[99] *Empire of Iran* (n 86) 80. Pursuant to Art 2(2) UNCSI, 'reference should be made primarily to the nature of the contract or transaction, but its purpose should also be taken into account' if relevant in the practice of the forum state.

[100] See J Finke, 'Sovereign Immunity: Rule, Comity or Something Else?' (2011) 21 *European Journal of International Law* 853; Yang (n 29) 35.

[101] J Crawford, 'International Law and Foreign Sovereigns: Distinguishing Immune Transactions' (1983) 54 *British Year Book of International Law* 75, 78.

[102] P de Visscher and J Verhoeven, 'L'immunité de juridiction de l'État étranger dans la jurisprudence belge et le projet de convention du Conseil de l'Europe' in *Immunité de juridiction et d'exécution des États* (Brussels, Institut de sociologie, 1971) 35, 60.

[103] Orakhelashvili, 'Jurisdictional Immunity' (n 98) 122; S El Sawah, *Les immunités des États et des organisations internationales – Immunités et procès équitable* (Brussels, Larcier, 2012) 101–201.

The reason why the foregoing distinction is widely regarded as a proxy for restrictive state immunity lies in the historical evolution of state immunity law. The 'private person test' originated in the domestic law of the states where absolute state immunity first came under challenge, and was initially applied to the domain of trade and commercial activities.[104] When a restrictive conception of immunity extended to other types of state activities, the pre-existing 'private person test' constituted a natural reference point. But the popularity of this test does not entail that restrictive state immunity identifies with it. In order for a rule of customary international law to exist, a general practice of states accompanied by a belief that this practice is required by law (*opinio juris*) should be in place.[105] Considering that the 'private person test' generates vastly different outcomes in national case law, the adoption of this same yardstick is in itself no indication of uniformity in state practice and *opinio* as regards the proceedings over which jurisdiction may not be exercised.

The diffusion of this test has inevitably produced some uniformity in state practice, notably with regard to those state acts that are widely or undisputedly regarded as being sovereign in character. This may give rise to a prima facie presumption that immunity attaches to claims relating to acts that are 'typically sovereign', eg military activities.[106] However, outside of these relatively uncontested cases, it would be incorrect to seek to extrapolate from abstract notions of public and private acts. Telling public from private is to a large extent an exercise of semantics, and it is no surprise that the conclusions are linguistically dependent. In the ample twilight zone between public and private, the only way of determining the content of state immunity law is to pierce the veil of the 'private person test' and proceed inductively from empirical observation of state practice.[107] It is not by chance that all international and domestic state immunity instruments seek to go past the simple *jure imperii*/*jure gestionis* distinction by pinpointing which specific types of claims are or are not covered by immunity – the so-called 'list method'.[108] This makes any discussion about the public or private nature of the act in principle irrelevant.[109] The use of the 'list method' highlights that the law of state immunity

[104] Yang (n 29) 22–23. For early examples, see Italy, Court of Cassation of Naples, *Typaldos Console di Grecia v Manicomio di Aversa* 16 March 1886 (1886-I) *Giurisprudenza d'Italia* 228; Belgium, Civil Tribunal of Brussels, *Société pour la fabrication de cartouches v Colonel Mutkuroff, Ministre de la guerre de Bulgarie* (1888), (1889-III) *Pasicrisie belge* 62.

[105] Statute of the International Court of Justice 1945, Art 38(1)(b).

[106] See, eg J-F Lalive, 'L'immunité de juridiction des États et des organisations internationales' (1953) 84 *Recueil des cours* 205, 286–87, arguing that certain state activities – namely, internal administrative acts, legislative acts, and acts concerning armed forces and diplomatic activities – should be considered as intrinsically sovereign.

[107] S Sucharitkul, 'Developments and Prospects of the Doctrine of State Immunity: Some Aspects of Codification and Progressive Development' (1982) 29 *Netherlands International Law Review* 252, 259.

[108] Van Alebeek, *The Immunity* (n 95) 60–61.

[109] 1991 Draft Articles (n 69) 45, re the so-called 'tort exception' (Art 12 UNCSI). Of course, the private/public dichotomy remains relevant where the instrument itself makes reference to that distinction: eg Art 2(1)(b)(ii) UNCSI, defining a state as comprising, inter alia, constituent units and political

cannot be reduced to one-size-fits-all standards; rather, different legal yardsticks may apply to different claims.

More hints of the insufficiency of the public–private dichotomy may be found in *Jurisdictional Immunities*. The main issue before the court in this case was whether claims arising out of acts of foreign armed forces amounting to violations of *jus cogens* were covered by immunity. The ICJ noted at the outset that the military activities at issue constituted sovereign acts,[110] but – what is most revealing – it did not stop there. One of Italy's arguments was that customary law recognised an exception to state immunity for tortious acts *jure imperii* performed in the forum state. The Court observed that the vast majority of states granted immunity over torts committed during armed conflicts and concluded for this reason that immunity could not be lifted.[111] Regardless of whether the Court correctly weighed the available practice,[112] this approach shows that the assessment of the law was conceptually independent from the public or private character of the underlying state act. Let us assume that, in its enquiry, the ICJ had found that substantial state practice militated against immunity for tortious conduct of foreign military forces. In such a case, it can be presumed that it would have held in favour of Italy. But clearly this would not have meant that the judgment would turn *delicta imperii* into private acts; it would simply have meant that state practice did not support the prohibition to exercise jurisdiction over those claims, irrespective of the underlying act's public character.

Having established that the content of the law of state immunity should be demonstrated through the inductive method, it is natural to wonder what exactly should be demonstrated – the prohibition to exercise jurisdiction or the absence of such a prohibition. The answer depends on the identification of the background presumption. A commonly held view is that immunity constitutes the general rule and areas of non-immunity see the light in the form of exceptions. This has the very practical consequence of establishing a presumption of immunity: where state practice is inconsistent or uncertain, immunity should be upheld.[113] Each exception to immunity should be established as a separate rule of customary international law supported by *usus* and *opinio*.[114] On closer inspection, however, this view makes the relaxation of immunity subject to an unduly cumbersome burden of proof. Support for the background presumption of immunity is usually derived from the idea that the areas of non-immunity historically developed in the form of exceptions to the initial rule of absolute immunity, and

subdivisions 'which are entitled to perform acts in the exercise of sovereign authority, and are acting in that capacity'. Unsurprisingly, provisions of this sort incur all the difficulties that are normally produced by the 'private person test': see T Grant, 'Article 2(1)(a)' in O'Keefe and Tams (eds) (n 26) 40, 49–50.

[110] *Jurisdictional Immunities* (n 3) paras 60–61.

[111] ibid paras 62 and 67–77.

[112] For criticism see ibid Dissenting Opinion of Judge Gaja; S El Sawah, 'Jurisdictional Immunity of States and Non-Commercial Torts' in Ruys and Angelet (n 25) 142.

[113] In this sense, see Yang (n 29) 37–41; B Conforti and M Iovane, *Diritto internazionale*, 12th edn (Naples, Editoriale scientifica, 2021) 284.

[114] Orakhelashvili, 'Jurisdictional Immunity' (n 98) 109–10.

from the fact that state immunity instruments set forth a general rule of immunity and enumerate an exhaustive list of exceptions.[115] However, the choice to adopt the 'exceptions to immunity' model is no more than a drafting technique, hence no general conclusion as regards the status of customary international law should be inferred.[116] Describing the areas of non-immunity as exceptions fundamentally misconceives the nature of immunity in international law, in that it transforms it from a rule *prohibiting* the (otherwise possible) exercise of territorial jurisdiction into a rule *allowing* for the exercise of jurisdiction.[117] Because immunity norms have a prohibitory character, it is necessary to prove that the prohibition exists, not otherwise. Thus the background presumption should be that the principle of territorial jurisdiction applies unless the existence of an obligation to grant immunity is proven.[118]

V. Scope of International Organisation Immunity

This section focuses on the scope of the jurisdictional immunity enjoyed by IOs under international law. Similarly to the previous section, the discussion starts from an analysis of the legal sources of IO immunity (section VA), then proceeds to investigate the standards governing the immunity's scope (section VB).

A. The Sources of the Law of International Organisation Immunity

Obligations to endow IOs with jurisdictional immunity arise first and foremost from international agreements. It should be noted at the outset that there exists no international instrument potentially applicable to all IOs, despite eminent voices having made the case for a universal convention in this field.[119] The ILC's work on the topic, which lasted for over 30 years, was discontinued in 1992 before the finalisation of a draft convention.[120] IO immunity provisions are therefore scattered across a variety of treaties.

[115] Yang (n 29) 37–38; *Nelson* (n 82) 355 (re US FSIA). For a practical application, see *Jones* (n 13) para 9 (Lord Bingham).

[116] Schreuer (n 94) 7; Sucharitkul (n 107) 261.

[117] See above s II.

[118] Higgins (n 61) 271; LJ Bouchez, 'The Nature and Scope of State Immunity from Jurisdiction and Execution' (1979) 10 *Netherlands Yearbook of International Law* 3, 13; I Sinclair, 'The Law of Sovereign Immunity: Recent Developments' (1980) 176 *Recueil des cours* 113, 215.

[119] See, eg G Gaja, 'Jurisdictional Immunity of International Organizations' in Report of the ILC on the work of its fifty-eighth session (1 May–9 June and 3 July–11 August 2006), ILC Yearbook 2006, vol II, Part 2, 201.

[120] The Commission produced a set of draft articles which were never referred back to the General Assembly: JG Lammers, 'Immunity of International Organizations: The Work of the International Law Commission' (2013) 10 *International Organizations Law Review* 276.

Many constitutive instruments provide at least some directives in matters of immunity, but the provisions often lack in detail and precision. The UN Charter, for instance, confines itself to stating that the UN 'shall enjoy in the territory of each of its Members such privileges and immunities as are necessary for the fulfillment of its purposes'.[121] A substantial number of constitutive instruments, by contrast, do not touch upon immunities at all.[122] For these reasons, IO constitutions are normally supplemented by more detailed treaty regimes, which may be found in either multilateral or bilateral instruments. The earliest and most prominent examples of dedicated multilateral treaties are the 1946 General Convention and the 1947 Specialized Agencies Convention, respectively regulating the privileges and immunities of the UN and its Specialized Agencies.[123] Just like the UN Charter, these two instruments have provided successful models for other IOs to follow.[124] As for bilateral treaties, immunity provisions may be laid down in instruments regulating an IO's legal relations with the state hosting its main or subsidiary offices.[125] The principle of *lex specialis* manages the interactions between different types of treaties: bilateral agreements should be prioritised over multilateral ones, and dedicated multilateral agreements over IO constitutions.[126] If no other treaty is binding on the state of the forum, it may well be possible that the constitutive instrument is the only relevant source of immunity, or a state may even find itself under no express treaty obligation to grant immunity to an IO.

It is a point of controversy whether there exist customary international obligations in the area of IO immunity.[127] Scholars answering this question in the affirmative have advanced a variety of arguments in support of this contention. In the early days of the development of the law of IOs, a popular view was that organisations had to be regarded as common organs of their member states: a person suing an IO would in fact be suing states, hence the application of the law of state immunity.[128] Others have argued that immunity automatically derives from the IOs' international legal personality,[129] or that state immunity law should apply to IOs by analogy.[130] Yet other authors maintain that state practice and

[121] Art 105(1) UN Charter.

[122] eg Constitutive Act of the African Union 2000; North Atlantic Treaty 1949; Charter of the Association of Southeast Asian Nations 2007.

[123] Convention on the Privileges and Immunities of the United Nations 1946; Convention on the Privileges and Immunities of the Specialized Agencies 1947.

[124] eg General Convention on the Privileges and Immunities of the Organization of African Unity 1965; Agreement on Privileges and Immunities of the Organization of American States 1949; General Agreement on Privileges and Immunities of the Council of Europe 1949.

[125] AS Muller, *International Organizations and Their Host States: Aspects of their Legal Relationship* (The Hague, Kluwer, 1995) especially 17–23.

[126] Austria, Supreme Court, *OSCE Case*, 1 December 2005, No 6 Ob 150/05k, para 2.

[127] C Wickremasinghe, 'International Organizations or Institutions, Immunities before National Courts' (2009) *Max Planck Encyclopedia of Public International Law*, para 28.

[128] D Anzilotti, 'Gli organi comuni nelle società di Stati' (1914) 9 *Rivista di diritto internazionale* 156.

[129] eg Lalive (n 106) 314.

[130] eg F Schröer, 'De l'application de l'immunité juridictionnelle des états étrangers aux organisations internationales' (1971) 75 *Revue générale de droit international public* 712, 723–28.

opinio juris support the existence of a specific norm of customary international law obliging states to grant immunity to IOs, although there is disagreement as to whether such a norm would be conditional upon a state's membership to a specific IO.[131] But none of these views seem persuasive. The first one is refuted by the autonomy that IOs enjoy from their member states and by their independent legal personality.[132] The claim that immunity is a necessary consequence of international legal personality is equally unsubstantiated, in that personality and immunity are conceptually distinct and neither implies the other.[133] Immunity may indeed be granted to organisations whose international personality is at best debated.[134] Thirdly, a generalised analogous application of state immunity to IOs appears problematic. Because IOs are not sovereign but functional entities, it cannot be easily assumed, without further elabouration, that the legal position of both entities should necessarily be governed by the same norms.[135] Most importantly, there seems to be scant evidence in state practice of a specific customary norm obliging states to refrain from exercising jurisdiction over IOs.[136] Not only are national cases affirming the existence of such a customary rule quite rare, but there is also no consistency within the same jurisdictions as regards this purported custom.[137] By contrast, there is abundant practice of national courts expressly stating that IOs do *not* derive any immunity from customary law.[138]

To conclude this review of legal sources, it should be stressed that domestic law plays a central role in the IO immunity regime.[139] This is because a significant

[131] C Dominicé, 'L'immunité de juridiction et d'exécution des organisations internationales' (1984) 187 *Recueil des cours* 145 (only member states); CH Brower, 'International Immunities: Some Dissident Views on the Role of Municipal Courts' (2001) 41 *Virginia Journal of International Law* 1, 19–20 (all states regardless of membership).

[132] S De Bellis, *L'immunità delle organizzazioni internazionali dalla giurisdizione* (Bari, Cacucci, 1992) 12–15.

[133] A Orakhelashvili, 'Jurisdictional Immunity of International Organizations: From Abstract Functionality to Absolute Immunity' in A Orakhelashvili (ed), *Research Handbook on Jurisdiction and Immunities in International Law* (Cheltenham, Edward Elgar, 2015) 497, 500.

[134] T Gazzini, 'The Relationship between International Legal Personality and the Autonomy of International Organizations' in R Collins and ND White (eds), *International Organizations and the Idea of Autonomy: Institutional Independence in the International Legal Order* (London, Routledge, 2011) 196, 198–99.

[135] *Reparation for Injuries Suffered in the Service of the United Nations (Advisory Opinion)* [1949] ICJ Rep 174, 179.

[136] M Wood, 'Do International Organizations Enjoy Immunity under Customary International Law?' (2013) 10 *International Organizations Law Review* 287.

[137] *cf* Italy, Court of Cassation, *INPDAI v FAO* 18 October 1982, No 196, basing IO immunity in general international law, with the same court's ruling in *Pistelli v European University Institute* 28 October 2005, No 20995, ILDC 297 (IT 2005), only relying on treaty law. Similarly cp *Mendaro v World Bank* 717 F.2d 610 (DC Cir 1983) 615, terming IO immunity 'an accepted doctrine of customary international law', with *Jam et al v International Finance Corp* 586 US (2019), not mentioning custom among the sources of IO immunity.

[138] Canada, *Amaratunga v Northwest Atlantic Fisheries Organization* 2013 SCC 66; Belgium, Court of Cassation, *League of Arab States v TM* 12 March 2001, No S.99.0103, ILDC 42 (BE 2001).

[139] J Klabbers, *An Introduction to International Institutional Law*, 3rd edn (Cambridge, Cambridge University Press, 2015) 150–51.

number of states have enacted general purpose legislation recognising privileges and immunities to designated IOs regardless of the existence of international obligations in this regard.[140] To the extent that they are not aimed at implementing treaty obligations in the domestic legal order, these acts should be seen as unilateral grants of privileges and immunities.[141] This marks an obvious difference from those adopted in the field of state immunity, which may be regarded as implementing customary international law (at least in the intentions of the drafters: their substantive content may, of course, deviate from custom to a greater or lesser degree). In *Jam*, the US Supreme Court recently stated that the immunities recognised under the US International Organizations Immunities Act (IOIA) only constitute a default regime without prejudice to different treaty obligations.[142]

B. The Variety of Standards of International Organisation Immunity

In the absence of customary obligations, the determination of the scope of IO immunity is essentially an issue of interpretation of the relevant provisions of immunity instruments. The wide fragmentation of legal sources does not prevent the identification of certain patterns in the scope of immunity: different instruments, both international and domestic, may indeed provide for the same standards. As a rule of thumb, the three legal yardsticks that are more frequently applied may be referred to as full, restrictive and functional immunity.[143]

The UN General Convention provides the prototype for the first of these standards. Article II, section 2 of this instrument states that the UN 'shall enjoy immunity from every form of legal process' save for express waiver. This clause was reproduced verbatim in Article III, section 4 of the Specialized Agencies Convention – which defines the legal status of, among others, the International Labour Organization (ILO), the Food and Agriculture Organization (FAO), the International Civil Aviation Organization (ICAO), the United Nations Educational, Scientific and Cultural Organization (UNESCO) and the World

[140] Foreign Missions and International Organizations Act 1991 (Canada); Privileges and Immunities Act 1970 (Kenya) Fourth Schedule; International Organisations (Immunities and Privileges) Act 1948 (Singapore); Federal Act on the Privileges, Immunities and Facilities and the Financial Subsidies granted by Switzerland as a Host State 2007 (Switzerland); International Organisations Act 1968 (UK); International Organizations Immunities Act 1945 (IOIA) (USA). See also Federal Act on the Legal Status of the OSCE Institutions 1993 (Austria).

[141] See PM Saunders, 'Canada' in A Reinisch (ed), *The Privileges and Immunities of International Organizations in Domestic Courts* (Oxford, Oxford University Press, 2013) 73, 84.

[142] *Jam* (n 137) 14.

[143] The same tripartition is in A Reinisch, 'Immunity of Property, Funds, and Assets (Article II Section 2 General Convention)' in A Reinisch (ed), *The Conventions on the Privileges and Immunities of the United Nations and its Specialized Agencies: A Commentary* (Oxford, Oxford University Press, 2016) 63, 67–68. Note that these categories may not be entirely homogeneous, nor do they rule out the existence of other less common standards.

Health Organization (WHO),[144] and has since been adopted by a great number of IOs not institutionally related to the UN.[145]

The second of the three most relevant standards, ie restrictive immunity, comes into play when IO immunity is made equivalent to that of states. Although, as seen previously, there are no grounds for a generalised analogy between the immunities of IOs and states, it may be the case that an immunity instrument expressly incorporates a similar standard. A prominent example is the IOIA, which grants designated IOs 'the same immunity from suit … as is enjoyed by foreign governments'.[146] Until recently, US case law was split on the interpretation of this provision. The dominant position construed it as granting absolute immunity, on the assumption that it made reference to the immunity enjoyed by states at the time the IOIA was adopted;[147] that was in 1945, well before the Tate Letter announced that the USA would switch to restrictive state immunity.[148] Other decisions took the view that the IOIA referred to the law of state immunity as applicable at the time of the proceedings, and therefore restrictive.[149] This controversy was recently settled in *Jam*, where the Supreme Court ruled in favour of the restrictive construction.[150] The situation would appear to be similar in the Kenyan legal system, where the Privileges and Immunities Act generically mentions 'immunity from suit and legal process' among the immunities and privileges bestowed upon designated IOs.[151] The Nairobi Court Appeal in *Tononoka* construed the immunity under this provision as not covering acts of commerce; remarkably, this decision was based solely on precedents concerning state immunity.[152] One should also mention the practice of Italy making reservations to certain IO immunity instruments providing for full immunity from suit. Such reservations limit the immunity recognised by Italy to that enjoyed by states under customary law.[153]

[144] The 17 annexes of the Specialized Agencies Convention generally do not touch upon the blanket immunity regime set forth by the Convention (but see Annex VI re the International Bank for Reconstruction and Development (IBRD)).

[145] eg Agreement on the Privileges and Immunities of the ASEAN 2009, Art 3(1); Agreement on the Privileges and Immunities of the International Criminal Court 2002, Art 6; Agreement on the Status of the North Atlantic Treaty Organization, National Representatives and International Staff 1951, Art V.

[146] IOIA, s 2(b). For a similar clause, see Headquarters Agreement Between the Government of Canada and the International Civil Aviation Organization 1990, Art 3(1) (note that Canada is not a party to the Specialized Agencies Convention).

[147] *Atkinson v Inter-American Development Bank* 156 F.3d 1335 (DC Cir 1998); *Jam et al v International Finance Corp* 860 F.3d 703 (DC Cir 2017).

[148] Letter from JB Tate, Acting Legal Adviser to the Department of State, to Acting Attorney General PB Perlman (Tate Letter), 19 May 1952 (1952) 26 *US Department of State Bulletin* 984.

[149] *Dupree Associates Inc v OAS* No 76-2335 (DDC 1977) 63 ILR 92; *Oss Nokalva, Inc v European Space Agency* 617 F.3d 756 (3rd Cir 2010).

[150] *Jam* (n 137) 7–10, relying on a textual reading of the IOIA as well as on the so-called 'reference canon' of statutory construction, whereby 'when a statute refers to a general subject, the statute adopts the law on that subject as it exists whenever a question under the statute arises'.

[151] Fourth Schedule, Part I(1).

[152] *Tononoka Steels Limited v Eastern and Southern Africa Trade and Development Bank* 13 August 1999, 2 EA 536 (CAK), ILDC 1283 (KE 1999).

[153] eg Agreement establishing the International Centre for Advanced Mediterranean Agronomic Studies 1962, Art 13(1); Supplementary Protocol No 2, Art 2. In 1952, an identical reservation to

A third possible standard of IO immunity is that of functional immunity. It will be recalled from the discussion in section III of this chapter that IO immunity is undisputedly functional as far as its general rationale is concerned; therefore, all standards of IO immunity are *lato sensu* functional. But the term 'functional immunity' also has a stricter meaning, ie it may refer to a particular standard of immunity whose prime example is enshrined in Article 105 UN Charter: 'The Organization shall enjoy … immunities as are necessary for the fulfillment of its purposes.' This provision is mirrored in the constituent treaties of many other organisations.[154] In most cases, as seen above, these generic clauses have been supplemented by other treaties laying down more detailed immunity regimes. Where no such regime is applicable, though, national courts have no other option than to draw the scope of immunity from the generic functional immunity clause.[155]

The problem, however, is that there is a fair amount of subjectivity in the idea of functional necessity; indeed, the attempts to translate this concept into a measure of immunity's scope have been wildly inconsistent.[156] The most common readings construe functional immunity as de facto absolute immunity. Some arguments rely mostly on policy considerations: for example, the necessity to protect IOs from biased or inexperienced national courts or hostile local governments.[157] Another strand of approaches, which argue that 'functional immunity' should cover all the acts made by IOs in the furtherance of their mission, is also normally conducive to blanket immunity. In a case concerning OPEC, for instance, the Austrian Supreme Court justified blanket immunity by noting that IOs are functional entities and therefore all their acts are necessarily connected to their functions.[158] Under this approach, a case may perhaps be made against granting immunity for acts ultra vires;[159] but this is far from self-evident, in that even such acts may be aimed at furthering the institutional purposes of an IO.[160] At the very least, as stated again

the UN Specialized Agencies Convention led the UN Secretary-General to refuse to deposit Italy's ratification. In 1985, Italy reacceded to the Convention without reservations: GL Burci, 'Immunity of Property, Funds, and Assets (Article III Section 4 Specialized Agencies Convention)' in Reinisch, *The Conventions* (n 143) 99.

[154] eg Statute of the Council of Europe 1949, Art 40(8); Constitution of the International Labour Organization 1919, Art 40(1); Charter of the Organisation of American States (OAS) 1948, Art 133; Agreement Establishing the World Trade Organization 1994, Art VIII(2).

[155] *cf* also Brower (n 131) 19, suggesting that IOs enjoy functional immunity under general international law.

[156] Reinisch, *International Organizations* (n 20) 206. To Klabbers (n 139), 132–33, the meaning of this standard is 'in the eyes of the beholder'.

[157] A Ehrenfeld, 'United Nations Immunity Distinguished from Sovereign Immunity' (1958) 52 *American Society of International Law Proceedings* 88, 90; K Ahluwalia, *The Legal Status, Privileges and Immunities of the Specialized Agencies of the United Nations and Certain Other International Organizations* (The Hague, Nijhoff, 1964) 200.

[158] Austria, Supreme Court, *Company Baumeister Ing Richard L v O* 14 December 2004, Case No 10 Ob 53/04y, ILDC 362 (AT 2004). See also Dutch Supreme Court, *Euratom Case* 13 November 2007, LJN: BA9173, No 01984/07 CW, re a violation of Dutch environmental regulations.

[159] In this sense, see M Arsanjani, 'Claims against International Organizations: *Quis Custodiet Ipsos Custodes*?' (1980–81) 7 *Yale Journal of World Public Order* 131, 153.

[160] Klabbers (n 139) 133.

by the Austrian Supreme Court, this time in the *EPO* case, one would expect there to be a rebuttable presumption that an organisation's acts are linked to its mission.[161]

The views favouring an equivalence between functional and full immunity have for the most part gone unchallenged in legal scholarship.[162] However, they are problematic in at least two respects. First, the premises from which they start are only partially plausible: while no one would question the need to ensure that an IO is able to pursue its mission without undue interference, the diffusion of an anti-IO bias among national courts or governments is a controvertible assumption. Secondly and more crucially, even accepting all these postulates, deriving absolute immunity is a *non sequitur*. The fact that *some* lawsuits may be unwarranted does not imply that *all* lawsuits are,[163] and 'The fact that an [IO] may perform an act in furtherance of its purposes … does not imply that it requires jurisdictional immunity for that act'.[164] Briefly put, the views in question simply posit that the functional needs of IOs require total isolation from domestic legal orders without actually proving why. As Gaillard and Pingel-Lenuzza persuasively opined, it is 'difficult to see why respect for the functional autonomy of an international organisation should necessarily entail the exclusion of the jurisdiction of national courts'.[165] In light of all this, a more restrictive construction of the functional necessity test would seem more appropriate. It has been suggested that the only way to make sense of this legal yardstick is for courts to enquire whether the exercise of jurisdiction may *effectively* disrupt the functions of an IO or somehow impair its capacity to achieve its institutional goals. This test may therefore be contingent upon a number of factors, including the type of claim brought against an IO, the type and functions of the impleaded IO, and generally the specific circumstances of the case.[166]

VI. Scope of Diplomatic and Consular Immunity

The present section concludes this chapter's introductory overview by focusing on the jurisdictional immunities of diplomatic and consular agents. Compared with the immunities of states and IOs, the landscape of the relevant legal sources here is much easier to describe. More than in any other sector of immunity law, the contours of the jurisdictional immunities enjoyed by diplomats and consuls have

[161] *EPO Case* 11 June 1992, Case No 7 Ob 627/91.
[162] Reinisch, *International Organizations* (n 20) 235.
[163] ibid 236.
[164] M Singer, 'Jurisdictional Immunity of International Organizations: Human Rights and Functional Necessity Concerns' (1995) 36 *Virginia Journal of International Law* 53, 163.
[165] E Gaillard and I Pingel-Lenuzza, 'International Organisations and Immunity from Jurisdiction: To Restrict or to Bypass' (2002) 51 *ICLQ* 1, 4–5.
[166] Reinisch, *International Organizations* (n 20) 365–66.

been definitively shaped and clarified by the codification process.[167] The matter is comprehensively regulated by the Vienna Convention on Diplomatic Relations (VCDR) and the Vienna Convention on Consular Relations (VCCR), two of the most widely ratified treaties ever concluded.[168] Their provisions on privileges and immunities are generally held to reflect customary international law, either because they already reflected well-established practice at the time of their drafting or because they became widely recognised in the ensuing years.[169] The principles enshrined in these provisions therefore also apply to non-parties.[170]

The universal applicability of the two Vienna Conventions makes it irrelevant to the present discussion to assess the general regime of state agents' immunity under customary international law. It is widely posited that all state agents are entitled to immunity *ratione materiae* for acts performed in their official capacity;[171] others, however, have objected that this view is not supported by state practice and that a category of state officials may only enjoy immunity if a specific customary norm entitles it to.[172] Either way, even if a rule providing for a generalised immunity *ratione materiae* existed, the Conventions would be applied in lieu of the general regime qua *leges speciales*. On the other hand, the VCDR and VCCR themselves allow some room for other legal sources. The former expressly allows states, 'by custom or agreement[, to] extend to each other more favourable treatment than is required by the provisions of the present Convention'.[173] Similarly, the VCCR is without prejudice to other international agreements in force between the parties.[174]

As regards the reach of immunity from civil jurisdiction under the two Conventions, the one enjoyed by diplomats *en poste* is particularly extensive, although not absolute like their immunity from criminal jurisdiction.[175] Article 31(1) VCDR establishes a general rule of immunity in civil and administrative proceedings subject to three exceptions: actions relating to (i) real property situated in the territory of the receiving state, (ii) succession and (iii) professional or commercial activities exercised in the receiving state. All three are subject to the proviso that the diplomat did not act in the discharge of his or her official

[167] K Bruns, 'On the Road to Vienna: The Role of the International Law Commission in the Codification of Diplomatic Privileges and Immunities' in P Behrens (ed), *Diplomatic Law in a New Millennium* (Oxford, Oxford University Press, 2017) 54.

[168] As of 2021, there are 193 parties to the VCDR and 181 parties to the VCCR.

[169] J Wouters, S Duquet and K Meuwissen, 'The Vienna Conventions on Diplomatic and Consular Relations' in AF Cooper et al (eds), *The Oxford Handbook of Modern Diplomacy* (Oxford, Oxford University Press, 2013) 510, 517.

[170] Supreme Court of Chile, *MH v Embassy of the Republic of China* 3 September 1969, 70 ILR 394, 395, applying Art 31 VCDR to a case brought against the ambassador of the Republic of China (a non-party to the VCDR).

[171] eg *The 'Enrica Lexie' Incident (Italy v India)* Award (21 May 2020), PCA Case No 2015-28, para 848.

[172] P De Sena, *Diritto internazionale e immunità funzionale degli organi statali* (Milan, Giuffrè, 1996).

[173] Art 47(2)(b) VCDR.

[174] Art 73(2) VCCR.

[175] Art 31(1) VCDR.

functions. In other words, diplomatic immunity extends to all official acts (*ratione materiae*) and also to those private acts that are not covered by Article 31's exhaustive list of exceptions (*ratione personae*).[176] The same norms extend to the family of the diplomatic agent.[177] After the end of a diplomat's functions, the individual continues to enjoy immunity only for official acts, while private acts return to being amenable to local jurisdiction: this is the so-called continuing, or residual, immunity.[178] It should be noted that diplomatic agents who are nationals or permanent residents of the receiving state only enjoy, during their posting, immunity for acts performed in the exercise of functions as members of the mission,[179] ie an immunity coextensive with residual diplomatic immunity.[180]

As regards consular agents, Article 43(1) VCCR provides that they 'shall not be amenable to the jurisdiction of the judicial or administrative authorities of the receiving State in respect of acts performed in the exercise of consular functions'. This formula is commonly interpreted as a synonym for official acts;[181] the different wording simply suggests that the notion of official acts should be construed by taking into account the (non-exhaustive) list of consular functions of Article 5 VCCR.[182] Article 43(2) then adds that immunity from civil suit is excluded in cases 'arising out of a contract concluded by a consular officer … in which he did not contract expressly or impliedly as an agent of the sending State'.[183] During the drafting of the VCCR, this provision was added *ex abundanti cautela*, and merely restates what is already established in paragraph 1, ie that a consular agent's private acts are not covered by immunity.[184] Damages arising from vehicle, vessel or aircraft accidents are also expressly excluded from immunity.[185] Similarly to diplomatic immunity, it is established that immunity *ratione materiae* (ie for acts performed in the exercise of consular functions) persists beyond the termination of consular functions 'without limitation of time'.[186] All such provisions extend to honorary consular officers who are domiciled in, and normally nationals of, the receiving state.[187]

[176] See generally Denza (n 22) 232–59; A Tanzi, *L'immunità dalla giurisdizione degli agenti diplomatici* (Padua, CEDAM, 1991).

[177] Art 37(1) VCDR.

[178] Art 39(2) VCDR. The term 'official functions' has the same meaning in the context of Arts 31 and 39 VCDR: see *Reyes v Al-Malki and Another* [2017] UKSC 61, para 20.

[179] Art 38(1) VCDR.

[180] Van Alebeek, 'Immunity, Diplomatic' (n 53) para 48; Denza (n 22) 358.

[181] Report of the ILC covering the work of its thirteenth session (1 May–7 July 1961), ILC Yearbook 1961, vol II, 88, 117.

[182] Pursuant to Art 5(m), consular functions include 'any other functions entrusted to a consular post by the sending State'.

[183] Art 43(2)(a) VCCR.

[184] GE do Nascimento e Silva, 'The Vienna Conference on Consular Relations' (1964) 13 *ICLQ* 1214, 1227.

[185] Art 43(2)(b) VCCR.

[186] Art 53(4) VCCR.

[187] Art 58(2) VCCR. See M Kowalski, 'Consuls' (2013) *Max Planck Encyclopedia of Public International Law*, para 2.

VII. Conclusions

As the overview in this chapter has made clear, the law of immunity from civil jurisdiction is a collection of norms of different origin and content. If there is any unity that underpins such norms, it can be found mostly at the conceptual level. As section II showed, all immunities share the same structural features, the most relevant of which is that they are purely procedural bars to the exercise of jurisdiction with no effect upon the substance of a claim. Moreover, as put forth in section III, all these immunities should be rationalised as pursuing a chiefly functional aim, ie the aim to ensure or facilitate the performance of sovereign/ institutional functions. It would, of course, be a mistake to forcibly translate this conceptual unity into a more uniform standardisation of the scope of immunity. Yet, a common thread unifying this legal regime is that, save for express exceptions laid down by specific international instruments, the standards of immunity from civil jurisdiction that international law mandates are non-absolute (or, in short, limited). Blanket immunity from civil adjudicatory jurisdiction is thus generally unwarranted: as a default rule, immunity norms require the distinction between admissible and non-admissible exercises of jurisdiction.

3

The Undue Persistence of Absolute Immunity in Employment Litigation

I. Introduction

The main takeaway of the previous chapter is that international law, save for express exceptions, is a selective rather than blanket bar to the exercise of civil adjudicative jurisdiction. However, this general statement might appear to be largely inaccurate when it comes to employment matters. Indeed, both judicial decisions and scholarly writings manifest a substantial resistance to the application of non-absolute standards of immunity in this category of civil litigation. As will be seen below, this trend is not based on a single legal ground. Rather, it arises from the combined effect of various legal or policy arguments which purportedly justify either absolute immunity *tout court* or, at best, an immunity so broad as to come close to being de facto absolute.

This chapter challenges the main rationales for the blanket exclusion of employment claims from the jurisdiction of national courts. Section II critiques the views whereby the courts of the territorial state lack subject-matter jurisdiction to adjudicate such cases. Section III discusses approaches that may be loosely described as relying on functionalist policy arguments. The subsequent sections comment on the opinions favouring blanket immunity in labour matters by considering the employment relationship en bloc as an act *jure imperii* (section IV) or as an official act (section V). Lastly, section VI focuses on instances where blanket immunity arises from express treaty provisions: these are, it is argued, the only cases where international immunity law actually requires total immunisation from domestic jurisdiction. In all other cases, section VII concludes, it is necessary to devise limited immunity standards applicable to employment litigation.

II. Alleged Lack of Subject-Matter Jurisdiction of the Territorial State

The first strand of approaches justifies the total exclusion of employment disputes from the territorial state's jurisdiction based on the assumption that such lawsuits fall *ab initio* outside of the subject-matter jurisdiction of municipal courts.

These arguments come in two distinct, but not necessarily alternative, variations: they allege either that foreign states and international organisations (IOs) have exclusive jurisdiction (section IIA) or that the IOs' internal remedies are entrusted with exclusive competence (section IIB) over employment disputes. As will be seen, these arguments currently retain a minor role in the context of staff claims against foreign states, but they have proved more influential with respect to IOs.

A. Exclusive Jurisdiction of Foreign States and International Organisations

The concept of exclusive jurisdiction provides a first possible justification for the territorial state's lack of jurisdiction over staff disputes involving other states and IOs. These employers – so the argument goes – would be entitled by international law to regulate their workforce and adjudicate over related litigation in full independence.

With respect to foreign states, this outcome would derive – according to Seyersted – from a purported principle of customary international law termed 'organic jurisdiction', which he described as having overriding force over any other grounds of jurisdiction recognised in international law.[1] Seyersted argued that 'The exclusive (and overriding) organic jurisdiction extends to all relationships of employment of the State concerned, without distinction between higher officials and subordinate employees'.[2] This approach, it should be noted, results in exclusion not only from local jurisdiction but also from local substantive law.[3]

There are both theoretical and practical reasons for questioning the validity of Seyersted's theory of 'organic state jurisdiction'. From a normative viewpoint, this argument greatly overstates the weight of the foreign state's interest in exercising jurisdiction over its staff. It is unclear, in particular, why the foreign state's jurisdiction would subdue in all cases any other grounds of jurisdiction, including the territorial principle: once we assume that more than one state may have an equally compelling interest in exercising jurisdiction over such disputes, there is no a priori reason why the foreign state's interest should always be prioritised. The International Law Commission (ILC) touched on this point in its commentary to the 1991 Draft Articles on state immunity.[4] Nowhere did the Commission suggest that the employer state has an overriding interest in applying its laws and exercising its jurisdiction. Rather, it reasoned that both states retain a legitimate interest in this regard, and each interest may well outweigh the other depending on the

[1] F Seyersted, *Common Law of International Organizations* (Leiden, Nijhoff, 2008) 82.

[2] ibid 89.

[3] ibid 82.

[4] Draft Articles on Jurisdictional Immunities of States and Their Property, with commentaries, ILC Yearbook 1991, vol II, Part 2, 13.

circumstances. By way of example, it noted that the employer state's interest may be overriding when it comes to the 'exercise of disciplinary supervision', but that

> the State of the forum appears to retain exclusive jurisdiction if not, indeed, an overriding interest in matters of domestic public policy regarding the protection to be afforded to its local labour force. Questions relating to medical insurance, insurance against certain risks, minimum wages, entitlement to rest and recreation, vacation with pay, compensation to be paid on termination of the contract of employment, and so forth, are of primary concern to the State of the forum.[5]

The ILC further argued that Article 11 of the Draft Articles, on contracts of employment, was aimed at maintaining a 'delicate balance' between these competing interests.[6] Thus, the Commission presupposed that subject-matter jurisdiction over such claims belongs *in abstracto* to both the employer and the territorial state, and that such contrasting policy inputs should be reconciled at the logically subsequent stage of immunity.

Moreover, the concept of 'organic jurisdiction' finds limited support in state practice. In all jurisdictions where relevant judicial or statutory practice has developed, the courts' subject-matter jurisdiction over labour claims against foreign states is governed by the normal rules of national procedural law on the subject, ie it is based, as a general rule, on a territorial or personal connection with the forum state. All instruments, both international and domestic, which expressly deal with employment claims against foreign states treat the question of the exercise of jurisdiction as an issue of immunity, at least for work performed within the territory of the forum state, and thus presuppose local jurisdiction.[7] Again, the ILC stated in its 1991 commentary that the territorial connection between the contract of employment and a state, including the nationality of habitual residence of the employee, 'distinctly and unmistakably' provides a basis for jurisdiction.[8] In *Mahamdia v Algeria*, the European Court of Justice (ECJ) held the jurisdictional regime of the Brussels I Regulation to be applicable to relationships of employment with third states' embassies to European Union Member States[9] in cases where the respondent states do not enjoy immunity from jurisdiction under

[5] ibid 42. See also Australian Law Reform Commission, 'Foreign State Immunity', Report No 24 (1984) 55–59, quoted in *Firebird Global Master Fund II Ltd v Republic of Nauru* [2015] HCA 43, para 198: 'where a foreign state enters into an employment contract in Australia or which is to be performed in Australia, the interest of Australia in providing a local forum outweighs the interest of the foreign state in exclusive jurisdiction'.

[6] 1991 Draft Articles (n 4) 42.

[7] A caveat is that certain instruments do not clearly distinguish between jurisdictional links and immunity rules, notably the European Convention on State Immunity 1972 (ECSI), on which see ch II, s IVA. This does not alter the substance: Art 5(1) ECSI provides that, as a general rule, a state 'cannot claim immunity … if the proceedings relate to a contract of employment … where the work has to be performed on the territory of the State of the forum'.

[8] 1991 Draft Articles (n 4) 42.

[9] Council Regulation (EC) No 44/2001 of 22 December 2000 on jurisdiction and the recognition and enforcement of judgments in civil and commercial matters [2001] OJ L12/1.

general international law.[10] Contrary to what Seyersted argued, a state's 'organic jurisdiction' does not seem to possess much, if any, of an overriding force.

The view that employment relationships with foreign states may never be subject to local laws and regulations is equally unsubstantiated.[11] The general rule that immunity from jurisdiction does not exempt from local laws holds true also in the case of employment and labour law.[12] For instance, the Brussels Cour du travail held that, in the absence of different stipulations in the employment contract, the Belgian legislation on social security applied to employment relationships with the Saudi Arabian embassy to Belgium.[13] The UK Supreme Court held in *Nolan*, a case where state immunity was not relied on because the USA defended itself on the merits, that the procedure for consultation of employee representatives in cases of dismissal on grounds of redundancy, as laid down by the UK Trade Union and Labour Relations (Consolidation) Act 1992, applied to employment at a US military base in the UK.[14] The Italian and French legislations expressly provide that the employment contracts of locally recruited staff of governmental offices abroad are subject to local law as a general rule.[15]

There is some evidence in case law of states trying to shield themselves from local jurisdiction (both prescriptive and adjudicative) by claiming that employment at diplomatic missions ought not to be considered as performed within the territory of the receiving state. This is probably what comes closest to an assertion by a respondent state of exclusive and overriding jurisdiction over its staff. National courts, however, have unwaveringly rejected this argument. In *Saville*, a labour case brought against the Embassy of Korea in Canberra, Korea construed the principle of inviolability of the premises of diplomatic missions, enshrined in Article 22 of the Vienna Convention on Diplomatic Relations (VCDR),[16] as implying that the mission was not legally situated in Australian territory.[17] The Australian Industrial Relations Commission correctly rejected this argument and considered the question whether the state could be sued as an issue of immunity law.[18] A similar argument came to the fore in *Migliorini*, a wrongful termination suit against

[10] Case C-154/11 *Mahamdia v People's Democratic Republic of Algeria* [2013] ECR 1. See also *Kais v Abu Dhabi Education Council et al* 2011 ONSC 75, affirming jurisdiction over claims brought by a Canadian national employed by an Emirati public educational institution headquartered in the UAE, on the grounds that the employee was Canadian and that the damages were suffered in Canada.

[11] L Sbolci, *Controversie di lavoro con Stati stranieri e diritto internazionale* (Milan, Giuffrè, 1987) 319–30.

[12] See ch 2, s II.

[13] *Saudi Arabia v KME* 19 June 2007, RG No 47.199, paras 11–12.

[14] *United States v Nolan* [2015] UKSC 63, 180 ILR 477.

[15] DPR 18 (1967) as amended by Legislative Decree No 103 (2000), Art 154 (Italy); Law No 2000-321 (2000), Art 34V (France).

[16] Vienna Convention on Diplomatic Relations 1961 (VCDR).

[17] On the obsolete concept of extraterritoriality of diplomatic missions, see E Denza, *Diplomatic Law: Commentary on the Vienna Convention on Diplomatic Relations*, 4th edn (Oxford, Oxford University Press, 2016) 111.

[18] *Saville v Embassy of the Republic of Korea* [2006] AIRC 598. Similarly, see the Netherlands, Sub-District Court of The Hague, *MK v Republic of Turkey* 1 August 1985, 94 ILR 350, 351.

the Pontifical Lateran University (PLU). The PLU is located in an annex building to the Basilica of St John Lateran in Rome, which, pursuant to the 1929 Lateran Treaty between Italy and the Holy See, is entitled to the 'immunity granted by International Law to the headquarters of the diplomatic agents of foreign States'.[19] The University contended, inter alia, that, on the basis of this provision, the plaintiff's work had been performed in an extraterritorial Vatican area enjoying a status analogous to foreign embassies and therefore not subject to Italian jurisdiction. While not expressly citing Article 22 VCDR, the Court of Cassation held that the Basilica's Article 15 immunity only referred to the inviolability of its premises and did not entail any extraterritoriality.[20] In line with previous Italian case law considering the Holy See as enjoying the same immunity bestowed upon states under international law, *Migliorini* was instead decided on grounds of immunity.[21]

While the argument of the lack of jurisdiction of the territorial state is almost universally discredited with regard to employment cases involving foreign states, this view has proved much more resilient as far as the legal status of IOs is concerned. It is a relatively widespread position among commentators that IOs retain exclusive jurisdiction over their internal matters, including employment relationships, and that issues of immunity arise only with respect to their external relations.[22] This view posits that an IO's internal legal system is entirely extraneous to domestic legal orders, including both their substantive law and their jurisdiction. As Amerasinghe put it, 'If the national law of the member states applied to relations between the organization and its staff, the courts of states would probably be competent to hear disputes', but in reality 'with respect to their internal organization and functioning [IOs] are outside the jurisdiction of national law'.[23] Brower similarly expressed the idea that, under customary international law, 'entities having international legal personality also possess exclusive legislative and adjudicative jurisdiction over their internal affairs'.[24]

This approach has exercised considerable influence on judicial practice. In *Profili*, one of the earliest domestic cases involving employment with IOs, the former head cashier of the International Institute of Agriculture (the predecessor

[19] Treaty of Conciliation between the Holy See and Italy 1929 (Lateran Treaty), Art 15.

[20] *Migliorini v Pontifical Lateran University* 18 September 2017, No 21541, ILDC 2887 (IT 2017) 16–17.

[21] See also Court of Cassation, *Cruz v Collegio Americano del Nord*, 1 August 2011, No 16847, ILDC 1783 (IT 2011).

[22] F Seyersted, 'Jurisdiction over Organs and Officials of States, the Holy See and Governmental Organisations (2)' (1965) 14 *ICLQ* 493, 523, applying the concept of 'organic jurisdiction' to IOs.

[23] CF Amerasinghe, *Principles of the Institutional Law of International Organizations*, 2nd edn (Cambridge, Cambridge University Press, 2005) 272. See also MB Akehurst, *The Law Governing Employment in International Organizations* (Cambridge, Cambridge University Press, 1967) 12.

[24] CH Brower, 'International Immunities: Some Dissident Views on the Role of Municipal Courts' (2001) 41 *Virginia Journal of International Law* 1, 67. For criticism, see A Orakhelashvili, 'Jurisdictional Immunity of International Organizations: From Abstract Functionality to Absolute Immunity' in A Orakhelashvili (ed), *Research Handbook on Jurisdiction and Immunities in International Law* (Cheltenham, Edward Elgar, 2015) 497, 499.

of the Food and Agriculture Organization), sued the organisation for wrongful dismissal before the Italian courts. In the absence of express provisions on jurisdictional immunity within the constituent instrument,[25] the Rome Court of Appeals affirmed jurisdiction.[26] However, this judgment was later reversed by the Court of Cassation, which held that Italian jurisdiction

> cannot be exercised against the International Institute of Agriculture insofar as [it] carries out activities relating to its own organization and consequently to the … relationship with its employees … [I]ts power of self-determination or autonomy, which includes that of organizing and regulating its own activities … rules out any interference by the State and any penetration by either substantive or procedural provisions of national law.[27]

A French court developed a similar reasoning in the 1945 *Chemidlin* case, an action for breach of employment contract brought by a former employee of the International Bureau of Weights and Measures. The court declined its jurisdiction on the grounds that 'the conventions and rules to which recourse is to be had … must lie outside the framework of French law so that they retain their purely international character. Hence French law is not, in all the circumstances, applicable.'[28] A more recent example is the 1992 *European School Employee Bonus Case*. The German Federal Administrative Court was seised by a former teacher of the European School in Karlsruhe. He had received the retirement bonus established under the School's personnel statute, but claimed a further bonus under German law. The Court found the claim inadmissible on the grounds of lack of jurisdiction: it held that the IO, as a self-governing independent body, was exclusively entitled to regulate its internal affairs, including employment relationships.[29]

It is important to note that, in domestic judicial practice, the distinction between lack of subject-matter jurisdiction and jurisdictional immunity is not always clearly marked – or, to be more precise, national courts may formally adjudicate on grounds of immunity while in fact relying on arguments akin to incompetence *ratione materiae*.[30] This mix-up is evident whenever a court describes as 'immunity' what is in fact an exemption from both substantive law and jurisdiction; this runs counter to the principle that immunities are purely procedural in nature

[25] Convention for the Creation of an International Institute of Agriculture 1905 (1908) 2 *American Journal of International Law Supplement* 358.

[26] *International Institute of Agriculture v Profili* 2 April 1930, 5 ILR 413, 414.

[27] *International Institute of Agriculture v Profili* 26 February 1931, 5 ILR 413. For a similar precedent, see Tribunal of Florence, *Mazzanti v Headquarters Allied Forces Southern Europe* 2 January 1954, 22 ILR 758, affirmed, Florence Court of Appeals, 23 August 1955, (1955) *Giustizia civile* 461.

[28] Tribunal Civil of Versailles, *Chemidlin v International Bureau of Weights and Measures* 27 July 1945, 12 ILR 281, 282. See also Conseil d'État, *In re Dame Adrien and Others* 17 July 1931, 6 ILR 33; *Weiss v International Institute for Intellectual Cooperation* 20 February 1953, (1953) 81 *Journal de droit international* 744, 745.

[29] *European School Employee Bonus Case* 20 October 1992, Case No 2 C 2.90, 108 ILR 664.

[30] A Reinisch, *International Organizations before National Courts* (Cambridge, Cambridge University Press, 2000) 113.

and do not exempt from substantive law.[31] In *Klarsfeld*, a wrongful termination suit against the Franco-German Youth Office, the Paris Court of Appeals – along the lines of *Chemidlin* – described the organisation as 'échappant aux règles de droit interne' ('outside the rules of domestic law'), but described this outcome as a jurisdictional immunity.[32] Also, the Mexican Supreme Court's *Diaz-Diaz* decision of 1953, a case concerning the payment of indemnities and overtime to a former UN staff member, employed immunity law terminology to sustain an IO's exemption from all of the 'positive legal Mexican provisions'.[33]

Terminological blunders aside, all such decisions are underpinned by a conviction that IOs operate in a buffer zone between domestic legal orders, from which their internal matters are totally insulated. However, this approach is not convincing for a number of compelling reasons. First of all, as per general rule, applicable law and jurisdiction are conceptually distinct issues.[34] Thus, even if employment relationships with IOs were exempt from national labour legislation, there would be no a priori reason why national courts should be deprived of adjudicative power: a domestic court may very well rule on the merits by applying the IO's internal law.[35] In *Siedler*, for instance, the Brussels Labour Court exercised jurisdiction over a dispute between the now defunct Western European Union (WEU) and one of its employees, and calculated the immunity allowance on the basis of the Belgian labour law.[36] The Court of Cassation reversed, holding that the allowance had to be determined by the Belgian courts on the basis of the WEU Staff Regulations.[37] Another example is the 1980 *Vuillod* case, where the French Court of Cassation was called upon to analyse the legitimacy of the dismissal of a former portfolio manager of the Central Bank of West African States. The Court disregarded the plaintiff's invocation of the French labour code and instead looked at

[31] See ch 2, s II.

[32] *Klarsfeld v Office franco-allemand pour la jeunesse* 18 June 1968, (1968) 15 *Annuaire Français de Droit International* 865, 866. The same confusion may be observed in certain judgments of the Italian Court of Cassation: see *ICEM v Chiti* 7 November 1973, (1976) 2 *Italian Yearbook of International Law* 348, 350–51; *Sindacato UIL (Bari Branch) v Bari Institute of the International Centre for Advanced Mediterranean Agronomic Studies* 4 June 1986, No 3732, 87 ILR 37, (1987) 70 *Rivista di diritto internazionale* 184, 189.

[33] *Diaz-Diaz v United Nations Economic Commission for Latin America* 7 August 1953, in Annual Report of the Secretary-General (1954) 9 UN GAOR, Supp No 1, UN Doc A/2663, 105, reversing a lower court's decision calculating the indemnities according to Mexican law.

[34] HG Schermers and NM Blokker, *International Institutional Law*, 6th edn (Leiden, Brill Nijhoff, 2018) 1037. See generally ch 2, s II.

[35] Reinisch, *International Organizations* (n 30) 383–84. The reverse is equally true: a forum for settling IO staff disputes different from national courts might be empowered to apply national labour legislation. See Amerasinghe, *Principles* (n 23) 278–79.

[36] *Siedler v Western European Union* 17 September 2003, ILDC 53 (BE 2003).

[37] *Western European Union v Siedler* 21 December 2009, No S 04 0129 F, ILDC 1625 (BE 2009). See also Brussels Tribunal of First Instance, *Sevens v NATO and Belgium* 12 March 2013, Case No 12/1586/C, dismissing a claim by a failed job applicant on the grounds that NATO complied with its own procedures of selection of personnel; Bangladesh Supreme Court (High Court Division), *World Bank Office, Dhaka and another v Ismet Zerin Khan* 2018(1) LNJ 82, para 35, applying the World Bank Staff Manual.

the termination in light of the Bank's internal law. Holding in favour of the Bank, it concluded that the termination, 'intervenu pour permettre la réalisation des buts fixés par les statuts de la Banque, avait une cause réelle et sérieuse'.[38]

Furthermore, even though an IO's relationship with its staff is subject to internal employment law as a general rule, the employment legislation of the territorial state is not necessarily irrelevant. The competence to regulate the recruitment of staff and the conditions of service is often attributed to the IOs by the constitutive instruments.[39] The law applicable to these employment relationships may arise from multiple sources, including the contract of employment, the IO constituent instrument, internal staff regulations and general principles of international administrative law.[40] Against this backdrop, commentators have traditionally been divided on the possible relevance of local employment legislation.[41] Current scholarship tends to favour an intermediate approach: while internal law should be prioritised, the law of the host country may apply as the default regime in the absence of internal rules or, in their presence, may supplement them.[42] This view is indeed the most consistent with the general principle that IOs are bound to respect the laws of the countries where they operate.[43] It is, moreover, undisputed that IOs may hire local personnel under local law or under a combination of internal and national law, as specified by the terms of the employment contract.[44]

In any event, the view that IOs are necessarily insulated from domestic legal orders is decisively disproved by numerous domestic decisions affirming jurisdiction over staff disputes with IOs. As will be seen in more detail in chapter six, many municipal courts reserve the right to adjudicate labour disputes in cases where IO employees are found not to have access to alternative means of redress. This approach has been endorsed by the European Court of Human Rights (ECtHR), starting from the seminal *Waite and Kennedy* and *Beer and Regan* judgments.[45] Obviously this would not be possible if national courts did not possess subject-matter jurisdiction in the first place. In fact, these cases indicate that, similarly

[38] *Vuillod v Banque centrale des Etats de l'Afrique de l'Ouest* 4 December 1980, (1980) 27 *Annuaire Français de Droit International* 841 ('aimed at enabling the achievement of the goals set by the Bank's statutes, had a real and serious cause').

[39] See, eg Art 101(1)–(3) Charter of the United Nations 1945.

[40] CF Amerasinghe, *The Law of the International Civil Service: As Applied by International Administrative Tribunals*, 2nd edn (Oxford, Oxford University Press, 1994). See also World Bank Administrative Tribunal, *de Merode and ors v World Bank* 5 June 1981, (1981) 1 WBAT Rep 734, OXIO 229.

[41] Against, Amerasinghe, *Principles* (n 23) 271–314; CW Jenks, *The Proper Law of International Organisations* (London, Stevens & Sons, 1962) 43–46. In favour, H Kelsen, *The Law of the United Nations. A Critical Analysis of Its Fundamental Problems* (New York, Praeger, 1950) 314.

[42] J Klabbers, *An Introduction to International Institutional Law*, 3rd edn (Cambridge, Cambridge University Press, 2015) 253; C Ryngaert, ILDC comment to *Western European Union* (n 37) A15. See further A Reinisch, 'Accountability of International Organizations According to National Courts' (2005) 36 *Netherlands Yearbook of International Law* 119.

[43] AS Muller, *International Organizations and Their Host States: Aspects of their Legal Relationship* (The Hague, Kluwer, 1995) 150.

[44] Seyersted, *Common Law* (n 1) 150.

[45] *Waite and Kennedy v Germany* App No 26083/94, 18 February 1999; *Beer and Reagan v Germany* App No 28934/95, 18 February 1999.

to what was said above with regard to foreign states, national courts assess their competence to adjudicate these disputes based on the ordinary grounds of jurisdiction.[46]

B. Exclusive Competence of International Organisations' Internal Remedies

Again in the ambit of employment cases involving IOs, another argument that is sometimes invoked to justify a lack of subject-matter jurisdiction is that such disputes would fall within the exclusive competence of a forum other than municipal courts. It should be noted that this argument is by no means alternative to an invocation of exclusive IO jurisdiction, and, indeed, the two justifications for abstaining from adjudicating IO staff disputes may coexist and overlap in judicial practice. Nevertheless, they remain conceptually distinct: here the emphasis is not so much on the supposedly watertight separation between the national legal system and IO internal law as on the perceived obligation to respect the exclusive competence of another forum.[47]

Before going into more detail, it is useful to provide a brief rundown of the remedies that IOs set up for settling staff disputes. Practically all major IOs have either created an administrative tribunal of their own or avail themselves of some other organisation's tribunal to resolve disputes with their staff.[48] Separate administrative tribunals have been established, for instance, by the Council of Europe, the World Bank and the North Atlantic Treaty Organization.[49] But the most notable examples of such judicial bodies are to be found within the frameworks of the UN and the International Labour Organization (ILO). With regard to the UN system, the General Assembly set up an Administrative Tribunal (UNAT) in 1949. Despite some initial controversy as to whether the Assembly had the power to disregard its decisions, in the 1954 *Effect of Awards* Advisory Opinion the International Court of Justice (ICJ) found the UNAT to be a proper judicial body and its judgments to be binding over other UN organs.[50] In response to criticism levelled at its

[46] See, eg France, Court of Cassation, *African Development Bank v X* 25 January 2005, No 04-41012, ILDC 778 (FR 2005) para 4, affirming that the French nationality of the employee, who worked for the African Development Bank in Ivory Coast, established a sufficient connection with France to entertain jurisdiction.

[47] Reinisch, *International Organizations* (n 30) 103.

[48] A Pellet, *Les voies de recours ouvertes aux fonctionnaires internationaux* (Paris, Pedone, 1982).

[49] O Elias and M Thomas, 'Administrative Tribunals of International Organizations' in C Giorgetti (ed), *The Rules, Practice, and Jurisprudence of International Courts and Tribunals* (Leiden, Nijhoff, 2012) 159.

[50] *Effect of awards of compensation made by the UN Administrative Tribunal* (Advisory Opinion) [1954] ICJ Rep 47.

scarce impartiality and efficiency,[51] the UN system for settling staff disputes was completely redesigned in 2009 with the creation of a court of first instance, the UN Dispute Tribunal (UNDT), and an appellate court, the UN Appeals Tribunal.[52]

Regarding the ILO Administrative Tribunal (ILOAT), its primary importance derives from the fact that a large number of other IOs – including certain UN Specialized Agencies, such as the Food and Agriculture Organization (FAO) and the World Health Organization (WHO) – have chosen to submit their staff disputes to its jurisdiction.[53] The ILOAT's judgments are final and binding, except for an exceptional possibility of review which does not extend to mistakes of law.[54] The decisions of both the UNAT and the ILOAT were originally subject to a review by the ICJ. The grounds, however, were limited to whether the Tribunals acted within the boundaries of their jurisdiction or committed a fundamental fault of procedure, and such a review was activated only three times within the UN framework[55] and two times in the ILOAT's case.[56] This procedure, which only the IOs and not the employee could initiate, attracted criticism as being contrary to the principle of equality of arms and was removed from the UNAT Statute in 1995 and from the ILOAT Statute in 2016.[57]

It is important to note that the IOs' internal remedies for staff disputes are by no means limited to administrative tribunals. Judicial remedies are normally complemented by non-judicial means of redress, including, for instance, the request for review of the contested decision by the hierarchical superior or the recourse to an internal advisory board which delivers non-binding recommendations to the IO's administration. The staff rules may require the prior exhaustion of such remedies as a condition for the initiation of proceedings before an administrative tribunal.[58] In smaller organisations where no tribunal has been created or that have not accepted the ILOAT's jurisdiction, such non-judicial remedies may constitute the only internal remedies available to the staff. Furthermore,

[51] UN, 'Expert Panel on United Nations Internal Justice Submits Report to Secretary-General, Says Fundamental Overhaul Essential for Management Reform Success', Press Release No ORG/1470 (20 July 2006).

[52] A Reinisch and C Knahr, 'From the United Nations Administrative Tribunal to the United Nations Appeals Tribunal – Reform of the Administration of Justice System within the United Nations' (2008) 12 *Max Planck Yearbook of United Nations Law* 447.

[53] For a full list, see ILOAT Membership, www.ilo.org/tribunal/membership/lang–en/.

[54] Art VI(1) ILOAT Statute 1946.

[55] *Application for Review of Judgment No 158 of the UNAT* (Advisory Opinion) [1973] ICJ Rep 166; *Application for Review of Judgment No 273 of the UNAT* (Advisory Opinion) [1982] ICJ Rep 325; *Application for Review of Judgment No 333 of the UNAT* (Advisory Opinion) [1987] ICJ Rep 18.

[56] *Judgments of the Administrative Tribunal of the ILO upon Complaints made against the UNESCO* (Advisory Opinion) [1956] ICJ Rep 77; *Judgment No 2867 of the Administrative Tribunal of the International Labour Organization upon a Complaint Filed against the International Fund for Agricultural Development* (Advisory Opinion) [2012] ICJ Rep 10.

[57] See UN General Assembly Resolution 50/54 (11 December 1995).

[58] S Villalpando, 'The Law of the International Civil Service' in JK Cogan et al (eds), *The Oxford Handbook of International Organizations* (Oxford, Oxford University Press, 2016) 1069, 1090–91.

the jurisdiction *ratione personae* of administrative tribunals is limited to staff members.[59] Individuals on contract with the IO who are not formally qualified as employees – such as temporary workers, consultants, contractors, interns or volunteers – may only have access to other means of redress, notably arbitration.[60]

Returning to the main object of this subsection, the existence of an internal remedy for staff disputes has sometimes been found to be a sufficient reason, or at least one of the deciding factors, for ousting the jurisdiction of domestic courts. The leading case is *Hetzel*: the Baden-Württemberg Higher Administrative Tribunal,[61] with a reasoning later espoused by the German Constitutional Court,[62] held that the ILOAT possessed exclusive competence to rule over staff disputes with Eurocontrol and therefore declined jurisdiction. Eurocontrol, it should be noted, is not granted any jurisdictional immunity under its constituent instrument save for some immunity from measures of constraint.[63] One of the key issues brought before the German courts related to the construction of a provision of the Eurocontrol staff regulations, according to which 'Any dispute between the Agency and one of the persons referred to in the present Conditions (Staff Regulations) … shall be referred to the [ILOAT], *in the absence of a competent national jurisdiction*'.[64] The German courts interpreted the last part of this provision as merely restating that the jurisdiction of the ILOAT was exclusive. That provision, in other words, was considered to be largely pleonastic, which suggests that the courts would have found the ILOAT to be exclusively competent even in the absence of said provision. It has been noted, however, that the staff regulation's ambiguous wording might as well have been construed as implying that the ILOAT's jurisdiction was only subsidiary to national courts.[65]

Aside from this narrow question of interpretation, the idea that the existence of administrative tribunals would *ipso facto* deprive national courts of subject-matter jurisdiction is perplexing. Domestic courts and IO internal remedies derive their jurisdiction from different legal bases: the former from domestic procedural law, the latter from international law and IO internal law. The abstract possibility to bring employment claims against IOs before domestic courts may give rise to a jurisdictional overlap with IO internal remedies, but this fact alone is insufficient

[59] A Riddell, 'Administrative Boards, Commissions and Tribunals in International Organizations' (2012) *Max Planck Encyclopedia of Public International Law*, paras 11–13.

[60] R Gulati and T John, 'Arbitrating Employment Disputes Involving International Organizations' in P Quayle (ed), *The Role of Administrative Law at International Organizations* (Leiden, Brill Nijhoff, 2021) 141.

[61] *Hetzel v Eurocontrol* Order of 7 August 1979, No IV 1355/79.

[62] *Eurocontrol II* Order of 10 November 1981, BverfGE 58, 1, 2 BvR 1058/79.

[63] International Convention relating to Cooperation for the Safety of Air Navigation 1960, Art 27.

[64] WEU Staff Regulations, Art 93(1), quoted in *Eurocontrol II* (n 62) s I(3) (emphasis added).

[65] Reinisch, *International Organizations* (n 30) 105–06. The latter construction was espoused in the Netherlands, Sittard Local Court, *Eckhardt v Eurocontrol* 25 June 1976, reversed by Maastricht District Court, *Eckhardt v Eurocontrol (No 2)* 12 January 1984, 94 ILR 331, on the grounds that the Eurocontrol staff regulations ruled out the competence of national courts *in toto* (337–38) and that Eurocontrol enjoyed immunity under customary international law (337–39).

to rule out a role for national courts. When it comes to the interplay of international and national fora, there exists no uniform model of regulation.[66] This interaction may be regulated by treaty,[67] in which case, of course, nothing would prevent the administrative tribunal's jurisdiction from being considered exclusive. However, such provisions are rarely found. One example is Article V of the Organization of American States (OAS) Headquarters Agreement, which provides that 'The Organization shall have exclusive jurisdiction over the resolution of any and all disputes and matters arising out of, related to, or deriving from employment in, by, or with the Organization'.[68] The rarity of such provisions should not be surprising. The intuitive reason is that the main tool employed at the international level to manage the scope of jurisdiction of national courts vis-à-vis IOs are jurisdictional immunity provisions, which – it will be remembered – presuppose the jurisdiction of national courts.[69] Immunity is indirectly concerned with the administrative tribunals' jurisdiction, insofar as it frees them from the competition of national courts. However, the reach of immunity and the scope of the internal IO remedy's jurisdiction may or may not be coextensive.

Apart from the above, there do not seem to be other grounds for affirming that international law limits national courts' adjudicative power over staff disputes with IOs. Hence, the possibility of a competing exercise of jurisdiction cannot be excluded, with the consequence that an employee may be entitled to choose between different remedies. It has been argued in scholarship that the ensuing risk of conflicting pronouncements would be 'compelling evidence against the argument favoring a role for domestic courts' in this matter.[70] But this is a flawed argument: by this logic, national courts should never pronouce over international legal matters that may potentially be adjudicated in international fora. However, it is widely recognised that national courts may perform a role in international law adjudication.[71] One sees no reason why this role should not in principle encompass IO staff disputes.[72]

Where immunity is not implicated, national courts may have recourse to a number of (discretionary or otherwise) judicial tools for managing the jurisdictional interplay with internal IO remedies, on the assumption that valid policy reasons – eg judicial economy and the principle of legal certainty – militate against

[66] Y Shany, *Regulating Jurisdictional Interactions between National and International Courts* (Oxford, Oxford University Press, 2007) 39.

[67] ibid 27–39.

[68] Headquarters Agreement between the Organisation of American States and the Government of the United States of America 1992.

[69] See ch 2, s II.

[70] RSJ Martha, 'International Financial Institutions and Claims of Private Parties: Immunity Obliges' in H Cissé, DD Bradlow and B Kingsbury, *The World Bank Law Review, vol 3: International Financial Institutions and Global Legal Governance* (The World Bank Group, 2011) 93, 114.

[71] Shany (n 66) 5.

[72] A Reinisch, 'To What Extent Can and Should National Courts Fill the Accountability Gap?' (2013) 10 *International Organizations Law Review* 572, 581.

the multiplication of proceedings over the same matter.[73] The type and functioning of such jurisdiction-regulating measures is highly contingent on domestic law. One example is the principle of *res judicata*, which in many jurisdictions may be applied vis-à-vis international awards and judgments.[74] Employment proceedings brought before national courts and administrative tribunals, being instituted between the same parties and based on the same object and cause, can meet the classic 'triple identity' requirement for the application of *res judicata*.[75] Consider, for instance, the *Popineau* case, where a European Patent Organisation (EPO) employee, after losing a wrongful termination claim before the ILOAT,[76] attempted to challenge the decision before the French courts. The Conseil d'État did not refer expressly to *res judicata*, but nonetheless affirmed that no international or national sources gave it competence to second-guess an ILOAT decision.[77] In other legal systems, by contrast, courts leave room for a potential duplication of proceedings. In *Broadbent*, for example, the DC District Court was seised of an action for wrongful termination brought by seven former staff members of the OAS. All seven had previously filed complaints with the OAS Administrative Tribunal, which had upheld their claims and awarded an indemnity.[78] Neither the District Court nor, on appeal, the DC Circuit Court of Appeals suggested their jurisdiction to be barred by the mere fact that the dispute had already been adjudicated. Instead, both courts refused to entertain jurisdiction on the sole grounds of immunity.[79] In *Khan*, the Bangladesh Supreme Court, having established that the World Bank did not enjoy immunity from civil jurisdiction under relevant treaty and statutory provisions, affirmed jurisdiction over an unfair dismissal claim even though the plaintiff had already obtained compensation from the World Bank Administrative Tribunal.[80] While this duplication of proceedings is undoubtedly problematic, this issue may not be resolved by arbitrarily extending the scope of immunity.

Other jurisdiction-regulating rules may operate at the level of contractual stipulations in the form of arbitration clauses or choice-of-forum clauses. A contract clause of the latter type, for example, was considered in the *Silberreis* case, an

[73] On the policy reasons against parallel proceedings, see G Zarra, *Parallel Proceedings in Investment Arbitration* (Turin/The Hague, Giappichelli/Eleven, 2017) 37–46. On judicial economy, see FM Palombino, 'Judicial Economy and Limitation of the Scope of the Decision in International Adjudication' (2010) 23 *Leiden Journal of International Law* 909.

[74] Shany (n 66) 160; A Reinisch, 'The Use and Limits of *Res Judicata* and *Lis Pendens* as Procedural Tools to Avoid Conflicting Dispute Settlement Outcomes' (2004) 3 *The Law and Practice of International Courts and Tribunals* 37.

[75] See V Lowe, '*Res Judicata* and the Rule of Law in International Arbitration' (1996) 8 *African Journal of International and Comparative Law* 38, 40–41.

[76] *In re Popineau* Judgment No 1363, 13 July 1994.

[77] *Popineau v Office Européen des Brevets* 15 February 1995, No 161784.

[78] *Chrétien v Secretary-General of the OAS* Judgment No 29, 1 June 1977; *Hebblewaite, Stone, Castro, Martinez and Broadbent v Secretary-General of the OAS* Judgment No 30, 1 June 1977.

[79] *Broadbent et al v Organization of American States et al* 481 F.Supp 907 (DDC 1978); *Broadbent et al v Organization of American States et al* 628 F.2d 27 (DC Cir 1980).

[80] *Ismet Zerin Khan* (n 37).

action brought by an auxiliary staff member of the EPO who claimed that the EPO's decision not to renew his contract of employment fell in breach of German labour law. The Berlin Landesarbeitsgericht eventually declined jurisdiction on grounds of immunity. However, one of the issues related to the interpretation of a clause of the employment contract, which read: 'Conditions of employment shall otherwise be governed by the employment and social welfare legislation in force at the place of employment; this shall also apply to matters of recourse to the national courts.' The contract, in other words, set forth a principle of residual applicability of municipal law and recognised the jurisdiction of national courts in such cases. The Court declined to exercise jurisdiction on the basis of this clause because it found the conditions applicable to fixed-term contracts to be regulated by the EPO's internal law and thus not to be subject to German law and jurisdiction.[81] The case was later adjudicated by the ILOAT, which adhered to the Berlin court's interpretation of the contract clause.[82]

A more detailed analysis of such jurisdiction-regulating tools exceeds the scope of this work. However, the key takeaway of the above discussion is that, as a default rule, national courts possess subject-matter jurisdiction over staff disputes with IOs as long as the required territorial and personal connecting links are present. The possibility to exercise such jurisdiction *in concreto* should normally be assessed at the later stage of immunity.

III. Absolute Immunity Based on Functionalist Policy Arguments

A second pathway for the total exclusion of employment disputes from domestic proceedings is the reliance on what may be described as functionalist policy arguments. While such views, as will be seen, come in several variations, they all share the core contention that the exercise of jurisdiction over labour claims should be avoided because it would unduly prevent the employers from performing their functions.

IO immunity is the area where this approach has been most pervasive. Besides being invoked when construing the meaning of 'functional immunity' under the many IO immunity instruments setting forth this standard,[83] policy considerations of this sort have been variously relied on to contend that IOs should be entrusted with blanket immunity in all circumstances, regardless of the immunity standard set forth by the applicable treaty or statutory provision. The underlying rationale is that any inquiry into the internal organic structure of an IO would inevitably result

[81] Berlin State Labor Court, *Silberreis v European Patent Organization* 12 September 1994, 16 Sa 58/94.

[82] *In re Kock, N'diaye and Silberreiss* Judgment No 1450, 6 July 1995, paras 15–18.

[83] See ch 2, s VB.

in some degree of encroachment, however indirect, upon its functions.[84] Another point to note is that these arguments, while generally invoked in the context of discussions on immunity, often do not clearly distinguish between immunity from jurisdiction and exemption from substantive law. This is mainly because the need to shield IOs from the application of local laws is itself invoked as one of the policy considerations justifying blanket immunity, on the assumption that 'municipal courts will not apply the [internal] laws of international organizations'.[85] Hence, in practice, these approaches may end up not differing much from the assertions of exclusive IO jurisdiction examined in the previous section. Take, for example, Brower's claim that functional necessity grounds justify immunity for all employment disputes involving IOs.[86] In this author's view, such grounds break down in an array of policy arguments where considerations of jurisdiction and applicable law are intertwined: notably, that the insulation from domestic legal systems is necessary to 'reinforce [IOs'] independence and neutrality' from their member states;[87] or that the relation between an IO and its staff resembles employment with the armed forces, in that both employers require their staff to adhere to 'strict codes of conduct [that are] vital to [their] survival'.[88]

Reliance on similar arguments is recurrent in judicial practice. A typical restatement can be found in a 1993 judgment of a Swiss court in an employment dispute against the Arab League. In the absence of treaty provisions granting immunity from suit, the court nonetheless granted immunity on the grounds that IOs 'can only carry out their tasks if they are beyond the censure of the courts of member states'.[89] Another example is *Killeen*, a judgment rendered by the Nairobi High Court.[90] The case was lodged by a visiting scientist under a two-year contract with the International Centre of Insect Physiology and Ecology (ICIPE), an IO based in Kenya. The ICIPE enjoyed immunity pursuant to a Kenyan statute that the Court of Appeal, in the leading case of *Tononoka*, had previously construed as granting an immunity analogous to restrictive state immunity.[91] While nominally adhering to *Tononoka*, the High Court in fact applied a functional immunity standard and justified it by quoting the functional immunity provision of Article 105 UN Charter. On this basis, it upheld immunity. It argued that doing otherwise 'would set a dangerous precedent and would adversely affect the hiring and control of staff employed to carry out the organizations purposes'.[92]

[84] See, eg A Quaglino, 'In tema di immunità del CIME dalla giurisdizione italiana nelle controversie in materia di lavoro' (1974) 10 *Rivista di diritto internazionale privato e processuale* 487, 500.

[85] Brower (n 24) 69.

[86] ibid.

[87] ibid. Similarly Amerasinghe, *Principles* (n 23) 272.

[88] Brower (n 24) 69.

[89] Geneva Labor Court, *ZM v Permanent Delegation of the League of Arab States to the UN* 17 November 1993, 116 ILR 643, paras 22–25.

[90] *Killeen v International Centre of Insect Physiology and Ecology* 27 May 2005, Civil Case No 1737 of 2002, ILDC 77 (KE 2005).

[91] *Tononoka Steels Limited v Eastern and Southern Africa Trade and Development Bank* 13 August 1999, Civil Appeal No 255 of 1998, ILDC 1283 (KE 1999).

[92] *Killeen* (n 90) para 9.

US courts have been at the forefront of the use of policy arguments in the construction of the concept of functional immunity. In the aforementioned 1980 *Broadbent* case, the DC Circuit upheld the immunity of the OAS from a wrongful termination suit. The court reasoned:

> An attempt by the courts of one nation to adjudicate the personnel claims of international civil servants would entangle those courts in the internal administration of those organizations. Denial of immunity opens the door to divided decisions of the courts of different member states passing judgment on the rules, regulations, and decisions of the international bodies. Undercutting uniformity in the application of staff rules or regulations would undermine the ability of the organization to function effectively.[93]

Three years later, in *Mendaro*, the same court further expounded on this reasoning. The case was an action for sexual harassment and discrimination filed by a researcher at the World Bank. She alleged to have been fired shortly after complaining about verbal and physical avances by other employees. The Bank's immunity was upheld. In the court's words:

> the purpose of immunity from employee actions is rooted in the need to protect international organizations from unilateral control by a member nation over the activities of the international organization within its territory. The sheer difficulty of administering multiple employment practices in each area in which an organization operates suggests that the purposes of an organization could be greatly hampered if it could be subjected to suit by its employees worldwide.[94]

Functional arguments of this kind have been constantly restated in subsequent US case law. In the 1990 case of *Chiriboga*, the DC District Court qualified as an employment lawsuit an action to recover benefits accruing from the accident insurance policy of the World Bank filed by relatives of a deceased employee. This led the Court to decline to exercise jurisdiction on the basis of *Broadbent* and *Mendaro*.[95] In *Boimah*, a district court upheld immunity by applying the 1946 General Convention's full immunity clause.[96] In a meaningful obiter, the court gave its view on the correct construction of the UN Charter's Article 105 functional immunity clause and opined that 'an international organization's self-regulation of its employment practices is an activity essential to the fulfillment of its purposes, and thus an area to which immunity must extend'.[97] *Broadbent* and *Mendaro* were cited with approval, again in obiter, in *Brzak*, where it was held that 'employment-related issues lie at the core of an international organization's immunity'.[98]

[93] *Broadbent* (n 79) 35.
[94] *Mendaro v World Bank* 717 F.2d 610 (DC Cir 1983) 615–16.
[95] *Chiriboga v International Bank for Reconstruction* 616 F.Supp 963 (DDC 1985) 967.
[96] Convention on the Privileges and Immunities of the United Nations 1946, Art II(2). On the construction of full immunity clauses in employment claims, see below s VI.
[97] *Boimah v United Nations General Assembly* 113 ILR 499, 664 F.Supp 69 (EDNY 1987) 71.
[98] *Brzak v United Nations* 551 F.Supp 2d 313 (SDNY 2008) 319, affirmed *Brzak and Ishak v United Nations et al* 597 F.3d 107 (2d Cir 2010).

US courts have also made use of functionalist policy considerations in another (but by no means alternative) way. Starting from the assumption that the US International Organizations Immunities Act 1945 (IOIA) granted IOs a de facto absolute immunity from employment suits, such courts have treated the immunity provisions of international agreements as possible exceptions to the default rule of absolute immunity – or, according to the prevailing terminology, as treaty-based waivers.[99] Functionalist arguments have been pivotal in the construction of such waivers. In particular, in order to assess whether to allow for derogation to absolute immunity, courts relied on a cost–benefit analysis of the exercise of jurisdiction over an IO: immunity could be considered as waived only where the exercise of jurisdiction could prove advantageous for an IO.[100] This line of reasoning was developed, again, in *Mendaro*, where one of the issues before the court was whether the World Bank's Articles of Agreement, which do not expressly provide for immunity from adjudicative jurisdiction but only bar measures of constraint,[101] could be interpreted as waiving the Bank's immunity in the context of employment disputes. The court approached this question on the basis of the following judicial test:

> Since the purpose of [IO immunities] is to enable the organizations to fulfil their functions, applying the same rationale in reverse, it is likely that most organizations would be unwilling to relinquish their immunity without receiving a corresponding benefit which would further the organization's goal.[102]

Unsurprisingly, this test resulted in blanket immunity from labour claims: it is hard to see how being sued by an employee could ever qualify as 'beneficial' for an employer. The *Mendaro* court found that the only type of suits that may be deemed beneficial to an international finance institution were those brought by private parties lending money to the IO: not allowing such suits may hamper the IO's functions by diminishing the investors' confidence and the IO's creditworthiness.[103] By contrast, it opined that a waiver of immunity from the Bank's internal operations, including employment, would risk creating 'devastating administrative consequences without materially advancing its chartered objectives':

> this waiver would lay the Bank open to disruptive interference with its employment policies in each of the thirty-six countries in which it has resident missions, and the more than 140 nations in which it could be involved in its lending and financing activities.

[99] M Singer, 'Jurisdictional Immunity of International Organizations: Human Rights and Functional Necessity Concerns' (1995) 36 *Virginia Journal of International Law* 53, 80–84, using the term 'constitutive waiver' in order to differentiate from ad hoc waivers.

[100] A Reinisch and J Wurm, 'International Finance Institutions before National Courts' in DD Bradlow and DB Hunter (eds), *International Finance Institutions and International Law* (Alphen aan den Rijn, Wolters Kluwer, 2010) 103, 117.

[101] Articles of Agreement of the International Bank for Reconstruction and Development 1944, Art VII(3).

[102] *Mendaro* (n 94) 617.

[103] ibid 618. See further A Viterbo, 'Immunità dalla giurisdizione della Banca mondiale e diritto di accesso al giudice' (2018) 12 *Diritti umani e diritto internazionale* 397, 402–03.

> Revising and administering consistent employment policies for a large administrative staff which includes citizens from more than 100 countries is difficult enough. If the Bank were required to adopt the local employment policies of each of its member countries this task would become nearly impossible.[104]

The application of the 'corresponding benefit' test in ensuing case law confirms that this approach is equivalent to a grant of absolute immunity in labour matters. In *Atkinson*, which concerned the different context of garnishment proceedings, the DC Circuit in obiter confirmed *Mendaro*'s point that labour lawsuits would be detrimental to an IO's functions.[105] Jurisdiction was again denied in three more recent cases against the World Bank: *Dujardin*, a suit filed by an individual who alleged to have been promised employment benefits by the Bank;[106] *Hudes*, a wrongful termination suit by a former lawyer at the Bank;[107] and *Smith*, a discrimination lawsuit.[108] All three cases were decided by applying the *Mendaro* 'corresponding benefit' test. The aforementioned *Chiriboga* judgment is more distinctive because the court curiously searched for a waiver not within the World Bank's Articles of Agreement but within the statute of the World Bank Administrative Tribunal. It ruled that no waiver had been granted because the Tribunal had jurisdiction over claims by staff members, their representatives and persons entitled to claim upon the rights of deceased employees.[109] This part of the judgment came close to an implicit assertion of exclusive competence of an administrative tribunal[110] (yet the court did not take the care to verify whether an action for denial of insurance benefits fell within the competence of the Tribunal). Outside of the USA, a strikingly similar approach was adopted by the Nigerian Supreme Court in *Abate Fantaye*, a wrongful termination case against the African Reinsurance Corporation. Similarly to the World Bank Articles of Agreement, this international finance institution's constituent treaty did not provide for immunity from adjudication. The court, however, assumed that IOs enjoy absolute immunity by default and refused to construe the relevant immunity provision as a waiver because it did not expressly allow for the exercise of jurisdiction.[111]

Express reliance on functionalist arguments is much less common in the context of state immunity and diplomatic and consular immunity. The reason is

[104] *Mendaro* (n 94) 618–19.

[105] *Atkinson v Inter-American Development Bank* 156 F.3d 1335 (DC Cir 1998) 1338. The respondent's immunity was modelled on the World Bank Articles of Agreement: Agreement Establishing the Inter-American Development Bank 1959, Art XI(3).

[106] *Dujardin v International Bank for Reconstruction and Development et al* 9 F App'x 19 (DC Cir 2001).

[107] *Hudes v Aetna Life Ins Co et al* 806 F.Supp 2d 180 (DDC 2011).

[108] *Smith v World Bank Group et al* 99 F.Supp 3d 166 (DDC 2015), affirmed *Smith v World Bank Group et al* 694 F App'x 1 (DC Cir 2017). See also *Price v Unisea Inc and Others* 289 P3d 914 (Alaska 2012), ILDC 2132 (US 2012), finding the International Pacific Halibut Commission, a bilateral US–Canadian IO, fully immune from suit on the basis of *Mendaro* and *Atkinson*.

[109] *Chiriboga* (n 95) 968.

[110] See above s IIB.

[111] *African Reinsurance Corporation v Abate Fantaye* 20 June 1986, 86 ILR 655.

easy to grasp: the existence of detailed legal standards of immunity leaves little room for adjudicating on the sole basis of policy considerations. Yet such arguments may still exert an impact on these sectors of immunity law by influencing, expressly or tacitly, the interpretation of the relevant immunity standards. The *Butters v Vance* case before the US Fourth Circuit provides an example where this influence was unequivocal. The respondent was a private company headquartered in Virginia which provided security to the US residence of a princess of the Saudi royal family. Butters, an employee of Vance, sued for gender discrimination, claiming not to have been promoted to a higher position due to her being a woman. The promotion had allegedly been denied upon Saudi officials' indications that, under Islamic law, a woman might not be assigned to higher functions. The court declined jurisdiction by applying the principles of state immunity. It found that, because the decision over the promotion of Butters was ultimately ascribable to Saudi Arabia, Vance was entitled to derivative immunity qua agent of a foreign state.[112] This finding defied the letter of the US Foreign Sovereign Immunities Act 1976 (US FSIA), according to which neither entirely private companies nor companies legally incorporated in the USA meet the definition of 'agency or instrumentality of a foreign state' for the purposes of applying state immunity.[113] This outcome was justified on functionalist grounds. In the court's words:

> All sovereigns need flexibility to hire private agents to aid them in conducting their governmental functions. This is especially true for foreign sovereigns given their lack of human resources while operating within the United States … [I]mposing civil liability on the private agents of Saudi Arabia would significantly impede the Saudi government's sovereign interest in protecting its leaders while they are in the United States.[114]

As is evident, *Butters* is strikingly reminiscent of the US precedents on IO immunity: the court embraced an absolutist understanding of state immunity for fear that exercising jurisdiction over employment claims might prevent a state from fulfilling its sovereign functions.

The approaches that have just been described raise a number of issues. There is, first of all, a methodological flaw in using policy arguments to justify blanket immunisation from employment-related claims. The fact that functional necessity is the rationale for granting privileges and immunities does not entail that the scope of immunity can be construed by drawing solely on the concept of functionality: functional necessity is merely the theoretical basis of immunity,

[112] *Butters v Vance International, Inc* 225 F.3d 462 (4th Cir 2000) 466.

[113] Foreign Sovereign Immunities Act 1976 (US FSIA), s 1603(a), pursuant to which an agency or instrumentality should meet three requirements, ie being (i) 'a separate legal person, corporate or otherwise', (ii) 'an organ of a foreign state … or a majority of whose shares or other ownership interest is owned by a foreign state' and (iii) 'neither a citizen of a State of the United States … nor created under the laws of any third country'. Vance International only met the first requirement: see AH Wen, 'Suing the Sovereign's Servant: The Implications of Privatization for the Scope of Foreign Sovereign Immunities' (2003) 103 *Columbia Law Review* 1538, 1551.

[114] *Butters* (n 112) 466.

not the measure of its scope.[115] Rather, what determines the reach of immunity is the standard contemplated by the applicable treaty or statutory provision (which should be construed according to the ordinary rules of treaty or statutory interpretation) or, in the case of state immunity, by customary international law. Because any immunity standard already reflects a balance of underlying policy concerns, discussions on grounds of policy should normally be considered as absorbed.

Admittedly, the situation is different when it comes to construing a specific standard of IO immunity, ie functional immunity, as notably enshrined in Article 105 UN Charter. Because this standard inherently refers to functional necessity considerations, a reliance on functionalist arguments may appear justified. But even if we restrict the analysis to the interpretation of this standard, there are several substantive reasons for being critical of the use of policy arguments to uphold blanket immunity from employment claims. First, the absolutist approaches described above are all premised on the idea that national courts would apply domestic employment law to an organisation. However, as seen above, this is not necessarily true.[116] The practice of certain municipal courts to apply IO internal law to the merits of a case has been lauded by prominent scholars as a way of limiting the intrusiveness of the judicial scrutiny in the internal affairs of an IO:[117] this proves that there are ways of safeguarding the independence of IOs also where national courts exercise jurisdiction over them.

But even assuming that, in certain countries, the judiciary might not be willing or empowered to apply IOs' internal laws, this would be far from a conclusive argument in favour of absolute immunity in employment matters. It is not very realistic to suggest, as in *Broadbent* and *Mendaro*, that the necessity to comply with the employment legislation of multiple countries would render IOs incapable of performing their functions. Certainly, it would be an administrative hassle;[118] but both private companies and sovereign states operating in the territory of foreign countries are well used to dealing with such complications without their operational capabilities being evidently affected. The plaintiff in *Mendaro* had a point in suggesting that the practice of multinational corporations showed that 'it may be possible to devise and administer consistent and fair employment policies in multiple jurisdictions'.[119] The court summarily rejected this submission by noting that IOs 'owe their primary allegiance to the principles and policies established by their organic documents, and not to the evolving legislation of any one member'.[120] But this is a circular argument: the reason why IOs cannot function

[115] See the discussion in ch 2, s III.

[116] Above s IIA.

[117] Reinisch, *International Organizations* (n 30) 244–45; J Wouters, C Ryngaert and P Schmitt, 'Western European Union v. Siedler, General Secretariat of the ACP Group v. Lutchmaya, General Secretariat of the ACP Group v. B.D.' (2011) 105 *American Journal of International Law* 560, 566.

[118] On the undeniable practical advantages of having an autonomous system of law governing employment relationships, see Villalpando (n 58) 1070; Amerasinghe, *Principles* (n 23) 277–79.

[119] *Mendaro* (n 94) 619.

[120] ibid.

subject to municipal employment law is that they are not subject to municipal employment law.

In sum, it would appear that the belief that IOs need full immunisation from domestic jurisdiction in order to be able to perform their functions is as questionable in the field of employment as it is in any other sector of civil litigation: it is more of a postulate than something that has been analytically proven.[121] The wealth of domestic employment cases in which IOs have been involved without suffering the 'devastating' administrative consequences foretold by the *Mendaro* court is a further indication that this equation is facile. Moreover, the existence of constitutive treaties or headquarters agreements expressly permitting employees to sue their IO employer before domestic courts raises doubts over the view that absolute immunity in this field is a *sine qua non* of the protection of the IOs' functional needs. This point was raised by the Constitutional Court of Georgia in a 2002 wrongful termination case involving the International Committee of the Red Cross (ICRC).[122] Even though the host agreement between the ICRC and Georgia included a typical full immunity provision (ie providing for 'immunity from every form of legal process'), the Court instead resolved to apply a 'functional immunity' standard modelled on Article 105 UN Charter.[123] In this respect, it is arguable that the Court erred in applying a standard different from the one expressly mandated by the applicable treaty. Nonetheless, what is relevant for the present discussion is that the concept of functional immunity was construed as not requiring immunity from employment claims. Interestingly, one of the reasons for this assessment was that the ICRC does not enjoy immunity from employment claims before the Swiss courts.[124] The ICRC–Switzerland Headquarters Agreement indeed contains an express exception to the ICRC's immunity from legal process 'in respect of a dispute, on relations of service, between the Committee and its staff, former staff or their rightful claimants'.[125] From this provision, the Georgian Constitutional Court inferred, in more general terms, that the ICRC did not necessitate immunity from labour lawsuits in order to perform its functions.

Mendaro's 'corresponding benefit' test is equally problematic. It is true, on the one hand, that the immediate reason why the constituent treaties of the World Bank and other international finance institutions do not contemplate immunity

[121] See ch 2, s VB.

[122] Although the ICRC is not an international organisation (see P Gargiulo, 'Croce rossa internazionale' in *Digesto delle discipline pubblicistiche*, vol IV (Turin, UTET, 1989) 488), its status is often analogous to that of IOs on the basis of headquarters agreements providing for privileges and immunities: see T Neumann and A Peters, 'Switzerland' in A Reinisch (ed), *The Privileges and Immunities of International Organizations in Domestic Courts* (Oxford, Oxford University Press, 2013) 241, 264.

[123] *A constitutional submission of Tbilisi Didube-Chughureti District Court*, 21 May 2002, Case No 8/177/2, ILDC 3103 (GE 2002), H3–H4.

[124] ibid A5.

[125] Agreement between the International Committee of the Red Cross and the Swiss Federal Council to determine the legal status of the Committee in Switzerland 1993, Art 5(1)(c).

from suit is that their drafters considered it preferable to allow such IOs to be sued by their creditors.[126] On the other hand, this underlying rationale is immaterial when it comes to interpreting unambiguous treaty provisions permitting civil lawsuits to be brought before domestic courts without distinguishing between creditors and other private parties. The construction of such instruments in *Mendaro* and its progeny is thus countertextual and the use of the term 'waiver' is technically improper, because there can only be a waiver where there is immunity in the first place.[127] More fundamentally, there is no basis in international law to presuppose that all IOs are absolutely immune from suit save for express or implicit exceptions to be found in treaty provisions. Quite the opposite, one should expect an IO to be absolutely immune only if a treaty so provides.[128] International finance institutions are no exception: unlike the World Bank, for instance, the International Monetary Fund is entitled to full immunity under its Articles of Agreement.[129]

As noted above, the 'corresponding benefit' test originated less from international law than from domestic law considerations: this test was used by US courts to carve out exceptions to the supposedly absolute immunity granted under the IOIA. The foundations of this approach, however, are now clearly incompatible with the 2019 US Supreme Court's *Jam* judgment, which construed the IOIA as granting IOs the same restrictive immunity enjoyed by foreign states.[130] In *Jam*, the respondent IO pleaded absolute immunity by relying on functionalist policy arguments straight from the *Mendaro* playbook. It argued, first, that the purpose of IO immunity is to allow IOs 'to freely pursue the collective goals of member countries without undue interference from the courts of any one member country';[131] and secondly, that 'to grant anything less than absolute immunity would lead to a number of undesirable results' including allowing member states 'to second-guess the collective decisions of the others' and exposing IOs to 'money damages, which would in turn make it more difficult and expensive for them to fulfill their mission'.[132] The Supreme Court disposed of these arguments by describing them as 'inflated', and noted that an IO would be free to equip itself with broader immunity via treaty if its work risked being impaired by restrictive immunity.[133] No consideration was given to whether the IO would receive a benefit from participating in

[126] Reinisch and Wurm (n 100) 105.
[127] Reinisch, *International Organizations* (n 30) 216.
[128] See below s VI.
[129] Articles of Agreement of the International Monetary Fund 1945, Art IX(10)(3).
[130] *Jam et al v International Finance Corp* 586 US (2019).
[131] ibid 8.
[132] ibid 13.
[133] ibid 14. See further P Rossi, 'The International Law Significance of *Jam v. IFC*: Some Implications for the Immunity of International Organizations' (2019) 13 *Diritti umani e diritto internazionale* 305, 311–15.

domestic litigation.[134] Although *Jam* was not an employment dispute, there is no reason why this passage's outright rejection of the equivalence between functional and absolute immunity should not be relevant to labour claims too, thus rendering *Broadbent* and *Mendaro* outdated precedents as regards their reliance on functionalist policy arguments.

IV. Absolute Immunity Based on the Public Nature of Employment

When it comes to employment claims brought against foreign states, it is common for courts and commentators to rely on the canonical formulation of restrictive state immunity, ie the distinction between *acta jure imperii* and *acta jure gestionis*.[135] On the basis of this standard, the total exclusion of labour claims from the jurisdiction of municipal courts is sometimes justified on the grounds that employment with foreign states would always have an intrinsically public nature. This approach was dominant in the early labour cases against foreign states. In the 1934 *Époux* case, an action for breach of employment contract against the Canadian Immigration Office of Antwerp, a Belgian court held that Canada, 'in engaging the plaintiff as its employee, was acting as a sovereign State and not in its capacity as a subject of private law'.[136] Shortly thereafter, in *Rosati*, an Italian court found the employment of an individual by the Russian Trade Delegation to be an act in public law.[137] Similar approaches can still be encountered in more recent legal thinking.[138] This can be explained in light of the fact that national courts commonly rely on some form of purposive analysis for applying the public–private distinction to the area of labour, ie they base their decisions, in whole or in part,

[134] cp *Jam* (n 130) Dissenting Opinion of Justice Breyer, 13–15, citing *Mendaro* and *Broadbent* with approval and supporting absolute immunity on the basis of functionalist arguments, eg: 'multilateralism is threatened if one nation alone, through application of its liability rules (by nonexpert judges), can shape the [IOs'] policy choices or actions' (14).

[135] See ch 2, s IVB. For employment cases decided on grounds of absolute immunity, see UK, *Omerri v Uganda High Commission* [1973] ITR 14; Romania, High Court of Cassation and Justice, *SDG v Canada and Prosecutor General (joining)* 1 April 2003, No 1292, ILDC 1024 (RO 2003); Ukraine, Kiev Court of Appeal, *Individual 2 v Delegation of the European Union to Ukraine* 7 October 2015, No 22-c796/12966/2015, ILDC 2499 (UA 2015), applying, for unclear reasons, absolute state immunity to a claim against the EU representation.

[136] Civil Tribunal of Antwerp, *Époux Perevostchikoff-Germeau v State of Canada* 10 October 1934, 9 ILR 249.

[137] Court of First Instance of Milan, *Rosati v Russian Trade Delegation* 13 February 1936 (1938) 30 *Rivista di diritto internazionale* 226. See also G Morelli, 'L'istituto internazionale di agricoltura e la giurisdizione italiana' (1931) 56 *Il Foro Italiano* 1424, 1430: 'il rapporto d'impiego è un rapporto di natura eminentemente pubblicistica'.

[138] eg EK Bankas, *The State Immunity Controversy in International Law. Private Suits against Sovereign States in Domestic Courts* (Berlin, Springer, 2005) 353, arguing that work for foreign states 'is always politically based and specifically geared towards the fulfilment of the sovereign function of the sending state', and 347, considering it 'incautious' to apply restrictive state immunity to employment matters.

on whether the employment relationship is aimed at the performance of public functions.[139] As seen in chapter two, the adoption of a test based on the purpose of the act may be naturally conducive to de facto absolute immunity.[140] This risk is particularly high when it comes to employment: any individual working for a state is a cog in the state machinery and is therefore somehow involved, however indirectly, in the performance of public purposes.[141] For this reason, it comes as no surprise that a reliance on purposive arguments has led courts to endorse all-embracing understandings of immunity in labour claims.

A typical example of this trend is *Sengupta*, a claim for unfair dismissal brought by a former low-grade clerk at the Indian High Commission in London. Because the UK State Immunity Act 1978 was not applicable, the contract of employment having been concluded before its adoption, the Employment Appeal Tribunal (EAT) upheld immunity based on general international law. The court rejected the submission by Dame Higgins, representing the plaintiff, that the classification of employment as private or public was dependent exclusively on the underlying contract; in other words, the nature of the act constituted the only relevant factor.[142] Under this approach, the contractual basis of employment would have sufficed to reject the plea of immunity. Browne-Wilkinson J responded that whether the contract was one that any private individual could enter into was only one aspect of the analysis. The application of the 'private person test' to the field of employment, he proposed, also depended on whether the performance of the employment contract 'involve[d] the participation of both parties in the public functions of the foreign state'.[143] Accordingly, he concluded:

> It is true that any private individual can employ another, ie can enter into a contract of employment. Therefore in that sense the entry into a contract of employment is a private act. But when one looks to see what is involved in the performance of the applicant's contract, it is clear that the performance of the contract is part of the discharge by the foreign state of its sovereign functions in which the applicant himself, at however lowly a level, is under the terms of his contract necessarily engaged.[144]

The use of purposive arguments of this sort has frequently led courts to similar results. In an unfair dismissal case brought by a former embassy driver, the Norwegian Supreme Court upheld immunity by noting that 'there is little doubt that activities at the foreign service missions of a State are in the core area of exercise

[139] X Yang, *State Immunity in International Law* (Cambridge, Cambridge University Press, 2012) 142; *Benkharbouche v Secretary of State for Foreign and Commonwealth Affairs and Secretary of State for Foreign and Commonwealth Affairs and Libya v Janah* [2017] UKSC 62, para 73, criticising *Sengupta v Republic of India* 17 November 1982, 64 ILR 352 (on which see below in text) on the grounds that 'the reasoning had more regard to the purpose than to the juridical character of the claimant's employment' and that this test 'was far too wide'.

[140] ch 2, s IVB.

[141] A Cassese (M Frulli, ed), *Diritto internazionale*, 3rd edn (Bologna, il Mulino, 2017) 121.

[142] *Sengupta* (n 139) 358.

[143] ibid 360.

[144] ibid.

of public authority' and that the 'exact position [of the employees] cannot have any bearing'.[145] In *Kato v Ishihara*, comparable reasoning led the Second Circuit Court of Appeals to decline jurisdiction over a sexual harassment suit filed by a marketing agent for the New York office of the Tokyo Metropolitan Government, an instrumentality of Japan involved in the promotion of trade and business with the USA. Applying the 'private person test' as enshrined in the US FSIA's 'commercial activity exception',[146] the court held that the plaintiff's work did not qualify as a commercial activity and thus remained covered by immunity. It reasoned that the plaintiff was employed by a branch of the state engaged in the promotion of commerce, 'a basic – even quintessential – governmental function'.[147] Considering that any foreign state's employee works *ipso facto* for an employer involved in the promotion of state interests, it is hard to imagine how a judicial test so conceived could ever lead to immunity being lifted in an employment dispute. Indeed, all subsequent US judicial decisions that have relied on the *Kato* principles have unfailingly ruled in favour of immunity.[148]

Similar arguments have sometimes also been advanced with respect to IO immunity, in circumstances where its scope is analogous to the immunity of states. The US IOIA, which grants designated IOs 'the same immunity from suit … as is enjoyed by foreign governments', is the most prominent example.[149] As seen above, the US Supreme Court judgment in *Jam* recently construed the IOIA as granting restrictive and not absolute immunity from suit; the IOIA restrictive immunity test thus corresponds to the 'private person test' laid down by the US FSIA.[150] But even though it repudiated the functionalist policy arguments for absolute immunity laid down in *Broadbent* and *Mendaro*, both of which were employment lawsuits, *Jam* did not touch upon the specific question of how restrictive immunity under the US FSIA applies to labour claims against IOs. Yet, this is a question that had already been addressed in the US case law from the pre-*Jam* era. All such cases had concluded that employment claims fell outside of the scope of the 'commercial activity exception'.

In *Broadbent* and in the following *Tuck* case, a racial discrimination lawsuit, the DC Circuit Court of Appeals refused to take a position on whether the IOIA made a *renvoi* to absolute or restrictive state immunity, a point on which US case law was split at the time. It reasoned that this question had no practical relevance because both tests would lead to the same result when it came to employment disputes: an IO would be granted immunity under the restrictive doctrine and thus a fortiori

[145] *A v Republic of B* 3 April 2004, ILDC 23 (NO 2004), 180 ILR 433, 439.

[146] US FSIA, s 1605(a)(2): 'A foreign state shall not be immune … in any case … in which the action is based upon a commercial activity carried on in the United States.' On the application of this provision to the field of employment, see below ch 4.

[147] *Kato v Ishihara* 360 F.3d 106 (2d Cir 2004) 112.

[148] On this case law, see ch 4, s IIIA.

[149] IOIA, s 2(b).

[150] *Jam* (n 130) 15, holding that, through the IOIA, 'the Foreign Sovereign Immunities Act governs the immunity of international organizations'.

under the absolute one.[151] This conclusion was based on the legislative history of the US FSIA, and notably on a passage of the House Report stipulating, inter alia, that employment by foreign states of civil service personnel should be considered as non-commercial, while 'the employment of American citizens or third country nationals by the foreign state in the United States' constituted a commercial activity. The Court held, first, that all administrative personnel of an IO qualified as 'civil service' and was therefore covered by immunity;[152] and secondly, that the nationality-based exceptions to immunity were not applicable to IOs: 'their civil servants are inevitably drawn from either American citizens or "third" country nations. In the case of international organizations, such an exception would swallow up the rule of immunity for civil service employment disputes.'[153] The *Broadbent* court reinforced this conclusion by invoking the functionalist policy arguments that have been analysed earlier in this chapter.

This reasoning has been affirmed in obiter in all subsequent US cases that have touched upon this issue. Notably, these cases have clarified that the principles espressed in *Broadbent* and *Tuck* apply not only to administrative personnel, but to all the 'internal staff' of IOs. The court in *Boimah*, for example, proclaimed that 'even if the [US FSIA] applies so as to limit the [IOIA]'s grant of immunity, an international organization's employment relationship with its internal staff is not "commercial activity"'.[154] Similarly, in *Morgan*, the DC District Court uncompromisingly stated that the commercial activity exception does not apply to 'the World Bank's employment practices' including the hiring of an external contractor performing secretarial duties.[155] These US precedents have influenced the approach of the Canadian courts as well. In *Trempe*, an action for wrongful dismissal brought by a former employee of the International Civil Aviation Organization (ICAO), the Superior Court of Quebec was called upon to interpret the scope of Article 3(1) of the ICAO Headquarters Agreement, pursuant to which 'The Organization … shall enjoy the same immunity from suit … as is enjoyed by foreign states'.[156] It held that employment relationships between an organisation and its staff were not to be qualified as private acts, and cited *Mendaro* and *Broadbent* as the most influential authorities.[157]

[151] *Broadbent* (n 79) 33; *Tuck v Pan American Health Organization* 668 F.2d 547 (DC Cir 1981) 550.

[152] The meaning of 'civil service' for the purposes of state immunity from employment claims is not clarified by the House Report and case law has devised various approaches to flesh out its meaning. On this point, see ch 4, s IV.

[153] *Broadbent* (n 79) 34; cited with approval in *Tuck* (n 151) 550.

[154] *Boimah* (n 97) 71. See also *Hunter v United Nations et al* 800 NYS.2d 347 (Sup Ct NY County 2004), ILDC 693 (US 2004).

[155] *Morgan v International Bank for Reconstruction and Development* 752 F.Supp 492 (DDC 1990) 494. See also *Weidner v International Telecommunications Satellite Organization* 392 A.2d 508 (DC 1978).

[156] Headquarters Agreement between the Government of Canada and the International Civil Aviation Organization 1990.

[157] *Trempe v Staff Association of the International Civil Aviation Organization and ors* 20 November 2003, ILDC 1748 (CA 2003) para 84. On the influence of *Broadbent* and *Mendaro* on *Trempe*, see PM Saunders, 'Canada' in Reinisch (n 122) 73, 93.

The main issue with these judicial trends is that the outcomes reached by the courts are entirely contingent upon highly subjective premises, as is frequently the case with the 'private person test'.[158] In effect, as noted at the beginning of this section, the labelling of all forms of employment as public acts is conceptually grounded on the *purpose* of employment, namely on its connection to the performance of the public functions of foreign states. But the approach based on the purpose of the act is only one of the two possible interpretations of the 'private person test', the other being based on the nature of the act: the above cases do not expound on the reasons why purposive considerations should have overriding importance in the field of employment. In fact, courts that have looked exclusively at the nature of the act – that is, at the contractual basis of employment – have achieved diametrically opposite outcomes. In *Bah*, for instance, the Industrial Court of Botswana broadly argued that a 'legal suit arising out of breach of the employment contract … involves a private law transaction and is justiciable'.[159] The Austrian Supreme Court proclaimed, in the 1989 *French Consular Employee* case, that 'a foreign State acts as the holder of private rights [when it] concludes a contract of employment for work to be performed on the territory of the State of the forum',[160] and its Czech equivalent similarly held that 'in proceedings concerning … labour contracts … the State does not act as the executor of public authority'.[161] The same conclusion has sometimes been reached with regard to employment with IOs. In *Sibanda*, the Zimbabwe Supreme Court adjudicated an employment claim against the ICRC on the basis of the restrictive state immunity doctrine. The Court withheld immunity on the grounds that a contract of employment clearly constituted 'an act of a private law character such as a private citizen might have entered into'.[162]

A prime example of the high subjectivity of the 'private person test' in employment matters is furnished by the decisions of the Dutch courts in the *Spaans* case. The plaintiff was a Dutch national who had worked for two years as an interpreter at the Iran–United States Claims Tribunal. He sued for unfair dismissal. In the absence of international treaty obligations binding upon the Netherlands to grant jurisdictional immunity to the Tribunal, both the first instance and the appellate court asserted that, under customary international law, the Tribunal was entitled to an immunity analogous to that of states. The two courts, however, reached radically different conclusions. To the former, an employment contract constituted an

[158] ch 2, s VB.

[159] *Bah v Libyan Embassy* No IC 956/2005, 142 ILR 167, ILDC 154 (BW 2005) para 25.

[160] *French Consular Employee Claim* 14 June 1989, Case No 9 Ob A 170/89, 86 ILR 583, 586. Similarly Superior Provincial Court of Vienna, *British Embassy Driver Case* 7 July 1978, 65 ILR 20, 22.

[161] Czech Supreme Court, *State Immunity in Labour Law Matters Case* 25 June 2008, 142 ILR 206, 207. See also Poland, Supreme Court, *Maciej K v Embassy of Foreign State* 11 January 2000, OSNAP 2000/19/723, www.cahdidatabases.coe.int/Contribution/Details/207.

[162] *International Committee of the Red Cross v Sibanda and Another* [2004] ZWSC 115.

act *jure gestionis* amenable to jurisdiction.[163] The latter, by contrast, considered that the duties performed by the employee were essential to the operations of the Tribunal, which pointed in the direction of an act *jure imperii*.[164] Notably, the Supreme Court rejected the applicability of the *jure imperii/jure gestionis* distinction altogether and resorted instead to a form of functional necessity analysis.[165]

The reason why the 'private person test' lends itself to generating erratic outcomes in labour matters is that the ambiguity between private and public is arguably entrenched in the very nature of employment. On the one hand, a contract of employment is certainly something that any private person may conclude.[166] On the other hand, this view instinctively appears incomplete, in that it misses something fundamental about the true nature of employment. As Webb has aptly argued, 'Employment is not a pure contractual, economic transaction. It is a relationship.'[167] Employees are indispensable parts of the machinery of states and IOs: without their personnel, none of these entities could perform their functions. This produces an inherent and structural tension between the private and public components of the employment relationship. This duality was captured well in *Re Canada Labour Code*. Referring to employment in a US military base, the Canada Supreme Court stated that 'While bare employment contracts are primarily commercial in nature, the management and operation of a military base is undoubtedly a sovereign activity'. It concluded that employment 'has a double aspect. *It is at once sovereign and commercial*.'[168] This passage was quoted with appreciation by the House of Lords in *Holland v Lampen-Wolfe*.[169] Similar doubts were expressed by the Seventh Circuit in *Segni*, with respect to a claim brought by an Argentine national employed by the Commercial Office of Spain; the case had a factual background similar to the aforementioned *Kato*. In the Court's words:

> In the case now before us, the nature/purpose distinction is further muddied by the fact that the public purpose behind Segni's hiring … is itself related to commerce. The Commercial Office asserts that Segni was hired to carry out a specific and articulated policy of the Spanish government … Thus, confusingly enough, we must decide whether

[163] Local Court of the Hague, *AS v Iran–United States Claims Tribunal* 8 June 1983, (1984) 15 *Netherlands Yearbook of International Law* 429.

[164] District Court of The Hague, *AS v Iran–United States Claims Tribunal* 9 July 1984, (1985) 16 *Netherlands Yearbook of International Law* 471.

[165] *Spaans v Iran-US Claims Tribunal* 20 December 1985, Case No 12627, ILDC 1759 (NL 1985).

[166] See, eg KE Boon, 'Immunities of the United Nations and Specialised Agencies' in T Ruys and N Angelet (eds), *The Cambridge Handbook of Immunities and International Law* (Cambridge, Cambridge University Press, 2019) 201, 206: 'Employment disputes are also considered private law claims' (re IOs).

[167] P Webb, 'The Immunity of States, Diplomats and International Organizations in Employment Disputes: The New Human Rights Dilemma?' (2016) 27 *European Journal of International Law* 745, 767.

[168] *United States of America v The Public Service Alliance of Canada and Others* [1992] 2 SCR 50, 94 ILR 264, 283 (emphasis added).

[169] *Holland v Lampen-Wolfe* [2000] UKHL 40, 119 ILR 367 (Lord Clyde): 'the relevant activity … may have a double aspect, being at once sovereign and commercial'.

> the *nature* of Segni's hiring is commercial, conscious of the fact that the underlying *purpose* is both commercial *and* public.[170]

Certain parties or courts have sought to solve the conundrum of the public or private nature of employment by adopting a narrower perspective: instead of focusing on the legal qualification of the initial transaction, ie the contract of employment or the relationship as a whole, they have enquired whether specific acts of the employer state – for example, a breach of the employment contract or the decision to dismiss an employee – have a private or public character.[171] Notably, 'the nature of the breach of contract or other act of the sovereign state giving rise to the proceedings' was considered in *Sengupta* to be one of the relevant factors for determining whether the employment claim before the court was covered by immunity.[172] The French Court of Cassation held in *Naira* that the respondent state's failure to notify the employment of the plaintiff to a French national insurance body, as required by French law, 'n'était qu'un acte de gestion administrative'.[173] This approach, however, does not bring much clarity from the standpoint of the 'private person test':[174] just as much as the underlying contract of employment, any subsequent decision of the employer state concerning the management of the employment relationship presents the same private–public ambiguity depending on whether one adopts the standpoint of the nature or the purpose of the act. For instance, dismissing an employee is obviously an act that any private employer could do. But if one looks into the motives of a state's choice to dismiss, one will in all probability find that the decision is underpinned by a public purpose – eg security or budgetary reasons.

Insofar as the private and the public dimensions coexist and overlap in the employment relationship, as the above cases correctly suggest, this inevitably means that the 'private person test' in its pure form is unworkable in this sector.[175]

[170] *Segni v Commercial Office of Spain* 835 F.2d 160 (7th Cir 1987), 98 ILR 55, 59 (emphasis in the original).

[171] On the question whether a breach of contract can qualify as an act *jure imperii* even if the initial transaction was an act *jure gestionis*, see R Higgins, 'Certain Unresolved Aspects of the Law of State Immunity' (1982) 29 *Netherlands International Law Review* 265, 269–70.

[172] *Sengupta* (n 139) 360.

[173] *Mme Naira X v École saoudienne de Paris* 20 June 2003, 127 ILR 163 ('was only an act of administrative management').

[174] See *El-Hadad v United Arab Emirates* 180 ILR 689, 496 F.3d 658 (DC Cir 2007) 663, 'focus[ing the] commercial activity analysis on the employment relationship [with] the UAE embassy as a whole, rather than narrowly on [the plaintiff's] termination alone or separately on [his] termination and defamation. Otherwise this case might entirely defy analysis (what would be a "commercial" or "noncommercial" breach of contract?)'; *Figueroa v Ministry for Foreign Affairs of Sweden et al* 222 F.Supp 3d 304 (SDNY 2016) 311, rejecting the plaintiff's assertion that specific retaliatory acts of the employer state were commercial activities under the US FSIA and focusing on whether the employment relationship as a whole had private or public character.

[175] R van Alebeek and R Pavoni, 'Immunities of States and Their Officials' in A Nollkaemper and A Reinisch (eds), *International Law in Domestic Courts: A Casebook* (Oxford, Oxford University Press, 2018) 100, 116; B Conforti and M Iovane, *Diritto internazionale*, 12th edn (Naples, Editoriale scientifica, 2021) 285; Cassese (n 141) 136; H Fox, 'Employment Contracts as an Exception to State Immunity: Is All Public Service Immune?' (1995) 66 *British Year Book of International Law* 97, 169.

Both the nature-based and purpose-based interpretations of the 'private person test' have an element of plausibility when applied to labour, but ultimately both may be convincingly accused of being too partial. In fact, it will be seen in the next chapter that the near totality of judicial decisions and immunity instruments does not subscribe to any of the two extremes but instead strikes an intermediate position between blanket immunity and no immunity at all. In particular, the necessity to devise workable restrictive immunity standards for labour litigation has resulted in the development of tests which seek to either adapt the distinction between *acta jure imperii* and *acta jure gestionis* to the peculiarities of employment litigation or eschew the divide between public and private acts altogether.

V. Absolute Immunity Based on the Official Nature of Employment

Another rationale for blanket immunity in labour disputes originates from considering employment as an official act. This is particularly the case for lawsuits brought against diplomatic and consular officers (section VA). The same may also be true for the operation of certain standards of IO immunity, most notably the interpretations of the 'functional immunity' test pursuant to which immunity should extend to all of an IO's official acts (section VB).

A. Employment as an Official Act of Diplomatic and Consular Agents

The immunity regimes of the VCDR and the Vienna Convention on Consular Relations (VCCR)[176] are thought out in such a way as to preclude the exercise of jurisdiction over acts performed in an official capacity in all circumstances. Immunity *ratione materiae* applies both during posting and after the termination of an agent's functions, and is enjoyed by diplomats and consuls who are nationals or permanent residents of the receiving state, including honorary consuls.[177] Against this backdrop, it is frequently argued that the act of hiring personal staff should be regarded as falling within an agent's official functions. This inevitably implies that all employment-related lawsuits filed against (both current and former) diplomatic and consular agents should be covered by immunity.

The leading case is *Tabion v Mufti*. The plaintiff, a Philippine national who worked for two years as a domestic servant of a Jordanian diplomat in Washington DC, alleged that her working conditions violated the minimum wage and overtime

[176] Vienna Convention on Consular Relations 1963 (VCCR).
[177] See ch 2, s VI.

prescriptions of US law and sought compensation. She also complained that she had been falsely imprisoned and discriminated against on grounds of race. Tabion sought to defeat the defendants' immunity plea by arguing that her employment was covered by the Article 31(1)(c) VCDR exception to diplomatic immunity, covering lawsuits 'relating to any professional or commercial activity exercised by the diplomatic agent in the receiving State outside his official functions'. The court upheld the immunity. With regard to the second aspect of the Article 31(1)(c) test, it affirmed that:

> Day-to-day living services such as dry cleaning or domestic help were not meant to be treated as outside a diplomat's official functions. Because these services are incidental to daily life, diplomats are to be immune from disputes arising out of them.[178]

This reasoning was fully confirmed in *Sabbithi*, a lawsuit brought by three domestic workers from India employed by an attaché to the Embassy of Kuwait to the USA. The plaintiffs claimed to have been forced to work over 16 hours a day, seven days a week, and to have been deprived of their passports and physically and sexually abused. Differently from *Tabion*, at the time of the proceedings the defendant had left his post and returned to Kuwait. Hence, the issue was whether he was entitled to residual diplomatic immunity under Article 39(2) VCDR.[179] Relying on *Tabion*, the *Sabbithi* court affirmed that all activities 'incidental to the daily life of a diplomat' were to be treated as performed in the exercise of diplomatic functions and thus concluded that claims brought by domestic employees were covered by continuing immunity.[180] A French appellate court adopted the same approach to assess the scope of immunity of a consular agent. The claim was brought by a Moroccan national who worked as a personal employee of the vice-consul of Morocco in Montpellier and his wife. After termination of her employment, she sued for compensation for exploitation and abuses. Reversing the decision of a first instance employment court, the Court of Appeal ruled that the vice-consul and his wife enjoyed immunity under Article 43(1) VCCR. Noting that the employee had been hired 'to work in [the vice-consul's] private home exclusively in his capacity of consular agent', it held that the employment contract was concluded by the vice-consul by contracting 'expressly or impliedly as an agent of the sending State'.[181]

[178] *Tabion v Mufti and Mufti* 73 F.3d 535 (4th Cir 1996). The Court also held that the employment of private servants does not constitute a commercial activity within the meaning of Art 31(1)(c) VCDR; this approach will be critiqued in ch 5, s IIIB.

[179] 'When the functions of a person enjoying privileges and immunities have come to an end … with respect to acts performed … in the exercise of his functions as a member of the mission, immunity shall continue to subsist.'

[180] *Sabbithi et al v Al Saleh et al* 605 F.Supp 2d 122 (DDC 2009), 180 ILR 703, 712–13. *Tabion* was also followed as an authoritative precedent in *Reyes and Suryadi v Al-Malki and Al-Malki* [2015] EWCA Civ 32, paras 13–14. However, this ruling was reversed by UK Supreme Court: *Reyes v Al-Malki and Another* [2017] UKSC 61, on which see further ch 5, s IIIA.

[181] Court of Appeal of Montpellier, *Mohamed X and Another v Fettouma Z* 17 October 2012, Case No 11/01255, 180 ILR 416.

In order to evaluate this jurisprudence, it should be noted at the outset that making the distinction between official and non-official acts of diplomatic and consular agents is frequently a controversial issue.[182] Neither the VCDR nor the VCCR provides detailed guidelines for identifying official acts. The lists of diplomatic and consular functions contained in Article 3 VCDR and Article 5 VCCR are expressly qualified as non-exhaustive. The lack of a *numerus clausus* of official functions means that whether or not an agent acted in an official capacity may require a case-by-case assessment: for instance, a diplomat instructed by the sending state to perform acts not falling into the ordinary diplomatic functions (say, a typically consular function, like promoting exports and commerce) would certainly be acting within *his or her own* official functions.[183]

Notwithstanding these difficulties, there is no disagreement as to the baseline definition of 'official functions': these are functions performed on behalf of the sending state and legally imputable to it, so that the resulting acts are 'in law the acts of the sending State'.[184] At a minimum, this definition allows some basic guidelines to be drawn as to the scope of official acts in the field of labour. Extrapolating from this definition, it follows that if an individual is a state employee, his or her hiring must have been an official act, ie an act legally imputable to the state. Thus, any acts of diplomatic and consular agents that are a parcel of the recruitment process of embassy or consular personnel cannot but be imputed to the sending state. An obvious example is that of an ambassador signing contracts of employment of embassy staff: regardless of the fact that such contracts bear the signature of the head of the mission, these individuals remain employees of the sending state. The same logic may reasonably apply to any ordinary acts of management of an employment relationship with a foreign state – eg an ambassador's decision to fire an embassy employee for gross misconduct. Accordingly, in *Ford v Clement*, a US court held that 'the management and supervision of the Vice Consul and other consular staff' was a part of the consular functions of a consul general, being 'fundamental to the efficient execution of all of the other consulate functions', and therefore fell within his official acts.[185]

In similar cases, the diplomatic or consular agent is simply not a party to the relevant employment relationship. This point has been the source of some confusion in domestic case law. For example, in *Robert*, the French Court of Cassation affirmed a decision of the Paris Court of Appeal upholding immunity over a wrongful dismissal claim filed by a security officer at the US embassy to France. The court affirmed that, because the plaintiff 'had been hired and then dismissed

[182] See, eg Report of the ILC to the General Assembly, ILC Yearbook 1961, vol II, 88, 117.

[183] Denza (n 17) 254.

[184] ibid 356–58; J Foakes and E Denza, 'Privileges and Immunities of Diplomatic Agents' in I Roberts (ed), *Satow's Diplomatic Practice*, 7th edn (Oxford, Oxford University Press, 2016) 246, 279.

[185] *Ford v Clement, Consul General of Panama in New York et al* 834 F.Supp 72 (SDNY 1993) 75. See also *Ewald v Royal Norwegian Embassy et al* Civil No 11-2116 SRN/SER (D Minn 2012) 7–10; *Jimenez v Delgado* 978 F.Supp 2d 726 (SD Tex 2013) 732–33; *Bardales v Consulate General of Peru* 1:17-cv-8897 (ALC) (SDNY 2020).

by the Ambassador', his claim was covered by immunity under Article 31(1) VCDR.[186] But the plaintiff was an employee of the foreign state: he had been hired and dismissed by the ambassador on behalf of the state employer. Therefore, the case should have been decided on grounds of state immunity rather than diplomatic immunity.

In this respect, the position of diplomatic and consular agents is no different from that of any other official of states or IOs tasked with the hiring and management of state or IO personnel. In the 1985 *Donald v Orfila* case, for example, a former OAS employee sued the former Secretary General for wrongful termination. The court ruled that personnel management, including hiring and firing, was part of the functional duties of the Secretary General and held the defendant to be immune from suit.[187] Another example is provided by a 1969 decision of the Supreme Court of Chile. A suit had been brought against the UN Economic Commission for Latin America (ECLA) before a Chilean labour court, which had summoned the ECLA Executive Secretary to make a statement under oath. Under the ECLA–Chile Headquarters Agreement, the Executive Secretary is entitled to 'diplomatic immunities and privileges'.[188] The Supreme Court set aside the summons served on the Executive Secretary, reasoning that, because the case concerned labour relations with the ECLA, the Secretary had been summoned as an IO representative and thus the diplomatic immunity provision deprived Chilean courts of jurisdiction.[189]

In cases factually similar to *Donald v Orfila*, where the defendant's labour-related acts are obviously official in nature, a court may discontinue a case not only on grounds of immunity, but also, perhaps more properly, because the official is the wrong defendant. The employee should instead sue the state (or the IO) qua his or her employer. This solution was reached by the Philippines Supreme Court in *Bautista*. A barracks boy at a US air base was dismissed after three US undercover agents caught him dealing drugs; he then sued the agents for damages for termination of employment. The Court held that the state agents, who had acted in an official capacity, had been wrongly impleaded.[190] In such cases, depending on national procedural law, a court may choose to terminate a case brought against a state agent as directed at the wrong defendant, to change the defendant's name into

[186] *Robert v Procureur de la République* 29 May 1990, 113 ILR 450, 452.

[187] *Donald v Orfila* 618 F.Supp 645 (DDC 1985) 648, affirmed 788 F.2d 36 (DC Cir 1986). For similar cases, see *Osman v Annan* 07-837-CV-W(NKL), 2008 WL 2477535 (WD Mo 2008), dismissing an action for wrongful dismissal against the UN Secretary-General on the grounds that 'functional immunity applies to employment-related suits against officials of international organizations'; *D'Cruz v Annan* 05 Cir 8918(DC), 2005 WL 3527153 (SDNY 2005), re claims for discrimination, harassment and retaliation; *Brzak and Ishak* (n 98) 113, holding that functional immunity covers 'personnel management decisions falling within the ambit of the [UN officials'] professional responsibility'.

[188] Agreement regulating conditions for the operation in Chile of the Headquarters of the United Nations Economic Commission for Latin America 1953, Art VII(15).

[189] *Decision concerning an action brought in a Labour Court against the Economic Commission for Latin America*, 8 November 1969, (1969) UN Juridical Yearbook 237.

[190] *United States of America and Others v Ceballos and Bautista* 26 February 1990, Case No 80018, 102 ILR 132.

the foreign state *ex officio* so as to reflect the proper defendant or to maintain the agent as the named defendant qua an alter ego of the state.[191]

The factual circumstances of *Tabion* and its progeny, however, were different. These cases were not concerned with individuals nominally employed by the foreign state (ie embassy or consular personnel), but with private domestic staff. The question raised by this jurisprudence is therefore whether *all* of the employment-related acts made by diplomats or consuls in the course of their posting, even those regarding individuals nominally employed by the agent in a personal capacity, should necessarily qualify as acts of the sending state. There are two main reasons why this interpretation does not seem tenable.

First, based on the above definition of official acts, to say that the hiring of a private employee is an official act is tantamount to saying that the agent concluded the employment contract on behalf of the sending state – that is, that the individual in question is the sending state's employee. But this would fly in the face of Article 1(h) VCDR, which defines a 'private servant' as 'a person who is in the domestic service of a member of the mission and *who is not an employee of the sending State*'.[192] If the hiring of all private servants were an official act, that of 'private servants' in VCDR terms would be an empty category: this construction would be logically absurd.

Secondly, the expansive reading of official acts encompassing all acts incidental to the agent's daily life, regardless of their actual benefit to the performance of official functions, is hardly justifiable in functional terms. As Milhaupt put it with regard to the VCCR (but the same arguments may apply to the VCDR as well):

> In answering whether immunity for the specific act in question is necessary for the performance of that function, it must be remembered that consular immunity is not intended to benefit the individual. Thus, the essence of the inquiry is not whether the defendant *consular officer* deserves immunity solely because he would have been unable, without the act, to perform the function, but whether the *consular process* would be impeded if consular officers were amenable to the jurisdiction of the receiving state for such acts.[193]

Along the same lines, Shi has persuasively argued that only ancillary or incidental acts which *directly* benefit the performance of the functions of the mission may fall within the scope of immunity *ratione materiae*.[194]

[191] See the case law cited in P De Sena, *Diritto internazionale e immunità funzionale degli organi statali* (Milan, Giuffrè, 1996) 242.

[192] Emphasis added. The employment of private servants who are not nationals or residents of the receiving state is subject to a number of substantive exemptions from local laws, including social security provisions (Art 33 VCDR) and taxes on the emoluments they receive (Art 37(4) VCDR).

[193] CJ Milhaupt, 'The Scope of Consular Immunity under the Vienna Convention on Consular Relations: Towards a Principled Interpretation' (1988) 88 *Columbia Law Review* 841, 857–58 (emphasis in the original).

[194] X Shi, 'Official Acts and Beyond: Towards an Accurate Interpretation of Diplomatic Immunity *Ratione Materiae* under the Vienna Convention on Diplomatic Relations' (2019) 18 *Chinese Journal of International Law* 669, 688.

This finds confirmation in national case law.[195] In *Park*, the respondent consul contended – relying on *Tabion* – that the plaintiff's duties were incidental to his life as a consular agent, in that 'he could not fulfill his other functions as a consular officer as effectively if he were required to cook, clean, take care of his children, and perform the other services that Plaintiff provided for the Shin family'.[196] But the US Ninth Circuit rejected this construction of consular functions as too broad: it reasoned that, under this test, immunity would encompass all personal services – 'from yard work to car repair' – saving consular officers the trouble of doing a chore themselves. It instead affirmed that, for an act to be official, 'A direct, not an indirect, benefit to consular functions is required'.[197] Similarly, in *Reyes*, the UK Supreme Court set aside a former diplomat's residual immunity in a labour lawsuit filed by a member of his domestic staff. The Court unanimously rejected the view that anything 'conducive' to the performance of official functions should itself be regarded as official, because 'that could be said of almost anything that made the personal life of a diplomatic agent easier'.[198]

A similar approach significantly raises the bar for assuming that acts that are only incidentally connected to the agent's functions constitute official acts. It cannot be presumed that an act is official simply because it was performed *during* the exercise of an agent's functions.[199] In light of the above, one should start from the premise that a diplomatic or consular agent may hire and manage employees both in an official and in a private capacity. This creates the need for a legal criterion for distinguishing immune and non-immune employment claims, a question that will be discussed more thoroughly in chapter five.

B. Employment as an Official Act of International Organisations

The concept of official acts may provide a rationale for absolute immunity in employment matters with respect to IOs as well. As seen in chapter two, the 'functional immunity' standard is frequently interpreted in the sense of immunising IOs from claims relating to acts performed in the exercise of their official functions.[200] National courts adopting this approach have generally declined to exercise jurisdiction over employment disputes, on the assumption that all labour-related acts fall within the scope of an IO's official acts.

The Italian Court of Cassation's *Pistelli* judgment is an example in point. Pistelli, a former contractor of the European University Institute (EUI), sued

[195] See further ch 5, s IIIA.
[196] *Park v Shin* 313 F.3d 1138 (9th Cir 2002) 1142.
[197] ibid.
[198] *Reyes* (n 180) para 48.
[199] Milhaupt (n 193) 854.
[200] ch 2, s VB.

for unlawful dismissal. She argued that, pursuant to the Italian legislation, her temporary employment contract had to be transformed into a permanent position. Pursuant to the EUI constituent treaty, 'The Institute and its staff shall enjoy such privileges and immunities as are necessary for the performance of their tasks, under the conditions laid down in the Protocol annexed to this Convention'.[201] The Court acknowledged that the Protocol in question made no mention of immunity from jurisdiction and only provided for 'immunity from enforcement in the exercise of its official activities', save for some specific exceptions,[202] but held that this provision *presupposed* immunity from jurisdiction for official activities. Because staff disputes fell within this category, it upheld the EUI's immunity.[203] Another example is *Killeen*, where the Nairobi High Court, besides invoking functionalist policy arguments in support of blanket immunity, also noted that an employment contract 'fell squarely within the operations of the Defendant in Kenya in respect of which [immunity] as one necessary for the fulfillment of the Defendants purposes may be invoked'.[204] This is a way of saying that an IO needs immunity for its official acts in order to fulfil its functions.

In both such cases, it is doubtful whether functional immunity was the right immunity standard to apply in the first place. In particular, it is difficult to share the Court of Cassation's contention that immunity for official activities arised by logical derivation from the EUI's immunity from execution: Article 4 of the EUI Convention is clear in limiting the Institute's 'functional' immunity to what the Protocol provides.[205] As for *Killeen*, the Kenyan Court of Appeal's authoritative precedent in *Tononoka* would have required the application of an immunity modelled on restrictive state immunity.[206] Be that as it may, the construction of functional immunity as entailing blanket immunity over all IO official acts is perplexing. As was argued in general terms in chapter two, the fact that an act may be official does not necessarily imply that, in order to perform its functions, the IO needs immunity from claims relating to that act. It is conceivable that an IO may defend itself in a lawsuit over an official act without its functions being disrupted.[207] Not unlike the other interpretations of functional immunity as de facto absolute immunity, the use of the notion of official acts as a yardstick of functional immunity is based mainly on an undemonstrated assumption.

The situation is admittedly different where a treaty *expressly* provides for immunity for all official acts of an IO. In such cases, the only question is whether

[201] Convention setting up a European University Institute 1972, Art 4(1).

[202] Protocol on the Privileges and Immunities of the European University Institute, Art 1, forming an integral part of the Convention pursuant to Art 4(1) of the Convention.

[203] *Pistelli v European University Institute* 28 October 2005, No 20995, ILDC 297 (IT 2005), para 13.2.

[204] *Killeen* (n 90) para 9.

[205] See, indeed, Court of Cassation, *European University Institute v Piette* 18 March 1999, No 149 (2000) 36 *Rivista di diritto internazionale privato e processuale* 472, affirming jurisdiction on account of the lack of a treaty clause granting the EUI immunity from jurisdiction.

[206] *Tononoka* (n 91).

[207] ch 2, s VB.

employment should be considered as an official act. The concept of official acts is essentially based on competence: this category includes all the acts performed within the boundaries of an IO's delegated authority, while those falling outside are deemed ultra vires.[208] As it is undisputable that IOs have the competence to hire and manage personnel in order to fulfil their functions, these labour-related acts cannot but be considered official as a general rule. This conclusion finds ample support in national case law. The Austrian Supreme Court, for example, construed a provision of the Austria–EPO Host Agreement whereby 'Within the scope of its official activities the Organisation shall have immunity from jurisdiction'[209] as covering employment matters.[210] In the 2009 *EPO* case,[211] the Dutch Hoge Raad (Supreme Court) reached the same conclusion when applying a textually identical provision of the EPO Protocol on Privileges and Immunities in an unlawful dismissal claim brought by a former patent examiner.[212] The Protocol specifies that, for its purposes, 'The official activities of the Organisation shall … be such as are strictly necessary for its administrative and technical operation'.[213] By all accounts, it can hardly be disputed that the hiring of staff is 'strictly necessary' to the operations of any organisation. The same construction has been espoused by the German courts in cases brought against the EPO or other IOs which, pursuant to the applicable treaty provisions, enjoy immunity within the scope of their official activities.[214]

But one may wonder if this general rule admits exceptions – that is, whether there exist labour-related IO acts which may be considered non-official. This question was addressed in two lawsuits brought against the European Bank for Reconstruction and Development (EBRD) before the UK courts. In *Mukoro*, a failed job applicant alleged to have been discriminated on grounds of race. The UK–EBRD Headquarters Agreement provides that 'Within the scope of its official activities the Bank shall enjoy immunity from jurisdiction', save for a number of enumerated exceptions.[215] While it was undisputed between the parties that

[208] A Reinisch, 'Privileges and Immunities' in Cogan et al (n 58) 1048, 1058. *cf* Orakhelashvili (n 24) 515, defining official acts as those *attributable* to an IO, thus including acts both intra and ultra vires. On the various understandings of acts ultra vires, see E Cannizzaro and P Palchetti, '*Ultra Vires* Acts of International Organizations' in J Klabbers and Å Wallendahl (eds), *Research Handbook on the Law of International Organizations* (Cheltenham, Edward Elgar, 2011) 365.

[209] Agreement between the Republic of Austria and the European Patent Organisation concerning the headquarters of the Vienna sub-office of the European Patent Office 1990, Art 4.

[210] *Manfred B v European Patent Organization* 30 March 1998, No 8 Ob A78/98y.

[211] *X v European Patent Organisation* 23 October 2009, No 08/00118, ILDC 1464 (NL 2009).

[212] Protocol on Privileges and Immunities of the European Patent Organisation 1973, Art 3(1).

[213] ibid Art 3(4).

[214] Appellate Administrative Court of Munich, *T v European Patent Organisation* 13 November 1991, No 3 B 91.1972; Higher Administrative Court of Hesse, *A v European Organisation for the Exploitation of Meteorological Satellites (EUMETSAT)* 17 February 2010, ILDC 2247 (DE 2010). Pursuant to Protocol on the Privileges and Immunities of the EUMETSAT 1986, Art 4, 'Within the scope of its official activities, EUMETSAT shall have immunity from jurisdiction'. Art 1(c) defines the EUMETSAT's official activities as including its administrative activities.

[215] Headquarters Agreement between the Government of the United Kingdom of Great Britain and Northern Ireland and the European Bank for Reconstruction and Development 1991, Art 4(1).

employment generally fell within the scope of this immunity provision, the plaintiff argued that racial discrimination could not be considered an official act. Citing from the Preamble to the EBRD constituent treaty, the plaintiff pointed out that discrimination went against the fundamental principles underpinning the creation of the Bank (democracy, rule of law and respect for human rights)[216] and that therefore it was not aimed at fulfilling the Bank's purposes: in essence, he submitted that the EBRD had, as it were, no 'competence to discriminate'. The EAT rejected this argument. In its view, the case concerned an activity which was undoubtedly official, ie the selection of staff for employment, and the alleged discrimination was only relevant as to the manner in which such activity was carried out.[217]

The reasoning in *Mukoro* was confirmed in the following *Bertolucci* case. Here the plaintiff complained about sexual discrimination in the course of her employment with the EBRD. She argued that the acts at issue had no connection with the administrative activities of the Bank but instead constituted 'free-standing acts of discrimination', thus falling outside the scope of official activities. The EAT, however, affirmed that 'the administration of the Bank, whether or not it is carried out in a way which involves acts of unlawful discrimination or indeed other civil wrongs, is one of the Bank's official activities'.[218] The approach followed in these two cases is defensible because the plaintiffs' arguments sought, in essence, to distinguish between official and non-official activities on the basis of the lawfulness of the activity in question. But this issue is a matter for the merits of the case.[219] If functional immunity could be defeated simply by arguing that an IO did not perform its functions faultlessly, immunity could always be outmanoeuvred by a skilful presentation of a party's legal arguments and would thus provide a merely illusory protection from legal process.[220]

However, the *Mukoro/Bertolucci* approach only works insofar as the activities at stake are ordinarily connected to an IO's managament of the relationship with its employees. A tortious act that simply happens to have been targeted at an employee without bearing direct links to the employment relationship may not be regarded as a mode of performance of the IO's administrative activities, but, to borrow the language employed by Bertolucci's defence, would constitute a truly 'free-standing' tortious act. The factual circumstances of the aforementioned *Morgan* case provide a clear example of a similar scenario.[221] The plaintiff worked for two years as a secretary at the World Bank on assignment from a temporary employment agency. He alleged that officials and security guards of the Bank forcibly detained him in the Bank's premises, accusing him, without evidence, of stealing money, and sought

[216] Agreement Establishing the European Bank for Reconstruction and Development 1990.

[217] *Mukoro v European Bank for Reconstruction and Development and Another* 19 May 1994, 107 ILR 604.

[218] *Bertolucci v European Bank for Reconstruction and Development and Others* 22 July 1997, EAT/276/97, 10.

[219] On the interaction between immunity and substantive norms, see ch 2, s II.

[220] Milhaupt (n 193) 855.

[221] *Morgan* (n 155).

damages for intentional infliction of emotional distress, false imprisonment, libel and slander. The court qualified the case as an employment claim, which led it to uphold the Bank's immunity based on the *Mendaro* doctrine of blanket immunity in labour disputes.[222] However, Morgan's claim was not directly connected to the employment relationship.[223] Hence, if this case were to be decided by applying the same immunity standard as in *Mukoro*, immunity ought not have been upheld in that the act of falsely imprisoning an employee does not constitute an IO's official act in the sphere of employment.

VI. Persistence of Absolute Immunity under Express Treaty Provisions

A last commonly invoked justification for absolute immunity in labour matters is based on treaty provisions granting IOs immunity 'from every form of legal process'. The prototypes of such provisions are Article II(2) of the UN General Convention and Article III(4) of the UN Specialized Agencies Convention; this formula has then been reproduced in numerous immunity instruments.[224]

US courts have consistently construed such treaty clauses as shielding the totality of staff disputes from jurisdiction. The leading case is *Boimah*. The plaintiff, employed by the UN under a fixed-term contract, alleged to have been denied a permanent position on account of his race. Immunity was upheld: 'Under the Convention the United Nations' immunity is absolute, subject only to the organization's express waiver thereof in particular cases.'[225] The *Boimah* precedent has been followed in all subsequent lawsuits filed by UN employees, including *De Luca*, an action for recovery of withheld income taxes;[226] *Hunter*, a discrimination lawsuit brought by a temporary employee of UNICEF;[227] and *Lempert*, an action for breach of contract, fraud and harassment brought by a fixed-term consultant of the UN Development Programme.[228] It is important to note that this jurisprudence remains unaffected by *Jam*, where the US Supreme Court held that restrictive immunity under the IOIA only constitutes a default rule and does not supersede international treaties granting broader immunity. It expressly referred to Article II(2) of the UN General Convention as an example of such provisions.[229]

[222] On *Mendaro* (n 94), see above s III.
[223] Reinisch, *International Organizations* (n 30) 165. For a critique of *Morgan*, see also D Hammerschlag, 'Morgan v. International Bank for Reconstruction and Development' (1992) 16 *Maryland Journal of International Law* 279.
[224] ch 2, s VB.
[225] *Boimah* (n 97) 71.
[226] *De Luca v United Nations Organization et al* 841 F.Supp 531 (SDNY 1994) 533.
[227] *Hunter* (n 154) 4.
[228] *Lempert v Rice, UN and UNDP* ILDC 2325 (US 2013), 956 F.Supp 2d 17 (DDC 2013) 23–24.
[229] *Jam* (n 130) 14.

The absolutist interpretation of the immunity of the UN and its Specialized Agencies is so well established in US case law that, in the most recent cases on the matter, plaintiffs have not even tried to dispute it. Instead, they have sought – in all cases, unsuccessfully – to have the UN immunity dismissed on other grounds. In *Bisson*, an action for injuries sustained in the course of employment with the UN World Food Programme, the plaintiff's main claim was that the UN had impliedly waived its absolute immunity from jurisdiction. This argument failed because the General Convention requires waivers to be express.[230] In *Brzak and Ishak*, two UNHCR employees complained about sex discrimination and retaliation. They argued that the General Convention was not a self-executing treaty in the US legal system according to the criteria laid down in *Medellín v Texas*, where the US Supreme Court adopted a particularly restrictive approach to the identification of self-executing treaties.[231] The Court of Appeals, however, found the General Convention to be self-executing and upheld immunity.[232] In the 2016 *Koumoin* case, the plaintiff, who asserted the non-renewal of his temporary employment contract by the UN to be discriminatory and retaliatory, attempted to bypass the organisation's immunity by naming Secretary-General Ban Ki-Moon as the sole defendant. However, because the Secretary-General is entitled by the General Convention to the same immunity enjoyed by diplomatic agents, his immunity was upheld.[233]

Such a broad understanding of the immunity of the UN and its Specialized Agencies is justified under the letter of the relevant treaty clauses, which does not appear to leave room for any interpretation to the contrary. While there have been instances where courts have sought to construe these clauses as entailing non-absolute immunity, similar attempts, as will be seen below, do not appear particularly persuasive.

Two such attempts may be distinguished. First, certain courts have simply refused to interpret the treaty clauses in question literally and have considered them as aimed at implementing more restrictive immunity standards. In the 1969 *Porru* case, for instance, a short-term staff member sued the FAO, alleging that they were entitled to certain social security benefits under Italian law. A first instance court interpreted Article VIII(16) of the Headquarters Agreement between the FAO and

[230] *Bisson v United Nations and Others* ILDC 889 (US 2008), 06 Civ 6352 (SDNY 2008) 5.

[231] *Medellín v Texas* 552 US 491 (2008). The Supreme Court made self-execution dependent on various factors, including the text of the relevant treaty, the post-ratification practice of other parties to the treaty and the executive branch's understanding of the treaty. In effect, this resulted in a presumption of non-self-execution: ME McGuinness, 'Medellín v. Texas, 128 S.Ct. 1346 (2008)' (2008) 102 *American Journal of International Law* 622, 627.

[232] *Brzak and Ishak* (n 98) 111–12. See also *Sei Fujii v State of California* 38 Cal.2d 718 (1952) 723–24, holding in obiter that the Art 105 UN Charter's immunity provision is self-executing.

[233] *Koumoin v Ban Ki-Moon* 16-cv-2111 (AJN) (SDNY 2016) 7–8. See Art V(17) UN General Convention. A similar precedent is *Kissi v De Larosière* No 82-1267 (DDC 1982), cited in 'Comments and Observations Received from International Organizations' UN Doc A/CN.4/545 (25 June 2004) 33, holding the Managing Director of the International Monetary Fund (IMF) immune from a claim for wrongful denial of a position at the Fund.

Italy, providing for immunity 'from every form of legal process', as merely restating a rule of customary international law purportedly granting IOs the same immunity as foreign states. *In concreto*, the court upheld the immunity, but only because it found that the acts by which an IO arranges its internal structure, including those relating to employment, were *acta jure imperii*.[234] Similar arguments have sometimes been developed by courts in France and Greece. In a 1982 unfair dismissal lawsuit filed by a former receptionist at an IO seated in France, the Bordeaux Court of Appeals was confronted with a provision of the headquarters agreement whereby the organisation 'jouit de l'immunité de juridiction sauf renonciation de sa part' ('enjoys immunity from jurisdiction unless it is waived') – a typical 'full immunity' provision. Nonetheless, the court held that IO immunity hinged upon the distinction between private and public acts, and on this basis upheld its jurisdiction.[235] Likewise, the Crete Court of Appeals applied the *jure imperii/jure gestionis* distinction to an employment dispute against the International Centre for Advanced Mediterranean Agronomic Studies, which enjoys 'immunity from every form of legal process' pursuant to its constituent treaty.[236] Full immunity treaty provisions have also been disregarded in a number of Brazilian precedents, which have upheld jurisdiction over labour disputes with the UN or its Specialized Agencies on the basis of the private law nature of employment contracts.[237]

This approach is, however, unwarranted, in that it runs counter to the letter of the treaties.[238] The General Convention does not contemplate exceptions to the immunity of the UN in situations where commercial activities are undertaken.[239] This position was expressed by the Argentine Supreme Court in *Duhalde*, an employment case against the WHO and the Pan American Health Organization (PAHO). A first instance court and an appellate court had denied immunity by invoking the principles expressed in *Manauta*, a Supreme Court decision which had recently applied restrictive immunity to labour claims with states.[240] The Supreme Court reversed, noting that IO immunity did not derive from general

[234] Pretore di Roma (First instance labour court), *Porru v Food and Agriculture Organization of the United Nations* 25 June 1969, 71 ILR 240.

[235] *Agence de Cooperation Culturelle et Technique v X* 18 November 1982, summarised in Court of Cassation, *Agence de Cooperation Culturelle et Technique v X* 24 October 1985, No 83-40918. The Court of Cassation affirmed the decision of the Bordeaux court, but on the grounds that the employment contract contained a choice of forum in favour of the French courts.

[236] *X v Mediterranean Institute for Agriculture* No 479/1991, cited in Reinisch, *International Organizations* (n 30) 191. See Agreement establishing the International Centre for Advanced Mediterranean Agronomic Studies 1962, Art 2.

[237] Superior Labor Court, *Estevao de Castro Melo v UN-UNDP* 1 April 2009, RR-295/2004-019-10-00; Superior Labor Court, *Cilene Maria Holanda Salaoio v UNESCO* 26 September 2007, RR-574/2004-013-10-001.

[238] Reinisch, *International Organizations* (n 30) 189.

[239] See 'Note to the Minister of Foreign Affairs of [State] to the United Nations concerning certain labour claims filed against the United Nations Logistics Base in [City] in the Court of [City] by five former individual contractors' [2012] *UN Juridical Yearbook* 459.

[240] *Manauta and Others v Embassy of the Russian Federation* 22 December 1994, CSJN Fallos 317:1880, 113 ILR 429.

international law but from treaty law, and that no analogy to state immunity, in the face of express treaty provisions to the contrary, was possible.[241]

Notably, both Italian and Brazilian courts have now discontinued their jurisprudence applying state immunity principles in lieu of 'full immunity' treaty provisions. The Brazilian Superior Labour Court has recently upheld the immunity of WHO and PAHO pursuant to the relevant treaties.[242] As for the Italian Court of Cassation, starting with the 1992 *Colagrossi* case, it has refused to analogise FAO's immunity to that of foreign states and has treated the relevant immunity instruments as self-contained bases of immunity.[243] Accordingly – as the Italian Court of Cassation held in *Carretti*, a wrongful dismissal case – the FAO is now considered to be entitled to full immunity from employment disputes under both the Headquarters Agreement with Italy and the Specialized Agencies Convention, and its employees are expected to bring their grievances to the ILOAT or other internal remedies.[244] This jurisprudence has been followed not only with regard to the UN and its Specialized Agencies, but in respect to any 'full immunity' provision included in international instruments. This was the case, for example, in *Lakomy*, an unfair dismissal claim against the Multinational Force and Observers (MFO). Pursuant to its Headquarters Agreement, this IO is entitled to immunity in all circumstances save for waiver.[245] The Court of Cassation expressly favoured a literal interpretation of this provision and described the MFO's immunity as 'treaty-based and substantially unlimited'.[246]

Another – more sophisticated – attempt at limiting the scope of full immunity clauses in labour matters construes these clauses in combination with other provisions of the same treaties which require IOs to establish remedies for the solution of disputes with private parties. A typical such clause is Article VIII, section 29 of the UN General Convention, pursuant to which the UN 'shall make provisions for appropriate modes of settlement of … disputes arising out of contracts or other disputes of a private law character to which the United Nations is a party'.[247] Some interpret similar provisions as conditioning the grant of immunity to the existence of appropriate alternative remedies: full immunity, in other words, would constitute the quid pro quo for the creation of effective means of redress within the IO.[248] A judicial application of this view can be found in the *Drago* decision of the Italian

[241] *Duhalde v Organización Panamericana de la Salud – Organización Mondial de la Salud Oficina Sanitaria Panamericana* 31 August 1999, CSJN Fallos 322:1905.

[242] *União, Centro Panamericano de Febre Aftosa – Projeto da Organização Panamericana da Saúde/Organização Mundial da Saúde v Lelis da Penha* 6 December 2016, AR 66241-82.2010.5.00.0000.

[243] *Colagrossi v FAO* 18 May 1992, No 5942, 101 ILR 386.

[244] *Carretti v FAO* 23 January 2004, No 180.

[245] Accordo di sede tra il Governo della Repubblica italiana e la Forza multinazionale e osservatori (MFO) per lo stabilimento in Italia del quartiere generale dell'Organizzazione 1982, Art 8(1).

[246] *Lakomy v Forza multinazionale e osservatori – MFO* 3 August 2000, No 531.

[247] The same obligation is set forth by Convention on the Privileges and Immunities of the Specialized Agencies 1947, Art IX, s 31.

[248] See, eg R Silverstein, 'Revisiting the Legal Basis to Deny International Civil Servants Access to a Fundamental Human Right' (2017) 25 *Michigan State International Law Review* 375, 383.

Court of Cassation. Pursuant to its headquarters agreement, the respondent IO was entitled to full immunity from suit.[249] The plaintiff alleged that the IO's failure to provide an internal remedy for settling staff disputes constituted a violation of the right of access to a court guaranteed by the Italian Constitution.[250] The Court dismissed the constitutional challenge to the IO's immunity (which would have required it to refer the matter to the Constitutional Court) because it refused to interpret the Headquarters Agreement in the sense of granting absolute immunity in the absence of internal means of redress. Instead, it held that Article 17 of the Agreement – 'The Institute shall establish suitable procedures for resolving disputes with its employees' – established a prerequisite for the application of immunity. Thus, in the Court's view, it was the Headquarters Agreement itself which did not require the granting of immunity in the instant case.[251]

On a policy level, this approach might find support in the likely rationale of treaty clauses requiring IOs to establish appropriate modes for settling private disputes. Conceptually, such provisions are evidently connected to those establishing jurisdictional immunities: as Schmalenbach has aptly argued with regard to the General Convention, section 29 signals an 'understanding that these immunities neither exonerate the UN from its duty to meet its … obligations nor that the immunities be seen as tantamount to a denial of justice'.[252] This rationale is particularly weighty when it comes to the legal relations between IOs and their staff. Quoting from what the ICJ held (although without referring expressly to section 29) in *Effect of Awards*:

> It would … hardly be consistent with the expressed aim of the Charter to promote freedom and justice for individuals and with the constant preoccupation of the [UN] to promote this aim that it should afford no judicial or arbitral remedy to its own staff for the settlement of any disputes which may arise between it and them.[253]

As seen earlier in this chapter, the vast majority of IOs establish some kind of judicial or administrative mechanism for resolving grievances in the workplace.[254]

However, the idea of a conditionality between full immunity and treaty provisions on dispute settlement probably pushes the nexus between these clauses too far. Nothing in the text of the relevant treaties or in the *travaux* of the General Convention suggests that an IO's failure to comply with its duty to provide for

[249] Agreement between the Italian Republic and the International Plant Genetic Resources Institute (IPGRI) regarding the headquarters seat of IPGRI 1991, Art V(1).

[250] Art 24: 'Anyone may bring cases before a court of law in order to protect their rights under civil and administrative law.'

[251] *Drago v International Plant Genetic Resources Institute (IPGRI)* 19 February 2007, No 3718, ILDC 827 (IT 2007) para 6.7.

[252] K Schmalenbach, 'Dispute Settlement (Article VIII Sections 29–30 General Convention)' in A Reinisch and P Bachmayer (eds), *The Conventions on the Privileges and Immunities of the United Nations and its Specialized Agencies: A Commentary* (Oxford, Oxford University Press, 2016) 529. See also K Wellens, *Remedies against International Organisations* (Cambridge, Cambridge University Press, 2002) 22; M Buscemi, *Illeciti delle Nazioni Unite e tutela dell'individuo* (Naples, Editoriale Scientifica, 2020) 238–41.

[253] *Effect of awards* (n 50) 57.

[254] See above s IIB.

appropriate modes of dispute settlement was intended to justify – let alone require – the lifting of immunity by national courts.[255] It is sufficient to point out that the duty under section 29 may be fulfilled by the UN even without instituting modes of settlement of individual complaints, eg by amicable settlement with the individual's state of nationality.[256] The idea of a conditionality between sections 2 and 29 UN General Convention has been expressly rejected by US courts in the context of labour cases.[257]

The key criticism that may be levied against the views favouring a link of conditionality between immunity and treaty provisions on dispute settlement is that they are overly reductive. It is arguably wrong to frame the problem of the IO employees' access to a remedy as a purely technical issue of treaty interpretation as it has a chiefly human rights dimension. In fact, as was already noted,[258] the ECtHR and a large number of national courts have developed a jurisprudence conditioning IO immunity on the availability to the employees of alternative means of redress. But such restrictions are not conceived of as deriving from the text of the relevant IO immunity instruments; instead, it is acknowledged that 'full immunity' provisions admit no exceptions *from the standpoint of immunity law*. The quid pro quo limitation on immunity is instead construed as deriving from constitutional or international human rights law provisions guaranteeing the right of access to a court: an extrinsic rather than intrinsic limit on immunity law, as it were. This point will be further discussed in chapter six.[259]

VII. Conclusions: The Need for Limited Immunity Standards in Employment Litigation

This chapter has taken a critical look at the most common justifications for blanket immunity in the context of employment disputes against foreign states, IOs and diplomatic and consular agents. It has been argued that international immunity law actually requires absolute immunity in employment matters only where this outcome arises from express treaty terms (sections VB and VI). Therefore, contrary to common belief, employment disputes do not warrant an immunity broader than is usually required in the context of civil claims. As a matter of fact, these disputes do not deviate from the general rule, described in chapter two, whereby civil cases are normally subject to limited rather than absolute immunity from jurisdiction. This entails a need to devise workable standards of limited immunity applicable to labour disputes – an issue that will be addressed in the next two chapters.

[255] Schmalenbach (n 252) 534; Boon (n 166) 208.

[256] Schmalenbach (n 252) 541.

[257] See, eg *Bisson* (n 230) para 10. For a rejection of the conditionality argument, although not in a labour dispute, see Belgium, Civil Tribunal of Brussels, *Manderlier v Organisation des Nations Unies and Etat Belge (Ministre des Affaires Etrangères)* 11 May 1966, 45 ILR 446.

[258] See above s IIA.

[259] ch 6, s III.

4

Restrictive State Immunity Standards in Employment Matters

I. Introduction

State immunity is the area where the greatest amount of practice has built up on how to adapt the concept of restrictive immunity to labour claims. Its leading role may be most obviously explained as a natural outgrowth of the demise of absolute state immunity in almost all jurisdictions. The transition to restrictive immunity has permeated most areas of civil litigation, labour lawsuits being no exception. But an equally important factor is the sheer number of employment cases – by far the most numerous lawsuits brought against foreign states[1] – which has produced a strong practical need for workable immunity standards.

This chapter examines how the restrictive state immunity doctrine has been adapted to employment litigation. Section II introduces the chapter's main claim, ie that this process of adaptation has taken place through the development of standards peculiar to labour matters and to a good extent alternative to the distinction between acts *jure imperii* and *jure gestionis*. The subsequent discussion looks in detail at each of these employment-specific standards. It starts from instances where the broader context where the employment takes place, notably the place of employment, is taken as decisive (section III). It then analyses approaches based on individual features of the plaintiff employees, namely their status within the foreign state's workforce, the tasks they are entrusted with (section IV) or their nationality or residence (section V). Subsequently, the chapter turns to cases where immunity is made dependent on the subject matter of the claim (section VI) or on the inclusion of forum selection clauses within the employment contract (section VII). In light of this survey of state practice, section VIII attempts to bring clarity to the status of customary international law in this field.

[1] H Fox and P Webb, *The Law of State Immunity*, 3rd edn (Oxford, Oxford University Press, 2013) 440.

II. The Emergence of Employment-Specific Approaches to Restrictive State Immunity

It will be recalled from chapter three that a restrictive immunity test based on the distinction between public and private acts comes across as particularly challenging in labour matters. The reason is that, when it comes to individuals in the employ of states, it is hard to untangle private from public: the employment relationship may reasonably be conceptualised as straddling the divide, ie as having a dual private–public character.[2] This, however, has not prevented the restrictive doctrine from applying to employment litigation. The difficulty has been overcome in practice through the emergence of restrictive immunity criteria tailor-made for employment. As will be seen below, the catalogue of such criteria in state immunity instruments and judicial practice boils down to five main items: (i) the nature of the workplace; (ii) the status of the employee or the functions he or she performs; (iii) the employee's nationality and residence; (iv) the claim's subject matter; and (v) the presence of a forum selection clause in the employment contract. While it is not uncommon that one factor alone is treated as dispositive, such criteria are by no means mutually exclusive. Accordingly, the application of restrictive immunity to employment is most often based on a 'multi-factor' analysis grounded on two or more of the above tests.[3]

In state immunity instruments, the prototype attempt at laying down restrictive immunity rules specifically devised for employment can be found in Article 5 of the 1972 European Convention on State Immunity (ECSI).[4] This provision reads:

> 1. A Contracting State cannot claim immunity … if the proceedings relate to a contract of employment between the State and an individual where the work has to be performed on the territory of the State of the forum.
> 2. Paragraph 1 shall not apply where:
>   a. the individual is a national of the employing State at the time when the proceedings are brought;
>   b. at the time when the contract was entered into the individual was neither a national of the State of the forum nor habitually resident in that State; or
>   c. the parties to the contract have otherwise agreed in writing, unless, in accordance with the law of the State of the forum, the courts of that State have exclusive jurisdiction by reason of the subject matter.
> 3. Where the work is done for an office, agency or other establishment referred to in Article 7, paragraphs 2.a and b of the present article apply only if, at the time the contract was entered into, the individual had his habitual residence in the Contracting State which employs him.

[2] See ch 3, s IV.

[3] R Garnett, 'State Immunity in Employment Matters' (1997) 46 *ICLQ* 81, 85; X Yang, *State Immunity in International Law* (Cambridge, Cambridge University Press, 2012) 164.

[4] European Convention on State Immunity 1972 (ECSI).

This article sets forth a general rule of non-immunity subject to three exceptions making immunity dependent on a complex interaction between nationality, residence and choice of forum. Claims may be brought against an employer state only by employees who were nationals or permanent residents of the forum state when the contract was concluded (paragraph 2(b)), with an exception made for those holding the nationality of the employer state when the proceedings are instituted (paragraph 2(a)).[5] Paragraph 3 gives some relevance to the criterion of the nature of the workplace by providing more lenient immunity rules for employees of commercial agencies of foreign states.[6] It is provided that employees who were not permanent residents of the employer state at the time the contract was made may sue whatever their nationality or residence. Otherwise, if the employee was an employer state's permanent resident when the contract was concluded, the general provisions of paragraphs 2(a) and (b) apply.

The language of Article 5 is peculiar in that it relies heavily on concepts originating from private international law.[7] This is the case with both criteria laid down in paragraph 2 (nationality/residence and choice of forum), and the same may be said with regard to the relevance given to the place of performance of work and the place of conclusion of the contract. The departure from typical immunity law schemes is evident also from paragraph 2(c), where the foreign state's 'immunity' is made conditional upon domestic law rules on jurisdiction. All this is distinctive because the assessment of jurisdiction is logically separate from and antecedent to any question concerning immunity.[8] The existence of a territorial connection to the forum state, for instance, is properly a question not of immunity, but purely of jurisdiction.[9] The usage of private international law terminology may be explained by the fact that the Convention's drafters chose to creatively combine immunity rules and jurisdictional links.[10] Thus, Article 5 is aimed at establishing that a sufficient jurisdictional connection with a state exists for the latter to exercise jurisdiction. As affirmed by the ECSI Explanatory Report with respect to the paragraph 2(a) and (b) immunity grounds, 'In both cases the links between the employee and the employing State … are generally closer than those between the employee and the State of the forum';[11] in other cases, the employee should be considered 'locally recruited'.[12]

[5] For details on how these variables affect the scope of immunity, see the table in U Köhler, 'Contracts of Employment under the UN Convention on Jurisdictional Immunities of States and Their Property' (2004) 9 *Austrian Review of International and European Law* 191, 196.

[6] Art 7 ECSI, to which Art 5(3) refers, regulates state immunity for acts performed by an 'office, agency or other establishment through which [the state] engages, in the same manner as a private person, in an industrial, commercial or financial activity'.

[7] H Fox, 'Employment Contracts as an Exception to State Immunity: Is All Public Service Immune?' (1995) 66 *British Year Book of International Law* 97, 141–45.

[8] See ch 2, s II.

[9] R Higgins, 'Certain Unresolved Aspects of the Law of State Immunity' (1982) 29 *Netherlands International Law Review* 265, 273. But see Yang (n 3) 173, listing the territorial connection among the judicial tests for delimiting immunity in labour claims.

[10] ch 2, s 4.1.

[11] Explanatory Report to the ECSI, ETS 74, para 30.

[12] ibid.

Article 5 ECSI's influence on state practice has been much greater than what the ECSI's limited membership would suggest. In fact, this provision has served as a model for many subsequent state immunity intruments. This trend was initiated by the UK State Immunity Act 1978 (UK SIA),[13] and continued in the provisions relating to employment contracts of state immunity statutes of several countries of common law, including the Singapore State Immunity Act 1979 (Singapore SIA),[14] the Pakistani State Immunity Ordinance 1981 (Pakistan SIO),[15] South Africa's Foreign States Immunities Act 1981 (South Africa FSIA),[16] Malawi's Immunities and Privileges Act 1984 (Malawi IPA),[17] and Israel's Foreign States Immunity Law 2008 (Israel FSIL).[18] Argentina's 1995 law on state immunity resorts to a streamlined version of the nationality/residence test by removing immunity from labour claims by Argentine nationals or residents arising from contracts concluded or having effects in Argentina.[19] The ECSI also exercised influence on the practice of countries where no state immunity legislation is in place. For example, in *Seidenschmidt*, a severance pay claim by a former employee of the US embassy Information Service, the Austrian Supreme Court applied Article 5 qua codification of customary international law and upheld Austrian jurisdiction because none of the paragraph 2 immunity grounds applied.[20] The Italian courts' approach too has been influenced by Article 5 ECSI, albeit in a more selective way. The Italian Court of Cassation (Corte di Cassazione) proclaimed in the 1977 *Jasbez* case that Article 5 was reflective of customary law, but curiously adjudicated on the basis of the employees' functions and not of the ECSI criteria.[21] Article 5's influence was more palpable in the 1989 *Toglia* decision, where the Corte di Cassazione invoked, inter alia, the ECSI with a view to justifying an innovative approach permitting jurisdiction over compensation claims regardless of the employees' functions.[22] When looking at the bigger picture, though, the ECSI's main legacy has consisted in propagating the idea that applying the restrictive doctrine to employment litigation requires ad hoc judicial tests – a method followed without exceptions in subsequent instruments and case law.

By contrast, the relevance in state practice of the specific criteria on which Article 5 relies has diminished significantly, particularly because the nationality/residence test has come to be regarded as introducing an unfair discrimination

[13] Of which s 4 is closely modelled on Art 5 ECSI.
[14] s 6.
[15] s 6.
[16] s 5.
[17] s 6.
[18] s 4 (unlike Art 5 ECSI, lacking a provision on contractual derogations).
[19] Art 2(d) Law No 24.488 (1995).
[20] *Seidenschmidt v United States* 8 July 1992, Case No 9 Ob A 116/96, 116 ILR 530.
[21] *Bari Institute of the ICAMAS v Jasbez* 21 October 1977, No 4502, (1978) 14 *Rivista di diritto internazionale privato e processuale* 788.
[22] *British Consulate-General in Naples v Toglia* 15 May 1989, No 2329, 101 ILR 380.

among workers.[23] The UK SIA and the Pakistan, South Africa and Malawi statutes attach greater importance to the nature of the workplace by barring jurisdiction over claims by all embassy and consulate employees, so that the rules based on nationality and residence apply only residually.[24] The Australian Foreign State Immunities Act 1985 (Australia FSIA) deviates even further from the ECSI model by formulating the nationality/residence test in terms less favourable to immunity: a state may be sued by any Australian or third-state employee who was not a resident of the employer state when the contract was concluded and even by the employer state's nationals already residing in Australia at the time of hiring, regardless of the employee's status when the proceedings are brought.[25] This instrument also introduces two further criteria unknown to the ECSI, namely status (barring claims by diplomatic or consular agents[26]) and functions (barring claims by administrative and technical personnel of embassies and consulates; but this only applies to non-residents of Australia at the time of hiring[27]).

The same trend can be clearly observed in the works of the International Law Commission (ILC) on state immunity. The first Draft Articles, as put forward in 1983 by Special Rapporteur Sucharitkul, included a provision on contracts of employment (Article 13) which reproduced Article 5 ECSI almost word for word. The only major difference was the inclusion of a further ground of immunity based on subject matter: paragraph 2(a) ruled out jurisdiction over proceedings relating to 'failure to employ an individual or dismissal of an employee'.[28] This initial draft was thoroughly altered over the course of the two decades leading up to the UN Convention on State Immunity (UNCSI).[29] Article 11 UNCSI – the final outcome of the drafting process – reads as follows:

> *Contracts of employment*
>
> 1. Unless otherwise agreed between the States concerned, a State cannot invoke immunity from jurisdiction before a court of another State which is otherwise

[23] H Fox, 'The Restrictive Rule of State Immunity – The 1970s Enactment and Its Contemporary Status' in T Ruys and N Angelet (eds), *The Cambridge Handbook of Immunities and International Law* (Cambridge, Cambridge University Press, 2019) 21, 28.

[24] s 16(1)(a) UK SIA; s 17(1)(a) Pakistan SIO; s 5(2)(b) South Africa FSIA; s 18(1)(a) Malawi IPA. *cf Benkharbouche v Secretary of State for Foreign and Commonwealth Affairs and Secretary of State for Foreign and Commonwealth Affairs and Libya v Janah* [2017] UKSC 62, holding that the blanket bar on jurisdiction does not apply to low-level embassy employees. Another difference relates to the territorial connection requirement: under these statutes, the employment exception also encompasses work performed only partly in the forum state (eg s 4(1) UK SIA; s 5(1)(a) South Africa FSIA), while Art 5(1) ECSI leaves this point uncertain: Yang (n 3) 147.

[25] s 12(3). See Australian Law Reform Commission, 'Foreign State Immunity', Report No 24, (1984), 56, para 96, explaining this choice as preventing employees from changing status 'simply in order to take advantage of a greater opportunity to sue [their] employer'.

[26] s 12(5).

[27] s 12(6).

[28] S Sucharitkul, 'Fifth Report on Jurisdictional Immunities of States and their Property', ILC Yearbook 1983, vol II, Part 1, 25, 38, para 62.

[29] United Nations Convention on Jurisdictional Immunities of States and Their Property 2004, not yet in force.

competent in a proceeding which relates to a contract of employment between the State and an individual for work performed or to be performed, in whole or in part, in the territory of that other State.

2. Paragraph 1 does not apply if:
   - (a) the employee has been recruited to perform particular functions in the exercise of governmental authority;
   - (b) the employee is:
     - (i) a diplomatic agent, as defined in the Vienna Convention on Diplomatic Relations of 1961;
     - (ii) a consular officer, as defined in the Vienna Convention on Consular Relations of 1963;
     - (iii) a member of the diplomatic staff of a permanent mission to an international organization or of a special mission, or is recruited to represent a State at an international conference; or
     - (iv) any other person enjoying diplomatic immunity;
   - (c) the subject matter of the proceeding is the recruitment, renewal of employment or reinstatement of an individual;
   - (d) the subject matter of the proceeding is the dismissal or termination of employment of an individual and, as determined by the head of State, the head of Government or the Minister for Foreign Affairs of the employer State, such a proceeding would interfere with the security interests of that State;
   - (e) the employee is a national of the employer State at the time when the proceeding is instituted, unless this person has the permanent residence in the State of the forum; or
   - (f) the employer State and the employee have otherwise agreed in writing, subject to any considerations of public policy conferring on the courts of the State of the forum exclusive jurisdiction by reason of the subject matter of the proceeding.

After providing a general rule of non-immunity in employment claims, Article 11 lays down a number of exceptions. As in all other immunity instruments, each exception is self-standing, in the sense that the occurrence of just one of the paragraph 2 immunity grounds entitles the employer state to immunity. Among such grounds, letters (e) and (f) are the only remnants of the approach followed by Article 5 ECSI, in that they broadly correspond respectively to paragraphs 2(a) and 2(c) of that provision.[30] Letter (a), by contrast, determines the scope of immunity on the basis of the employees' functions, and letter (b) on the basis of status. Letters (c) and (d) differentiate according to the subject matter of the claim.

Similarly to the ECSI, Article 11 – despite the UNCSI not being yet in force – has also exercised a relevant impact on state practice. Its content has been textually reproduced in the most recent domestic enactments on state immunity, including Article 11 of the 2015 Russian statute, Article 10 of Spain's 2015 legislation

[30] Note, however, that letter (e) departs from Art 5 ECSI where it allows for jurisdiction over claims brought by nationals of the employer state who are permanent residents of the forum state at the start of the proceedings.

and Article 9 of the 2009 Japanese legislation.[31] Starting from the 2010 judgment in *Cudak*, the European Court of Human Rights (ECtHR) has resorted to Article 11 UNCSI as reflective of the current status of customary international law.[32] The courts of several European countries, including the Italian[33] and French Courts of Cassation,[34] have aligned their approach to the ECtHR and applied Article 11 accordingly. Article 11 was also applied qua codification of custom by the Delhi High Court in the 2010 case of *Shyam Lal*[35] and by the Dutch Hoge Raad in the 2010 *Moroccan Secretary* case.[36] Regardless of whether this approach is sound from the standpoint of customary law ascertainment – a point which will be explored below[37] – what matters the most for the present discussion is that Article 11 has further contributed to the diffusion in state practice of employment-specific restrictive immunity tests.

Employment-specific criteria of restrictive immunity have also been in use in the case law of the USA and Canada, whose foreign state immunity statutes do not contain articles specifically devoted to employment contracts. The courts of these countries have addressed the issue of immunity from employment claims within the context of the so-called 'commercial activity exception' to state immunity – that is, section 1605(a)(2) of the US Foreign Sovereign Immunities Act 1976 (US FSIA), withholding immunity in cases 'in which the action is based upon a commercial activity carried on in the United States by the foreign state'; and the similarly worded section 5 of the Canada State Immunity Act 1985 (Canada SIA). Both provisions use the concept of commercial activity in such a broad sense as to function as a synonym for act *jure gestionis*.[38] It is therefore unsurprising that the application to employment of the 'commercial activity exception' has required the same process of adaptation seen in other jurisdictions in order to overcome the issues raised by the 'private person test'. The FSIA House Report (ie the FSIA's legislative history) had already suggested that the application of section 1605(a)(2) to labour disputes could be based on the functions performed by the individual employee: among activities falling into the definition of commercial activity the Report listed, by way of example, the 'employment or engagement of laborers, clerical staff or public relations or marketing agents'.[39] As will be seen below,

[31] Law No 297-FZ (2015) (Russia); Law No 16 (2015) (Spain); Act on Civil Jurisdiction over Foreign States (2010) (Japan).

[32] *Cudak v Lithuania* App No 15869/02, 23 March 2010.

[33] *Embassy of Spain to the Holy See v De la Grana Gonzales* 11 March 2014, No 9034, ILDC 2436 (IT 2014).

[34] *B v Republic of Ghana* 27 November 2019, No 18-13790, ILDC 3070 (FR 2019).

[35] *Shyam Lal v Union of India et al* 16 September 2010, WP(C) 10185/2009.

[36] *Kingdom of Morocco v X* 5 February 2010, BK 6673.

[37] See below s VIII.

[38] s 1603(d) US FSIA circularly defines 'commercial activity' as 'either a regular course of commercial conduct or a particular commercial transaction or act'. Similarly, see s 2 Canada SIA. On the use of 'commercial activity' as a synonym for private act, as opposed to a narrow sense only referring to acts of trade and commerce, see Yang (n 3) 75.

[39] House of Representatives Committee of the Judiciary, Report on Jurisdiction of United States Courts in Suits Against Foreign States, 9 September 1976, No 94-1487, 16.

US and Canadian courts have also resorted to a variety of other tests, including the nationality of the employee, the nature of the workplace and the subject matter of the claim.[40]

III. Approaches Based on the Nature of the Workplace

The chapter now starts a more detailed analysis of the above-mentioned employment-specific criteria of restrictive state immunity. The present section focuses on the approaches based on the nature of the employee's workplace. The distinguishing feature of the 'workplace test' is that it makes immunity dependent on the foreign state's establishment where the work is performed, irrespective of the individual situation of the plaintiff employee. The likely rationale for this approach is the assumption that certain state establishments – most commonly embassies, consulates and military bases – are inherently geared for performing sovereign activities, which is seen as attaching a sovereign label to any work performed in them. Vice versa, it is considered permissible to exercise jurisdiction over lawsuits by employees at establishments deemed not to perform sovereign activities – most commonly state agencies engaged in trade and commerce. The following analysis describes the most relevant examples of the use of the 'workplace test' (section IIIA). It then focuses on the key shortcomings of this approach and the reasons why it appears to be losing centrality in national case law (section IIIB).

A. The 'Workplace Test' in Immunity Instruments and Judicial Practice

The most relevant example of the 'workplace test' can be found in state immunity statutes providing for blanket immunity from claims by employees at embassies and consulates. A similar provision was first included in the UK SIA, whose section 16(1)(a) excludes the application of section 4 (closely modelled on Article 5 ECSI) in 'proceedings concerning the employment of the members of a mission within the meaning of the [Vienna Convention on Diplomatic Relations (VCDR)] or of the members of a consular post within the meaning of the [Vienna Convention on Consular Relations (VCCR)]'. The expressions 'members of the mission' and 'members of the consular post' are defined by the two Vienna Conventions as encompassing the whole staff of embassies and consulates.[41]

[40] R Garnett, 'The Perils of Working for a Foreign Government: Foreign Sovereign Immunity and Employment' (1998) 29 *California Western International Law Journal* 133, especially 139.

[41] Vienna Convention on Diplomatic Relations 1961 (VCDR), Art 1(b): 'The "members of the mission" are the head of the mission and the members of the staff of the mission', and Art 1(c): 'The "members of the staff of the mission" are the members of the diplomatic staff, of the administrative

Hence, section 16(1)(a) lays down a de facto absolute immunity over claims brought by these individuals. Such a blanket immunity no longer reflects the state of UK law, where *Benkharbouche* permitted members of the embassies' service staff to sue their employer states,[42] but provisions akin to section 16(1)(a) remain fully operational in several countries whose immunity legislation drew heavily from the UK model. For instance, under section 5 South Africa FSIA, the general rule of non-immunity in labour claims shall not apply if

> the proceedings relate to the employment of the head of a diplomatic mission or any member of the diplomatic mission or any member of the diplomatic, administrative, technical or service staff of the mission or to the employment of the head of a consular post or any member of the consular, labour, trade, administrative, technical or service staff of the post.

Provisions to the same effect are contained in section 17(1)(a) Pakistan SIO and section 18(1)(a) Malawi IPA.[43] It is noteworthy that, according to some interpretations, the saving clause of Article 32 ECSI ('Nothing in the present Convention shall affect privileges and immunities relating to the exercise of the functions of diplomatic missions and consular posts and of persons connected with them') would exclude all employment disputes with embassies and consulates from the purview of Article 5, thus creating an area of blanket immunity identical to section 16(1)(a) UK SIA and akin provisions.[44] This construction, however, has been convincingly refuted in legal doctrine: the better interpretation is that Article 32 only refers to diplomatic and consular immunities and not to state immunity, thus not excluding the application of Article 5 to employment disputes with diplomatic missions and consular posts.[45] The Explanatory Report to the ECSI supports this view by stating that Article 32 refers to the immunities enshrined in the VCDR and VCCR.[46]

Even in absence of express statutory provisions of the type just described, the use of the 'workplace test' has frequently led courts to bar jurisdiction over the totality of staff disputes with embassies and consulates. A notable example is the

and technical staff and of the service staff of the mission'; Vienna Convention on Consular Relations 1963 (VCCR), Art 1(g): '"members of the consular post" means consular officers, consular employees and members of the service staff'.

[42] On which see further below in this section.

[43] See also Revised Draft Articles for a Convention on State Immunity (1994) 66 *ILA Reports of Conferences* – Report of the Sixty-Sixth Conference held at Buenos Aires, Argentina, 14–20 August 1994, 488, 490, containing an 'employment exception' modelled on Art 5 ECSI. But Art 3(c)(1) reinstates immunity if 'The employee was appointed under the public (administrative) law of the foreign State, such as, inter alia, members of the mission, diplomatic, consular or military staff'.

[44] See Germany, Federal Labor Court, *German citizen v Kingdom of Belgium* 25 October 2001 (2002) Betriebs-Berater 787, Council of Europe Committee of Legal Advisers on Public International Law's Report on Germany, 2005, 29, www.coe.int/en/web/cahdi/database-immunities.

[45] Köhler (n 5) 197–98; Fox, 'Employment' (n 7) 140.

[46] Explanatory Report to the ECSI (n 11) para 117. Nor can a different conclusion be reached based on the Explanatory Report's comment on Art 5, ambiguously stating that 'As regards contracts of employment with diplomatic missions or consular posts, Article 32 shall also be taken into account' (ibid para 30).

decision of the English Employment Appeal Tribunal (EAT) in *Sengupta*,[47] a case to which the UK SIA did not apply because the employment contract predated the SIA's entry into force.[48] Browne-Wilkinson held that the customary law of state immunity, as received into the common law, endorsed blanket immunity over claims by embassy staff. He reasoned:

> One of the classic forms of sovereign acts by a foreign state is the representation of that state in a receiving state … A contract of work at a diplomatic mission in the work of that mission is a contract to participate in the public acts of the foreign sovereign.[49]

A Dutch local court held in a 1978 wrongful termination lawsuit that the employment of a Dutch national in the administrative service of the Belgian Consulate-General was an act done in a public capacity, because the plaintiff was 'employed by [the foreign] state to render services to a public body'.[50] More recently, in the 2004 *A v B* case, the Norwegian Supreme Court upheld immunity in a labour case brought against a foreign embassy, holding that 'activities at the foreign service missions of a State are in the core area of exercise of public authority'. The court expressly refused to make distinctions based on the functions performed by the employees.[51] Almost identical was the Canadian Federal Court's reasoning in the 2015 *Zakhary* case over the question whether employment of a cashier at the US consulate in Toronto constituted a 'commercial activity' within the meaning of section 5 Canada SIA.[52] The court held that employment of personnel by foreign embassies and consulates is not a commercial activity. In its words:

> employment within the embassy is integral to its operations and is immune from review in domestic courts. Nor can any principled distinction be drawn between employment in [a consulate and an embassy]. The nature of the functions and responsibilities of the employee, whether administrative, clerical or, as in this case, financial, do not limit the immunity … the Court will not engage in a dissection of specific employment responsibilities within embassies or consulates.[53]

Other examples of the use of the 'workplace test' have to do with employment at foreign states' military bases. Certain judicial decisions have declined to adjudicate lawsuits filed by all employees at such facilities, on the assumption that employment in a military base always amounts to an immune public act.

[47] *Sengupta v Republic of India* 17 November 1982, 64 ILR 352.

[48] See s 23(3), pursuant to which 'sections 3, 4 and 9 do not apply to any transaction, contract or arbitration agreement, entered into before [the date of the coming into force of this Act]'.

[49] *Sengupta* (n 47) 358.

[50] Local Court of Rotterdam, *AAMG v The Kingdom of Belgium* 13 April 1978, (1979) 10 *Netherlands Yearbook of International Law* 442, paras 13–14.

[51] *A v Republic of B* 3 April 2004, ILDC 23 (NO 2004), 180 ILR 433.

[52] On s 5 Canada SIA, see above s II.

[53] *United States of America v Zakhary* 2015 FC 335, paras 30–31. Similarly, see Romania, High Court of Cassation and Justice, *SDG v Canada and Prosecutor General (joining)* 1 April 2003, ILDC 1024 (RO 2003), upholding immunity over a wrongful dismissal claim by a security agent at the Canadian embassy. See also Lithuania, Supreme Court, *Stukonis v Embassy of the United States of America* 5 January 1998, Civil Case No 3K-1/1998.

Before getting into details, this jurisprudence requires some context. In particular, it should be noted that the treaties governing the status of visiting friendly forces – which often include provisions regulating privileges and immunities of the forces and their members in the receiving state – normally do not expressly address the issue of jurisdiction over employment disputes with military facilities personnel. Consider, for example, the 1951 North Atlantic Treaty Organization (NATO) Status of Forces Agreement (SOFA).[54] This treaty distinguishes between three categories of people working at military facilities in the NATO framework: (i) military personnel stationed abroad ('forces');[55] civilian personnel employed by the visiting forces, who cannot be nationals or ordinarily resident in the receiving state ('civilian component');[56] and (iii) local personnel, a residual category whose employment, unlike the military and civilian component, is subject to the substantive employment law of the receiving state.[57] The SOFA only addresses the exercise of criminal jurisdiction (Article VII) and of civil jurisdiction over third party claims (Article VIII) against the forces and the civilian component. Employment claims therefore fall outside the scope of these provisions. It has been suggested that, by submitting local personnel to the laws of the forum, the SOFA implicitly qualifies such individuals' employment as having a private law nature, thus subjecting it to local jurisdiction.[58] But this is hardly a conclusive argument. As a general rule, substantive law does not determine jurisdiction: foreign states are routinely held immune from claims based on local law.[59] Moreover, Article IX(4) merely restates the default rule that employment with foreign states is subject to the territorial state's legislation; it is rather the exclusion of the civilian component from local law that is exceptional.[60] Finally, where the SOFA intended to regulate the exercise of jurisdiction, as in Articles VII and VIII, it did so expressly. Hence, a better view is that the SOFA remains silent as to which courts should adjudicate employment claims with personnel at military bases.[61]

[54] Agreement between the Parties to the North Atlantic Treaty regarding the Status of their Forces 1951 (SOFA).

[55] ibid Art I(1)(a).

[56] ibid Art I(1)(b).

[57] ibid Art IX(4).

[58] N Ronzitti, 'Rapporti di lavoro con Stati membri dell'Alleanza atlantica ed esenzione dalla giurisdizione' [1972-IV] *Giurisprudenza di merito* 25, 27. See, eg Italy, Court of Cassation, *United States v Gereschi* 14 October 1977, No 4372, 77 ILR 598, holding that the SOFA sets forth a self-contained immunity regime for employment claims excluding the customary rules of state immunity; *United States v Porciello* 27 January 1977, No 400, (1978) 4 *Italian Yearbook of International Law* 174; *Bruno v United States* 25 January 1977, No 355, 65 ILR 316; *United States Government v Bellotto* 2 March 1964, No 467 (1965) 88 *Il Foro Italiano* 913. But see Tribunal of Naples, *Francischiello v Government of the United States* 13 February 1959, 28 ILR 158, holding that Art XI(4) SOFA only refers to substantive employment law and not to jurisdiction; Court of Cassation, *Department of the Army of the United States v Savellini* 17 October 1955, 23 ILR 201.

[59] See ch 2, s II.

[60] As noted in Leeds Employment Tribunal, *Harrington v United States of America* 27 March 2015, 180 ILR 454, 465.

[61] A Dickinson, 'Status of Forces under the UN Convention on State Immunity' (2006) 55 *ICLQ* 427, 433–34; EH Schwenk, 'Jurisdiction of the Receiving State over Forces of the Sending State under the NATO Status of Forces Agreement' (1972) 6 *International Lawyer* 525, 538–39.

Domestic state immunity statutes are also sometimes reticent to engage with the issue of jurisdiction over employment at military facilities. In fact, some expressly remove claims against military forces from their scope.[62] Most notably, section 16(2) UK SIA excludes the application of the Act's Part I (including section 4 on employment contracts) to 'proceedings relating to anything done by or in relation to the armed forces of a State while present in the United Kingdom',[63] and so do the statutes of Singapore and Pakistan.[64] The UK Visiting Forces Act 1952 partially fills this gap by ruling out jurisdiction over employment claims by members of the 'forces' and the 'civilian component'.[65] This Act, however, says nothing as to the possibility to entertain jurisdiction over claims by other categories of employees at military bases. This question has been decided at common law by UK courts,[66] which have attributed primary relevance to the nature of the workplace.

This was the case with the EAT's 1995 *Hicks* judgment, an unfair dismissal claim brought by a US national working as a repairer at a US Airforce base's bowling centre. The first instance court affirmed jurisdiction based essentially on the activities performed by the employee: it held that 'The applicant was not engaged in the discharge of the sovereign act of a foreign state; the US Airforce is not here to run bowling alleys'. The appeal court reversed: it considered a bowling centre to be instrumental to the performance of sovereign functions, in that 'The primary purpose of providing recreational facilities [at the] base must be to sustain the effectiveness of its central military activity'.[67] In the more recent *Harrington* case, an employment tribunal was confronted with a discrimination claim by a computer operator (of UK nationality and employed under UK law) at an Army and Air Force Exchange Facility (AAFES) store of a US military base. AAFES stores are set up by US armed forces to sell food and merchandise to members of the US military. The court reasoned that the management of an exchange store within a military base is an act *jure imperii*, because such facility 'is specifically linked to maintaining military readiness' and therefore 'plays a part, however small' in the sovereign activities of the state.[68] Notably, the court

[62] In the absence of similar saving clauses, there are no grounds for not applying the ordinary immunity regime to military establishments. See, eg s 6 Australia FSIA and s 16 Canada SIA, merely prioritising statutory provisions regulating the status of visiting forces in case of inconsistency, and s 22 Israel FSIL, prioritising inconsistent international treaties. The saving clause of Art 31 ECSI ('Nothing in this Convention shall affect any immunities … in respect of anything done … by … armed forces when on the territory of another Contracting State') may be construed as barring application of Art 5 ECSI only where another treaty stipulates otherwise: see Fox, 'Employment' (n 7) 140, arguing that Art 5 applies to employment with visiting forces.

[63] Yet this provision does not prevent the application of s 4 SIA to cases regarding work for foreign forces performed outside the UK: Garnett, 'State Immunity in Employment Matters' (n 3) 106.

[64] s 19(2)(a) Singapore SIA; s 17(2)(a) Pakistan SIO.

[65] UK Visiting Forces Act 1952, s 6.

[66] See, although not with regard to an employment claim, *Holland v Lampen-Wolfe* [2000] UKHL 40, ILDC 223 (UK 2000), re a defamation lawsuit against a US official at a military base in the UK.

[67] *United States of America v Hicks* [1995] UKEAT 1021_94_1107.

[68] *Harrington* (n 60) 469.

acknowledged that, had section 4 UK SIA been applicable, immunity would not have been upheld.[69]

By contrast, in cases where the employer is a state establishment engaged in trade and commerce, the application of the 'workplace test' has frequently led courts to affirm jurisdiction, on the grounds that such establishments are perceived as not – or not primarily – involved in the performance of sovereign functions. An example is *Gilligan*, a Canadian decision over a claim for compensation for discriminatory dismissal by a secretary at the Swedish Trade Council (STC), an agency of the Swedish government established with a view to helping Swedish companies do business in Canada. The STC was hosted in the premises of the Swedish consulate in Toronto but was legally distinct from it. The adjudicator rejected Sweden's immunity plea on the grounds that the STC's only institutional aim was to facilitate commercial activities.[70] A somewhat similar case is *Rodrigo and Genove*, where an employee at a US military base recreation centre sued for wrongful dismissal. In order to rule on immunity, the Philippines Supreme Court analysed the activities performed by the centre and concluded that it was a commercial activity operated for profit. This led it to hold that 'by entering into the employment contract … in the discharge of its proprietary functions, [the USA] impliedly divested itself of its sovereign immunity from suit'.[71]

It should also be recalled that state immunity instruments often establish more lenient immunity rules for claims by employees at foreign states' commercial institutions. Notably, under Article 5(3) ECSI, immunity only applies to claims involving offices, agencies or instrumentalities performing industrial, commercial or financial activities if the plaintiff was habitually resident in the employer state at the time of hiring.[72] It should be noted incidentally that this provision – reproduced, inter alia, in section 4(3) UK SIA – constitutes *lex specialis* vis-à-vis the rules generally governing the immunity of agencies and instrumentalities of foreign states (ie state entities set up to participate in economic and commercial activities). In the ECSI, for instance, such establishments are not immune if the proceedings relate to activity performed by them 'in the same manner as a private person'.[73] But this provision is utterly unhelpful in matters of employment insofar as it merely restates the classic 'private person test'.

As frequently happens in matters of state immunity, there have been conflicting pronouncements. In the context of claims by employees at foreign states'

[69] ibid 460.

[70] Ontario Ministry of Labour, Office of Adjudication, *Gilligan v Ministry of Labour and Swedish Trade Council and Swedish Trade Office (Canada) Inc* 2 February 1998, No ESC 97-91, 8. Similarly, Quebec Superior Court, *Orvieto v Government of the Republic of Italy – Italian Trade Commission* 28 November 2001, No 500-05-068162-013, affirmed, Quebec Court of Appeal, *Government of the Republic of Italy – Italian Trade Commission v Orvieto* 11 September 2002, No 500-09-011655-016.

[71] *United States of America, Lamachia and Others v Rodrigo and Genove* 26 February 1990, Case No 79470, 102 ILR 132, 145–46.

[72] See above s II.

[73] Art 7(1) ECSI. Art 27 ECSI, of similar content, applies to entities having a distinct legal personality from the state. See also s 14(2) UK SIA.

commercial establishment, US courts traditionally gave primary regard to the functions performed by the employees and their nationality.[74] However, more recent case law appears to have shifted the main focus of the inquiry to the broader context of the employment. This trend was initiated by the 2004 *Kato* decision.[75] The plaintiff, who sued for sexual harassment, worked in the administrative staff of the New York office of the Tokyo Metropolitan Government (TMG), a Japanese instrumentality whose institutional aim is the promotion of commerce. In order to assess whether the claim fell under the FSIA's 'commercial exception' to immunity, the test on which the court relied needed to establish 'whether TMG's activities in New York were typical of a private party engaged in commerce'. The Court answered in the negative and affirmed immunity. It opined:

> the fact that a government instrumentality … is engaged in *the promotion of commerce* does not mean that the instrumentality is thereby engaged in *commerce*. The promotion abroad of the commerce of domestic firms is a basic – even quintessential – governmental function …[76]

Subsequent decisions relying on *Kato* have interpreted its dicta as requiring a two-pronged examination: first, on 'the nature of the sovereign's activities in the United States of which the plaintiff's employment is a part'; and secondly, on 'the extent to which the plaintiffs individual duties are themselves either integral or incidental to any governmental function'.[77] In other words, this combines the 'workplace test' with the test based on the functions of the employee. In practice, though, the former test retains a decisive role. This emerges clearly from the 2017 *Salman* case. The plaintiff, a US citizen, worked as academic advisor at the Saudi Arabian Cultural Mission, and agency created by the Saudi government to deliver educational services to Saudi nationals in the USA. He sued for sexual harassment in the workplace. The plaintiff sought to overcome the *Kato* bar on jurisdiction by submitting that he was engaged in activity which is regularly performed in private institutions, eg by teachers at private universities. The court rejected this argument:

> the question is not whether an individual employed by a foreign state performed job functions with an analogue in the private sector. Rather, the inquiry centers on *the nature of the conduct undertaken by the foreign state itself* and the individual's role in that activity'.[78]

[74] *Segni v Commercial Office of Spain* 835 F.2d 160 (7th Cir 1987) 165: 'the mere fact that Segni was an employee of the Commercial Office will not, by itself, render his hiring commercial activity … We must also examine the nature of Segni's "employment activities" in order to determine whether they are governmental or private.' See further below s IV.

[75] *Kato v Ishihara* 360 F.3d 106 (2d Cir 2004).

[76] ibid 112 (emphasis in the original). cp *Mukaddam v Permanent Mission of Saudi Arabia* 111 F.Supp 2d 457 (SDNY 2000) 466, declining to give relevance to the 'broader context of plaintiff's employment [ie the workplace] and whether it was designed to fulfill a sovereign function'.

[77] *Hijazi v Permanent Mission of Saudi Arabia to the United Nations* 689 F.Supp 2d 669 (SDNY 2010) 674, affirmed, 403 Fed.Appx 631 (2d Cir 2010).

[78] *Salman v Saudi Arabian Cultural Mission* 2017 WL 176576 (ED Va 2017) (emphasis added).

The court qualified educational services as public benefits and concluded that a state's distribution of public benefits was a 'quintessentially' sovereign activity.

B. Drawbacks of the 'Workplace Test' and its Declining Relevance

The *Kato* jurisprudence highlights the main conceptual difficulty raised by the 'workplace test'. On the one hand, the *Kato* court had a point in affirming that the acts of a foreign state establishment engaged in commerce-related activity are not all necessarily commercial. Notwithstanding a certain variety among national approaches, it is widely accepted that agencies or instrumentalities – which by definition are engaged in commerce-related activities – *can* perform acts of sovereign authority, being entitled to immunity in such cases.[79] Therefore the approach in *Gilligan* comes across as somewhat simplistic: a state entity's engagement in commerce-related activity is not a decisive argument for non-immunity per se. Further elaboration as to why the employment of an individual fell outside of the 'commercial activity' exception would have been required.

But the reverse is also true: the fact that a state establishment is involved in sovereign activities (such as embassies, consulates and military bases, as well as, to a certain extent, agencies and instrumentalities) is not a sufficient ground for affirming that all the acts by such establishments are immune from suit. This logic errs on the side of absolute immunity. Since any activity of foreign states is ipso facto connected (more or less closely) to public purposes, by that logic anything done by a foreign state could be immune. But this contradicts a fundamental tenet of the restrictive doctrine, which has historically developed around the idea that the sovereign status of the defendant is not decisive in itself and that only specific activities of foreign states may attract immunity from jurisdiction.[80] Put differently, under restrictive state immunity the broader context in which a state act is performed is not decisive in isolation from other factors. Thus, that an act is done by an embassy says nothing as to whether that act is immune: an embassy can act *jure imperii* or *jure gestionis*.[81]

The same goes for military bases. It is useful to recall the principles laid out by the English Court of Appeal in *Littrell*. This was not an employment dispute: the

[79] Fox and Webb (n 1) 359. See also Art 2(1)(b)(iii) UNCSI, considering an agency or instrumentality as part of a foreign state for immunity purposes only if it is 'entitled to perform and [is] actually performing acts in the exercise of sovereign authority of the State'.

[80] Yang (n 3) 132: it is an 'elementary rule' that what is decisive under restrictive state immunity is 'the *nature of the act*, rather than the *status of the actor*' (emphasis in the original).

[81] Case C-154/11 *Mahamdia v People's Democratic Republic of Algeria* [2013] ECR 1, para 49: 'the functions of an embassy … consist essentially in representing the sending State, protecting the interests of the sending State, and promoting relations with the receiving State. In the exercise of those functions, the embassy, like any other public entity, can act *iure gestionis* … in particular as a result of concluding private law contracts.'

plaintiff, a US serviceman stationed in the UK, contended to have been the victim of negligent treatment at a US base's hospital. Yet, the court offered guidelines that could apply to all activities performed at military bases. Notably, it refused to consider context as a conclusive factor. It affirmed:

> The context in which the act took place was the maintenance by the United States of a unit of the United States Airforce in the United Kingdom. This looks about as imperial an activity as could be imagined. But it would be facile to regard this context as determinative of the question. Acts done within that context could range from arrangements concerning the flight of the bombers (plainly *jure imperii*) to ordering milk for the base from a local dairy or careless driving by off-duty airmen on the roads of Suffolk. Both of the latter would seem to me to be *jure gestionis* ...[82]

Against this backdrop, the court upheld immunity, but only because it considered that adjudicating over the running of a military hospital directly interfered with military matters.[83] The aforementioned *Hicks* and *Harrington* cases, which both cited *Littrell* as a leading precedent, ironically did what *Littrell* qualified as 'facile', ie treated the 'context in which the act took place' – in *Hicks* and *Harrington*, the place of employment – as the only decisive factor.

The above shows that the 'workplace test' is nothing but a reappearance in a different form of the logic underpinning absolute immunity. One fails to see why this approach should retain a controlling character in matters of employment whereas it has been relinquished in other sectors of state immunity law. Accordingly, the approaches followed in the majority of jurisdictions do not consider the workplace as dispositive, but instead narrow down the inquiry to the characteristics of the individual employment relationship or of the specific claim. In fact, the 'workplace test' appears to be a receding trait in domestic case law. This can be explained by the impact exercised on state practice by Article 11 UNCSI, which does not include this test among the factors relevant to the assessment of immunity,[84] and by the case law of the ECtHR.

As noted above in section II, starting from its seminal *Cudak* judgment, the ECtHR has applied Article 11 qua codification of custom. The court has reached this conclusion while assessing the compatibility of grants of state immunity with the right of access to court under Article 6 of the European Convention on Human Rights (ECHR).[85] Because, according to its well-established jurisprudence, the ECtHR finds no breach of Article 6 where a grant of immunity complies with customary international law, treating Article 11 as codificatory has meant the court turning this provision into a yardstick of compliance with Article 6 ECHR: a state granting an immunity broader than envisioned by Article 11 breaches the

[82] *Littrell v United States of America (No 2)* [1995] 1 WLR 82, 100 ILR 438, 463 (Hoffman LJ).
[83] ibid 464.
[84] Also note that the UNCSI contains no saving clause regarding military forces, thus its provisions apply to military matters: see Dickinson (n 61) 429–31.
[85] Convention for the Protection of Human Rights and Fundamental Freedoms 1950 (ECHR).

plaintiff employee's right of access to court.[86] Against this backdrop, the use of the 'workplace test' may lead a state to violate the ECHR because Article 11 does not condone blanket grants of immunity to diplomatic and consular missions or any other state establishment. It is therefore not surprising that the necessity to comply with the ECHR has led national courts in several European states to abandon the 'workplace test' in favour of other approaches. This process may be illustrated by two examples taken from the practice of Lithuania and the UK.

Until relatively recently, the 'workplace test' had pride of place in the Lithuanian case law on employment suits against foreign states. In the 2001 *Cudak v Embassy of Poland* case, an unlawful dismissal claim by a secretary and switchboard operator at the Polish embassy, the Supreme Court declared that the entitlement to immunity depended on multiple factors, including the character of the workplace, the employee's status, the territorial connection to the forum state and the nature of the claim. With regard to the first factor, the court noted that the functions of an embassy were directly related to the exercise of sovereignty; this, along with the finding that secretarial functions 'facilitated, to a certain degree, the exercise by the Republic of Poland of its sovereign functions', sufficed to uphold immunity.[87] The Supreme Court was even more forthright in its 2007 *Naku* decision, where it granted Sweden immunity in relation to an unfair dismissal claim by an employee of the Swedish embassy's press office. In a textbook restatement of the 'workplace test', the court proclaimed that 'everyone who works in a diplomatic representation of a foreign State … in one way or another contributes to the performance of the sovereign rights of a represented State, carrying out public-law functions'.[88] In the cases of *Cudak* and *Naku*, however, both these Supreme Court decisions were found by the ECtHR to have breached the applicants' right to a court: the Strasbourg Court rejected the blanket immunity accruing to diplomatic missions and held – relying on Article 11 UNCSI – that the Lithuanian courts ought to have considered the specific duties performed by the applicants.[89] As a result, the Lithuanian courts seem now to have aligned their approach to the Strasbourg Court's jurisprudence. Notably, after the Supreme Court set aside its ruling in *Cudak v Embassy of Poland* and ordered a retrial, a Vilnius court dismissed the immunity plea and awarded compensation for unfair dismissal.[90]

In the UK legal system, the 'workplace test' has also lost its previous centrality under the influence of the Strasbourg Court's case law. The 2015 Court of Appeal ruling in *Benkharbouche and Janah* and, at last instance, the Supreme Court's aforementioned *Benkharbouche* judgment struck down the saving regime

[86] For a more thorough analysis, see ch 6, s II.

[87] *Cudak (Senkevič) v Embassy of the Republic of Poland* 25 June 2001, Case No 3K-3-203/2001, (2003) 3 *Baltic Yearbook of International Law* 320.

[88] *Sniegė Naku v Embassy of the Kingdom of Sweden* 6 April 2007, Case No 3K-3-142/2007; English translation in *Naku v Lithuania and Sweden* App No 26126/07, 8 November 2016, para 38.

[89] *Cudak* (n 32) paras 70–72; *Naku* (n 88) para 95.

[90] Vilnius Court of Appeal, 11 November 2011, Case No 2-1212-553/2011.

of section 16(1)(a) UK SIA, which barred all claims by employees at diplomatic and consular missions.[91] Both courts reached this conclusion by applying the ECHR-derived doctrine that a grant of immunity is only justifiable from a fair trial standpoint insofar as it is required by general international law. It may be noted that, because neither court was persuaded by the ECtHR's qualification of Article 11 UNCSI as codificatory of custom, their decisions were based on a *de novo* assessment of general international law.[92] However, the final outcome conformed to the substance of the ECtHR's jurisprudence. The scope of immunity under section 16(1)(a) UK SIA, to the extent it covered claims by service staff whose work was unrelated to sovereign functions, was held to be exorbitant vis-à-vis customary international law and thus in breach of Article 6 ECHR.[93] In so doing, the courts introduced within UK law a judicial test based on the functions performed by the employee.

IV. Approaches Based on the Status and Functions of the Employee

This section analyses a second common approach for adapting the restrictive immunity doctrine to labour disputes – one based on the functions performed by the employee. Under the 'functions test', immunity is granted where the employee's duties and tasks are deemed connected to the employer's sovereign powers. In some cases, decisive weight is attributed to employee's status rather than the specific duties. But despite its more formalistic undertone, the logics of the 'status test' and the 'functions test' are closely intertwined, so much so that they may be regarded as variations of the same approach. A reference to status may in fact be interpreted as establishing an unrebuttable presumption that an employee's role is connected to the sovereign functions of the employer, thus absorbing any examination of individual tasks.[94]

[91] *Benkharbouche and Janah v Embassy of the Republic of Sudan, Libya and the Secretary of State for Foreign and Commonwealth Affairs* [2015] EWCA Civ 33; Supreme Court, *Benkharbouche* (n 24). For pre-*Benkharbouche* application of s 16, see EAT, *Arab Republic of Egypt Embassy v Gamal-Eldin and Another* 2 March 1995, 104 ILR 673, upholding immunity over claims by two drivers at the Egyptian embassy's Medical Office.

[92] For a more detailed discussion on the state of customary international law in employment disputes, see below s VIII.

[93] Supreme Court, *Benkharbouche* (n 24) para 76. s 16(1)(a) was also disapplied (in claims derived from European Union law on employment rights) for breaching the Charter of Fundamental Rights of the European Union 2000, whose Art 47 is coextensive with Art 6 ECHR: see WA Schabas, *The European Convention on Human Rights: A Commentary* (Oxford, Oxford University Press, 2015) 266.

[94] J Foakes and R O'Keefe, 'Article 11' in R O'Keefe and CJ Tams (eds), *The United Nations Convention on Jurisdictional Immunities of States and Their Property: A Commentary* (Oxford, Oxford University Press, 2013) 183, 200, noting that Art 11(2)(b) UNCSI is *lex specialis* vis-à-vis the Art 11(2)(a) 'functions test'.

The following discussion analyses the diffusion of this test in state practice (section IVA), its application *in concreto* to the various categories of state personnel (section IVB) and its scope under Article 11 UNCSI (section IVC).

A. The Diffusion of the 'Status and Functions Test' in State Practice

The test based on the status or functions of the employee is without a doubt the most widespread approach in state practice.[95] While this test is unknown to the ECSI and the national statutes that are directly derived from it (although, as seen above, *Benkharbouche* introduced it into UK law), it is enshrined in section 12(5)–(6) Australia FSIA and in Article 11(2)(a)–(b) UNCSI. Notably, Article 11(2)(a) UNCSI – pursuant to which the foreign state is immune from claims by employees 'recruited to perform particular functions in the exercise of governmental authority' – refers to the tasks of the employee, while paragraph 2(b) bars jurisdiction on the basis of status: precluded claims include those by diplomatic and consular agents and some other categories of persons enjoying individual immunities. Apart from these instances, in the majority of legal systems the 'status and functions test' is a product of judicial construction.

The use of this approach (either in isolation or in combination with other tests, primarily nationality and residence or the claim's subject matter) is particularly common in continental Europe. Both European regional courts have endorsed this approach in some form: the ECtHR resorts to this test as a consequence of its application of Article 11 UNCSI qua codification of international custom, whereas the Court of Justice of the European Union (CJEU) declared in *Mahamdia* that 'the embassy, like any other public entity, can act *iure gestionis* … That is the case where it concludes contracts of employment with persons who do not perform functions which fall within the exercise of public powers.'[96]

As far as national courts are concerned, in the 1997 *Saignie* judgment, the French Cour de cassation resorted to a test based on whether the employee had 'special responsibility for the performance of the public service' of a mission.[97] Similarly, the yardstick employed by the Hague Court of Appeal in *Morocco v HA* was whether the employee 'played an essential role for the diplomatic mission'.[98] Belgian courts have consistently held that immunity should be recognised when an employee's functions involve 'attributes of public power'.[99] In *S v India*, the Swiss

[95] Garnett, 'State Immunity in Employment Matters' (n 3) 784.

[96] *Mahamdia* (n 81) para 49.

[97] *Saignie v Embassy of Japan* 11 February 1997, 113 ILR 492, 493.

[98] *Kingdom of Morocco v HA* 27 July 2007, (2008) 39 *Netherlands Yearbook of International Law* 392, 396, cumulating this requirement with nationality and residence.

[99] Labour Court of Brussels, *Castanheira v Commercial Office of Portugal* 1 February 1980, 82 ILR 100, 103; Labour Court of Brussels, *Rousseau v Republic of Upper Volta* 25 April 1983, 82 ILR 118, 120; Labour Court of Brussels, *United States of America v Van Averbeke* 7 October 2015, RG 2013/AB/1.051, 15.

Federal Tribunal distinguished between claims brought by employees 'with relatively senior functions' and lower level employees.[100] Also, the Oslo District Court – departing from a Norwegian Supreme Court precedent applying blanket immunity to employment at embassies[101] – held in 2015 that the nature and purposes of the work duties were determinants of the scope of immunity.[102]

The 'functions test' occupies a central place in Portuguese case law too. In 1984, the Supreme Court categorically held that all administrative employees should be 'recognized as forming a necessary part of the performance of the public functions of the diplomatic mission', and did not indulge in an analysis of the particular duties of the plaintiff employee.[103] However, in a 2002 ruling, the same court distinguished between employees performing 'subordinate' and 'more senior' functions: 'only employment contracts concluded with a person of a higher grade are really capable of being linked with the exercise of public authority (*jure imperii*)'.[104] German courts normally inquire into whether an employee's tasks belong to the core sphere of sovereign state activity.[105] And in Finland, the Supreme Court's 1993 *Heusala* judgment proclaimed that immunity should be upheld whenever an employee's functions 'were meant to serve the official duties' of the state.[106]

The relevance of the employee's tasks is less clear in Italy. Until the late 1980s, the 'functions test' was the main criterion on which Italian courts relied.[107] However, with the 1989 landmark judgment in *Toglia*,[108] the Court of Cassation inaugurated a trend according to which immunity was lifted not only in cases where an employee's tasks were unrelated to sovereign functions, but also, *irrespective of the functions*, where the claims only concerned monetary compensation (save – according to the prevalent judicial trend – for claims for unfair dismissal, where immunity persisted). This way, the 'functions test' lost its prominence in favour of a test based on subject matter: Italian courts routinely affirmed jurisdiction over monetary claims by employees whose tasks were expressly qualified

[100] *S v India* 22 May 1984, 82 ILR 13, 19.

[101] *A v Republic of B* (n 51).

[102] *Sostrand v United States* 2015, No 14-111748 TVI-OTIR/05, 25.

[103] *Brazilian Embassy Employee Case* 11 May 1984, Case No 706, 116 ILR 625, 633. See also High Court of Lisbon, *Ramos and Others v United States of America* 4 May 1994, 116 ILR 634; see Supreme Court, *A (Individual) v France* 9 December 1998, www.cahdidatabases.coe.int/Contribution/Details/219, re an embassy driver.

[104] *X v Israel* 13 November 2002, 127 ILR 310, 311–12.

[105] See, eg Federal Labor Court, *X v Argentina* 3 July 1996, 114 ILR 502, 506.

[106] *Heusala v Turkey* 30 September 1993, KKO:1993:120, ILDC 576 (FI 1993).

[107] L Sbolci, *Controversie di lavoro con Stati stranieri e diritto internazionale* (Milan, Giuffrè, 1987) 121–29. See, most recently, Court of Cassation, *Ambasciata della Repubblica del Ghana v Barbini* 9 July 1991, No 7548; *Republic of France, French Embassy in Italy and Lycée Chateaubriand v Jacuzio* 16 December 1987, No 9322, 87 ILR 53, 55; *Panattoni v Repubblica federale di Germania* 15 July 1987, No 6172 (1988) 71 *Rivista di diritto internazionale* 902; *Special Representative of State of the City of the Vatican v Pieciukiewicz* 5 July 1982, No 4005, 78 ILR 120.

[108] Above n 22. See G Cataldi, 'I recenti sviluppi della giurisprudenza italiana in materia di controversie di lavoro con Stati stranieri' (1991) 27 *Rivista di diritto internazionale privato e processuale* 691; B Conforti, 'Ancora sull'atteggiamento della Corte di cassazione in tema di immunità degli Stati stranieri dalla giurisdizione italiana' (1990) 73 *Rivista di diritto internazionale* 911.

as 'sovereign-related'.[109] This approach remained dominant until the 2014 *De la Grana* judgment, where the Court of Cassation, under the direct influence of the ECtHR, applied Article 11 UNCSI qua codification of customary law.[110] Because Article 11(2)(a) attributes decisive relevance to the tasks of the employee, the 'functions test' may be said to have regained its old importance. However, quite confusingly, the Court of Cassation occasionally invokes principles developed in its pre-2014 jurisprudence, on the likely assumption that the two approaches are interchangeable.[111] But clearly they are not: under the UNCSI, the employee's functions are a threshold issue which cannot be bypassed by reason of subject matter.[112] Hence the actual importance of the 'functions test' in Italian case law is uncertain.[113]

While the European practice is particularly abundant, the adoption of the 'status and functions test' is in no way limited to Europe. In *Sutton*, an unfair dismissal claim against the British High Commissioner, the New Zealand Court of Appeal held that jurisdiction may not be exercised where 'the employee is engaged in carrying out public functions of the foreign State'.[114] The Supreme Court of Sri Lanka held in *Jansen* that immunity depended on whether the duties of the employee 'were integral to the core sphere of sovereign activity'.[115] This approach also bears relevance in US case law. As seen above, because the US FSIA lacks a provision on employment contracts, labour cases are handled within the framework of section 1605(a)(2)'s 'commercial activity exception' to state immunity. In the FSIA House Report, to which US courts commonly refer when interpreting the statute, the status and functions of the employee come across as key factors for distinguishing immune and non-immune claims. The Report suggests, by way of example, that employment contracts of 'laborers, clerical staff or public relations or marketing agents' ought to be considered as commercial and the employment of 'diplomatic, civil service or military personnel' as governmental in nature.[116]

The application of the test at hand by US courts, however, is not entirely straightforward. It might appear from the House Report's exemplification that, when it comes to diplomatic, civil service or military personnel, the formal status of the employee should suffice to pronounce on immunity independently of the

[109] R Pavoni, 'La jurisprudence italienne sur l'immunité des États dans les différends en matière de travail: tendances récentes à la lumière de la Convention des Nations Unies' (2007) 53 *Annuaire Français de Droit International* 211. On the role of the subject matter of the claim in Italian case law, see also below s VI.

[110] *De la Grana* (n 33).

[111] Compare *Chibomba v Embassy of the Republic of Zambia to the Italian Republic* 6 June 2017, No 13980, ILDC 2703 (IT 2017), applying Art 11 UNCSI; *Embassy of Qatar v Awad* 27 February 2017, No 4882, ILDC 2699 (IT 2017), applying pre-2014 case law; *British Council v Dickinson* 8 March 2019, No 6884, ILDC 3010 (IT 2019), mentioning but not applying Art 11 UNCSI.

[112] F Salerno, *Diritto internazionale. Principi e norme*, 5th edn (Padua, Cedam, 2019) 340.

[113] P Rossi, 'Conflicting Approaches of the Court of Cassation to State Immunity in Employment Disputes' (2017) 27 *Italian Yearbook of International Law* 431.

[114] *Governor of Pitcairn and Associated Islands v Sutton* [1995] 1 NZLR 426, 104 ILR 508, 522.

[115] *British High Commission v Jansen* 10 July 2014, SC Appeal No 99 of 2012, 15.

[116] House of Representatives Committee of the Judiciary (n 39) 16.

employee's specific tasks. Yet, what the Report refers to as 'civil service' is unclear, particularly because this expression may bear different meanings in different countries and may be unknown to some state apparatuses.[117] US courts have thus resorted to various criteria as determinants of civil service status, including the functions performed by an employee and his or her nationality. In 2000, the DC Circuit in *El-Hadad* described civil service status as depending on multiple factors, including the nature of the employee's work.[118] In the 2013 *Shanchez-Ramirez* case, a court held that the plaintiffs were to be considered part of Mexico's civil service because their work 'could not have been performed by private persons in commerce'.[119] Furthermore, US courts often resort to the 'functions test' in order to determine whether to exercise jurisdiction over claims by employees who are not considered members of the civil service. As the DC Court of Appeals put it in its 2007 *El-Hadad* decision:

> A foreign government's employee might not be a civil servant (or diplomat or soldier) and still be engaged in quintessentially governmental work – like, for example, a judge. Thus, if El-Hadad is a civil servant, our analysis stops for we have determined that the UAE is immune from his suit. If El-Hadad is not a civil servant, we go on to scrutinize whether his work involves the exercise of powers that can also be exercised by private citizens, as distinct from those powers peculiar to sovereigns.[120]

This approach, however, is not unanimously followed in US case law. Other courts have suggested that the employment of any individual not belonging to the diplomatic, civil service or military personnel should be treated as commercial.[121] Also different, as seen above, is the *Kato* test, which nominally requires consideration of both the nature of the workplace and the employee's tasks.[122] Evidently, however,

[117] As acknowledged in *El-Hadad v United Arab Emirates* 180 ILR 689, 496 F.3d 658 (DC Cir 2007) 664–65.

[118] *El-Hadad v United Arab Emirates* 216 F.3d 29 (DC Cir 2000) 34. Other factors considered by the court were: (i) the foreign state's definition of civil service; (ii) whether the claim is based solely on the foreign country's civil service laws; (iii) whether the employee had previously performed the same functions in the employer state; and (iv) the employee's nationality, also in light of whether the foreign country employs non-nationals in governmental positions.

[119] *Sanchez-Ramirez v Consulate General of Mexico in San Francisco* No C 12-3485 PJH (ND Cal 2013) 15.

[120] *El-Hadad* (2007) (n 117) 664; followed in *Dahman v Embassy of Qatar* Civil Action No 17-2628 (JEB) (DDC 2018) 9; *Harmouche v Consulate General of Qatar* 313 F.Supp 3d 815 (SD Tex 2018) 820; *Howe v Embassy of Italy* 68 F.Supp 3d 26 (DDC 2014) 34, note 4 (but not applying the test and dismissing the case on grounds of improper service); *Lee v Taipei Economic Cultural Representative Office* No 4:09-cv-0024 (SD Tex 2010) 3–4. See also *Mukaddam* (n 76) 466, analysing the employee's work duties in order to determine whether she belonged to 'diplomatic personnel', and answering in the negative. This assessment was unnecessary in that the employee, a researcher performing clerical duties, was undisputedly not endowed with diplomatic status.

[121] See, eg *Holden v Canadian Consulate* 92 F.3d 918 (9th Cir 1996) 921: 'employment of diplomatic, civil service or military personnel is governmental and the employment of other personnel is commercial'.

[122] *Hijazi* (n 77) 674, holding that immunity 'depends both on the nature of the sovereign's activities … and the extent to which the plaintiffs' individual duties are themselves either integral or incidental to any governmental function'.

the former element has overriding relevance: if a state establishment is categorised as performing sovereign activities, a court may be expected to uphold immunity without dissecting the employee's specific duties.

Another jurisdiction where the 'functions test' is frequently applied is Canada, whose immunity legislation is also silent on employment contracts.[123] An example is *Roy*, a wrongful dismissal lawsuit by a former clerk at South Africa's High Commission. The test on which the Ontario Superior Court of Justice relied was whether the employee participated 'in the creation of government policy or its administration'.[124] In other cases, however, under the direct influence of US precedents, Canadian courts have treated the civil service status of the employee as decisive without apparently taking duties into account.[125]

Finally, it should be noted that a consideration of the plaintiff's tasks might be implicit in pronouncements which do not expressly mentioned this criterion, notably those including decisions seemingly considering all forms of employment with foreign states as *acta jure gestionis*. Regardless of the breadth of such statements of principle, practically all such decisions have been concerned with claims by relatively low-level employees. For example, in *Dube and Rabasha*, the Industrial Court of Botswana exercised jurisdiction over claims for compensation for wrongful retrenchment by two locally recruited accounting technicians and financial assistants. The court justified its decision by broadly affirming that contracts of employment are a matter of private law.[126] The Czech Supreme Court similarly held in the context of a claim by a driver that, in labour matters, a state 'does not act as the executor of public authority'.[127] As has been rightly noted, it is doubtful that these courts would have adopted the same approach in proceedings involving higher-level embassy or consular employees.[128]

B. The Varied Outcomes of the 'Status and Functions Test'

The widespread adoption of this test in state practice has not translated into coherent outcomes in national case law. Rather, as this subsection will show, it is difficult in most cases to discern a general agreement as to how this test should be applied.

In order to distinguish between different grades of staff, the following discussion relies mainly on the VCDR terminology. This Convention classifies personnel

[123] R Garnett, 'State Immunity and Employment Relations in Canada' (2015) 18 *Canadian Labour and Employment Law Journal* 643, 649–50.

[124] *Roy v South Africa* 2013 ONSC 4633 (CanLII) para 61.

[125] *Gouvernement du Royaume du Maroc v El Ansari* 2010 QCCA 2256.

[126] *Dube and Rabasha v American Embassy/Botusa* 30 October 2008, No IC 897/2006, ILDC 1347 (BW 2008).

[127] *State Immunity in Labour Law Matters Case* 25 June 2008, 142 ILR 206, 214–15.

[128] J Brower, 'State Practice on Sovereign Immunity in Employment Disputes Involving Embassy and Consular Staff. A Report of the Center for Global Legal Challenges' (Yale Law School, 2015) 19–20, https://law.yale.edu/sites/default/files/state_immunity_in_employment_disputes.pdf.

working at diplomatic missions in three tiers: (i) 'members of the diplomatic staff', ie persons having diplomatic rank;[129] (ii) 'administrative and technical staff';[130] and (iii) 'service staff'.[131] The distinguishing factor between technical/administrative staff and service staff is the element of intellectual responsibility.[132] In particular, the former category is made up of employees working in highly responsible positions who 'may be dealing at a lower level with diplomatic matters',[133] including, among others, secretaries, clerks, operators and computer technicians. The service staff, by contrast, are not directly in contact with official matters, and include eg drivers, cooks, cleaners and doorkeepers.[134] A similar categorisation is adopted in the VCCR, which partitions the members of the consular post into 'consular officers' (ie persons entrusted with consular functions), 'consular employees' (ie technical/administrative staff) and service staff.[135] This distinction may also be applied to other state establishments *mutatis mutandis*.

There seems to be general agreement that jurisdiction over labour claims by individuals having diplomatic or consular rank should be barred on grounds of status. Although a few instruments provide so expressly – this is the case with Article 11(2)(b)(i)–(iii) UNCSI and section 12(5) Australia FSIA – in other instruments this categorical exclusion is implicit, being covered by the blanket immunity provisions applicable to suits by embassy or consulate personnel.[136] The same may be said of the US FSIA, whose legislative history expressly stipulates that governmental character should be attached to employment of diplomatic personnel. In other legal systems, the prohibition to adjudicate such claims may be drawn *a fortiori* by the practice concerning technical/administrative and service staff, which will be analysed shortly. Moreover, the UNCSI's *travaux* further highlight a widespread agreement as to the exclusion of employment claims by diplomatic and consular employees from local jurisdiction. While the scope of the 'functions test' was fiercely debated,[137] no state expressed opposition to the provisions eventually enshrined in Article 11(2)(b)(i)–(iii).[138]

It would appear that very few courts have ever had the chance of ruling about the scope of immunity in labour claims between diplomatic and consular agents

[129] Art 1(d) VCDR.

[130] Art 1(f) VCDR.

[131] Art 1(g) VCDR. The VCDR relies on status and functions to differentiate levels of individual immunity: see Art 37.

[132] R van Alebeek, 'Immunity, Diplomatic' (2009) *Max Planck Encyclopedia of Public International Law*, para 44.

[133] J Foakes and E Denza, 'Privileges and Immunities of Diplomatic Agents' in I Roberts (ed), *Satow's Diplomatic Practice*, 7th edn (Oxford, Oxford University Press, 2016) 246, 278.

[134] ibid 281. The distinction between these two categories may not always be clear-cut. It is within the sending state's discretion to classify the staff, but the receiving state may ask to reclassify: ibid 278–79.

[135] Art 1(d), (e), (f) VCCR.

[136] On which see above s IIIA.

[137] See further below s IVC.

[138] UN General Assembly Sixth Committee, Convention on jurisdictional immunities of States and their property: Report of the Chairman of the Working Group, UN Doc A/C.6/55/L.12 (10 November 2000) paras 42–52.

and their sending states, possibly because similar lawsuits are very rarely initiated in the first place. A notable exception is the 1998 *Butcher* case. Butcher had been offered the position of Consul General of Saint Lucia in Toronto, but the offer was withdrawn when he was revealed to be an ex-convict. He sued Saint Lucia for breach of employment contract. The Ontario Court of Justice upheld immunity: it reasoned that, although Butcher's relationship with Saint Lucia had a commercial component, ie performing services in exchange of compensation, 'The significance of [the governmental] aspect of the activity far outweigh[ed] in importance the commercial aspect'. This is because Butcher's claim would have encroached upon

> the right of the Government of Saint Lucia to decide how and when its consulates abroad will be established, who will be in charge of those consulates … the objectives to pursue in the area of foreign affairs and international trade, etc. A Consul General represents a state in the same way as an ambassador. Each country is entitled to retain control over the choice of such individuals and their tenure in this capacity.[139]

The treatment of military personnel seems to be very similar. Such personnel are generally prevented from bringing claims against their employer before another state's courts.[140] Judicial practice in this area, too, is limited but consistent. Italian courts, for example, only exercise jurisdiction over suits by locally recruited civilian staff of visiting forces, but not over claims by military personnel or the 'civilian component'.[141] In *Friedar*, a US national who suffered injuries while serving in the Tsahal sued Israel before the US courts, seeking compensation for medical expenses. While the court did not expressly qualify it as such, this case fell squarely within the ambit of labour claims – the plaintiff was trying to hold Israel liable for work-related injuries. The court determined that both the act of recruiting an army and that of determining eligibility for veterans' benefits were activities that were sovereign in nature, and on this basis upheld immunity.[142] This line of reasoning was restated in a case involving the hiring of contractors by the Royal Saudi Air Force (RSAF). The Fifth Circuit qualified their employment as sovereign insofar as the 'employees were integrated into the RSAF and can be considered military personnel'.[143]

Butcher and *Friedar* illuminate the two key reasons why labour claims involving diplomatic and consular agents and military personnel are uniformly treated as immune. A first, quite obvious reason is that the discharge of diplomatic, consular and military affairs is a typically sovereign act, whose qualification as *jure imperii* is uncontested.[144] The employment of personnel directly implicated in such

[139] *Butcher v Government of St Lucia* [1998] 61 OTC 208, affirmed [1999] OJ SCCA No 322.

[140] A Sari, 'The Immunities of Visiting Forces' in Ruys and Angelet (n 23) 559, 560.

[141] See, eg *Gereschi* (n 58). See also Belgium, Labour Court of Mons, *Piha v Belgium* 19 January 1982, 82 ILR 109. On the distinction between these personnel categories within the NATO SOFA, see above s III.

[142] *Friedar v Government of Israel* 614 F.Supp 395 (SDNY 1985) 399.

[143] *UNC Lear Services, Inc v Kingdom of Saudi Arabia* 581 F.3d 210 (5th Cir 2009) 216.

[144] See Supreme Court, *Benkharbouche* (n 24) para 55: 'Diplomatic agents participate in the functions of a diplomatic mission … These functions are inherently governmental. … Every aspect of the employment of a diplomatic agent is therefore likely to be an exercise of sovereign authority.'

activities is unsurprisingly regarded as a discharge of sovereign functions, as the *Friedar* court declared. But the exclusion of these claims from local jurisdiction is also grounded on avowedly functional rationales, as the above passage of *Butcher* suggests. It is generally perceived that foreign states should be provided ample freedom in managing their diplomatic and consular corps. This extends to the armed forces, whose functional needs require respecting the chain of command, military organisation and internal disciplinary procedures.[145] The same rationales can apply to other high-ranking officials in the areas of defence and intelligence, whose legal status may be analogous to military personnel. A rare example of such lawsuits is the *Eringer* case. The plaintiff, who alleged to have been 'Director of [Monaco Intelligence Services] and … its spymaster', sued Monaco for back pay and expenses. The Ninth Circuit tersely noted that '[this] is not the type of employment private parties can undertake'.[146]

Conversely, when it comes to claims by service staff members, a majority of national courts have pronounced in favour of jurisdiction. Drivers and chauffeurs at diplomatic or consular missions have been permitted to sue their employers in Portugal,[147] Belgium,[148] Spain,[149] Austria,[150] the USA[151] and Australia.[152] The Swiss Federal Tribunal held in *M v Egypt* that the condition of chauffeurs was 'equilavent to that of porters, gardeners, kitchen workers', thus suggesting that jurisdiction would be affirmed over claims by any service staff.[153] In *X v Israel*, the Portuguese Supreme Court found a cleaner's duties to be unrelated to sovereign functions,[154] and the French Court of Cassation held the same with regard to a doorman and caretaker at the embassy of Japan.[155] The Austrian Supreme Court affirmed jurisdiction over a lawsuit by an embassy's photographer;[156] an Australian court did so over claims by an embassy's gardener;[157] and a Dutch court did so over a claim by an embassy's butler.[158]

[145] Sari (n 140) 560.

[146] *Eringer v Principality of Monaco* 533 F App'x 703 (9th Cir 2013).

[147] Lisbon Court of Appeal, *A v Islamic Republic of Pakistan* 23 June 2004, www.cahdidatabases.coe.int/Contribution/Details/223.

[148] Labor Court of Brussels, *Kingdom of Morocco v DR* 6 November 1989, 115 ILR 421; *Rousseau* (n 99).

[149] Supreme Court, *Emilio BM v Embassy of Equatorial Guinea* 10 February 1986, 86 ILR 508.

[150] Superior Provincial Court of Vienna, *British Embassy Driver Case* 7 July 1978, 65 ILR 20.

[151] *Lee* (n 120) 12–14, re a chauffeur and repair person.

[152] *Hussein v The People's Bureau of the Great Socialist People's Libyan Arab Jamahiriya* 2006 AIRC 486.

[153] *M v Arab Republic of Egypt* 16 November 1994, 116 ILR 656. See also Geneva Labour Court, *Nicoud v United States of America* 27 April 1994, 116 ILR 650.

[154] *X v Israel* (n 104).

[155] *Saignie* (n 97).

[156] *Roswitha W v United States of America* 21 November 1990, Ob A244/90, summarised in *Wallishauser v Austria* App No 156/04, 17 July 2012, paras 6, 7 and 62.

[157] *Robinson v Kuwait Liaison Office* [1997] IRCA 170.

[158] The Hague Sub-District Court, *MDDA v Australian Embassy* 3 March 1986, (1988) 19 *Netherlands Yearbook of International Law* 438, note 27.

There exist, however, some significant exceptions. Finnish and Irish courts have held that a chauffeur's duties warrant a grant of immunity,[159] and so have US courts relying on the *Kato* jurisprudence.[160] In the 2013 *Greene* case, the Irish Employment Appeals Tribunal declined jurisdiction over claims by an embassy gardener, seemingly suggesting that the work of any embassy employee would be considered sovereign-related.[161] That same year, however, the same tribunal affirmed jurisdiction over a lawsuit by an embassy cleaner.[162] The practice of New Zealand is also more nuanced: in *Sutton*, the Court of Appeal affirmed that:

> Cleaners and others engaged to maintain the physical fabric may be able to make such a claim depending on whether their work brings them into a sufficient association with the sovereign functioning of the office. Domestic staff, who are often in a position of trust and confidence, may find it harder to establish a sufficient separation.[163]

Italian courts have traditionally adopted a broad definition of sovereign-related functions which encompass large swaths of the service staff. In the 1931 *Mazzucchi* case, the US consulate in Naples was sued by a former employee tasked with disinfecting emigrants before embarkation and stamping certificates to say that they had been medically examined. The court held the consulate immune on the grounds that, 'although [the] duties were simple, they were nevertheless still relative to a service of a political nature which the American State carries on … by means of its consuls'.[164] More recently, in the 1987 *Panattoni* case, the Court of Cassation refused jurisdiction on a compensation claim over pension benefits by a parcel deliverer and usher at the German embassy to the Holy See. In the court's view, only claims by workers performing 'manual or temporary duties … extraneous to the organization of an embassy' would be amenable to jurisdiction, while immunity would cover 'clerical employment relationships which involve a stable position within the structure of a diplomatic mission'.[165] Not even the aforementioned 1989 *Toglia* judgment caused the Italian courts to depart from such a broad construction of sovereign functions. Yet, *Toglia* diminished its

[159] Helsinki District Court, *Oliva Carrasco v Republic of Venezuela* 14 November 2000, Case No 00/1467, affirmed, Helsinki Court of Appeal, www.cahdidatabases.coe.int/Contribution/Details/98; Supreme Court of Ireland, *Canada v Employment Appeals Tribunal and Burke* [1992] ILRM 325, 95 ILR 467, 481 (O'Flaherty J): 'the element of trust and confidentiality that is reposed in the driver of an embassy car creates a bond with his employers that has the effect of involving him in the employing government's public business'.

[160] *Crum v Kingdom of Saudi Arabia* 2005 WL 3752271 (ED Va 2005); *Figueroa v Ministry for Foreign Affairs of Sweden et al* 222 F.Supp 3d 304 (SDNY 2016) 313; *Martinez v Consulate General of Algeria* 16 Civ 2390 (HBP) (SDNY 2016) 7, approving a settlement agreement between the parties and noting in obiter that litigation would have likely been unfavourable to the employee; *Bardales v Consulate General of Peru* 1:17-cv-8897 (ALC) (SDNY 2020) 12; *Ayekaba v Mba* 18 Civ 12040 (PGG) (SDNY 2020) 3.

[161] *Greene v Embassy of India* [2013] 9 JIEC 0301, 2: 'as embassies have sovereign immunity, the Tribunal has no alternative but to refuse jurisdiction'.

[162] *Adan v Embassy of the Republic of Kenya* [2013] 4 JIEC 0508, relying on the 'functions test' as set out in *Mahamdia* (n 81).

[163] *Sutton* (n 114) 522 (Richardson J).

[164] Court of Appeal of Naples, *Mazzucchi v American Consulate* 7 April 1931, 6 ILR 336.

[165] *Panattoni v Federal Republic of Germany* 15 July 1987, No 6172, 87 ILR 42, 46–47.

practical relevance by allowing jurisdiction over monetary compensation claims regardless of the employee's tasks:[166] this led Italian courts to exercise jurisdiction over lawsuits whose plaintiffs were openly qualified as performing tasks *de jure imperii*, provided the necessary requirements were met as regards subject matter.[167] More recently, the Italian courts' approach to the 'functions test' appears to have shifted towards a narrower construction, arguably under the influence of the ECtHR's jurisprudence on the point.[168]

The case law on technical and administrative staff is even more diverse. Here, it is hard to discern coherent patterns: domestic decisions range from de facto blanket immunity to blanket jurisdiction. In countries where the service staff are not allowed to sue, immunity obviously applies to claims by technical and administrative staff a fortiori.[169] By contrast, in certain legal systems, claims by all administrative and technical staff can be subject to jurisdiction. This is notably the case of section 12(6) Australia FSIA, provided the employee was an Australian national or permanent resident when the contract was signed.[170] Many such cases are decided directly on the merits without consideration of immunity issues, arguably because, in light of section 12(6), foreign states tend not to plea immunity in lawsuits brought by embassy and consulate employees before Australian courts.[171] Along similar lines, the Geneva Labour Court argued in 1995 that immunity does not cover proceedings brought by 'a locally recruited member of the *administrative, technical or service staff* of its diplomatic or consular mission … such employees do not perform an activity closely linked to the exercise of the public sovereignty'.[172]

The majority of national courts, however, adopt a more nuanced approach and draw the line somewhere across the category of administrative and technical staff,

[166] See above s IVA.

[167] See, eg Court of Cassation, *Capitolo della Patriarcale Arcibasilica di San Giovanni in Laterano v Zammerini* 17 November 1989, No 4909, (1991) 27 *Rivista di diritto internazionale privato e processuale* 489, affirming jurisdiction over monetary claims by the Basilica of St John Lateran's chief organist despite considering his functions to be strictly intertwined with the core religious functions of the Holy See. *cf* Court of Cassation, *Giaffreda v Stato della Repubblica di Francia e Consolato generale di Francia* 18 November 1992, No 12315, 114 ILR 558, considering an embassy usher's tasks to be *jure imperii* and upholding immunity because the employee requested reinstatement.

[168] See further below s IVC.

[169] See, eg the UK case law preceding *Benkharbouche*: *Al-Kadhimi et al v Saudi Arabia* [2003] EWCA Civ 1689, re an interpreter in the Military Attaché's Department at the Saudi embassy; EAT, *Military Affairs Office of the Embassy of Kuwait v Caramba-Coker* 10 April 2003, ILDC 251 (UK 2003), re a shipping clerk; *Saudi Arabia v Nasser* [2000] UKEAT 672_99_2607, re an interpreter and driver; EAT, *United Arab Emirates v Abdelghafar and Another* 10 July 1995, 107 ILR 626, re two employees of the UAE embassy medical office; EAT, *Government of the Kingdom of Saudi Arabia v Ahmed* 8 October 1993, 104 ILR 629, re an embassy secretary; EAT, *Jayetilleke v High Commission of the Bahamas* 14 December 1994, 107 ILR 622, re a senior accounts clerk.

[170] See *Kassis v Republic of Lebanon* [2014] FCCA 155, para 4, considering jurisdiction over a consular employee's claims 'not controversial'; *Hussein* (n 152) re a driver/receptionist; *Thomas v Consulate General of India* [2002] NSWIR Comm 24, re a typist.

[171] See, eg *Kumar v Consulate General of India* [2018] FCCA 7; *Gibbs v Embassy of Mexico* [2011] FWA 7853; *Sidhwa v British Consulate General* [1997] IRCA 129.

[172] Switzerland, Geneva Labor Court, *X v United States* 16 February 1995, 116 ILR 668, 670–71 (emphasis added).

even though there seems to be no agreement about where precisely to draw it. The resulting picture is confusing: conflicting pronouncements have been issued on practically all categories of technical and administrative staff.

Secretarial functions, for example, have been found by courts in Italy and Finland to be 'closely connected' with the employer state's governmental authority.[173] The Corte di Cassazione held in *Trobbiani* that the duties of a secretary and telephonist 'clearly denote a position of trust within the organization, inasmuch as they are directly bound up with the work of its officials and also inevitably involve access in practice to information concerning the agency's official activities';[174] in *Lo Gatto*, the same court reached this conclusion in respect of the duties of a clerk and telephone operator.[175] In *Sutton*, New Zealand's Court of Appeal held that the duties of a clerk and typist, although 'not entail[ing] any significant responsibility for decision-making ... were close to the heart of the administrative process. She was an important cog in the administrative wheel.'[176] However, opposite conclusions on secretarial tasks have been reached by courts in the Netherlands,[177] Portugal,[178] Belgium,[179] France[180] and the USA;[181] the Swiss courts have consistently exercised jurisdiction over claims by telephone operators;[182] and the French Cour de cassation has affirmed that a senior clerk did not perform any 'particular functions' in the exercise of a consulate's public service.[183]

Conflicting views have also been expressed with regard to embassy and consular officials tasked with issuing visas or passports. In *X v Argentina*, the German Federal Labour Court upheld immunity because the issuing of visas constitutes one of the typical consular functions under the VCCR.[184] In France, the Court of

[173] Italy, Court of Cassation, *Norwegian Embassy v Quattri* 28 November 1991, No 12771, 114 ILR 525 (however, following *Toglia* (n 22), affirming jurisdiction over unpaid allowances); *Heusala* (n 106).

[174] *Libyan Arab Jamahiriya v Trobbiani* 16 January 1990, No 145, 114 ILR 520, 522–23. Similarly, *Barbini* (n 107) re a secretary and telephone operator; Court of Cassation, *Embassy of the Republic of Korea v BS* 17 January 2007, No 880, re a typist (but affirming jurisdiction over purely pecuniary claims).

[175] *United States of America v Lo Gatto* 21 April 1995, No 4483, 114 ILR 555.

[176] *Sutton* (n 114) 514.

[177] *Morocco v HA* (n 98) 395–96; The Hague Sub-District Court, *MK v Republic of Turkey* 1 August 1985, 94 ILR 350.

[178] Supreme Court, *AA v Austrian Embassy* 18 February 2006, ILDC 826 (PT 2007).

[179] Brussels Labor Court, *Sawas v Saudi Arabia* 11 January 2007, ILDC 1146 (BE 2007).

[180] Court of Cassation, *Barrandon v United States of America* 10 November 1998, 116 ILR 622, re a nurse and medical secretary at the US embassy.

[181] *Zveiter v Brazilian National Superintendency of Merchant Marine* 833 F.Supp 1089 (SDNY 1993) 1093: 'employment of a secretary is hardly within the unique sphere of sovereign authority ... It is of no consequence that the purpose of employing the secretary was to further the sovereign mission'. See also Spain, Supreme Court, *Diana A v Republic of South Africa* 1986, No 7231, 86 ILR 512, affirming Spanish jurisdiction over a secretary's claims; but the reasoning, although mentioning both Art 5 ECSI and the ILC works (514–15), does not clarify the relevance, if any, of the employee's functions.

[182] *X v United States* (n 172); Geneva Labor Court, *Landano v United States of America*, 16 April 1987, 116 ILR 636; *S v India* (n 100).

[183] *Mme X v Consulat d'Algérie à Nanterre* 14 December 2005, No 03-45973.

[184] *X v Argentina* (n 105). See also *Sanchez-Ramirez* (n 119) 15, re consular employees tasked with assisting the public in filling visa and passport applications.

Cassation held that an interpreter at the passport section of a consulate 'participait à la mission de service public du consulat et y exerçait une responsabilité particulière en rapport avec cette mission' ('participated in the consulate's public service mission and exercised a special responsibility in relation to this mission'), thus finding the consulate immune.[185] Conversely, the Austrian Supreme Court affirmed jurisdiction over a claim by the former head of the visa section at the French consulate in Innsbruck.[186] In *Roy*, the Ontario Superior Court of Justice similarly exercised jurisdiction over claims by a consular employee tasked with processing visa applications and with diplomatic protocol.[187]

Financial assistants and accountants were held to perform sovereign-related functions by courts in Germany[188] and Canada;[189] in the USA, though, the DC Circuit reached the opposite conclusion with regard to an accountant who, despite managing 'large sums of money', 'had no role in the creation of … government policy and was not privy to … political deliberations'.[190] The functions of a commercial officer were qualified as sovereign by the Italian Court of Cassation in *Cargnello*[191] and as commercial by the Ninth Circuit in *Holden*.[192] The French Court of Cassation affirmed jurisdiction over claims by a press office assistant,[193] and a Texas district court did so over a discrimination lawsuit brought by a consulate's public relations manager;[194] courts in Italy[195] and the Belgian Congo,[196] on the other hand, considered cases brought by librarians in foreign states' information offices to be covered by immunity. Translating and interpreting was treated as a sovereign-related function in Italy[197] but not in Switzerland, where the Federal Tribunal found the 'confidential nature' of the job to be irrelevant for immunity purposes.[198] Individuals employed in teaching and academic activities were allowed to sue in Belgium and Italy[199] but not in the USA.[200] The Brussels Labour

[185] *Mohamed X v Consulat d'Egypte en France* 9 October 2001, No 98-46214.

[186] *French Consular Employee Claim* 14 June 1989, Case No 9 Ob A 170/89, 86 ILR 583.

[187] *Roy* (n 124).

[188] Regional Labour Court of Hesse, *Muller v United States of America* 11 May 1998, No 10 Sa 1506/97, 114 ILR 513.

[189] *Zakhary* (n 53) para 33: 'The respondent's duties … however administrative they may be, engaged elements of trust and confidentiality, and were thus integral to the operations of the consulate.'

[190] *El-Hadad* (2007) (n 117) 666. More recently, see *Dahman* (n 120) 11–12, re an embassy's chief accountant.

[191] *Canada v Cargnello* 20 April 1998, No 4017, 114 ILR 559.

[192] Above n 121.

[193] *Coco v State of Argentina* 2 April 1996, 113 ILR 491.

[194] *Harmouche* (n 120).

[195] Court of Cassation, *De Ritis v Government of the United States of America* 25 November 1971, No 3441 (1975) 1 *Italian Yearbook of International Law* 235.

[196] Court of Appeal of Leopoldville, *De Decker v United States of America* 29 May 1956, 23 ILR 209.

[197] *Pieciukiewicz* (n 107) re a translator and announcer at the Vatican radio.

[198] *R v Republic of Iraq* 13 November 1994, 116 ILR 664, 668.

[199] Brussels Labor Court, *De Queiroz v State of Portugal* 22 September 1992, 115 ILR 430; Italy, Court of Cassation, *Stato francese v Guerriero et al* 13 February 1992, No 1716, re a French language teacher.

[200] *Salman* (n 78). See also *Holland* (n 66), holding that teaching at a military base would 'at least indirectly' benefit a state's military functions (Lord Clyde).

Court held in *Van Averbeke* that a computer assistant did not perform sovereign functions, but implied that it might have reached a different conclusion had it been established that the employee had access to classified information.[201]

A further element of complexity as regards the position of technical and administrative personnel arises from the US practice whereby members of a foreign state's civil service are analogous en masse to persons having diplomatic and consular rank. As a consequence, all claims brought by such people are barred by immunity even though they may formally belong to the technical and administrative staff; in fact, their functions might be indistinguishable from those of other staff who are permitted to lodge claims.[202] US courts have considered a multiplicity of factors in order to distinguish between civil service personnel and non-civil service technical and administrative staff. As seen earlier in this section, certain decisions have relied (primarily, or in combination with other factors) on the employees' functions and nationality.[203] Other courts have based the assessment of civil service status on a multi-factor test which does not include the functions of the employee, for example enquiring

> whether the plaintiff/employee competed by examination for any position before being hired; … was entitled to tenure; … was provided the same benefits as the foreign service officers (such as an allowance for moving expenses, a round-trip ticket home every two years, an official civil service passport, or a sales tax exemption); and … received any civil service protections from the [foreign] government.[204]

Applying this test, the *Holden* court held that a commercial officer at the Canadian consulate was not a member of the civil service. By contrast, in *El Ansari*, the Quebec Court of Appeal – relying on US precedents, including *Holden* – considered a private secretary to be a member of a foreign state's civil service. The plaintiff, a Moroccan national, had worked for 30 years in various Moroccan diplomatic missions before moving to Canada for reasons unrelated to her work for Morocco. She was then rehired and assigned first to the Moroccan consulate in Montreal and then to the Moroccan embassy in Ottawa, where she performed the duties of private secretary and 'implementation officer'. She had meanwhile become a Canadian national. After being dismissed, she sued Morocco for compensation and reinstatement. The court considered her to be a member of the civil service, noting, inter alia, that she was a *fonctionnaire* of the Moroccan government, her employment was regulated by Moroccan law, she did not pay taxes in Canada and she received a number of benefits that local employees did not enjoy. On this basis, it upheld immunity.[205]

[201] *Van Averbeke* (n 99) 13. See also Brussels Labor Court, *François v State of Canada* 1989, 115 ILR 418, affirming jurisdiction over claims by a technician.

[202] As noted by Köhler (n 5) 199, in most countries positions traditionally deemed as civil service are increasingly covered by people hired under private law contracts.

[203] See, eg *Sanchez-Ramirez* (n 119); *El-Hadad* (2007) (n 117) 665–68, re an Egyptian national employed at the UAE embassy.

[204] *Holden* (n 121) 921.

[205] *El Ansari* (n 125) especially para 78.

This approach is peculiar to US and Canadian courts. In other countries, the civil service status of the employee is normally not treated as dispositive. Claims by civil service members are instead handled according to the ordinary employment-specific immunity criteria in use in a given jurisdiction.[206] This appears reasonable, first, because the US approach gives rise to a disparity of treatment between employees working in the same role; and secondly, because it is unclear why exercising jurisdiction over claims by employees tagged as 'civil servants' should, for that reason alone, prove more intrusive of the foreign state's sovereignty than claims by non-civil service personnel.[207] The civil service status of the employee was expressly dismissed as irrelevant by the Supreme Court of Victoria in *Reid*, where an airline pilot employed by Nauru's flag carrier sued the state for breach of the employment contract. The court wrote:

> There has been some dispute concerning whether the plaintiff was … a member of the public service. However … I consider that the resolution of that question is not particularly important. The employment of Mr Reid as a public servant does attach to his position a 'governmental' character, but the significance of that categorization in this case is limited … The nature of the employment itself and the relationship between the role performed by the employee and the sovereign functions of the State need to be scrutinized.[208]

The court thus dismissed immunity on the basis of the 'functions test': it considered the plaintiff's work to be unconnected with public powers in that the tasks were 'not very different in any significant respect from those performed by a commercial pilot in private employment'.[209]

C. The 'Status and Functions Test' under the UN Convention on State Immunity

This subsection focuses on the scope of the 'status and functions test' under Article 11 UNCSI. One key question is whether this provision's influence on state practice may bring about greater uniformity of national approaches as regards the importance given to the tasks of the employee, and whether and to what extent this process has already occurred.

Pursuant to Article 11(2)(a), a state is entitled to immunity if 'the employee has been recruited to perform particular functions in the exercise of governmental authority'. No indication is provided as to what functions should be deemed 'in the exercise of governmental authority' or which such functions should be

[206] See, eg Fox, 'Employment' (n 7) 147, noting that nationality often absorbs any relevance of the employee's civil service status.

[207] Garnett, 'State Immunity and Employment Relations in Canada' (n 123) 659.

[208] *Reid v Republic of Nauru* 17 February 1992, 101 ILR 193, 200.

[209] ibid. Because the Australia FSIA was not applicable *ratione temporis*, the court applied what it saw as the restrictive state immunity doctrine at common law.

considered 'particular'.[210] Yet, some guidance may be found in the UNCSI's *travaux préparatoires*.[211] Special Rapporteur Sucharitkul's 1983 original draft – which followed closely in the footsteps of Article 5 ECSI[212] – did not contain any reference to the functions of the plaintiff employee,[213] but the antecedent of paragraph 2(a) appeared shortly afterwards in the revised first draft submitted to the Drafting Committee, which read: 'paragraph 1 does not apply if … the individual has been appointed under the administrative law of the employer State, and is performing functions in the exercise of governmental authority'.[214]

After revision by the Drafting Committee, the text provisionally adopted by the ILC in 1984 retained immunity over claims by employees 'recruited to perform services *associated with* the exercise of governmental authority'.[215] The commentary clarified that this provision was meant to cover all technical and administrative staff[216] and not, by contrast, 'employees of lower echelons performing menial tasks'.[217] It is unclear how the service staff of *higher echelons*, such as embassies and consulates, were meant to fare under this provision, but the broad wording provided a strong argument for shielding their contracts from local jurisdiction. Indeed, this clause received criticism by states for being 'so vague as to lead to an extremely wide interpretation which might substantially negate the exception to State immunity in case of differences relating to the contracts of employment'.[218]

After initially proposing to delete this provision altogether,[219] Special Rapporteur Ogiso opted to retain it in his following drafts.[220] In his view, however, the provision was intended to cover exclusively technical and administrative staff, thus allowing the whole of the service staff to sue.[221] In order to reflect this intended scope and to avoid 'unduly extensive interpretation' – as the Commission aptly

[210] Foakes and O'Keefe (n 94) 208, describing Art 11(2)(a) as 'unhelpfully general' and 'liable to lead to the scratching of judicial heads'.

[211] Pursuant to Vienna Convention on the Law of Treaties 1969 (VCLT), Art 32, recourse may be had to the *travaux* when recourse to the Art 31 general rule of interpretation 'leaves the meaning ambiguous or obscure'.

[212] See above s II.

[213] Sucharitkul, 'Fifth Report' (n 28) para 62.

[214] Report of the ILC on the work of its thirty-fifth session (3 May–22 July 1983), ILC Yearbook 1983, vol II, Part 2, 20, note 58 (Art 13(2)(a)).

[215] Report of the ILC on the work of its thirty-sixth session (7 May–27 July 1984), ILC Yearbook 1984, vol II, Part 2, 62 (emphasis added).

[216] ibid 65, para 11: 'Examples … are librarians of an information service, code clerks, security guards, watchmen, interpreters, translators and other administrative or technical staff of higher echelons.'

[217] ibid 64, para 8: 'examples … are contracts of employment of individuals for the cleaning or maintenance of an office, a library, a cemetery or a museum'.

[218] M Ogiso, 'Preliminary Report on Jurisdictional Immunities of States and Their Property', ILC Yearbook 1988, vol II, Part 1, 96, 110, para 128 (comments by Belgium, the Federal Republic of Germany and the UK).

[219] ibid para 132.

[220] M Ogiso, 'Third Report on Jurisdictional Immunities of States and Their Property', ILC Yearbook 1990, vol II, Part 1, 3, 13.

[221] ibid 14, para 3. He also proposed an alternative phrasing: 'the employee is administrative or technical staff of a diplomatic or consular mission who is associated with the exercise of governmental authority' (ibid 13).

noted, any 'contract of employment concluded by a State [stands] a good chance of being associated with the exercise of governmental authority, even very indirectly'[222] – the clause in question was modified in the 1991 Draft Articles: the new text referred to employees performing 'functions *closely related* to the exercise of governmental authority'.[223] Crucially, though, the ILC Working Group manifested an intention to further restrict the scope of this clause to 'persons performing functions *in* the exercise of governmental authority'[224] – a formula finally inserted in the Convention with an additional caveat: '*particular* functions'.[225] This further restriction at the hands of the Working Group constituted a rejection of the 1991 Draft Articles' blanket immunity approach to claims by technical and administrative staff.[226] Proposals by Working Group members to specifically list technical and administrative staff of foreign missions among the employees not permitted to sue an employer state were expressly turned down, on the grounds that the Working Group 'had … not seen any reason why administrative staff, for whom the practice of the courts was still not well established, should be included in one particular category'.[227]

In sum, what may be drawn with certainty from the *travaux* is that Article 11(2)(a) does not establish any presumption of immunity for claims by technical and administrative staff.[228] Moreover, if at least certain members of the technical and administrative personnel are allowed to sue, a fortiori this clause should not cover claims by the service staff.[229] Within these loose boundaries, it seems correct to say that the UNCSI leaves states broad discretion to establish the scope of 'particular functions in the exercise of governmental authority'.[230]

The Strasbourg Court has so far adopted a narrow construction of Article 11(2)(a) in its jurisprudence on the relation between state immunity and Article 6 ECHR.[231] The court's general position as regards the interpretation of Article 11 is that its

[222] Draft Articles on Jurisdictional Immunities of States and Their Property, with commentaries, ILC Yearbook 1991, vol II, Part 2, 13, 43, para 9.

[223] ibid 41 (emphasis added). See also ibid 42, para 9: 'Examples of such employees are private secretaries, code clerks, interpreters, translators.'

[224] Report of the Working Group on Jurisdictional Immunities of States and Their Property, ILC Yearbook 1999, vol II, Part 2, 149, 167, para 104 (emphasis added).

[225] Art 11(2)(a) UNCSI (emphasis added).

[226] R Garnett, 'State and Diplomatic Immunity and Employment Rights: European Law to the Rescue?' (2015) 64 *ICLQ* 783, 789–90; G Hafner, 'United Nations Convention on Jurisdictional Immunities of States and Their Property (2004)' (2010) *Max Planck Encyclopedia of Public International Law*, para 26.

[227] Summary records of the meetings of the fifty-first session (3 May–23 July 1999), ILC Yearbook 1999, vol I, 259, para 33.

[228] Garnett, 'State and Diplomatic Immunity' (n 226) 789.

[229] See *Van Averbeke* (n 99) 14–15, holding that, for the Art 11(2)(a) immunity ground to apply, it is not sufficient that the employee's function is 'essentielle au bon fonctionnement de la fonction publique … tant du point de vue organisationnel que sécuritaire' ('essential to the proper functioning of the public service … from both an organisational and a security point of view'); rather, the employee should exercise 'prerogatives caractéristiques de la puissance souveraine de cet Etat' ('prerogatives characteristic of the sovereign power of this state') (citations omitted).

[230] R Nigro, 'Immunità degli Stati esteri e diritto di accesso al giudice: un nuovo approccio nel diritto internazionale?' (2013) 96 *Rivista di diritto internazionale* 812, 836.

[231] On which see above s IIIB.

immunity grounds 'must be strictly interpreted'.[232] In *Cudak*, it held that claims by an embassy's switchboard operator, whose duties included 'recording international telephone conversations, typing, sending and receiving faxes, photocopying documents, providing information and assisting with the organisation of certain events', were not barred by Article 11(2)(a), the respondent state not having shown 'how these duties could objectively have been related to [its] sovereign interests'.[233] The ECtHR added that 'the mere allegation that the applicant could have had access to certain documents or could have been privy to confidential telephone conversations in the course of her duties is not sufficient'.[234] In ensuing cases, the court has reached the same conclusion with regard to the head of an embassy's account department;[235] an assistant in the publications service of a French public institution;[236] an embassy's photographer;[237] an embassy's protocol specialist/translator, whose duties included organizing official receptions, official calls and visits, drafting correspondence and translating documents;[238] and an embassy's cultural, information and press officer.[239] In *Radunović*, the ECtHR considered the tasks of two security guards at the US embassy in Montenegro as non-governmental;[240] this is noteworthy in that, in previous domestic case law, claims by security personnel had most frequently failed on the grounds that the plaintiffs' duties were deemed 'integral to the core sphere of sovereign activity'.[241] *Radunović* may be contrasted with the earlier *Sostrand* judgment, where the Oslo District Court held that a security agent's claims fell within the Article 11(2)(a) UNCSI grounds for immunity.[242] In short, employees performing highly responsible duties have been found by the Strasbourg Court to fall outside the scope of Article 11(2)(a).

The ECtHR's restrictive approach to the 'functions test' has already spilled over into national case law. This trend is particularly visible in Italy, whose courts, as seen earlier, traditionally subscribed to a broad understanding of sovereign-related duties, often as broad as including large portions of the service staff.[243]

[232] *Sabeh El Leil v France* App No 34869/05, 29 June 2011, para 66.
[233] *Cudak* (n 32) para 70.
[234] ibid para 72.
[235] *Sabeh El Leil* (n 232) para 62.
[236] *Guadagnino v Italy and France* App No 2555/03, 18 January 2011.
[237] *Wallishauser* (n 156) concerning service of process, but holding in obiter that none of the Art 11(2) grounds of immunity applied to the case (para 71).
[238] *Radunović and Others v Montenegro* App Nos 45197/13, 53000/13 and 73404/13, 25 October 2016, paras 6–8.
[239] *Naku* (n 88) para 15.
[240] *Radunović* (n 238) paras 9 and 75.
[241] *Jansen* (n 115) 15. See also *Butters v Vance International, Inc* 225 F.3d 462 (4th Cir 2000) 465; Italy, Court of Cassation, *Consolato generale dell'Ecuador v Marchetti* 1 February 1999, No 18, re a night shift security guard (but affirming jurisdiction over the plaintiff's claims for compensation); UK Employment Tribunal, *Buttet v Ambassade de France au Royaume Uni* 22 August 2019, Case No 2204921/2012, paras 115–21, re a security guard at an ambassador's private residence, distinguishing *Benkharbouche* (n 24) on grounds of the claimant's functions (para 119).
[242] *Sostrand* (n 102) 25.
[243] See above s IVB.

In post-2014 cases, where, under the influence of the Strasbourg Court, Article 11 has been applied qua codification of customary law, the Italian Court of Cassation has never declined jurisdiction on the basis of Article 11(2)(a). The following employees have been considered not to perform sovereign-related functions: the *sécretaire de direction* (whose duties included the management of the press office and the organisation of ceremonies) of a French public body established for the dissemination of arts and science;[244] a consular employee;[245] an embassy driver;[246] and an embassy's high-level administrative employee.[247] In *De la Grana*, a claim by an archivist, translator and typist, immunity was upheld pursuant to Article 11(2)(c), which suggests that the court did not consider the employee's duties to be covered by Article 11(2)(a).[248] A restrictive approach to Article 11's 'functions test' was also embraced by the Hoge Raad in the *Moroccan Secretary* case, where immunity was denied on the grounds that, 'although [the employee] had access to confidential documents and had to maintain secrecy, it has neither been asserted nor established that her activities were of a diplomatic nature'.[249]

While certainly influenced by an underlying policy choice of interpreting Article 11(2)(a) in a sense favourable to the employees' rights, there can be no doubt that the approach followed by the Strasbourg Court is tenable from the standpoint of treaty interpretation. Because the text of the provision leaves broad discretion to the interpreter, nothing precludes this margin of manoeuvre from being exploited with a view to expanding the avenues of redress available to the employees. A further notable feature of the Strasbourg Court's approach is that, as the court has repeatedly made clear, the burden of proving that an employee's functions meet the standard of Article 11(2)(a) lies with the employer state.[250] This is equally defensible, considering that – as argued above – paragraph 2(a) establishes no presumption of immunity in claims by members of the technical and administrative staff. Hence, it is correct to consider that an opposite presumption exists and that the state should rebut it.[251]

However, under which circumstances the presumption may be rebutted remains dubious. The ECtHR has never expressly clarified what functions should be deemed 'objectively' related to state sovereignty, nor has the Corte di Cassazione ever elaborated on the reasons why a certain employee's tasks fell outside the scope

[244] *Académie de France à Rome v Galamini di Recanati* 17 June 2014, No 19674, ILDC 2437 (IT 2014).
[245] *Lasaracina v Embassy of the United Arab Emirates* 7 October 2014, No 22744, ILDC 2438 (IT 2014), para 24 (immunity upheld on other grounds).
[246] *Rohitha v Embassy of the Republic of Korea to the Holy See* 9 June 2016, No 11848, ILDC 2697 (IT 2016).
[247] *Chibomba* (n 111).
[248] *De la Grana* (n 33). cp *Real Academia de España de Bellas Artes en Roma v Escudero García* 22 December 2016, No 26661, ILDC 2698 (IT 2016), affirming jurisdiction pursuant to Art 11 UNCSI but without discussing the employee's tasks.
[249] *Morocco v X* (n 36) para 3.4.
[250] See, eg *Guadagnino* (n 236) para 72.
[251] Garnett, 'State and Diplomatic Immunity' (n 226) 793.

of Article 11(2)(a).[252] In *Sabeh El Leil*, the ECtHR reprimanded the French courts for justifying their decision to grant immunity to Kuwait on the basis of alleged, but not proven, 'additional responsibilities' performed by the employee besides his role as head accountant;[253] such responsibilities included administrative matters, legal affairs, the payment of certain financial contributions and the supervision of bank accounts.[254] But the court said nothing as to whether proof of such duties would have sufficed to meet the Article 11(2)(a) threshold.

More concrete hints may perhaps be found in the 2019 *Ndayegamiye* judgment. The applicant worked at Burundi's permanent mission to the UN in Geneva performing highly responsible tasks: she oversaw the mission's secretariat and accounting, was in charge of consular services including passport and visa applications, and qualified herself as 'assistante de l'ambassadeur'.[255] Because this case was decided on the basis of Article 11(2)(e) (ie nationality and residence), the ECtHR considered it unnecessary to rule on whether the applicant's tasks fell within the ambit of Article 11(2)(a).[256] However, some passages suggest that they might: the court indeed opined that, 'considérant les faits de l'espèce et les tâches effectivement confiées à la requérante au sein de la mission permanente, il y a un chevauchement complexe entre les actes *jure imperii* et *jure gestionis* accomplis par celle-ci'.[257] This was the first time the ECtHR qualified an employee's functions as (partly) *de jure imperii*. Considering that, in previous cases, secretarial and accounting duties had already been found not to trigger Article 11(2)(a)'s immunity ground, it is reasonable to infer that the duties which the court saw as (to some extent) governmental in nature were those involving the performance of consular services. But this still provides no certainty as to whether, according to the ECtHR, an employee carrying out similar duties should be prevented from suing under Article 11(2)(a).

In view of the Strasbourg Court's avowed aim to interpret the Article 11 immunity grounds strictly, it may be suggested that such an employee should not be barred from suing. Neither being in charge of processing passport or visa applications nor working in close cooperation with an ambassador renders an employee's work any less administrative in nature – even more so since *Cudak* ruled that an employee's access to confidential information was no sufficient reason for granting immunity. As seen previously, employees performing tasks similar to those discussed in *Ndayegamiye* have been permitted to sue in jurisdictions like Austria and Canada. It would be more appropriate for the ECtHR to follow in the footsteps

[252] See, eg *Galamini di Recanati* (n 244) para 6, merely noting that 'It is evident that these tasks, although being not purely executive and of high organizational level, were not connected with the excercise of public functions'.

[253] *Sabeh El Leil* (n 232) paras 63–64.

[254] ibid para 15.

[255] *Ndayegamiye-Mporamazina v Switzerland* App No 16874/12, 5 February 2019, para 10.

[256] ibid para 65.

[257] ibid para 50 ('Considering the facts of this case and the tasks actually entrusted to the applicant within the permanent mission, there is a complex overlap between the acts *jure imperii* and *jure gestionis* performed by the applicant').

of these domestic courts and embrace the strictest possible interpretation of the 'functions test'. Article 11(2)(a) may therefore be construed as only referring to employees who are by general agreement prevented from suing their employer states before another state's courts, namely members of the armed forces and high-ranking officials involved in matters of defence and security.[258] This construction is defensible because these employees are not enumerated in Article 11(2)(b), which only refers to persons entitled to diplomatic or consular immunity. By contrast, it may be legitimate to interpret Article 11(2)(a) as *not* encompassing either the service staff or the technical and administrative staff.

Regrettably, the text of Article 11(2)(b) might appear to pose some obstacles to this restrictive approach to the 'functions test'. On the one hand, subparagraphs (i), (ii) and (iii) of this provision are unproblematic in that they refer to various persons having diplomatic or consular status. These are: (i) diplomatic agents as defined in the VCDR;[259] (ii) consular officers as defined in the VCCR;[260] and (iii) persons enjoying diplomatic status for the purpose of a permanent mission to an international organisation or a special mission.[261] The second part of subparagraph (iii), addressing employees 'recruited to represent a State at an international conference', may reasonably be construed as referring to the same type of employees as the first part of the same subparagraph, ie persons having diplomatic rank.[262]

On the other hand, subparagraph (iv), barring claims by 'any other person enjoying diplomatic immunity', is decidedly more puzzling. The VCDR bestows immunity *ratione materiae* upon members of the technical, administrative and service staff of diplomatic missions who are not nationals or permanent residents of the receiving state.[263] Moreover, the receiving state may unilaterally extend privileges and immunities to any other member of the staff of the mission.[264] Thus, if one takes subparagraph (iv) literally, it might have the effect of barring claims by any employees of diplomatic missions, however lowly their position, who are entitled to *some amount* of diplomatic immunity. This would be a serious limitation on the possibility to exercise jurisdiction over employment relations with foreign embassies, and would come close to reintroducing the 'workplace test' into the UNCSI through the back door.

The literature is divided over the interpretation of this provision. According to Foakes and O'Keefe, a literal reading should be rejected for 'fly[ing] in the face

[258] See above s IVB.

[259] ie the head of the mission and all persons having diplomatic rank: Art 1(d) and (e) VCDR.

[260] ie 'any person, including the head of a consular post, entrusted in that capacity with the exercise of consular functions' (Art 1(1)(d) VCCR), including honorary consuls (Art 1(2) VCCR).

[261] Vienna Convention on the Representation of States in their Relations with International Organizations of a Universal Character 1975, Art 1(1)(28), not yet in force; Convention on Special Missions 1969, Art 1(h).

[262] Foakes and O'Keefe (n 94) 201.

[263] Art 37(2) and (3) VCDR. Technical and administrative employees falling into this category also enjoy full immunity from criminal jurisdiction.

[264] Art 38(2) VCDR.

of the *travaux préparatoires*'.[265] These commentators have pointed out that the antecedent of Article 11(2)(b), as initially proposed by the ILC Working Group in 1999, was merely intended to 'further clarify' the meaning of Article 11(2)(a) by listing, as examples of employees performing functions *jure imperii*, diplomatic and consular officers as well as 'Other persons enjoying diplomatic immunity, such as persons recruited to represent a State in international conferences'.[266] Because subsequent discussions in the ILC and the Ad Hoc Working Groups do not reveal any intention to radically alter this provision's meaning, the current wording of subparagraph (iv) should be treated as a mishap and read as only encompassing claims by persons of diplomatic rank who are not covered by the previous three subparagraphs.[267] Pavoni, by contrast, has criticised this restrictive reading as untenable, considering that the language of subparagraph (iv) is facially unambiguous.[268] Contrasting views as to the meaning of this provision were expressed by the UK courts in *Benkharbouche*. Quoting from the work of Foakes and O'Keefe, the Court of Appeal fully espoused the restrictive reading.[269] The Supreme Court, however, was unconvinced:

> It was suggested to us that subparagraph (iv) might also have been intended to cover diplomats at international conferences, and there are passages in the *travaux* which support that view … But since … these categories are already covered by article 11(2)(b)(i) and (iii), and the language of (iv) is unequivocal, I doubt whether these suggestions can be supported.[270]

While the wording of subparagraph (iv) is unfortunate, the arguments in favour of a restrictive reading are compelling. First, the construction of treaty terms does not stop at their ordinary meaning but requires their context, including the whole of the treaty text, and their object and purpose, to be looked at.[271] Hence subparagraph (iv) cannot be construed in isolation from Article 11(2)(a) – which, as seen above, adopts a quite restrictive stance to the 'functions test', *irrespective of the place or context of employment* – or from the remainder of Article 11(2)(b), which only refers to high-ranking officials having diplomatic or consular rank. It is reasonable to construe subparagraph (iv) so as not to contradict the logic underpinning paragraphs 2(a) and (b), ie that only personnel performing particularly high functions on behalf of the foreign state should be prevented from suing. Furthermore, recourse to the *travaux* is permissible not only when the text leaves the meaning ambiguous or obscure, but also when the outcome of the interpretation

[265] Foakes and O'Keefe (n 94) 201.
[266] 1999 Report of the Working Group (n 224) 167, para 105.
[267] Foakes and O'Keefe (n 94) 202.
[268] R Pavoni, 'The Myth of the Customary Nature of the United Nations Convention on State Immunity: Does the End Justify the Means?' in A van Aaken and I Motoc (eds), *European Convention on Human Rights and General International Law* (Oxford, Oxford University Press, 2018) 264, 274–76.
[269] *Benkharbouche and Janah* (n 91) para 38.
[270] *Benkharbouche* (n 24) para 72.
[271] Art 31(1) VCLT.

is manifestly unreasonable.[272] The *travaux*, in their turn, provide no meaningful support to the expansive interpretation: as seen earlier in this subsection, the Working Group expressly and unmistakably rejected any proposals having the effect of barring claims by low-level employees of diplomatic missions. Finally, it may be noted that there is no evidence in state practice of any national approach vaguely resembling the expansive reading of subparagraph (iv), ie denying jurisdiction over claims by mid- or low-level embassy employees solely on the grounds that they enjoy some amount of functional immunity. For all such reasons, subparagraph (iv) should be construed as referring to persons enjoying the full range of diplomatic immunities, ie individuals having diplomatic rank.

V. Approaches Based on the Nationality and Residence of the Employee

A third common approach for differentiating immune and non-immune labour claims looks at the nationality and residence of the employee. As mentioned in section II, this test occupies a central position in Article 5 ECSI and in domestic instruments that have drawn direct inspiration from the ECSI. These instruments provide that immunity shall be upheld where the employee (i) is a national of the employer state at the time the proceedings are commenced or (ii) was not a permanent resident of the state of the forum at the time the contract was made.[273] Claims by nationals of the employer state are thus barred in toto, even if such individuals hold dual nationality (unless, of course, the plaintiff renounces the employer state's nationality before bringing the action[274]). So are claims by persons who, despite not being nationals of the employer state, were not already residing in the forum state when they were hired; it should be stressed that this applies not only to third-country nationals, but also to nationals of the forum state, and that the acquisition of permanent residency *after* concluding the contract is immaterial. For instance, in *Arias* – a case to which Article 5 ECSI was applied because it was considered to reflect general international law – a Dutch court upheld immunity in a wrongful dismissal lawsuit filed by a secretary at Venezuela's embassy. Born in Argentina, the plaintiff had obtained Dutch nationality after working at the embassy for seven years and before instituting the case. However, because she was neither a national

[272] Art 32(b) VCLT. Note, for instance, that the expansive reading would bar jurisdiction over mid- or low-level embassy employees while allowing it over high-level consular employees.

[273] Art 5(2)(a)–(b) ECSI; s 4(2)(a)–(b) UK SIA (but partially struck down by *Benkharbouche* (n 24), on which see below); s 6(2)(a)–(b) Singapore SIA; s 6(2)(a)–(b) Pakistan SIO; s 5(1)(b)–(c) South Africa FSIA; s 6(1)(b)–(c) Malawi IPA. Pursuant to s 4(a)(3)–(b) Israel FSIL, a state shall not enjoy immunity if, 'when the cause of action arose, the employee … was an Israeli citizen or was habitually resident in Israel', unless the employee was a national of the employer state not resident in Israel when the proceedings commenced.

[274] Yang (n 3) 145.

nor a resident of the Netherlands at the time of her recruitment, her claims fell outside the reach of Dutch jurisdiction.[275]

Other instruments which resort to the 'nationality and residence test' do so in less stringent terms. Argentina's state immunity legislation allows for the exercise of jurisdiction over claims by both nationals and residents of Argentina.[276] This means that jurisdiction may be entertained over claims by both non-resident Argentine nationals and resident foreign nationals, including citizens of the employer state. Australia's FSIA stipulates that immunity covers claims by nationals of the employer state who are not 'permanent residents' of Australia or by habitual residents of the employer state;[277] the category of 'permanent resident' is defined as including both nationals and residents of Australia.[278] Hence, people allowed to sue an employer state encompass all Australian nationals (including dual nationals), third-state nationals who are habitual residents of a country other than the employer state and nationals of the employer state permanently residing in Australia. In the case of administrative and technical staff of diplomatic and consular missions, however, jurisdiction may be exercised only over claims by employees who were already 'permanent residents' (ie nationals or residents) of Australia at the time the contract was made.[279] The statutes of the UK, Singapore and Pakistan, while reproducing Article 5 ECSI's approach to nationality and residence, lay down more favourable special rules for employees of commercial establishments. Such individuals are only prevented from suing if they were permanent residents of the employer state when the contract was made, regardless of their nationality.[280]

In other jurisdictions, courts may attach importance to the employee's nationality or residence also in the absence of statutory provisions to this effect. In *Borrisow*, for example, the Colombian nationality of the plaintiff (a secretary at the Lebanese embassy) was apparently the key factor why the Colombian Supreme Court of Justice affirmed jurisdiction over a claim for compensation for unjust dismissal.[281] In *Morocco v HA*, the Court of Appeal of The Hague ruled that the foreign state's entitlement to immunity depended not only on the plaintiff's functions, but also on his nationality and residency status, and upheld jurisdiction because the employee, a Moroccan national, was already a resident of the Netherlands at the time of hiring.[282] Conversely, in *X v Morocco*, the same court declined jurisdiction over a claim by another Moroccan national who worked as a driver at the

[275] The Hague District Court, *Arias v Venezuela* 4 February 1998, 128 ILR 684.

[276] Art 2(d) Law No 24.488 (1995), codifying principles formulated by the Supreme Court in *Manauta and Others v Embassy of the Russian Federation* 22 December 1994, CSJN Fallos 317:1880, 113 ILR 429.

[277] s 12(3) Australia FSIA.

[278] s 12(7).

[279] s 12(6).

[280] s 4(3) UK SIA; s 6(3) Singapore SIA; s 6(3) Pakistan SIO.

[281] *García de Borrisow v Embassy of Lebanon* 13 December 2007, Case No 32096, ILDC 1009 (CO 2007), ILDC para 27. Similarly, see Venezuela, Supreme Tribunal of Justice, *López v Libyan nation* 19 September 2001, No 01967, re a Venezuelan secretary at the Libyan embassy.

[282] *Morocco v HA* (n 98) 395–96.

Moroccan consulate general. Central to the court's reasoning was the fact that the plaintiff resided in Morocco at the time of hiring and had not acquired permanent residency status in the Netherlands when he was dismissed.[283] The Swiss Federal Tribunal too gave relevance to both functions and nationality in *S v India*, a lawsuit filed by an Italian national formerly employed at the Indian embassy. The court ruled that claims by junior employees could always be amenable to local jurisdiction as long as 'the employee does not enjoy the nationality of the sending state and has been recruited on the spot'.[284] Furthermore, in a subsequent case between Egypt and an Egyptian national employed as chauffeur, the Federal Tribunal clarified that 'The fact that the plaintiff is a national of the defendant State' is not per se decisive, but 'constitutes merely one factor, amongst others, which should be taken into consideration'. The court rejected Egypt's immunity plea primarily on account of the functions performed by the plaintiff.[285]

US courts have adopted conflicting views as to the relevance of the employee's nationality. Doubts arise mainly from a passage of the FSIA House Report reading that 'public or governmental, and not commercial in nature, would be the employment of diplomatic, civil service, or military personnel, *but not the employment of American citizens or third country nationals by the foreign state*'.[286] In an obiter in *Broadbent*, the DC Circuit construed this phrasing as implying that the employment of US or third country nationals by a foreign state – regardless of their civil service status – ought to be treated as non-governmental per se.[287] But this interpretation is not easy to reconcile with other passages of the Report which refer to the employee's functions as a key factor in immunity determinations, without clarifying how to coordinate the 'functions test' and the 'nationality test'.[288] In fact, the later *Segni* judgment more hesitantly stated:

> The legislative history of the FSIA suggests that an employee's status as a third country national … is relevant to the commercial nature of his employment. We need not determine how important this factor is, though; it is sufficient to observe that a person hired by his own country's government to work abroad should have a somewhat lesser expectation of suing his homeland in his host nation's courts.[289]

In *El-Hadad*, the DC Circuit expressly distanced itself from its own dictum in *Broadbent* and suggested that the Report's mention of 'American citizens or third country nationals' should be read as a generic reference to non-civil service personnel. Its wording would simply betray an assumption by Congress that the hiring of US or third country nationals in a foreign state's civil service was 'unlikely'.[290]

[283] *X v Morocco* 27 July 2007, ILDC 548 (NL 2007) para 7.
[284] *S v India* (n 100) 19–20.
[285] *M v Egypt* (n 153) 663.
[286] House of Representatives Committee of the Judiciary (n 39) 16 (emphasis added).
[287] *Broadbent et al v Organization of American States et al* 628 F.2d 27 (DC Cir 1980) 34.
[288] On the scope of the 'functions test' under the House Report, see above s IVA.
[289] *Segni* (n 74) 165.
[290] *El-Hadad* (2000) (n 118) 33.

But the court noted that the correctness of this assumption depended on a specific state's approach to civil service appointment, and accordingly considered nationality to be only one out of many indicia of civil service status, along with, inter alia, the employer state's own definition of civil service and the tasks performed by the employee.[291] Under this multi-factor test, the employee's nationality is not decisive in itself, but its relevance

> becomes a matter of context. Where a country rarely if ever hires non-citizens for its civil service … non-citizenship strongly indicates that someone is not a civil servant. And in our view, citizenship makes someone more likely to qualify as a civil servant even if a country sometimes hires noncitizens as civil servants.[292]

Other than in the assessment of civil service status, US courts do not seem to attach any meaningful relevance to nationality or habitual residence.[293] In *Hansen*, jurisdiction was upheld over a discrimination claim brought against Denmark by a Danish citizen employed at the Danish Tourist Board's New York office. While the judgment's description of facts mentioned that the plaintiff was a US permanent resident, this did not play any role in the court's discussion on immunity.[294] In *Sanchez-Ramirez*, two Mexican nationals were barred from suing the Mexican consulate exclusively on account of their functions; nationality was not treated as a relevant factor.[295] The same may be said of *Kato*: as seen above, the court declined jurisdiction over a claim by a Japanese national against a political subdivision of the Japanese state, but only on grounds of the nature of the workplace and not of her nationality.[296]

This last feature of US case law is shared by several other jurisdictions where the plaintiff's nationality does not appear to bear any relevance to the scope of immunity. In fact, it is quite common for national courts not to mention the employee's nationality or residence status at all and to focus exclusively on other immunity tests.[297] It should be noted that this applies not only to third country nationals, but also to citizens of the employer state. In the *French Consular Employee* case, for example, the Austrian Supreme Court exercised jurisdiction over claims by a French national dismissed by the French consulate.[298] The Brussels Labour Court did the same in *Castanheira*, where the plaintiff was a Portuguese national,[299] and in *Kingdom of Morocco v DR* it proclaimed that 'The nationality of the employee

[291] ibid 34, wondering: 'Is the UAE a country in which, as the House Report assumed, non-nationals are unlikely to be employed as governmental officers? Or does the UAE often employ non-nationals in governmental positions?'

[292] *El-Hadad* (2007) (n 117) 667. *El-Hadad* was followed in *Mukaddam* (n 76) 465–66. cp *Lasheen v Embassy of the Arab Republic of Egypt* No 10-17034 (9th Cir 2012) 6–8, holding that an Egyptian university professor on sabbatical in the US was not a member of Egypt's civil service.

[293] Yang (n 3) 162.

[294] *Hansen v Danish Tourist Board* 147 F.Supp 2d 142 (SDNY 2001) 146 and 151.

[295] *Sanchez-Ramirez* (n 119).

[296] *Kato* (n 75), on which see above s IIIA.

[297] Yang (n 3) 162, with further references to case law.

[298] *French Consular Employee Claim* (n 186).

[299] *Castanheira* (n 99).

has no bearing on the laws applicable to contracts of employment executed in Belgium'.[300] In *Sendanayake*, Zambia asserted that it was immune from the Italian courts' jurisdiction in that the plaintiff employee was a third state national. However, the Court of Cassation reasoned that, 'under the Italian Constitution … everyone – not just Italian citizens – is entitled to take legal action'.[301] Later on, in *De Vianna*, the Cassazione proved indifferent to the fact that the employee held his employer's nationality and only upheld immunity because he sought reinstatement in employment.[302]

There is furthermore evidence of a dimished relevance of nationality also in countries where this criterion was traditionally very much in vogue. Most notably, one of the issues examined by the UK Supreme Court in *Benkharbouche* was whether section 4(2)(b) UK SIA – whereby a state is immune if 'at the time when the contract was made the individual was neither a national of the United Kingdom nor habitually resident there' – found correspondence in general international law; section 4(2)(b) reproduces the content of Article 5(2)(b) ECSI. As will be recalled from the previous pages, in *Benkharbouche*, following in the footsteps of the ECtHR, the Supreme Court abided by the principle that state immunity is only justifiable under Article 6 ECHR if it is required by general international law.[303] A comparative analysis of foreign case law led the court to conclude that section 4(2)(b) did not meet this criterion in that it found no correspondence in the judicial practice of the majority of states.[304] This provision was thus declared incompatible with the ECHR. The court had no chance to pronounce itself on the legitimacy of section 4(2)(a) – granting immunity over claims by nationals of the employer state – because this issue was not brought before it.[305]

When compared to its ECSI antecedent, Article 11 UNCSI clearly reflects the declining relevance of the 'nationality and residence test' in state practice. A provision equivalent to Article 5(2)(b) ECSI (that is, barring jurisdiction over claims by employees who were neither nationals or residents of the forum state at the time of hiring), still present in the 1991 final Draft Articles,[306] was later deleted upon the suggestion of the ILC Working Group as it was found impossible to 'reconcil[e] with the principle of non-discrimination based on nationality'.[307] Under Article 11(2)(e) UNCSI, the only employees barred from suing on grounds

[300] *Kingdom of Morocco v DR* (n 148) 422.

[301] *Zambian Embassy v Sendanayake* 18 May 1992, No 5941, 114 ILR 532, re a Sri Lankan employee. See also Court of Cassation, *Embassy of the Kingdom of Saudi Arabia v Al Bayaty* 15 July 1999, No 395, (2000) 36 *Rivista di diritto internazionale privato e processuale* 757, re an Egyptian national.

[302] *Brazil v De Vianna Dos Campos Riscado* 13 February 2012, No 1981, ILDC 2037 (IT 2012).

[303] See above s IIIB.

[304] *Benkharbouche* (n 24) paras 66–67.

[305] ibid para 64. But on this point see *Buttet* (n 241) para 114, re a French security guard at the French ambassador's residence, finding s 4(2)(a) compatible with customary international law but not pronouncing on the possible relevance of permanent residence because the claimant had not pleaded it (para 111).

[306] Art 11(2)(c) 1991 Draft Articles (n 222) 41.

[307] 1999 Report of the Working Group (n 224) 167, para 106.

of nationality are citizens of the employer state who are not permanent residents of the state of the forum upon commencement of proceedings.[308] Pursuant to this provision, the Dutch Supreme Court in *Moroccan Secretary* upheld jurisdiction over a dispute between Morocco and a Moroccan national who was a habitual resident of the Netherlands.[309] In the case of claims by nationals of the forum state or a third country, Article 11(2)(e) permits jurisdiction to be exercised regardless of their residence (provided, however, that the employee is not a dual national of the employer state[310]).

The UNCSI drafters' choice to depart from the ECSI's formulation of the 'nationality and residence test' should be regarded as a laudable development of the law of state immunity. The discrimination between workers of different nationality or residence realised by Article 5 ECSI is not justifiable by any convincing legal or policy rationale. According to Yang, the logic underpinning the ECSI's approach would be that of barring 'an individual without any connection whatsoever with the forum State from bringing proceedings'.[311] But it is difficult to see how an individual working in the forum state might be regarded as lacking a meaningful connection to the forum state simply because he or she was not a national or permanent resident at the time of hiring, even if such a status was acquired later on. It is also hardly conceivable that such an individual should necessarily have a weaker connection to the forum state than to the employer state. Consider, for example, the aforementioned *Arias* case. The plaintiff was a third country national holding both nationality and permanent residency status of the forum state; for all the court knew, she might have never set foot in the employer state before. Yet the employee was not permitted to sue. The absurdity of a similar outcome was well captured by the Supreme Court in *Benkharbouche*:

> I do not see how the absence of British nationality or residence at the time of the contract can be a proper ground for denying an employee access to the courts in respect of their employment in the United Kingdom. They have no territorial connection with their employer, other than that which is implicit in the employment relationship itself. The fact that they may have had no connection with the United Kingdom either before they came to work here does not prevent them from being part of the domestic labour force afterwards.[312]

[308] The UNCSI does not define the concept of 'permanent residence'. The same term is employed, without being defined, in Arts 33(2)(a), 37, 38 and 39(4) VCDR. UK diplomatic practice considers individuals as 'permanent residents' for VCDR purposes if they would reside in the UK independently of their work for the sending state. This depends on various factors, including whether the person has been locally recruited, intends to remain in the UK after the appointment ends and has a prospect of being posted to another state: see Foakes and Denza (n 133) 284–85. See *Jimenez v Inland Revenue* [2004] UKSC SPC00419, para 69, considering this UK practice as 'subsequent practice' under Art 31(3)(b) VCLT in that it had never been challenged by any foreign missions to the UK.

[309] *Morocco v X* (n 36).

[310] Foakes and O'Keefe (n 94) 205.

[311] Yang (n 3) 146.

[312] *Benkharbouche* (n 24) para 68.

The ECSI's criteria may also discourage foreign states from employing nationals or residents of the forum state at the time their contract is made.[313] It would be clearly advantageous for a state to hire people not meeting such criteria in order to shield itself from future employment litigation.

Still, the UNCSI may be criticised for not going far enough in scrapping the 'nationality and residence test'. Paragraph 2(e) differentiates the treatment of employer state nationals depending on whether they are permanently residing in the forum state. It might be speculated that what the drafters had in mind were cases where an employer state national works only occasionally in the forum state, as in the case of employees sent abroad on temporary assignments. Yet, this provision may have perverse effects for individuals permanently working in the forum state. An illuminating example is the ECtHR's *Ndayegamiye* judgment. The applicant, a national of Burundi, had been living with her family in Prévessin-Moëns, a French municipality just across the Swiss border, since 1993. In 1995, she was hired by Burundi's mission to the UN in Geneva. In 2007, she sued Burundi for discriminatory termination before the Swiss courts, which upheld immunity.[314] She then turned to the ECtHR, contending that Switzerland had breached her right of access to justice. The court, however, ruled in favour of Switzerland because the applicant's claim was covered by Article 11(2)(e) UNCSI: she was a national of the employer state not residing in the forum state.[315] As seen previously, Article 11 is used by the ECtHR as a yardstick of compliance of grants of immunity with Article 6 ECHR.[316]

This decision shows that treating workers differently solely on account of their residency status is grossly unfair. In fact, Article 11(2)(e) UNCSI draws an arbitrary line between otherwise indistinguishable employees: had the applicant lived a few hundred metres down the road in Swiss territory, Article 11 would have warranted an opposite conclusion. Hence, it would appear preferable on a policy level not to treat nationality and residence as determinants of immunity. The requirement that the employment relationship presents sufficient jurisdictional links to the forum state may already be ensured by national norms delimiting the courts' jurisdiction, which, depending on domestic law, may refer to factors including the place where the work is performed, the contract signed or the damages suffered.[317]

[313] G Gaja, 'Quale immunità degli Stati esteri per le controversie di lavoro?' (1991) 74 *Rivista di diritto internazionale* 920, 921.

[314] Federal Tribunal, *Ndayegamiye-Mporamazina v République du Burundi* 4 August 2011, Case No 4A_386/2011, para 6.

[315] *Ndayegamiye* (n 255) paras 62–63.

[316] See above s IIIB.

[317] See, eg *M v Egypt* (n 153) 662: 'It is also necessary to establish that the relationship in question has certain links with Swiss territory ... that is to say that it arose there, must be performed there, or at least that the debtor performed certain acts such as to make it a place of performance of the contract.'

VI. Approaches Based on the Subject Matter of the Claim

Another possible way of distinguishing immune and non-immune labour lawsuits has to do with the claim's subject matter. This approach develops from the assumption that certain forms of litigation – or, alternatively, certain remedies that may be sought through litigation – are less intrusive of the employer state's sovereign prerogatives than others. Most commonly, the 'subject-matter test' is applied so as to bar jurisdiction over claims for non-monetary relief, eg reinstatement in employment, while at the same time allowing monetary claims to proceed on the merits. This evidently attempts to strike a balance between the granting of remedies to disgruntled employees and the foreign states' freedom to choose and manage their staff.[318] It is noteworthy that the VCDR and VCCR expressly stipulate the sending state's freedom to appoint all diplomatic and consular personnel, from the heads of post down to the service staff.[319] This section first covers in greater detail the distinction between monetary and non-monetary claims as applied in domestic immunity instruments and judicial decisions (section VIA). It then turns to the scope of the 'subject-matter test' under Article 11 UNCSI (section VIB).

A. The Distinction between Monetary and Non-monetary Claims

Courts resorting to the 'subject-matter test' commonly draw the line between claims for monetary compensation (eg concerning unpaid wages, severance pay or damages for breach of contract) and other types of claims. In the former case, jurisdiction is exercised whenever the court is satisfied that the requirements of other, if any, relevant immunity tests are met. Among the cases discussed in previous sections where jurisdiction was affirmed, the vast majority concerned financial aspects of the employment relationship. By contrast, state practice is nearly uniform in opposing exercises of jurisdiction where an employee pleads to be appointed to a position or reinstated in employment, or more generally directly impinge on the employer state's internal organisation.

[318] See G Gaja, 'Immunity from Jurisdiction of the International Centre for Advanced Mediterranean Agronomic Studies' (1977) 3 *Italian Yearbook of International Law* 310, 313: 'it would be more satisfactory to abandon the distinction between categories of employees altogether and draw a line between different aspects of employment. One could for instance recognize the local State's jurisdiction over compensation, working hours, social security, etc.'

[319] Art 7 VCDR; Art 19(1) VCCR. The same freedom may be spelled out in other instruments. See, eg Agreement to Supplement the Agreement Between the Parties to the North Atlantic Treaty Regarding the Status of Their Forces with Respect to Foreign Forces Stationed in the Federal Republic of Germany 1959, as amended in 1971, 1981 and 1993, Art 56(6), conferring a 'right of engagement, placement, training, transfer, dismissal and acceptance of resignations' of local personnel upon the authorities of the military force or its civilian component.

Thus, in *AA v Austrian Embassy*, having ascertained that the plaintiff's secretarial functions qualified as *de jure gestionis*, the Portuguese Supreme Court held that the request for reinstatement was covered by immunity, but that the proceedings could continue with regard to payment of salaries, holiday bonuses, compensation for violation of the right to holidays, damages arising from the unlawful dismissal and compensation in lieu of reinstatement.[320] The Italian Court of Cassation posited in *Toglia* that monetary claims could be subject to jurisdiction whatever the functions performed by the employee, in that such claims – unlike those for reinstatement – were unable to meaningfully interfere with the 'essential core' of a state's public functions.[321] In *Di Francesco*, the same tenets were applied to claims concerning job reclassification or unfair downgrading: the Cassazione affirmed jurisdiction on the grounds that the plaintiff only sought a compensatory remedy and did not request to be assigned to a higher position.[322] The Swiss courts do not exercise jurisdiction over claims that 'require an intrusion into the internal life of a diplomatic or consular mission or an examination of its staff policy', but do affirm jurisdiction over financial consequences of unlawful dismissals.[323]

Along the same lines, in *Cudak*, the claim's subject matter was one of several factors considered by the Lithuanian Supreme Court, along with the nature of the workplace and the status of the employee. Although the last two factors led the court to decline jurisdiction, it was acknowledged that 'a claim for recognition of unlawful dismissal and for compensation cannot be regarded as violating the sovereignty of [a] State, since … there is no claim of reinstatement'.[324] The French Cour de cassation went so far as to affirm jurisdiction over an action for payment of compensation for termination of employment due to the shutting down of the US consulate general in Martinique. The court held that, while the decision to close a consulate was undisputedly an act *jure imperii*, the French courts could rule over the financial consequences of the resulting layoffs.[325]

A comparable approach is adopted under various domestic instruments. Most notably, while Australian courts routinely exercise jurisdiction over claims for compensation for wrongful dismissal,[326] section 29(2) Australian FSIA prevents courts from 'mak[ing] an order that a foreign State employ a person or re-instate a person in employment'. In other instruments, including the UK SIA, the general prohibition on relief by way of injunction or order for specific performance is to

[320] *AA v Austrian Embassy* (n 178) paras ix and x. Similarly, see *A v Pakistan* (n 147) re a driver.

[321] *Toglia* (n 22) 384. See also *De Vianna* (n 302), declining jurisdiction over a request for reinstatement.

[322] *Ambassador of the Federative Republic of Brazil to the Italian Republic v Di Francesco* 20 October 1995, No 10932, (1996) 32 *Rivista di diritto internazionale privato e processuale* 807.

[323] *X v United States* (n 172) 675; *Nicoud* (n 153) 654–55.

[324] *Cudak (Senkevič)* (n 87), quoted by the ECtHR in *Cudak* (n 32) para 18.

[325] *Mme X v Consulate General of the United States of America in Martinique* 31 March 2009, 07-45.618, Bulletin 2009, V, No 92.

[326] *Robinson* (n 157); *Thomas* (n 170); *Adam v High Commission of Malaysia* [2005] AIRC 882; *Hussein* (n 152); *Riskalla v The Consulate General of Portugal in Sydney trading as AICEP Portugal* [2009] NSWIRComm 185; *Kim v Embassy of the People's Democratic Republic of Algeria* [2016] FWC 4726.

the same effect as section 29(2).[327] It may be noted that these provisions are not framed jurisdictionally,[328] in the sense that, strictly speaking, they do not bar the exercise of jurisdiction over non-pecuniary claims but merely prohibit the grant of non-pecuniary relief.[329] But this drafting choice does not produce any meaningful difference with the aforementioned case law from countries of civil law.[330] In fact, because the bar on non-pecuniary relief results either in plaintiffs not requesting non-pecuniary remedies or in courts not ruling over the relative claims,[331] requests for reinstatement fall de facto outside of local jurisdiction. More importantly, these statutory provisions are underpinned by the same logic of non-interference with the internal management of a foreign state's offices. In *Zakhary*, reversing a decision granting reinstatement to a dismissed cashier at a consulate, the Canadian Federal Court pointed out that 'An order reinstating an employee interferes with a foreign state's ability to conduct the operations of its consulate in Canada, a quintessentially sovereign activity'.[332]

Decisions exercising jurisdiction over labour claims for non-pecuniary remedies are extremely infrequent. In 1991, the Amsterdam Sub-District Court ordered Italy to reinstate an employee who had been dismissed by the Italian Cultural Institute – a branch of the Italian embassy – without prior authorisation from the regional employment office, as required under a 1945 Dutch statute on labour law.[333] This decision was later overturned, but this was only because the statute was found to be inapplicable and Italy had validly terminated the contract.[334] Other Dutch lower courts' decisions on wrongful dismissals delivered during the 1980s and 1990s appear to only have granted pecuniary remedies, but it is unclear from their reasonings whether this reflected a conviction that ordering reinstatement would

[327] s 13(2)(a) UK SIA; s 11(1) Canada SIA; s 15(2)(a) Singapore SIA; s 14(2)(a) Pakistan SIO; s 15(1)(a) Malawi IPA; s 14(1)(a) South Africa FSIA. Note that work injury claims may sometimes be brought under these instruments' 'tort exception' to immunity: eg *The Federal Republic of Nigeria v Ogbonna* 12 July 2011, Appeal No UKEAT/0585/10/ZT, re illness allegedly caused by summary dismissal. The 'tort exception', too, only applies to pecuniary compensation: S El Sawah, 'Jurisdictional Immunity of States and Non-Commercial Torts' in Ruys and Angelet (n 23) 142, 144; Art 12 UNCSI.

[328] Brower (n 128) 33.

[329] *cf* Agreement regarding the Status of United States Armed Forces in Japan 1960: while US armed forces' local personnel is subject to Japanese jurisdiction (Art XII(5)), if US authorities do not approve reinstatement, the USA shall only pay monetary compensation (Art XII(6)).

[330] R Garnett, 'The Rights of Diplomatic and Consular Employees in Australia' (2018) *University of Melbourne Law School Research Series* 5, noting that s 29(2) Australia FSIA is 'entirely consistent with international practice'.

[331] See, eg *Thomas* (n 170) para 44; *Sidhwa* (n 171) (applicants not seeking reinstatement).

[332] *Zakhary* (n 53) para 36. See also Supreme Court, *Benkharbouche* (n 24) para 70: 'the right freely to appoint embassy staff means that a court of the forum state may not make an order which determines who is to be employed by the diplomatic mission of a foreign state'.

[333] *BV v Istituto Italiano di Cultura per i Paesi Bassi and the Republic of Italy* 3 October 1991, (1993) 24 *Netherlands Yearbook of International Law* 341, 346.

[334] Amsterdam District Court, *Republic of Italy v BV* 26 May 1993, (1995) 26 *Netherlands Yearbook of International Law* 338. See also Germany, Administrative Court of Mainz, *French Consulate Disabled Employee Case* 5 May 1988, No AZ 1K 4/88, 114 ILR 508, holding that prior consent to dismissal from the local welfare office would have interfered excessively with the consulate's internal affairs.

be impermissible.[335] Probably the most relevant outlier cases are two 1986 decisions by the Spanish Supreme Court where claims for reinstatement brought by a former chauffeur and a former secretary at foreign embassies were upheld.[336] These Dutch and Spanish precedents, however, may now be considered outdated. The practice of both countries is currently aligned with Article 11 UNCSI, which – as will be seen shortly – bars jurisdiction over claims for reinstatement in employment.[337]

There is furthermore evidence of decisions adjudicating claims for reinstatement being the subject of protests by respondent states. An example may be drawn from the Austrian *Wallishauser* case. The applicant, a photographer at the US embassy, was dismissed after enduring a work-related accident and sued for unfair dismissal. A first instance court denied immunity on account of the plaintiff's functions being unrelated to the sovereign activities of the embassy and, because dismissal had not been authorised by the public authority overseeing employment of disabled persons, declared the termination void. The Supreme Court upheld, although it seemingly did so because the USA had not maintained the objection of state immunity in the course of the proceedings.[338] The USA refused to reinstate the plaintiff and complained that the application of the prior authorisation procedure to embassy employees interfered with its sovereignty.[339] Notably, though, the protests were not directed at the monetary aspect of the decision. In fact, due to the continued validity of her employment contract, the plaintiff was able to request payment of salary arrears in subsequent proceedings. Following a 1995 decision rejecting the USA's immunity plea over the claim for front pay damages, she obtained payment from the USA of approximately seven years of lost salary.[340]

Leaning more on the side of immunity, other (minority) interpretations of the 'subject-matter test' bar jurisdiction over wrongful termination lawsuits without differentiating between monetary and non-monetary claims. The underlying rationale is that any enquiry into the reasons for dismissal would interfere with the employer state's functions, conflict with security reasons or more generally relate to state acts done in a public capacity. Italian decisions rendered between the early 1990s and 2014 are prime examples of this trend. Although the 1989 *Toglia* judgment differentiated between monetary and non-monetary claims without further qualification,[341] the majority of subsequent cases refrained from

[335] See, eg The Hague Sub-District Court, *MHC v The Republic of Cuba* 15 April 1992, (1996) 27 *Netherlands Yearbook of International Law* 319.

[336] *Emilio BM v Embassy of Equatorial Guinea* 10 February 1986, Case No 727, 86 ILR 508, 511; *Diana A* (n 181).

[337] Art 10 Law No 16 (2015) (Spain); *Morocco v X* (n 36), applying Art 11 qua codification of customary law.

[338] *Roswitha W* (n 156). Note that the ECtHR judgment only concerned immunity from service of process, which prevented the plaintiff from bringing further proceedings relating to salary payments: see Austria, Supreme Court, *W v United States* 11 June 2011, 8 Ob A201/00t, ILDC 358 (AT 2001).

[339] *Wallishauser* (n 156) para 8.

[340] ibid para 9.

[341] See *Quattri* (n 173), affirming jurisdiction over a claim for payment of arrears accruing from the dismissal.

adjudicating the financial consequences of acts of dismissal. This was justified on the grounds that dissecting the dismissal's reasons would intrude into the foreign state's powers of self-organisation.[342] In *Trobbiani*, the same principles were applied to a request for compensation filed by an employee complaining of having been assigned to a lower job category than appropriate. As the Court of Cassation put it, immunity should cover staff disputes where

> the plaintiff requests … to pass judgment on acts of the defendant coming within the scope of its right of self-organization … [T]his is the case, even where the claim involves only a factual enquiry (and not the handing down of a judgment) into the sovereign internal activities of the foreign State, such as those relating to the scope of the duties performed by the plaintiff.[343]

Aside from wrongful dismissals and grading of employees, the general rule of amenability of monetary claims to the Italian jurisdiction stood unchanged. Drawing a line often required intricate hair-splitting. In cases where the Court of Cassation declined jurisdiction over unfair dismissal compensation claims, jurisdiction was instead affirmed over requests for payment of thirteenth and fourteenth month salary, pay differences based on seniority, payment in lieu of notice and severance pay;[344] damages suffered due to irregular working conditions and workplace bullying;[345] and unpaid social security contributions.[346]

Closely reminiscent of this jurisprudence of Italy's courts is the Ontario Superior Court of Justice's ruling in *Greco*, an action for breach of employment contract by a former administrative employee of the Apostolic Nunciature to Canada. While the plaintiff's claim for lost wages owed under the employment contract was allowed to proceed on the merits, the court declined jurisdiction over the claim for wrongful dismissal: it affirmed that such an enquiry would 'necessarily have an impact on the right of the defendant state to decide how it manages and deals with its personnel', thus producing 'an unacceptable interference with [its] sovereignty'.[347] In *Lovell*, another Canadian court exercised jurisdiction over a claim for redundancy severance pay on the grounds that the plaintiff – a former marketing officer at New Zealand's tourist board – did not question the legality of the layoff but merely sought to enforce a term of the employment contract.[348]

[342] A Atteritano, 'Immunity of States and Their Organs: The Contribution of the Italian Jurisprudence in the Past Ten Years' (2009) 19 *Italian Yearbook of International Law* 31, 43. See, eg Court of Cassation, *Kuna – Kuwait News Agency v Musa* 12 June 1999, No 331; *Consolato britannico in Milano v Papa* 27 May 1999, No 313, (1999) 35 *Rivista di diritto internazionale privato e processuale* 628.

[343] *Trobbiani* (n 174) 524. Similarly, see Court of Cassation, *École française de Rome v Guadagnino* 9 September 1997, No 8768, (1998) 34 *Rivista di diritto internazionale privato e processuale* 816.

[344] *Korea v BS* (n 174).

[345] *Embassy of the State of Kuwait v AEGAMM* 10 July 2006, No 15626.

[346] *Republic of Peru v LMC* 10 July 2006, No 15620, para 2; *Consulate of the Republic of Tunisia v AM* 10 July 2006, No 15628, para 3.

[347] *Greco v Holy See (State of the Vatican City)* [2000] OJ No 5293, para 6; followed in *Bentley v Consulate General of Barbados/Invest Barbados* 2010 HRTO 2258, 2010 CarswellOnt 9446, para 43, re a claim of unfair dismissal during pregnancy.

[348] *Lovell v New Zealand Tourism Board* 37 ACWS (3d) 930, 1992 CanLil 1502 (BCSC), paras 15 and 18.

Traces of this approach may sometimes be found in decisions of other countries too. One example is *Hicks*. Although, as seen above, the case was decided on the basis of the 'workplace test',[349] the UK EAT also briefly touched upon the relevance of the nature of the claim. In reversing the first instance judgment, it held that the lower court had not considered

> what would be involved in [the] investigation of, in particular, the claim of unfair dismissal … the Tribunal would have had to investigate the question of reasonableness … Should there have been consultation; was the applicant fairly selected for redundancy at the time he was; what possibilities were there for employment on other US bases? Such investigations could well intrude into the public or sovereign acts of the US Government.[350]

And in *Muller*, a German appellate labour court held that immunity barred any investigation into the legality of a termination prompted by an 'organisational restructuring' of a consulate. The court feared that the exercise of review powers over decisions concerning its internal structure 'would adversely affect the guarantee under international law of the unimpeded fulfilment of the tasks of the Consulate'.[351]

The interpretation of the 'subject-matter test' barring all unfair dismissal claims is problematic in two key respects. First, at least some of the above decisions essentially treat all acts of dismissal as *acta jure imperii*. Yet, as was discussed more in depth in chapter three, the distinction between acts *jure imperii* and *jure gestionis* is not readily applicable to specific acts and decisions of the employer state.[352] Secondly, and more crucially, it is unclear why investigating the reasons of a dismissal for the sole purpose of awarding monetary compensation should be more intrusive into the internal organisation of a foreign state's office than a claim for compensation based on other grounds, eg irregular working conditions.[353] An argument in this sense was made by the UK Supreme Court in *Benkharbouche*:

> I would accept that the right freely to appoint embassy staff means that a court of the forum state may not make an order which determines who is to be employed by the diplomatic mission of a foreign state … But a claim for damages for wrongful dismissal does not require the foreign state to employ any one. It merely adjusts the financial consequences of dismissal … Therefore, no right under the Vienna Convention would

[349] See above s IIIA.

[350] *Hicks* (n 67).

[351] *Muller* (n 188) 519. *cf* Botswana, Industrial Court, *Bah v Libyan Embassy* 28 November 2005, No IC 956/2005, 142 ILR 167, ILDC 154 (BW 2005). The applicant sought payment of benefits arising from the termination but did not challenge the dismissal (paras 8–9). Although the court broadly affirmed that an employment dispute 'involves a private law transaction and is justiciable' (para 25), it also added: 'The applicant in this matter … is merely seeking compliance with the Employment Act in so far as he is merely claiming payment of severance pay, notice pay and the payment of wrongfully withheld wages' (para 26).

[352] See ch 3, s IV.

[353] Garnett, 'State Immunity and Employment Relations in Canada' (n 123) 655; Pavoni, 'La jurisprudence' (n 109) 218–19, criticising Italian case law on the point as incoherent.

be prejudiced by the refusal of the forum state to recognise the immunity of the foreign state as regards a claim for damages.[354]

The Supreme Court's argument is compelling: pecuniary compensation has no direct bearing on the state's actual freedom to choose and manage its staff, as most notably enshrined in Article 7 VCDR.

B. The 'Subject-Matter Test' under the UN Convention on State Immunity

The test based on the claim's subject matter features prominently in Article 11 UNCSI, which broadly keeps to the distinction between monetary and non-monetary claims. According to paragraph 2(c), immunity applies if 'the subject matter of the proceeding is the recruitment, renewal of employment or reinstatement of an individual'. While this provision certainly covers all actions aimed at obliging states to recruit, renew or reinstate, it does not bar claims for wrongful dismissal compensation.[355] This reading of the paragraph – which might not be self-evident should this clause be taken in isolation – is compelled by the following paragraph, 2(d), pursuant to which, where 'the subject matter of the proceeding is the dismissal or termination of employment of an individual', immunity only applies if the foreign state determines that the proceedings interfere with its security interests.

This construction is also supported by the *travaux*. The ILC described the 1991 Draft Articles' antecedent of paragraph 2(c) as safeguarding the state's 'discretionary power of appointment or non-appointment' of an individual to any employment position, 'without prejudice to the possible recourse which may still be available in the State of the forum for compensation or damages for wrongful dismissal'.[356] The provision, which in previous drafts read 'the proceeding *relates to* the recruitment, renewal of employment or reinstatement of an individual',[357] was amended by the Drafting Committee precisely with a view to avoiding overly extensive interpretation and clarifying that it was not meant to bar compensation claims.[358]

Article 11's application in state practice further corroborates the view that this provision does not bar unfair dismissal compensation claims. Article 9 of the 2009 Japanese state immunity statute, which for the most part textually repeats the words of Article 11, more directly stipulates that a state is immune from 'An action or petition regarding the existence or nonexistence of the contract for the employment or re-employment of the individual (excluding those seeking compensation

[354] Supreme Court, *Benkharbouche* (n 24) para 70.
[355] Foakes and O'Keefe (n 94) 203.
[356] 1991 Draft Articles (n 222) 43, re Draft Art 11(2)(b).
[357] Ogiso, 'Third Report' (n 220) 13 (emphasis added). *cf* Sucharitkul, 'Fifth Report' (n 28) para 62, Art 13(2)(a): 'the proceedings relate to failure to employ an individual or dismissal of an employee'.
[358] 1991 Draft Articles (n 222) 43–44.

for damages)'.[359] The same interpretation has been consistently reaffirmed in case law. In *Shyam Lal*, the respondent construed Article 11(2)(d) as indicating that all proceedings whose subject matter is termination of employment interfere with the employer state's security interests. This reading was rejected by the Delhi High Court: 'Article 11 ... does not give any such blanket immunity to a foreign embassy from claims for compensation by a local employee who alleges illegal termination of his services'; immunity may only arise from a determination under paragraph 2(d) made by the impleaded government.[360] When confronted with cases where the applicants had requested both reinstatement and compensation for unfair dismissal in proceedings before the respondent state's courts, the ECtHR, applying Article 11(2)(c), has ruled that national courts erred in considering both such claims to be covered by immunity. As the ECtHR put it in *Naku*:

> The fact that the applicant had sought reinstatement ... was undisputed. The invocation and subsequent granting of immunity for that part of the claim had thus undoubtedly been correct. [This] rule was, however, without prejudice to the possible recourse that might still be available in the forum State for compensation or damages for wrongful dismissal, which was also part of the applicant's claims.[361]

The same position has been espoused by the Italian Court of Cassation in the 2014 *Galamini di Recanati* ruling and in all subsequent decisions on the point.[362] The earlier *De la Grana* judgment appears to be slightly at odds with this pattern. Here, the plaintiff raised several claims relating to the termination of her employment by the Spanish embassy. Among other things, she sought a declaration that the dismissal was null and void, claimed payment of financial benefits and requested 'in any case' immediate reinstatement. The Cassazione upheld immunity over all of the plaintiff's claims. This anomaly, however, did not arise from a rogue interpretation of Article 11 UNCSI. Rather, the court inferred that the words 'in any case' made all other claims inseparable from the claim for reinstatement and held all aspects of the lawsuit to be barred under paragraph 2(c).[363] This decision was thus superficially compliant with Article 11, although one may raise doubts as to whether such a highly formalistic approach would pass the scrutiny of the Strasbourg Court.

Article 11(2)(d), which only bars proceedings relating to compensation for unfair dismissal if, 'as determined by the head of State, the head of Government or the Minister for Foreign Affairs of the employer State, such a proceeding would interfere with the security interests of that State', was added late in the drafting

[359] Art 9(2)(3) Act on Civil Jurisdiction over Foreign States (2010) (Japan).
[360] *Shyam Lal* (n 35) para 11.
[361] *Naku* (n 88) para 71. See also *Radunović* (n 238) para 76. By contrast, the applicant in *Cudak* (n 32) did not seek reinstatement (para 16).
[362] *Galamini di Recanati* (n 244) paras 6 and 8; *Escudero García* (n 248) para 3; *Chibomba* (n 111) para 26.
[363] *De la Grana* (n 33) ILDC para 25.

process without any recorded explanation.[364] Perhaps this clause draws ispiration from isolated precedents upholding blanket immunity over proceedings involving employees dismissed for security reasons.[365] Such was the 1989 Dutch Supreme Court's decision in *Van der Hulst*. Faced with claims by an embassy secretary dismissed for security reasons one month after hiring, the court granted immunity by opining that states should be free to terminate their employment relationships following security checks on their employees.[366] Still, there is a fundamental difference between this precedent and paragraph 2(d). The *Van der Hulst* jurisprudence only applied to employees whose dismissal had been justified by the employer state on security grounds. Paragraph 2(d), by contrast, seemingly entitles a state to bring up security reasons in the course of the proceedings in all circumstances, even though it did not initially justify the dismissal on such grounds.

The key question raised by paragraph 2(d) is the measure of discretion to which the foreign state is entitled in its determination. On its face, the provision appears to treat said determination as final – and, indeed, commentators have contended that the veracity of the state's declaration is removed from the court's review.[367] So interpreted, paragraph 2(d) would introduce a dangerous loophole into Article 11. If foreign states were empowered to portray any unfair dismissal lawsuit as one interfering with security interests, this provision would have 'the potential of conferring absolute immunity in mission disputes, since the majority of such claims are unfair dismissal pleas'.[368] However, an argument against the view that a foreign state's discretion under paragraph 2(d) is unbound may be put forward on the basis of the Annex to the UNCSI, which has the same legal value as the Convention.[369] The understanding with respect to Article 11 reads: 'The reference in article 11, paragraph 2(d), to the "security interests" of the employer State is intended primarily to address matters of national security and the security of diplomatic missions and consular posts.' Although the word 'primarily' makes the exemplification contained therein forthrightly non-exhaustive, to treat the understanding as superfluous would run counter to the well-established principle of treaty interpretation that phrases should not be read in such a way as to render them devoid of any effect (*ut res magis valeat quam pereat*).[370] At a minimum, the

[364] Report of the Ad Hoc Committee on Jurisdictional Immunities of States and Their Property (24–28 February 2003), UN Doc A/58/22, Annex I, 8.

[365] Köhler (n 5) 212.

[366] *Van der Hulst v United States* 22 December 1989, 94 ILR 373, 376–77. See also *United States of America v The Public Service Alliance of Canada and Others (Re Canada Labour Code)* [1992] 2 SCR 50, 94 ILR 264, 283, holding in obiter (citing *Van der Hulst*) that 'cases have recognized that foreign states are immune from wrongful dismissal claims when the dismissal was for national security reasons'.

[367] Foakes and O'Keefe (n 94) 205; Köhler (n 5) 212; G Hafner and L Lange, 'La convention des Nations Unies sur les immunités juridictionnelles des États et de leurs biens' (2004) 50 *Annuaire Français de Droit International* 45, 65.

[368] R Garnett, 'The Precarious Position of Embassy and Consular Employees in the United Kingdom' (2005) 54 *ICLQ* 705, 717.

[369] Art 25 UNCSI.

[370] See, inter alia, *Anglo-Iranian Oil Co Case* Judgment (Preliminary Objections) [1952] ICJ Rep 93, 105. Although not expressly mentioned in Art 31(1) VCLT, this principle is implicit in the obligation to

understanding represents an attempt to exert an influence on the state's measure of discretion and therefore supports the idea that such discretion should not be absolute. It does not follow from the fact that the understanding does not specify exactly the limits to this discretion that there should be no limits; a better view is that finding an appropriate balance is deferred to the states and their courts.

This view is confirmed by the most recent judicial practice. In *Sabeh El Leil*, the ECtHR held that the paragraph 2(d) immunity ground was inapplicable because there was no record of any declaration made by the employer state's authorities before the courts of the respondent.[371] This was interpreted in scholarship as implying that such declaration would have been treated as conclusive.[372] But later, in *Radunović*, the ECtHR suggested a much stricter test. It reasoned: 'Paragraph 2(d) … was not applicable in the present case since neither the domestic courts nor the Government have shown how the applicants' duties could objectively have been linked to the security interests of the USA.'[373] This passage extends to paragraph 2(d) the 'objective link' requirement devised by the court in the context of the interpretation of Article 11(2)(a). It will be recalled that, in order for the paragraph 2(a) immunity ground to apply, the ECtHR requires foreign states to prove that the employee's duties are 'objectively related' to sovereign functions. This effectively gives rise to a rebuttable presumption that employees do not perform sovereign-related duties.[374] Likewise, *Radunović* seemingly creates a presumption that proceedings concerning unfair dismissal do not affect national security interests, unless the foreign state proves otherwise. As was the case with paragraph 2(a), however, the conditions for rebutting this presumption are unclear, particularly since the ECtHR has never been faced with a case where the employer state had actually made a paragraph 2(d) declaration. In any event, the threshold for rebutting the presumption should be high. The mere fact that an employee was dismissed for security reasons does not prove that proceedings relating to that dismissal would impair the foreign state's security. Rather, it appears reasonable to suggest that the employer state may substantiate its declaration by proving, for example, that examining the employee's claims would cause divulgence of confidential or highly sensitive information.

The above finds further support in a 2019 ruling of the French Court of Cassation where a state's paragraph 2(d) declaration was expressly disregarded.[375] The plaintiff, who had worked as a secretary at the embassy of Ghana, had been dismissed for serious misconduct: Ghana alleged that she failed to ensure proper maintenance of the embassy computers and that her negligence led to a security

interpret a treaty in good faith: see J-M Sorel and V Boré Eveno, 'Article 31 – General Rule of Interpretation' in O Corten and P Klein (eds), *The Vienna Conventions on the Law of Treaties: A Commentary* (Oxford, Oxford University Press, 2011) 804, 816.

[371] *Sabeh El Leil* (n 232) para 61.

[372] Foakes and O'Keefe (n 94) 205.

[373] *Radunović* (n 238) para 77.

[374] See above s IVC.

[375] *B v Ghana* (n 34).

breach. She sought compensation for illegal termination. Before the first instance and appellate courts, Ghana filed a letter from its Minister of Foreign Affairs attesting that the proceedings would interfere with security interests. Both courts rejected Ghana's immunity plea on the grounds that the plaintiff did not perform tasks *de jure imperii* and granted compensation.[376] In its appeal to the Cour de cassation, Ghana argued that the Minister's letter should have been treated as conclusive. But the court affirmed the appellate court's judgment. It held that the declaration did not 'exempt the court from determining the existence' of a risk of interference with the state's security interests. The fact that the employee had not performed confidential duties satisfied the court that no such risk existed.[377]

Paragraphs 2(c) and (d) do not clarify how to handle claims by individuals currently employed by foreign states but complaining about the position to which they are assigned. Still, it seems straightforward to analogise such claims to those concerning dismissal. If compensation for illegal termination constitutes a generally admissible relief, claims for compensation for unfair downgrading should be amenable to jurisdiction a fortiori. By contrast, where an employee aims to obtain a higher position, the bar on claims which seek to directly limit state freedom to choose and manage staff should reasonably apply. This solution mirrors the long-standing case law of the Italian Court of Cassation according to which the principles governing immunity from unfair dismissal claims also apply to claims for job reclassification or unfair downgrading.[378]

A further issue is whether, pursuant to Article 11(2)(c), jurisdiction may be exercised over claims for monetary compensation for reasons other than dismissal, eg for discrimination in the recruitment process. This problem arises from the fact that, as seen above, a plain reading of paragraph 2(d) only allows (save for declarations by the employer state) for jurisdiction over claims for compensation for illegal termination; other types of compensation claims fall outside its scope. Thus, the bar on proceedings concerning 'recruitment or renewal of employment' under paragraph 2(c) might be construed as encompassing all claims – both monetary and non-monetary – relating to recruitment or renewal. But a contextual reading does not support this construction: if the term 'recruitment' in paragraph 2(c) only refers to claims for non-monetary relief, the most reasonable construction is to interpret 'recruitment' and 'renewal of employment' as only referring to non-monetary relief too. The *travaux* strongly support this reading in that the Commission described the (textually identical) 1991 precursor of paragraph 2(c) as 'not prevent[ing] an employee from bringing action … to seek redress for damage arising from recruitment, renewal of employment or reinstatement of an individual'.[379] At the time, Article 11 contained no equivalent of current

[376] Paris Labour Court, 6 November 2013, No 12/00081; Paris Court of Appeal, 24 January 2018, No 14/09595.

[377] *B v Ghana* (n 34).

[378] *Trobbiani* (n 174); *Di Francesco* (n 322). See further above s VIA.

[379] 1991 Draft Articles (n 222) 43.

paragraph 2(d). Hence, paragraph 2(c) should be regarded as only covering claims for non-monetary relief independently of paragraph 2(d). This is the approach adopted by Japan's implementing legislation of the UNCSI, which does not bar compensation claims regarding 'the existence or nonexistence of the contract for the employment or re-employment of the individual'.[380]

Moreover, the distinction between the three subject matters mentioned in paragraph 2(c) – ie recruitment, renewal and reinstatement – is not always clear-cut. This provides further argument against differentiating between monetary claims according to whether they relate to dismissal or recruitment and renewal. Consider, for example, the Italian Court of Cassation's 2019 *Dickinson* judgment.[381] An employee of the Rome office of the British Council, a UK public institution, alleged that he had worked under a series of unlawful temporary contracts. He sued before the Italian courts, seeking conversion of his temporary contract into a permanent one, as provided by Italian law, and compensation for the difference between the salary he received and that of permanent employees. In the course of the proceedings, he concluded a permanent job contract with the British Council. As a result, by the time the lawsuit reached the Court of Cassation, his claim only concerned compensation for the difference in pay. Still, compensation was contingent upon the recognition that the previous temporary contracts were to be converted into a permanent one. It is arguably hard to classify a similar compensation claim as one purely relating to termination, renewal of employment or possibly recruitment. This difficulty might be the reason why the court – despite acknowledging that Article 11 reflected custom[382] – curiously departed from its most recent precedents and did not apply Article 11. Instead, it resorted to the straightforward distinction between monetary and non-monetary claims, and affirmed jurisdiction on the grounds that assessing the legality of previous temporary contracts only served the purpose of calculating pecuniary benefits accruing to the employee.[383]

One last issue that is not expressly addressed in the UNCSI (nor, for that matter, in any other immunity instrument) is whether jurisdiction may be exercised over collective disputes, most notably trade union claims. These lawsuits are often contemplated by municipal industrial relations legislation and relate to issues such as collective bargaining, employee representation, allocation of work or disciplinary matters. Article 11's silence about collective disputes opens up various possibilities. On the one hand, because Article 11 only entitles to immunity under the circumstances enumerated in paragraph 2, and because paragraph 2 makes no mention of such claims, it might be concluded that collective claims fall into paragraph 1's general rule of non-immunity. This interpretation is, however, unwarranted, considering that trade union claims may prove particularly intrusive

[380] Act on Civil Jurisdiction over Foreign States (2010) (Japan), Art 9(2)(3).
[381] *Dickinson* (n 111).
[382] ibid ILDC para 9.
[383] ibid ILDC para 11.

into a foreign state's organisational choices[384] (think of a trade union seeking to prevent a mass layoff or to change a state's general recruitment policies). Others, on the other hand, have contended that the UNCSI bars collective claims in toto. This argument is based on a literal interpretation of Article 11(1), which sets forth a default rule of non-immunity for proceedings 'relat[ing] to a contract of employment'. In Garnett's words, 'Since a collective claim is brought … on behalf of a *group* of employees, it is not a proceeding in respect of a *single* contract of employment and so arguably would fall outside this provision'.[385] This textual argument is, however, quite weak. The *travaux* offer no support to the view that the singular form was intentionally directed at barring proceedings relating to more than one contract; it is more realistic to see the singular as purely stylistic, all the more since Article 11's title uses the plural form – 'contracts of employment'. Also, this interpretation may have the illogical consequence of barring lawsuits filed jointly by two or more employees whose claims would individually be amenable to jurisdiction, such as group actions by service staff members to recover unpaid wages. In fact, it seems hard to deny that collective claims are proceedings which relate – at least broadly – to a contract of employment in the sense of Article 11(1).[386]

A preferable solution is to handle collective claims according to the ordinary 'subject-matter test', and particularly to the distinction between monetary and non-monetary claims. Indeed, there is no reason why a lawsuit's collective character per se should indicate higher intrusiveness into the foreign state's sovereign prerogatives; this arguably depends on what the collective claim aims to achieve. Thus, bringing collective claims should be impermissible whenever they aim to directly impinge upon the state's freedom to choose its staff and manage its internal organisation. Conversely, jurisdiction should, in principle, remain possible over collective claims dealing only with financial aspects of the employment.

This solution is consistent with existing domestic case law. For example, an Italian court declined jurisdiction over a claim challenging a consulate's alleged anti-union behaviour – conduct that Italian legislation broadly defines as anything aimed at limiting trade union activity or the right to strike[387] – by reason that the remedies sought by the union were too intrusive. The union had requested to order changes into the consulate's preordained procedures of employment in order to remove certain aspects considered to be harmful to its own interests. The court wrote:

> In order to protect these interests effectively, the judge is called upon to interfere considerably in all the various powers of the employer (organisational, managerial

[384] Yang (n 3) 162.

[385] Garnett, 'State and Diplomatic Immunity' (n 226) 813 (emphases in the original).

[386] See Yang (n 3) 146, re Art 5 ECSI (which, just like Art 11 UNCSI, refers to 'proceedings relat[ing] to a contract of employment'). *cf* Fox, 'Employment' (n 7) 139, arguing that trade union claims fall outside the scope of s 4(6) UK SIA, defining non-immune 'proceedings relating to a contract of employment' as 'proceedings *between the parties to such a contract*' (emphasis added), but expressing doubts as to whether the same approach can be applied to Art 5 ECSI, which contains no such textual limitation (ibid).

[387] Art 28 Law No 300 (1970) (Italy).

> and disciplinary powers, etc.) and impart direct 'orders' to put an end to the offending behaviour and to rectify the situation and he has to apply repressive measures which … impinge upon the employer's prerogatives in their entirety.[388]

Other courts have exercised jurisdiction over collective claims whose subject matter only concerned economic aspects of the employment. The leading precedent is the Second Circuit's judgment in *Goethe House*. A union had commenced a certification procedure for the non-German employees of Goethe House, a New York cultural centre administered by West Germany. The National Labor Relations Board (NLRB) had ordered a representation election to determine whether the employees wished to be represented by that union. A district court, however, issued a preliminary injunction in favour of Goethe House. It held that submission to NLRB jurisdiction 'might well conflict or otherwise interfere with the German government's employment objectives' in that the centre 'would then be forced either to bargain with the union in contravention of some or all of the German government's personnel mandates or, alternatively, to obtain review it would have to commit an unfair labor practice'.[389] The Court of Appeals reversed. While its decision was based on a narrow domestic law ground, ie that NLRB orders are not reviewable in court, the court did address the lower court's arguments on immunity in a meaningful obiter dictum. The majority challenged the idea that the union certification would realise an unacceptable interference with sovereign prerogatives:

> Even if the Union were certified as the bargaining agent of Goethe House's non-German employees, we fail to see how the presence of the Union would interfere with Goethe House's implementation of West German cultural foreign policy … Goethe House would have a duty to bargain with the Union over *wages, hours and other terms and conditions of employment* … Goethe House would have no duty to bargain over how it performed its mission of promoting German culture.[390]

Thus, in essence, what the court found decisive was that the suit addressed issues which could have been litigated individually by the state employees and that the relief sought by the union did not meaningfully affect Germany's freedom to manage its offices. In this latter respect, the court also noted that Goethe House's German employees were already unionised. This confuted Germany's claim that the presence of a union for non-German employees would obstruct Goethe House's operations.[391]

In *Re Canada Labour Code*, Canada's Supreme Court resorted to the 'subject-matter test' in the context of collective labour claims. The case concerned union

[388] Examining Magistrate of Milan, *Italian Trade Union for Embassy and Consular Staff v United States* 14 April 1981, 65 ILR 338, 342–43.
[389] *Goethe House New York, German Cultural Center v National Labor Relations Board et al* 7 June 1988, 685 F.Supp 427 (SDNY 1988) 429.
[390] *Goethe House New York, German Cultural Center v National Labor Relations Board* 869 F.2d 75 (2d Cir 1989) 79 (emphasis added), certiorari denied 493 US 810 (1989).
[391] ibid.

certification procedures for Canadian service staff at a US military base. The military authorities had agreed to collective bargaining according to US labour law. When US law turned out not to be applicable to labour relations at the base, a Canadian trade union applied for collective bargaining certification under Canadian labour law before the Canada Labour Relations Board (CLRB). The USA challenged the CLRB's jurisdiction before the Canadian Supreme Court, which upheld the plea of immunity. The key rationale was that collective bargaining under Canadian law would have empowered the CLRB to 'impose terms in a collective agreement, reinstate employees and rescind disciplinary actions taken by the base commander'; all remedies deemed too intrusive into the military authorities' control of the base.[392]

Interestingly, the Supreme Court acknowledged that it would have affirmed jurisdiction had the collective claim only concerned economic aspects of employment at the base. As the majority put it, 'If the only effect of union certification proceedings was … a duty to bargain over terms of employment, then I would agree with the result in *Goethe House*. However, as we have seen, the impact is much greater.'[393] Hence, even though the Supreme Court distinguished *Goethe House*, both decisions applied the same test: assessing the capacity of the relief sought by the union to disrupt state functions. Furthermore, both courts agreed that the mere duty to bargain with a union over the conditions of employment would not amount to a disruption of state functions. What set the two decisions apart was very much factual, ie the different scope of collective bargaining powers in the labour legislations of Canada and the USA.

VII. Approaches Based on Forum Selection Clauses in the Employment Contract

Most existing immunity instruments containing an employment-specific provision stipulate that the 'employment exception' to state immunity shall not apply where the employment contract confers jurisdiction upon the courts of the employer state.[394] The existence of forum selection clauses is thus treated as a further determinant of state immunity, in addition to the criteria described in the previous sections. The operation of such clauses is normally made conditional on their compatibility with the forum state's legislation.[395] For instance, pursuant to Article 11(2)(f) – closely modelled on Article 5(2)(c) ECSI – paragraph 1's general rule of non-immunity does not apply if 'the employer State and the employee have otherwise agreed in writing, subject to any considerations of public policy

[392] *Re Canada Labour Code* (n 366) 286.
[393] ibid 288.
[394] But no such provision is contained in s 4 Israel FSIL and Art 8 Law No 297-FZ (2015) (Russia).
[395] With the exceptions of s 5(2)(a) South Africa FSIA and s 6(2)(c) Pakistan SIO.

conferring on the courts of the State of the forum exclusive jurisdiction by reason of the subject matter of the proceeding'.[396]

While these provisions do not raise major interpretive issues, the language they employ is somewhat misleading as regards their relationship to immunity. In fact, a contract clause assigning jurisdiction to the employer state has little to do with immunity law at all, in the sense that it is not reflective of any international legal obligation upon the forum state not to exercise jurisdiction. The fact that most intruments set forth domestic law limitations on these opt-out clauses clearly confirms that no such obligation exists.[397] Furthermore, if a court seised with an employment claim against a foreign state finds itself under a legal obligation to grant immunity, a choice of the courts of the employer state is immaterial because the seised court may not exercise jurisdiction anyway. Hence, from the standpoint of the forum state's courts, similar contract clauses are relevant only insofar as jurisdiction is not barred by a rule of immunity. In such cases, these clauses produce the effects ordinarily associated with exclusive choice-of-court agreements, to the extent that this outcome is permissible under the law of the forum state.

A confirmation may be drawn from the CJEU judgment in *Mahamdia*. The court held that the rules on jurisdiction of the Brussels I Regulation are applicable to employment disputes with third states' diplomatic missions to EU Member States, but only insofar as the employer state does not enjoy immunity under international law.[398] To put it more precisely, the Regulation was found to be applicable to such labour disputes in cases 'where the functions carried out by the employee do not fall within the exercise of public powers'.[399] But it is clear from the judgment's reasoning that the 'status and functions test' was invoked as a proxy for the customary rule of state immunity.[400] Therefore, regardless of how the court identified the specific content of international custom, the gist of this passage simply reflects the broader principle that EU law should not be construed as infringing upon general international law.[401] Within these limits, the Regulation's provisions

[396] Similarly, see Act on Civil Jurisdiction over Foreign States (2010) (Japan), Art 9(2)(vi); Law No 16 (2015) (Spain), Art 10(2)(f), providing that the agreement in writing shall result in immunity 'salvo que la competencia de los órganos jurisdiccionales españoles fuese irrenunciable para el trabajador' ('unless the jurisdiction of the Spanish courts was not waivable by the worker'); s 4(2)(c) and (4) UK SIA; s 6(2)(c) and (4) Singapore SIA; s 6(2) Malawi IPA; s 12(4) Australia FSIA.

[397] On the relationship between jurisdiction and immunity, see ch 2, s II.

[398] *Mahamdia* (n 81) paras 56–57.

[399] ibid para 57.

[400] See ibid para 56: 'in view of the content of that principle of customary international law concerning the immunity of States from jurisdiction … it does not preclude the application of Regulation No 44/2001 … where the court seised finds that the functions carried out by that employee do not fall within the exercise of public powers'.

[401] S Migliorini, 'Immunità dalla giurisdizione e Regolamento (CE) 44/2001: riflessioni a partire dalla sentenza *Mahamdia*' (2012) 95 *Rivista di diritto internazionale* 1089, 1101. On this principle, see F Casolari, *L'incorporazione del diritto internazionale nell'ordinamento dell'Unione europea* (Milan, Giuffrè, 2008) 260–71.

limiting the autonomy of parties to an employment contract to determine the courts having jurisdiction were held to apply to employment contracts with foreign states.[402] All this, in essence, restates that state immunity and provisions such as Article 11(2)(f) UNCSI operate at different levels: the effects envisioned by these provisions can only occur if the proceedings are not barred by immunity.

The main reason why contract terms conferring exclusive jurisdiction to the employer state are often treated as determinants of immunity may be explained by the impact of Article 5 ECSI on subsequent state practice. But this is not only the case with domestic instruments, such as the UK SIA, that were drafted under the ECSI's direct influence; the same goes for Article 11(2)(f) UNCSI, which constitutes one of the few remnants of the earliest draft article on contracts of employment (then Article 13) proposed by Special Rapporteur Sucharitkul in his 1983 Report to the ILC.[403] Draft Article 13 was generally identical to Article 5 ECSI, save for an additional ground of immunity based on subject matter.[404] Unlike the other provisions of Draft Article 13 reproducing Article 5, which were all heavily amended at later stages, the one currently included in paragraph 2(f) went unscathed through the drafting process. This was, however, an inappropriate drafting choice by the ILC. The inclusion into the ECSI of a similar provision could be explained by the ECSI being generally aimed at setting forth both immunity rules and jurisdictional links.[405] Paragraph 2(f), by contrast, does not blend well with the previous five subparagraphs of Article 11(2), all of which exclusively encompass proper grounds of immunity.

A different matter entirely is the legal value of contract clauses conferring jurisdiction upon courts of states other than the employer state. These clauses directly affect the scope of immunity insofar as they can be construed as waivers of immunity from proceedings before the courts of the chosen state. It is widely accepted that submitting to the forum state's jurisdiction through prior written agreement amounts to express waiver of immunity: Article 7(1)(b) UNCSI, for instance, stipulates that a state may consent 'to the exercise of jurisdiction … in a written contract'.[406] An example of application of these principles in employment matters is the 1987 *Schiavetti Magnani* case. The plaintiff was a journalist at the Rome office of the Bavarian public broadcasting network. She sued for discrimination and unfair downgrading, and requested reinstatement to her previous functions. The Court of Cassation affirmed jurisdiction on the grounds that the contract expressly designated an Italian court as the forum for claims arising from

[402] *Mahamdia* (n 81) paras 58–66.

[403] Sucharitkul, 'Fifth Report' (n 28) para 62, Draft Art 13(2)(d).

[404] Above s II.

[405] See ch 2, s IVA.

[406] See generally C Amirfar, 'Waivers of Jurisdictional Immunity' in Ruys and Angelet (n 23) 167, 169–74. See also s 2(2) UK SIA; s 4(2) Singapore SIA; s 4(2) Malawi IPA; s 3(2) South Africa FSIA; s 10(2) Australia FSIA; Art 2(a) Law No 24.488 (1995) (Argentina); Act on Civil Jurisdiction over Foreign States (2010) (Japan), Art 5(1)(ii); Art 5(b) Law No 16 (2015) (Spain); Art 5(1)(2) Law No 297-FZ (2015) (Russia).

the employment relationship: such clause was held to supersede any immunity enjoyed by the respondent.[407] In its commentary to the 1991 Draft Articles, the ILC cited *Schiavetti Magnani* as a case that would be covered by Article 7(1)(b).[408]

Curiously, more recent decisions of the Cassazione have refused to interpret contractual submissions to the Italian jurisdiction as waivers. In *De la Grana*, the employee sought to defeat Spain's immunity by invoking, inter alia, an employment contract clause which read: 'Ambas partes para dirimor lo conflictos que se puedan originar en la interpretación del siguiente contrato, se someten de mutuo acuerdo a la jurisdicción de los Juzgados y Tribunales de Italia'.[409] The court upheld immunity. It asserted that, under Article 11(2)(f) UNCSI, a prior agreement between the parties may only derogate from the forum state's jurisdiction and never decrease the scope of immunity (what the court termed 'inverse' derogation).[410] It is, however, a serious mishandling of the UNCSI to interpret Article 11 in isolation from the rest of the treaty. Article 11 does not set forth a self-contained regime of immunity in labour disputes: other provisions of the Convention regulating general aspects of immunity law remain fully applicable. In light of Article 7 UNCSI, the court should have treated the contract clauses in question as submissions of the foreign state to the Italian courts' jurisdiction. Furthermore, the court's allegation that party autonomy is unlimited when it comes to derogations from Italian jurisdiction is in direct breach of EU law as interpreted in *Mahamdia*. It is, ironically, also in breach of Article 11(2)(f) itself, which makes the legality of such derogations conditional on their compatibility with the forum state's legislation.

It is a matter of contract interpretation whether the employer state should be regarded as having waived its immunity in full or only with regard to certain aspects of the employment relationship. Again, the Court of Cassation in *De la Grana* opined that, were 'inverse derogations' admissible under Article 11(2)(f), the contract clause in question – which purely concerned disputes over contract 'interpretation' – would not have granted Italian courts the power to adjudicate claims for reinstatement in employment.[411] In this respect, the judgment is more defensible. A foreign state's waiver of immunity from legal process has no bearing on its (substantive) right under the VCDR and VCCR to freely appoint the staff of diplomatic and consular missions.[412] As seen earlier, the rationale for immunising foreign states from claims for recruitment or reinstatement is precisely to preserve

[407] *Bayerischer Rundfunk v Schiavetti Magnani* 12 January 1987, No 110, 87 ILR 38, 40–41.

[408] 1991 Draft Articles (n 222) 27, note 75. The employer state may also waive immunity after commencement of proceedings, either expressly (Art 7(1)(c) UNCSI) or impliedly, by intervening in the proceedings and defending on the merits (Art 8 UNCSI): see, eg *Sidhwa* (n 171); *Ashraf-Hassan v Embassy of France in the United States* Civil Action No 11-805 (JEB) (DDC 2012) 4.

[409] *De la Grana* (n 33) ILDC para 26 ('Both parties, in order to resolve disputes that may arise in the interpretation of the following contract, submit themselves by mutual agreement to the jurisdiction of the courts and tribunals of Italy').

[410] ibid ILDC para 28. Similarly, see *Escudero García* (n 248) ILDC para 8.

[411] *De la Grana* (n 33) ILDC para 29.

[412] Art 7 VCDR; Art 19(1) VCCR.

their freedom of appointment of staff.[413] Thus, at least with regard to employment at establishments to which the VCDR and VCCR apply, it is reasonable that a generic waiver of immunity should not affect such freedom of the employer state, but that a waiver of this portion of immunity should be specific and unequivocal.

Also broadly accepted is the principle that the choice of the forum state's law as the law governing the employment contract does not amount to a waiver of immunity. Most instruments, including the UNCSI, clearly stipulate that choice-of-law clauses may never be construed as submissions to jurisdiction.[414] The reverse should also be true – that is, a choice of the law of the employer state should not be construed as a derogation from the forum state's jurisdiction.[415] This is nothing but a corollary of the conceptual separation between jurisdiction and substantive law:[416] the court of the country where the work is performed may well apply the laws of the employer state, to the extent that this is possible under its private international law rules (notably in terms of compatibility with public policy).[417]

VIII. Restrictive State Immunity in Employment Matters under Customary International Law

The wide variety of approaches to restrictive state immunity in labour matters that can be found in national and international practice begs the question of what is the current status of customary international law in this field – that is, to what extent the exercise of jurisdiction over employment claims should be considered as barred by general international law.

This issue is a matter of scholarly discussion. It is often contended that practice is too diverse to distil any common ground, so that no customary rules would exist in this field for want of the necessary degree of uniformity in the elements of custom, ie *usus* and *opinio*.[418] For example, Advocate General Mengozzi argued in *Mahamdia* that, when it comes to labour claims against foreign states, 'national differences are so pronounced that [they] may even cast doubt on the actual

[413] See further above s VI.

[414] Art 7(2) UNCSI. In domestic instruments, see, eg s 2(2) UK SIA; Act on Civil Jurisdiction over Foreign States (2010) (Japan), Art 5(2). See also Italy, Court of Cassation, *Lakomy v Forza multinazionale e osservatori – MFO* 3 August 2000, No 531. cp *Re Canada Labour Code* (n 366) 271, quoting a Canada Labour Relations Board decision holding that choice-of-law clauses may 'at most' amount to implied waivers of immunity.

[415] *Republic of Italy (Minister of Foreign Affairs and International Cooperation – Adelaide Consulate) v Benvenuto* [2018] FCAFC 64, para 63, rejecting Italy's argument that, although the employees' contracts did not include a forum selection clause, a choice of Italian courts was implicit in the choice of Italian legislation as the law governing the contracts: 'There is no reason to suppose that the [Australian courts] could not, on proper evidence, determine the parties' entitlements by reference to the law of Italy, if that was applicable.'

[416] For a more in-depth discussion see ch 2, s II.

[417] *Benvenuto* (n 415) para 63.

[418] Statute of the International Court of Justice 1945, Art 38(1)(b), defining international custom as 'evidence of a general practice accepted as law'.

existence of a rule of customary international law in this regard'.[419] However, such a view should not be accepted uncritically for two main reasons. First, it appears too hasty to postulate a lack of customary norms by generically referencing the variety of domestic approaches. State practice is riddled with inconsistencies in many areas of state immunity, but this does not prevent consideration of state immunity as an undisputed rule of customary law – it simply makes it more cumbersome to ascertain the content of such a rule.[420] Secondly, the implications of a lack of customary norms in this field would be perplexing. Because – as seen in chapter two – the jurisdiction of the territorial state applies by default unless the existence of a rule requiring to grant immunity is proven,[421] this would mean that general international law poses no limits to entertaining jurisdiction over staff disputes with states. Yet, at least prima facie, this would be difficult to reconcile with existing state practice. If there is one thing virtually all instruments and judicial decisions seem to agree on, it is a conviction that *some* immunity should be granted to employer states.

The ILC works and the UNCSI may be used as a starting point for the present analysis. As seen earlier in the chapter, in a consistent line of cases starting with *Cudak*, the ECtHR has affirmed that Article 11 UNCSI constitutes in its entirety a codification of customary law.[422] The same conclusion has been reached by courts in, inter alia, France, India, Italy and the Netherlands.[423] It is remarkable that none of these courts have conducted any meaningful survey of state practice.[424] For instance, the only state practice actually examined in *Cudak* was the legislation and case law of Lithuania.[425] As for the practice of other countries, the ECtHR merely noted that 'there were no particular objections by States to the wording of [Draft] Article 11'.[426] Instead, the main argument invoked by the court in support of the codificatory character of Article 11 was a passage of the ILC commentary to the 1991 Draft Articles where it was stated that Draft Article 11 'appear[ed] to be consistent with the emerging trend in the recent legislative and treaty practice of a growing number of States'.[427] The court interpreted this passage as implying that Draft Article 11 was meant to codify existing state practice,[428] and affirmed

[419] Opinion of Advocate General Mengozzi, Case No C-154/11 *Mahamdia v Algeria* 24 May 2012, para 24. See also Yang (n 3) 197: 'It is impossible to make any generalization out of current State practice, much less to distil any uniform rule'; EK Bankas, *The State Immunity Controversy in International Law. Private Suits Against Sovereign States in Domestic Courts* (Berlin, Springer, 2005) 352, describing the current state of the law as 'far from clear'.

[420] See further ch 2, s IV.

[421] ch 2, s IVB.

[422] *Cudak* (n 32) para 67.

[423] *B v Ghana* (n 34); *Shyam Lal* (n 35); *De la Grana* (n 33); *Morocco v X* (n 36). See also *Borrisow* (n 281) ILDC paras 25–26, relying on the UNCSI as evidence of the state of customary law.

[424] See, eg *Shyam Lal* (n 35) para 6, relying on an affidavit filed by the Union of India; *De la Grana* (n 33) ILDC para 21, relying on the ECtHR judgment in *Guadagnino* (n 236).

[425] *Cudak* (n 32) paras 19–24.

[426] ibid para 66.

[427] 1991 Draft Articles (n 222) 44.

[428] *Cudak* (n 32) paras 66–67.

that what the Commission said with regard to Draft Article 11 'must also hold true for the 2004 United Nations Convention'.[429] The ECtHR also noted, as a side note, that no objections to Draft Article 11 and the UNCSI were voiced 'at least' by the respondent state.[430] But this passage, which has been interpreted as an implicit reference to the persistent objector doctrine,[431] is baffling to say the least. Even assuming that the status of persistent objector can actually shield a state from a customary norm, which is debated,[432] this only applies where the opposition is consistently maintained during the formation of said norm.[433] If Article 11 really codified pre-existing custom, as the ECtHR opined, an opposition towards that provision alone should not exempt the opposing state from the underlying customary rule.[434]

Aside from this last issue, the most relevant aspect of the *Cudak* jurisprudence in matters of custom ascertainment lies in the relevance given to the works of the Commission. The ECtHR is far from isolated in its reliance on ILC works or codification conventions for determining the content of customary law.[435] On multiple occasions, the International Court of Justice (ICJ) has considered provisions of such instruments to embody customary norms without conducting an autonomous evaluation of state practice, most notably with respect to the Vienna Convention on the Law of Treaties[436] and the Articles on the Responsibility of States for Internationally Wrongful Acts.[437] This practice may be justified as a way for a court to 'outsource' the ascertainment of customary law to the ILC, which is institutionally better positioned than a court to perform extensive surveys of state practice.[438] However, it is only possible to speak of 'outsourcing' if the ILC did conduct such a survey of state practice in the first place and if it did intend a certain provision to be reflective of such practice.[439] There can be no guarantee that every product of ILC works meets similar standards. The Commission's goals comprise not only the codification of customary law, but also its progressive development[440] – meaning that the ILC might intend a certain provision *not* to reflect state practice

[429] ibid para 66.

[430] ibid. Similarly, see *Sabeh El Leil* (n 232) para 57, re French practice.

[431] Garnett, 'State and Diplomatic Immunity' (n 226) 795.

[432] See generally P Dumberry, 'Incoherent and Ineffective: The Concept of Persistent Objector Revisited' (2010) 59 *ICLQ* 779.

[433] *Fisheries Case (United Kingdom v Norway)* Judgment [1951] ICJ Rep 116, 131.

[434] See also Pavoni, 'The Myth' (n 268) 270–71.

[435] M Iovane, 'L'influence de la multiplication des juridictions internationales sur l'application du droit international' (2017) 383 *Recueil des cours* 233, 394–97.

[436] eg *Oil Platforms (Islamic Republic of Iran v United States of America)* Judgment (Preliminary Objections) [1996] ICJ Rep 803, para 23, re Art 31.

[437] See, eg *Armed Activities on the Territory of the Congo (Democratic Republic of the Congo v Uganda)* Judgment [2005] ICJ Rep 168, para 160, re Arts 4, 5 and 8.

[438] FL Bordin, 'Reflections of Customary International Law: The Authority of Codification Conventions and ILC Draft Articles in International Law' (2014) 63 *ICLQ* 535, 549–58.

[439] M Wood, 'Third Report on Identification of Customary International Law', UN Doc A/CN.4/682 (27 March 2015) 45, para 65.

[440] Art 1(1) ILC Statute. See also Art 13(1)(a) UN Charter.

if this contributes to the progress of general international law. Moreover, states may be heavily involved in the drafting of a convention's provision, which may thus be reflective less of existing state practice and more of political compromise. An analysis of ILC works often provides sufficient indications of whether a provision was intended to codify custom. For example, in *North Sea Continental Shelf*, the ICJ excluded that Article 6 of the 1958 Geneva Convention on the Continental Shelf embodied customary principles by affirming that:

> The status of the rule in the Convention … depends mainly on the processes that led the Commission to propose it. [Article 6] was proposed by the Commission with considerable hesitation, somewhat on an experimental basis, at most *de lege ferenda*, and not at all *de lege lata*.[441]

In light of the above, what is most problematic about *Cudak* is not the ECtHR's reliance on ILC works per se, but the fact that – contrary to what the Court opined – the ILC has never remotely suggested that Article 11 was intended to reflect existing state practice in its entirety. In fact, this provision was one of the most hotly debated during the ILC works on state immunity.[442] Special Rapporteur Sucharitkul wrote in his 1983 Report that state practice was 'relatively silent on contracts of employment as a possible area of exceptions to State immunity'[443] and that the limited practice available at the time presented a 'startling number of inconsistencies and contradictions'.[444] There can thus be no doubt that Sucharitkul's Draft Article 13 – the precursor of Article 11 UNCSI – was mostly an exercise in progressive development. As noted above, the original contours of this provision drew heavily from Article 5 ECSI.[445] The state practice cited by the Special Rapporteur was limited: it boiled down to a handful of state immunity instruments of countries of common law (themselves modelled on Article 5 ECSI, like the UK SIA) and to Italian and French judicial precedents.[446] The provision was then subject to extensive changes during the drafting process, but the works of the ILC and the two Ad Hoc Working Groups do not necessarily support the view that such changes were aimed at better reflecting state practice. For example, when the provision now included in Article 11(2)(a) UNCSI – barring claims by employees performing tasks *de jure imperii* – was added to the text of Draft Article 11,[447] the only practice cited to motivate the addition were three decisions of the Italian Court of Cassation.[448] Other additions – such as Article 11(2)(d) UNCSI – were not accounted for at all.[449]

[441] *North Sea Continental Shelf (Federal Republic of Germany/Denmark; Federal Republic of Germany/Netherlands)* Judgment [1969] ICJ Rep 3, para 62.
[442] Foakes and O'Keefe (n 94) 189.
[443] Sucharitkul, 'Fifth Report' (n 28) para 59.
[444] ibid para 39.
[445] See above s II.
[446] Sucharitkul, 'Fifth Report' (n 28) paras 42–54.
[447] See further above s IVC.
[448] 1991 Draft Articles (n 222) para 10.
[449] See above s VIB.

In sum, all of Article 11's drafting process reflected difficult compromises and considerable second-guessing.[450] This trait, which is shared by many other UNCSI provisions,[451] entails that the correspondence of the Convention with customary law should not be taken for granted.[452] This was acknowledged by the ICJ in *Jurisdictional Immunities* with regard to Article 19 UNCSI: it noted that 'When the [UNCSI] was being drafted, these provisions gave rise to long and difficult discussions', and considered it unnecessary to decide whether all aspects of Article 19 reflected international custom.[453]

Looking back at the ILC commentary's passage quoted in *Cudak*, it is clear that the Commission was much more cautious than the ECtHR suggested: not only did it refer to *emerging* rather than existing state practice, but it also pointed to an *increasing* (though unspecified) number of states. This is a far cry from saying that state practice had already reached the threshold for the existence of custom. Indeed, when the ILC actually believed a certain portion of Draft Article 11 to be reflective of existing state practice, it said so expressly: for instance, Draft Article 11(2)(b) – the precursor of Article 11(2)(c) UNCSI, barring claims for recruitment, renewal and reinstatement – was described as 'designed to confirm the existing practice of states'.[454] Finally, even assuming that the Commission really meant to say that Draft Article 11 was entirely codificatory, this assessment may hardly extend to Article 11 UNCSI, considering that the two versions differ in significant respects. It is therefore reasonable to affirm, as the Court of Appeal did in *Benkharbouche*, that 'it is questionable whether Article 11 of the ILC Draft Articles … or Article 11 of the UN Convention … can be taken to be a definitive statement of the extent of State immunity required by international law' in employment disputes.[455]

All of the above is not to say, of course, that Article 11 UNCSI is entirely inconsistent with custom. Specific provisions of it may well reflect existing state practice. Furthermore, a codification convention may itself exert an influence on subsequent state practice, thus contributing to the crystallisation of a rule which was already *in statu nascendi* or to the emergence of a new customary rule.[456] From this

[450] Pavoni, 'The Myth' (n 268) 277.

[451] DP Stewart, 'The UN Convention on Jurisdictional Immunities of States and Their Property' (2005) 99 *American Journal of International Law* 194, 210.

[452] R van Alebeek, 'Part III: Proceedings in Which State Immunity Cannot Be Invoked' in O'Keefe and Tams (n 94) 153, 163: 'the broad contours of Part III of the Convention reflect customary international law … The real question, however, is whether the precise formulation of each provision is also consonant with custom. To this the answer is at present very likely to be no.' See also Supreme Court, *Benkharbouche* (n 24) para 32: 'it is not to be assumed that every part of the Convention restates customary international law'; Sweden, Svea Court of Appeal, *Republic of Kazakhstan v Ascom Group SA et al* 17 June 2020, Case No ÖÄ 7709-19, para 20: 'since the convention … in several respects constitutes a compromise between the views of different states, each separate provision cannot without further consideration be accepted as applicable customary law'.

[453] *Jurisdictional Immunities of the State (Germany v Italy: Greece intervening)* Judgment [2012] ICJ Rep 99, para 117.

[454] 1991 Draft Articles (n 222) para 10.

[455] *Benkharbouche and Janah* (n 91) para 30.

[456] Wood (n 439) paras 38–39; *North Sea Continental Shelf* (n 441) Dissenting Opinion of Judge Sørensen, 244.

standpoint, the very fact that a number of national and international courts have applied Article 11 qua custom shows that this provision's impact on state practice is already palpable.[457] Yet, for the reasons detailed above, Article 11 may not constitute the only source for ascertaining the state of custom. It is only a survey of state practice and *opinio juris* that can illuminate the relationship between Article 11 and customary law. This analysis should be directed at verifying whether there are categories of employment-related proceedings upon which, by sufficiently general agreement, the territorial state is obliged to refrain from exercising jurisdiction.

As regards the selection of relevant sources of state practice and *opinio*, one may follow the script laid down by the ICJ in *Jurisdictional Immunities*. The court held that national judicial decisions constitute 'the most pertinent state practice' in state immunity matters.[458] Other sources of state practice are national statutes concerning immunities, claims to immunity advanced by impleaded states before foreign courts and the opinions voiced by states in the course of the ILC work on state immunity and with respect to the UNCSI.[459] *Opinio*, for its part, may be drawn from

> the assertion by States claiming immunity that international law accords them a right to such immunity … the acknowledgment, by States granting immunity, that international law imposes upon them an obligation to do so; and … the assertion by States in other cases of a right to exercise jurisdiction over foreign States.[460]

Also relevant is the voicing of protests *ex post facto* by respondent states whose pleas of immunity are rejected: the lack of protests, in particular, may be evidence of an *opinio* that jurisdiction over such claims is admissible.[461]

Revisiting the domestic practice surveyed in previous sections of this chapter, it is possible to point to two key areas where a high degree of uniformity can be observed. The first such area is that of employment claims filed by individuals having diplomatic or consular rank and military personnel, a category which may be extended to include top civilian officials in matters of defence, intelligence and security.[462] The second such area is that of non-monetary claims by which an employee requests appointment, promotion or reinstatement,[463] to which collective claims aiming at causing changes into the state's general employment policies

[457] On the possible contribution of Art 11 to the development of the law of state immunity, see further P Rossi, 'Controversie di lavoro e immunità degli Stati esteri: tra codificazione e sviluppo del diritto consuetudinario' (2019) 102 *Rivista di diritto internazionale* 5.

[458] *Jurisdictional Immunities* (n 453) para 73.

[459] ibid para 55. See also S Sucharitkul, 'Developments and Prospects of the Doctrine of State Immunity: Some Aspects of Codification and Progressive Development' (1982) 29 *Netherlands International Law Review* 252, 260, listing as relevant practice national case law, the practice of the executives, domestic legislation, and bilateral and multilateral treaties.

[460] *Jurisdictional Immunities* (n 453) para 55.

[461] GM Badr, *State Immunity: An Analytical and Prognostic View* (The Hague, Martinus Nijhoff, 1984) 33–34.

[462] Above s IVB.

[463] Above s VIA.

may be equated.[464] There can be little doubt that any exercise of jurisdiction over such claims would be inadmissible as a matter of general international law. Indeed, there is little to no sign of jurisdiction ever being entertained over similar proceedings. In rare cases where jurisdiction has been exercised, there is evidence of protests by the respondent state.[465] This is remarkable in that, in labour disputes at large, there is generally no evidence of foreign states protesting *ex post facto* against the territorial state's exercise of jurisdiction, even if such states did plead immunity *in limine litis*.

Doubts may arise as to the consonance with customary law of the 'functions test', ie the approach upholding immunity if the plaintiff employee is found to perform functions *de jure imperii*. The popularity of this test in judicial practice might appear to make it a good candidate for a customary rule,[466] and the view that international custom requires differentiation according to the employees' functions has indeed been expressed in scholarship and case law.[467] Reliance on this test would actually seem to be increasing in state practice, especially as a consequence of the combined influence of Article 11 UNCSI and the ECtHR's jurisprudence.[468] However, for as much as this test is relatively widespread, there is little agreement among courts as to which claims should be barred because of the sovereign/public character of the employee's duties.[469] As just mentioned, the only point over which there is agreement is that claims by diplomatic, consular and military personnel should fall outside the scope of local jurisdiction. But this is an evaluation based on status rather than functions – that is, it is not based on an *individual* assessment of the tasks performed by a given employee. By contrast, for claims by service, technical and administrative staff, the diversity of state practice indicates that jurisdiction over such claims is permissible irrespective of the individual duties of the plaintiff employee.

This conclusion is unequivocal at least when it comes to proceedings involving service staff. In the vast majority of countries where relevant jurisprudence has developed, domestic courts routinely adjudicate such claims.[470] Hence, state practice certainly does not support any bar on jurisdiction over them. This point was cogently restated by the UK Supreme Court in *Benkharbouche*. The Secretary of State had submitted that a rule of customary law barred the exercise of jurisdiction over proceedings brought by all embassy staff, including the service staff (as the two plaintiffs were).[471] This argument was not accepted by the court. An

[464] Above s VIB.
[465] Above s VIA.
[466] On the diffusion of the 'functions test', see above s IVA.
[467] See, eg Garnett, 'State and Diplomatic Immunity' (n 226) especially 796; *Mahamdia* (n 81) paras 56–57.
[468] Above s IVC.
[469] Above s IVC.
[470] Above s IVB.
[471] Supreme Court, *Benkharbouche* (n 24) para 70.

analysis of available domestic case law showed, in the Supreme Court's view, that decisions upholding immunity over claims by the service staff were 'occasional' and that it was 'clear beyond argument is that there is no international consensus on this point sufficient to found a rule of customary international law' preventing the exercise of jurisdiction over the two plaintiffs' claims.[472]

Although *Benkharbouche* was only concerned with service staff, similar considerations may apply to the technical and administrative personnel. Domestic practice regarding such proceedings is particularly diverse. In a minority of countries, these claims are entirely barred; in others, they are entirely amenable to jurisdiction. Yet other courts differentiate among technical and administrative employees according to inconsistent judicial tests.[473] According to available records, in no case has the assumption of jurisdiction over similar claims attracted protests from respondent states. Quite evidently, in this case too there is no convergent state practice or *opinio juris* in the sense that these claims should be barred by immunity, in whole or in part. General international law therefore would seem to pose no obstacles to jurisdiction over claims by technical and administrative staff, nor would it seem to require courts to operate a distinction according to an individual employee's functions.

The same holds true with regard to differentiations based on nationality or residence. Although it retains paramount importance in Article 5 ECSI and in the domestic statutes directly inspired by it, this test's relevance in municipal case law is receding.[474] In most countries, jurisdiction over claims by nationals of third states or the employer state is routinely exercised without any discussion of their residency status, where other relevant criteria for the exercise of jurisdiction are met. Many courts do not even mention the employee's nationality among the relevant factors in immunity determinations.[475] Again, the UK Supreme Court persuasively noted in *Benkharbouche* that a 'considerable body of comparative law material … suggests that unless constrained by a statutory rule the general practice of states is to apply [restrictive immunity] irrespective of the nationality or residence of the claimant'.[476]

The above discussion shows that Article 11 UNCSI reflects the current development of the customary law of state immunity only in part.[477] Article 11(2)(c), barring proceedings whose subject matter is 'recruitment, renewal of employment or reinstatement', certainly mirrors well-established state practice. So does

[472] ibid para 73.

[473] See above s IVB.

[474] Above s II.

[475] Above s V.

[476] Supreme Court, *Benkharbouche* (n 24) para 66. But see *Buttet* (n 241) para 114, holding that Art 11(2)(e) UNCSI represents customary international law.

[477] See also P Franzina, 'L'immunità giurisdizionale degli Stati rispetto alle controversie di lavoro, fra equo processo e diritto internazionale generale: il caso Guadagnino' (2011) 10 *Int'l Lis: supplemento di documentazione e discussione sul diritto giudiziario transnazionale* 81.

Article 11(2)(b)(i), (ii) and (iii), preventing jurisdiction over claims by persons having diplomatic and consular rank. Article 11(2)(b)(iv), barring jurisdiction over claims by 'any other person enjoying diplomatic immunity', may be regarded as declaratory of existing customary law only if construed (as was suggested in section IVC) as referring exclusively to persons enjoying the full range of diplomatic immunities. In *Benkharbouche*, the Supreme Court espoused a different interpretation whereby subparagraph 2(b)(iv) would encompass individuals enjoying any amount of diplomatic immunity, including members of the service staff; so interpreted, this provision was rightly held to be inconsistent with international custom.[478] As for Article 11(2)(a), which enshrines the test based on the employee's functions, this provision may be deemed to reflect custom only if interpreted (again, as suggested in section IVC) as only barring claims by military personnel and high-ranking officials involved in matters of defence and security – ie personnel, other than diplomatic and consular agents, whose employment claims are generally considered not amenable to jurisdiction. Should Article 11(2)(a) be interpreted so as to require immunity over (part of the) claims by service, administrative or technical staff, this provision would not be reflective of general international norms. Article 11(2)(d) and 11(2)(e) do not seem to reflect sufficiently general state practice. As to paragraph 2(f), affirming immunity where 'the employer State and the employee have [so] agreed in writing' to the extent that this is allowed by the forum state's legislation, it was seen earlier in the chapter that this provision has no bearing on the scope of immunity required under international law and, in fact, does not concern immunity law at all.[479] On balance, Article 11 UNCSI can thus be deemed to grant an immunity that in many respects is broader than required by customary law.

IX. Conclusions

In conclusion of this analysis, it may be natural to wonder how one should conceptualise the relationship between the employment-specific immunity tests and the time-honoured distinction between *acta jure imperii* and *acta jure gestionis*. Some scholars have described such criteria as a way of *adapting* the distinction to the peculiarities of employment – or, to put it differently, as tools for classifying employment relationships as acts *jure imperii* or *jure gestionis*.[480] Others,

[478] Supreme Court, *Benkharbouche* (n 24) para 72: 'if article 11(2)(b)(iv) means what it says, it is legislative rather than declaratory of existing international law. It may one day bind states qua treaty. It may come to represent customary international law if and when the Convention attracts sufficient support. But it does not do either of these things as matters presently stand.'

[479] Above s VII.

[480] Sbolci (n 107) 181; Garnett, 'State Immunity in Employment Matters' (n 3) 83, contending that these criteria's function is to assess 'whether the foreign State, in entering into the contract of employment, is engaging in "private" or "sovereign" activity'.

by contrast, have treated such criteria as altogether alternative to the distinction between private and public acts.[481]

In fact, both camps have an element of truth on their side. On the one hand, some employment-specific criteria are quite evidently inspired by the 'private person test'. The 'workplace test', for example, reflects the idea that certain state entities should be regarded as inherently involved in sovereign (or private) activities, so that any work performed in them would be tainted with a sovereign (or private) character. The test based on status or functions, too, draws heavily from the distinction between acts *jure imperii* and *jure gestionis*, in that it distinguishes between employees according to whether their status or duties are considered to relate to the sovereign or private law functions of the foreign state.[482] On the other hand, factors like an employee's nationality or residence have little to do with any common-sense definition of what is a public or private state act. But the clearest evidence of the irreducibility of the employment-specific immunity criteria to the 'private person test' is provided by the criterion of the claim's subject matter. Such an approach obviously prescinds from any assessment of specific qualities of the underlying employment relationship, let alone its private or public nature. It may even lead to the drawing of a line between different claims relating to the same underlying act of the employer state: for instance, as has been seen, it is common for courts to exercise jurisdiction over claims for compensation for unfair dismissal while at the same time declining jurisdiction over claims for reinstatement.[483]

The attempts at describing the use of employment-specific criteria solely as an adjustment of the distinction between private and public acts betray the assumption that restrictive state immunity necessarily revolves around the distinction between *acta jure imperii* and *acta jure gestionis*: everything that can be subject to jurisdiction is labelled as an act *jure gestionis* and everything that cannot is an act *jure imperii*. Yet, this is an unfounded assumption for reasons set out in chapter two.[484] Employment litigation may therefore be regarded as a prime confirmation that, although the distinction between public and private acts still retains some centrality in the law of state immunity, restrictive state immunity *can* be grounded on different tests. More than just drawing lines between different types of state acts based on their supposedly private or public character, the prevailing approaches to state immunity in employment matters appear to be primarily aimed at barring jurisdiction over proceedings perceived as excessively intrusive into the foreign state's inner organisation, in accordance with a chiefly functional approach to state immunity.

[481] See, eg R van Alebeek, *The Immunity of States and Their Officials in International Criminal Law and International Human Rights Law* (Oxford, Oxford University Press, 2008) 56: 'immunity decisions in labour disputes … cannot be explained on the basis of a strict public–private *act* distinction'.

[482] M Nino, 'State Immunity from Civil Jurisdiction in Labor Disputes: Evolution in International and National Law and Practice' (2014) 50 *Rivista di diritto internazionale privato e processuale* 819, 834–35, describing the test based on the employee's functions as a restatement of the distinction between *acta jure imperii* and *acta jure gestionis*.

[483] See above s VI.

[484] ch 2, s IVB.

5

Limited Immunity Standards for Employers Other than the State

I. Introduction

The absolute immunity of international organisations (IOs) and diplomatic and consular agents in labour matters has proved much more resilient than that of states. The number of judicial decisions entertaining jurisdiction over such employers on grounds of limited immunity is thus comparatively small. Yet, as chapter three has demonstrated, it is also necessary to develop non-absolute immunity standards for employers other than the foreign state. This chapter aims to delineate such standards. It puts forward that it is possible to flesh out clear standards of limited immunity from staff claims against IOs and diplomatic and consular agents, and that restrictive state immunity may to some extent be relevant to this end *mutatis mutandis*.

The structure of the present chapter is as follows. Section II addresses the interpretation of non-absolute standards of IO immunity in labour matters. Section III discusses the scope of immunity in employment claims against diplomatic and consular agents. This section enquires when employment relationships with such agents may fall within the scope of their official acts; and, with specific regard to the immunity of diplomats *en poste*, whether the employment of private staff may be treated as a commercial, and thus non-immune, act of the agent in terms of Article 31 of the Vienna Convention on Diplomatic Relations (VCDR).

II. Limited Standards of International Organisation Immunity in Employment Matters

This section is concerned with the interpretation of two IO immunity standards commonly found in treaties and domestic instruments, ie 'restrictive' and 'functional' immunity. The former entitles an IO to immunity coextensive with that owed to foreign states, while the latter allows it as much immunity as is necessary for it to fulfil its purposes.[1] It will be recalled from chapter three that neither

[1] On the various standards of IO immunity see ch 2, s VIB.

standard may be construed as supporting blanket immunity from labour claims.[2] This requires the translatation of these clauses into workable standards of limited immunity for employment litigation.

Starting from the concept of restrictive IO immunity, the wording of the relevant provisions leaves little doubt that the law of state immunity should be the benchmark for the scope of IO immunity.[3] In its recent judgment in *Jam*, for example, the US Supreme Court held that section 2(b) of the International Organizations Immunities Act – granting designated IOs 'the same immunity from suit … as is enjoyed by foreign governments' – should, in accordance with its ordinary meaning, 'be understood to link the law of international organization immunity to the law of foreign sovereign immunity, so that the one develops in tandem with the other'.[4]

The applicability of state immunity rules to disputes involving IOs has often been brought into question. This argument goes that IOs, unlike states, are functional and not sovereign entities, so the concepts of sovereign and private acts are extraneous to the law of IOs.[5] According to Webb, this would find confirmation in the 'odd results' generated by the *jure imperii/jure gestionis* distinction whenever applied to IOs.[6] She has pointed, in particular, to the *Spaans* saga, where Dutch courts reached inconsistent conclusions on whether employment of a translator at the Iran–US Claims Tribunal should be classified as a public or private act.[7] But the fact that the distinction between public and private acts has proved unable to offer clear legal guidance in labour claims against IOs, as was the case in *Spaans*, is by no means conclusive proof that principles of state immunity law are generally inapplicable to IO employers. It is not the application of that distinction to employment disputes with IOs that is problematic, but its application to employment disputes *tout court*: in fact, this test is just as unworkable in the realm of state immunity.[8] This is precisely the reason why, as seen in chapter four, applying

[2] See particularly ch 3, ss III and IV.

[3] A Reinisch and J Wurm, 'International Financial Institutions before National Courts' in DD Bradlow and DB Hunter (eds), *International Finance Institutions and International Law* (Alphen aan den Rijn, Wolters Kluwer, 2010) 103, 115, re US International Organizations Immunities Act 1945, s 2(b).

[4] *Jam et al v International Finance Corp* 586 US (2019), 9–11, relying on a textual canon of statutory construction as well as the so-called 'reference canon', whereby 'when a statute refers to a general subject, the statute adopts the law on that subject as it exists whenever a question under the statute arises'.

[5] CF Amerasinghe, *Principles of the Institutional Law of International Organizations*, 2nd edn (Cambridge, Cambridge University Press, 2005) 322; P Webb, 'Should the 2004 UN State Immunity Convention Serve as a Model/Starting Point for a Future UN Convention on the Immunity of International Organizations?' (2013) 10 *International Organizations Law Review* 319, 323; H Fox and P Webb, *The Law of State Immunity*, 3rd edn (Oxford, Oxford University Press, 2013) 581–82 and 586.

[6] Webb (n 5) 323.

[7] ibid 323–24, referring to The Hague Local Court, *AS v Iran-United States Claims Tribunal* 8 June 1983, (1984) 15 *Netherlands Yearbook of International Law* 429; The Hague District Court, *AS v Iran-United States Claims Tribunal* 9 July 1984, (1985) 16 *Netherlands Yearbook of International Law* 471; Hoge Raad, *Spaans v Iran–US Claims Tribunal* 20 December 1985, Case No 12627, ILDC 1759 (NL 1985).

[8] See ch 3, s IV.

restrictive state immunity to labour disputes has required the development of employment-specific immunity criteria that are only partly inspired by the *jure imperii/jure gestionis* dichotomy.

An argument has been made that even such employment-specific state immunity standards would be inapplicable to labour disputes with IOs. Again, Webb has contended that Article 11 of the UN Convention on State Immunity (UNCSI), on contracts of employment, cannot offer any guidance in matters of IO immunity because it is based on 'state-centric' notions, such as the performance of 'particular functions in the exercise of governmental authority', the 'interference with the security interests' of a state and whether the employee is a national of the employer state.[9] In her words:

> How do we translate these criteria to international organizations? Only a few organizations would have 'security interests' (such as NATO) or powers analogous to governmental authority (UN territorial administration). An international organization does not have a territory or a bond of nationality with its staff: it has no 'nationals'.[10]

But this argument is equally inconclusive. Because the UNCSI deals with state immunity, it is no wonder that Article 11 is worded so as to best suit state employers. This, however, does not imply that the employment-specific immunity criteria it codifies are all inapplicable to entities other than states. Some clauses of Article 11 do not rely on 'state-centric' concepts at all: for instance, the paragraph 2(c) immunity ground – the subject matter is 'recruitment, renewal of employment or reinstatement of an individual' – may apply without difficulty to any employers. As for nationality, there is no question that Article 11(2)(e) – pursuant to which a state is immune if 'the employee is a national of the employer State at the time when the proceeding is instituted', save for permanent residents of the forum state – may only apply to states, they being the only employers with their own nationals. Yet, not all nationality-based tests are intrinsically inapplicable to IOs. Nothing would theoretically prevent distinctions from being drawn based on whether the employee has the nationality or residence of the state where the work is performed.[11] Relying on state immunity precedents, for instance, a Venezuelan labour court in *Dorta* affirmed jurisdiction over a claim for social security benefits against the Food and Agriculture Organization on the grounds that the employee was a Venezuelan citizen.[12]

Italian judicial practice provides copious evidence that employment-specific approaches to state immunity can be applied to labour lawsuits against IOs. Italian courts have frequently relied on restrictive state immunity principles when

[9] Webb (n 5) 327.

[10] ibid.

[11] As in European Convention on State Immunity 1972 (ECSI), Art 5(2)(b): a state is immune if 'at the time when the contract was entered into the individual was neither a national of the State of the forum nor habitually resident in that State'.

[12] Tribunal Septimo de Primera Instancia de Juicio del Trabajo de Caracas, *Dorta v FAO* 27 June 2007, File No AP21-L-2006-003372. Note that Venezuela is not a party to the Convention on the Privileges and Immunities of the Specialized Agencies 1947.

adjudicating such disputes.[13] This jurisprudence has been based on a variety of legal grounds, including purported customary law norms on IO immunity,[14] Italy's reservations to certain constitutive instruments[15] or a restrictive construction of treaty clauses granting immunity 'from every form of legal process'.[16] Such legal grounds may not always have been sound (both the existence of customary norms on IO immunity and the possibility to construe full immunity clauses restrictively are questionable, for reasons more thoroughly discussed earlier in this book[17]), but this issue is beside the point here. What matters to the present discussion is that, in such cases, the scope of IO immunity in employment matters has been determined on the basis of tests developed in the context of labour litigation against states, and that their extension to IOs has not proved problematic.

Two criteria in particular have been employed by Italian judges to expound the concept of restrictive IO immunity, namely the functions performed by the employee and the claim's subject matter.[18] As to the former, it may be recalled from chapter four that Italian courts traditionally subscribed to a broad understanding of tasks *de jure imperii* and only affirmed jurisdiction over claims by workers performing 'manual or temporary duties … extraneous to the organization' of the state.[19] A consequence of this jurisprudence was that immunity shrouded claims not only by the technical and administrative staff, but even by parts of the service staff.[20] When applied to IOs, the 'functions test' required some nominal adjustment: the benchmark was whether the worker's duties were closely related to the performance of (not sovereign but) organisational functions.[21] But the outcomes were in all respects identical to those encountered in state immunity cases. In *Di Banella Schirone*, for instance, the Italian Court of Cassation (Cassazione) upheld immunity over a lawsuit by an Intergovernmental Committee for European Migration's employee performing secretarial duties. The court maintained that the plaintiff's work, although 'instrumental in character', was 'directly connected with the pursuit of that [IO's] institutional aims', but acknowledged that it would have set aside immunity had the employee been performing purely manual work or 'irregular or casual services'.[22] In *Cristiani*, the same principles led to decline

[13] *Ex multis* G Adinolfi, 'L'immunità delle organizzazioni internazionali dalla giurisdizione civile nella giurisprudenza italiana' (2007) 23 *Comunicazioni e studi* 233; F Schröer, 'De l'application de l'immunité juridictionnelle des Etats étrangers aux organisations internationales' (1971) 75 *Revue générale de droit international public* 712, 721–23.

[14] ch 2, s VA.

[15] ch 2, s VB.

[16] ch 3, s VI.

[17] ch 2, s VA; ch 3, s VI.

[18] BI Bonafè, 'Italian Courts and the Immunity of International Organizations' (2013) 10 *International Organizations Law Review* 505, 524–27.

[19] Court of Cassation, *Panattoni v Federal Republic of Germany* 15 July 1987, No 6172, 87 ILR 42, 46–47.

[20] See further ch 4, ss IVA and IVB.

[21] Bonafè (n 18) 525.

[22] *Intergovernmental Committee for European Migration (ICEM) v Di Banella Schirone* 8 April 1975, No 1266, 77 ILR 572, (1976) 2 *Italian Yearbook of International Law* 351, 353.

jurisdiction over claims by the former director of the audiovisual documentation centre of the Italo-Latin American Institute. His responsibilities were described as having a direct and immediate relationship to the organisation's cultural purposes as detailed in the constitutive instrument.[23] By contrast, the Cassazione considered the duties of a cleaning woman and an interpreter at the International Centre for Advanced Mediterranean Agronomic Studies (ICAMAS) to be unrelated to 'the decision-making process for implementing the institutional purposes' of the organisation.[24]

As regards the 'subject-matter test', too, Italian courts' decisions have conformed entirely to the approaches followed in state immunity cases, based on the assumption that immunity should bar claims that most directly impair an employer's freedom to choose and manage its own staff.[25] Thus, jurisdiction has been denied over claims for reinstatement, a relief deemed too intrusive into an IO's internal organisation.[26] Trade union claims challenging an organisation's 'anti-union behaviour' – ie employer behaviour limiting the exercise of trade union rights – have also been deemed impermissible. In *Sindacato UIL*, a trade union sought an order annulling the ICAMAS's decision to reorganise its management structure on the grounds that this decision allegedly infringed the union's rights under Italian legislation. The Court of Cassation, however, ruled that the annulment would have inevitably encroached upon the IO's internal organisation and upheld immunity.[27] Following in the footsteps of the *Toglia* decision on foreign state immunity,[28] the Cassazione held in *Chirico* that Italian courts could adjudicate claims for monetary compensation whatever the functions of the IO employee.[29] Some courts,

[23] Court of Cassation, *Cristiani v Istituto italo-latino-americano* 23 November 1985, No 5819, 87 ILR 20, (1986) 69 *Rivista di diritto internazionale* 147, 152. See also Court of Cassation, *Maida v Administration for International Assistance* 27 May 1955, 23 ILR 510, (1956) 39 *Rivista di diritto internazionale* 546, 548, re a doctor on contract with the International Refugee Organization; *Nacci v Bari Institute of the ICAMAS* 8 June 1994, No 5565, 114 ILR 540, (1994) 77 *Rivista di diritto internazionale* 838, 845, re the director of the ICAMAS Bari branch documentation centre; *Galasso v Istituto italo-latino-americano* 3 February 1986, No 667, (1987) 23 *Rivista di diritto internazionale privato e processuale* 827, re a library clerk.

[24] *ICAMAS v Perrini* 21 October 1977, No 4512, (1979) 102 *Foro italiano* 472, 476, re a cleaner; *Iasbez v ICAMAS* 21 October 1977, No 4502, (1978) 61 *Rivista di diritto internazionale* 577, 581, re an interpreter. But see Court of Cassation, *Paradiso v ICAMAS* 13 February 1991, No 1513, (1992) 28 *Rivista di diritto internazionale privato e processuale* 603, upholding immunity on an interpreter's claim.

[25] On which see further ch 4, s VIA.

[26] See, eg Court of Cassation, *Paradiso v Bari Institute of the ICAMAS* 4 June 1986, No 3733, (1987) 70 *Rivista di diritto internazionale* 190, re an attempt to enforce a lower court's provisional reinstatement order.

[27] *Sindacato UIL (Bari Branch) v Bari Institute of the ICAMAS* 4 June 1986, No 3732, 87 ILR 37, (1987) 70 *Rivista di diritto internazionale* 184, 190. See also Court of Cassation, *Camera Confederale del Lavoro CGIL and Another v Bari Institute of the ICAMAS* 27 April 1979, No 2425, 78 ILR 86. For decisions barring 'anti-union behaviour' claims against foreign states see ch 4, s VIB.

[28] Court of Cassation, *British Consulate-General in Naples v Toglia* 15 May 1989, No 2329, 101 ILR 380.

[29] *Chirico v Bari Institute of the ICAMAS* 21 November 1989, No 4968, (1991) 27 *Rivista di diritto internazionale privato e processuale* 490, re an interpreter. *cf* Tribunal of Bari, *Chirico v Bari Institute of the ICAMAS* 10 October 1985, 87 ILR 19, upholding immunity based on the plaintiff's functions.

however, carved out an exception for claims relating to the financial consequences of wrongful dismissals;[30] this followed, once again, state immunity precedents.[31]

As to the second standard of limited IO immunity, ie 'functional immunity', valid reasons suggest that this should also be construed by reference to employment-specific state immunity tests. The preferable interpretation of functional immunity requires differentiating between claims according to their effective ability to disrupt an IO's functions.[32] This begs the question of what types of employment proceedings should be barred under this non-interference rationale. In order to make this assessment, many commentators have proposed benchmarks entirely analogous to those devised by national courts in employment litigation against states, namely the claim's subject matter and the employee's status or functions.[33] Notably, it has been put forward that claims for monetary damages do not generally possess the ability to prevent IOs from functioning independently, while claims for injunctive relief would most certainly incur this risk.[34] Others have submitted that an IO's functioning would not be meaningfully affected by domestic proceedings involving workers 'who have not been accorded the status of agents',[35] primarily including members of the service staff.[36]

The idea of drawing inspiration from employment-specific state immunity criteria is a sensible one. The conditions are indeed present for importing these criteria into the law of IO immunity by way of analogical reasoning. As demonstrated by Bordin, analogy – defined as 'a form of systemic reasoning whereby existing rules are extended to novel situations with which they share a relevant similarity'[37] – is a feature of the international legal reasoning when dealing with situations of uncertainty,[38] and it can justify extending rules from states to IOs to the extent allowed by the structural differences between these legal persons.[39] In the present case, the 'relevant similarity' justifying recourse to analogy is that, as argued earlier in this book, the rationale of both state and IO immunity is to provide these entities

[30] *Nacci* (n 23).

[31] *Libyan Arab Jamahiriya v Trobbiani* 16 January 1990, No 145, 114 ILR 520.

[32] A Reinisch, *International Organizations before National Courts* (Cambridge, Cambridge University Press, 2000) 365–66. See ch 2, s VB.

[33] See, eg MF Orzan, 'International Organizations and Immunity from Legal Process: An Uncertain Evolution' in R Virzo and I Ingravallo (eds), *Evolutions in the Law of International Organizations* (Leiden, Brill Nijhoff, 2015) 364, 374: 'the nature of the claim has to be taken into account in deciding whether to grant immunity and, secondly, … the position held by the employee'.

[34] Reinisch (n 32) 365; A Orakhelashvili, 'Jurisdictional Immunity of International Organizations: From Abstract Functionality to Absolute Immunity' in A Orakhelashvili (ed), *Research Handbook on Jurisdiction and Immunities in International Law* (Cheltenham, Edward Elgar, 2015) 497, 502; K Cully, 'Jurisdictional Immunities of Intergovernmental Organizations' (1982) 91 *Yale Law Journal* 1167, 1179.

[35] E Gaillard and I Pingel-Lenuzza, 'International Organisations and Immunity from Jurisdiction: To Restrict or to Bypass' (2002) 51 *ICLQ* 1, 7.

[36] L Ferrari Bravo, 'Le controversie in materia d'impiego presso enti internazionali e la giurisdizione italiana' (1956) 39 *Rivista di diritto internazionale* 550, 564.

[37] FL Bordin, *The Analogy between States and International Organizations* (Cambridge, Cambridge University Press, 2019) 7.

[38] ibid 47–48.

[39] ibid 49–86 and 240–41.

with a quantum of autonomy for performing their functions.[40] Because both types of immunity rest of functional necessity grounds, applying state immunity standards is *ipso facto* a form of functional necessity analysis.[41] The employment-specific state immunity criteria reflect a delicate balancing between the exercise of territorial jurisdiction over employment relationships and an employer's freedom to manage its workforce. Considering that ad hoc criteria so specific have not been consolidated in the more meagre domestic case law on IO staff disputes, one may resort to the solutions devised in the more developed field of law.

The above should not be regarded as contradicting the argument, made in chapter two, that a generalised analogy between the immunities of states and IOs is unwarranted.[42] This section advances the narrower thesis that analogy should be employed to construe the specific standard of 'functional' IO immunity. Within these boundaries, the use of the analogical reasoning to fill lacunae or clarify ambiguities in immunity law reflects the methodology employed by the International Court of Justice (ICJ) in *Arrest Warrant*. The issue concerned the scope of immunity from criminal jurisdiction enjoyed by ministers of foreign affairs under customary international law. The court reasoned that immunities are conferred to foreign ministers 'to ensure the effective performance of their functions'.[43] It further observed that the legal position of foreign ministers is akin to that of heads of state or government, and is central to the conduct of diplomatic relations.[44] From this, the ICJ drew that ministers of foreign affairs require, for performing their functions, the same absolute immunity from criminal jurisdiction to which diplomats and heads of state or government are entitled.[45] *Arrest Warrant* was therefore decided on the basis of analogy, and this resulted from the immunities in question sharing the same functional rationale.[46]

Several municipal courts have construed IO employers' 'functional' immunity by recourse to employment-specific immunity tests ordinarily applied to foreign states. In *Spaans*, for example, the Dutch Supreme Court rejected the approach followed by the lower courts, which relied on the distinction between acts *jure imperii* and *jure gestionis*, and pronounced on the basis of a purported customary

[40] ch 2, s III. See also M Singer, 'Jurisdictional Immunity of International Organizations: Human Rights and Functional Necessity Concerns' (1995) 36 *Virginia Journal of International Law* 53, 65.

[41] C Ryngaert, 'The Immunity of International Organizations Before Domestic Courts: Recent Trends' (2010) 7 *International Organizations Law Review* 121, 127: 'the immunity exception in case of *acta jure gestionis* is based on their not being necessary for the performance of the State's sovereign functions'; Bonafè (n 18) 524, in the sense that the Italian courts' application of state immunity criteria in IO staff disputes 'derive[s] from a teleological interpretation of the functional necessity principle … identify[ing] … a set of core institutional activities that should be protected from external interference'.

[42] ch 2, s VA.

[43] *Case Concerning the Arrest Warrant of 11 April 2000* Judgment [2002] ICJ Rep 3, para 53.

[44] ibid.

[45] ibid para 54.

[46] Bordin (n 37) 18. See *Arrest Warrant* (n 43) Dissenting Opinion of Judge Ad Hoc Van den Wyngaert, para 14, criticising the majority because 'the Judgment … proceeds from a mere analogy with immunities for diplomatic agents and Heads of State'.

norm requiring functional immunity to be granted to IOs. This concept was interpreted as shielding the organisation from 'labor disputes which may arise [with] those in its service who play an essential role in the performance of [its] functions'.[47] 'Functional immunity' was thus construed by reference to the employees' tasks, ie the criterion traditionally employed by Dutch courts to flesh out restrictive state immunity in labour disputes.[48] The Supreme Court upheld immunity because it found this test to be met by the duties of the plaintiff, a Farsi interpreter.[49]

Other examples may be drawn from the Canadian *Amaratunga* case. The Northwest Atlantic Fisheries Organization (NAFO) was sued by a former senior official for compensation for unfair dismissal and payment of separation indemnity. The main legal issue boiled down to the interpretation of a domestic law provision entitling NAFO to privileges and immunities 'to such extent as may be required for the performance of its functions' – a typical functional immunity clause.[50] Despite reaching inconsistent conclusions, the trial court, the appellate court and the Supreme Court of Canada all relied on judicial tests which are also in use in employment litigation against foreign states, namely the employee's functions and the subject matter of the claim.

The first instance court rejected NAFO's contention that the provision in question immunised any act 'related to' its functions and espoused a plain-meaning reading of the term 'required' as 'necessary or essential'.[51] Upon this premise, the claim's subject matter played a key role against immunity. Because the plaintiff's claims were limited to monetary damages for breach of contract and he did 'not claim any right to interfere with the internal organization, management or governance' of his employer,[52] the court reasoned that it had 'not been made aware of any aspect of NAFO's official functions which would be significantly impeded by the imposition of an obligation to pay monetary entitlements to a former employee'.[53] The appellate court reversed, holding that functional immunity had to be construed more broadly as encompassing any immunity necessary to 'the preservation of the organization's autonomy to carry out its functions'.[54] It further stated that a labour lawsuit's capacity to encroach upon IO autonomy hinged primarily on the functions of the employee.[55] The tasks of the plaintiff, who was NAFO's Deputy Executive Secretary, were such that exercising jurisdiction would 'inevitably put NAFO's core operations under a microscope', affecting its autonomy.[56]

[47] *Spaans* (n 7) para 3.3.5.

[48] ch 4, s IVA.

[49] See T Henquet, 'The Jurisdictional Immunity of International Organizations in the Netherlands and the View from Strasbourg' (2013) 10 *International Organizations Law Review* 538, 543–44.

[50] Northwest Atlantic Fisheries Organization Privileges and Immunities Order 1980, s 3(1).

[51] *Amaratunga v Northwest Atlantic Fisheries Organization* 2010 NSSC 346, para 67.

[52] ibid para 69.

[53] ibid para 70. Also relevant was that the employee did not invoke Canada's employment legislation and that no 'sovereign, political or security elements' were present (para 69).

[54] *Northwest Atlantic Fisheries Organization v Amaratunga* 2011 NSCA 73, para 42.

[55] ibid: 'the closer an aggrieved employee's tasks come to the organization's core function, the more likely its autonomy will be affected and, therefore, the greater likelihood that immunity will be required'.

[56] ibid para 58.

The claim's subject matter was also given some relevance: the court affirmed that 'wrongful dismissal actions by their very nature represent critical exposés of the employer/employee relationship'.[57]

The final appeal judgment held, first, that Canadian legislation granted NAFO the immunity needed to be 'shielded from undue interference'; and secondly, that what constitutes undue interference should be established on a case-by-case basis.[58] In practice, the Supreme Court took an intermediate position between the lower courts' rulings and relied on a combination of the 'functions test' and the 'subject-matter test'. As regards the former, its reasoning did not differ much from the Court of Appeal's. The court stated:

> the appellant was the Deputy Executive Secretary of NAFO, the second-in-command in the Secretariat … That alone would be sufficient to conclude that immunity is required in this case in order for NAFO to perform its functions. NAFO must have the power to manage its employees, especially those in senior positions, if it is to perform its functions efficiently. To allow employment-related claims of senior officials to proceed in Canadian courts would constitute undue interference with NAFO's autonomy in performing its functions and would amount to submitting its managerial operations to the oversight of its host state's institutions.[59]

Interestingly, however, the Supreme Court held that the above rationales for immunity only applied to the official's claims relating to his allegedly unlawful dismissal (namely, the claims for salary in lieu of reasonable notice, general damages and punitive or aggravated damages) and not to the claim for separation indemnity: a distinction based on subject matter. The court wrote that to adjudicate claims for unfair dismissal would require it to 'pass judgment on NAFO's management of its employees. That … would constitute interference with NAFO's internal management, which goes directly to its autonomy'.[60] No interference, by contrast, would result from the separation indemnity proceedings because, according to NAFO's employment regulations, all departing employees should receive such indemnity: a court exercising jurisdiction over such claim would thus not be required to inquire into the reasons for termination.[61] Although the Supreme Court did not cite those precedents, its reasoning in *Amaratunga* was very similar to earlier Canadian judgments in matters of employment with foreign states. These precedents declined jurisdiction over the monetary consequences of wrongful dismissals on the grounds that doing so would 'necessarily have an impact on the right of the defendant state to decide how it manages and deals with its personnel'.[62] According to this jurisprudence, other types of monetary claims

[57] ibid para 57.
[58] *Amaratunga v Northwest Atlantic Fisheries Organization* 2013 SCC 66, paras 49 and 53.
[59] ibid para 57.
[60] ibid para 58.
[61] ibid para 65.
[62] *Greco v Holy See (State of the Vatican City)* [2000] OJ No 5293, para 6. Similarly, see *Bentley v Consulate General of Barbados/Invest Barbados* 2010 HRTO 2258. On these Canadian precedents see further ch 4, s VIA.

(eg a claim for severance pay) would not cause the same interference with the employer's internal organisation and may therefore be adjudicated on the merits.[63]

It should be noted that construing non-absolute IO immunity standards by reference to employment-specific criteria of restrictive state immunity – as is suggested here – may create a problem of consistency. The Italian, Dutch and Canadian judgments analysed above show that, whenever national courts have applied employment-specific immunity standards to IO staff disputes, they have by and large replicated the approaches to state immunity in use in their own jurisdiction. Because there is a great diversity of such criteria in domestic practice, organisations may risk being subject to differential treatment even in cases where the same immunity standard should apply. In order to increase consistency, it is advisable that the IO immunity clauses in question be construed in light of the content of the customary law of state immunity rather than the approach followed in a given domestic jurisdiction, which may well diverge from what international law requires. The content of Article 11 UNCSI should be equally immaterial, to the extent that this provision does not correspond to international custom.

As argued in chapter four, the customary law of state immunity in labour disputes articulates around two key factors: the claim's subject matter and the status of the employee. As to the former aspect, custom bars jurisdiction over non-monetary claims aimed at directly impinging into the internal organisation of the employer, eg by seeking an order for recruitment or reinstatement, or by requesting changes to its general employment policies.[64] The application of this criterion to IOs is straightforward, as demonstrated by the Italian case law discussed above. In this respect, the Canadian Supreme Court's interpretation of the 'subject-matter test' in *Amaratunga* may be subject to the same criticism levelled against the analogous Canadian precedents in state immunity matters. It is unclear why investigating the reasons for a dismissal for the sole purpose of awarding compensation would meddle with an employer's functions more than any other compensation claims: all other things being equal, paying compensation causes the same amount of hindrance to an employer whatever its legal reasons.[65] The Supreme Court's argument that the separation indemnity claim would be less intrusive of NAFO's functions being based on the IO staff rules and not on Canadian employment law is equally moot, because the question whether local courts have jurisdiction is unrelated to the applicable substantive law.[66] If the Supreme Court felt that Canadian law was inapplicable, or that applying it would have caused undue interference with NAFO's functions, nothing prevented it from adjudicating the merits of the unlawful dismissal claim under the contract terms and NAFO's administrative law.[67]

[63] *Lovell v New Zealand Tourism Board* 37 ACWS (3d) 930, 1992 CanLil 1502 (BCSC).

[64] ch 4, s VIII.

[65] See further ch 4, s VIA.

[66] See ch 2, s II.

[67] For examples of national courts applying IOs' internal staff rules, see ch 3, s IIA.

The Supreme Court's handling of the separation indemnity claim demonstrates that it was possible for the Canadian courts to apply NAFO's internal staff rules.[68]

As far as the status of the plaintiff employee is concerned, again in chapter four it was contended that customary law bars claims by state employees having diplomatic or consular rank, military personnel and possibly top civilian officials in matters of defence, intelligence and security. By contrast, there would seem to be no prohibition to assert jurisdiction over claims by the service, technical and administrative staff, irrespective of an employee's individual duties.[69] The application of this test to IOs is not particularly problematic either. Claims by IO employees performing menial, administrative or technical duties may be considered amenable to jurisdiction within the limits posed by the 'subject-matter test'. Insofar as a state employee's being part of the 'civil service' of the employer state is normally immaterial in matters of state immunity,[70] the mere status of 'international civil servant' should be expected to have no role in immunity determinations.

As to the staff members whose claims should be barred by reason of status, the relevant principles of state immunity law require some adaptation. Few IOs are equipped with a diplomatic corps (like the European Union[71]) or with personnel involved in matters of defence, intelligence and security (like the North Atlantic Treaty Organization). However, the rationale for immunising states from claims by these categories of officials – ie providing employers with ample freedom to manage staff whose duties come closest to the employers' core functions[72] – can reasonably apply also to an IO's 'top echelon' officials.[73] Similarly to the activities of diplomatic, consular or military personnel for their state employers, the responsibilities of its highest officials are of a 'vital nature' to the functions of an organisation.[74] While IO officials are generally entitled to immunity only for acts performed in the exercise of their functions, an organisation's highest officials are frequently assigned the full range of immunities enjoyed by national diplomats, notably including personal immunity.[75]

Clearly, the category of 'top echelon' officials may vary significantly in scope depending on an IO's internal structure. In the case of the UN, for example, the

[68] For a criticism of the appellate court's *Amaratunga* judgment (n 54), but with arguments that may mostly apply to the Supreme Court's judgment, see PM Saunders, 'Canada' in A Reinisch (ed), *The Privileges and Immunities of International Organizations in Domestic Courts* (Oxford, Oxford University Press, 2013) 73, 97–98.

[69] ch 4, s VIII.

[70] ch 4, s IVB.

[71] See generally D Spence and J Bátora (eds), *The European External Action Service: European Diplomacy Post-Westphalia* (Basingstoke, Palgrave Macmillan, 2015).

[72] ch 4, s IVB.

[73] This expression is borrowed from AJ Miller, 'Privileges and Immunities of United Nations Officials' (2007) 4 *International Organizations Law Review* 169, 223.

[74] Y-L Ling, 'A Comparative Study of the Privileges and Immunities of United Nations Member Representatives and Officials with the Traditional Privileges and Immunities of Diplomatic Agents' (1976) 33 *Washington and Lee Law Review* 91, 131.

[75] C Walter and F Preger, 'Immunities of Civil Servants of International Organisations' in T Ruys and N Angelet (eds), *The Cambridge Handbook of Immunities and International Law* (Cambridge, Cambridge University Press, 2019) 542, 545–49.

General Convention contemplates that the Secretary-General and the Assistant Secretaries-General enjoy diplomatic immunities;[76] following subsequent reorganisations of the Secretariat, this status is now extended to Under Secretaries-General. The ranks of Assistant and Under Secretaries-General include all heads and deputy heads of UN offices, funds and programmes, special representatives, envoys and advisers to the Secretary-General.[77] Diplomatic immunities are also enjoyed by other categories of high IO officials, including, for example, international judges, prosecutors and registrars.[78] In smaller organisations, the number of 'top echelon' officials may be much lower, or even limited to the Secretary-General (or equivalent positions) and possibly his or her deputies. In any event, these senior officials are singled out by their active involvement in an IO's highest level of management and not only in technical or administrative duties. An example of a lawsuit which would plainly attract immunity under a similar test is the French *Hintermann* case, where the former Deputy Secretary-General of the Western European Union (WEU) sued for payment of certain indemnities allegedly accruing from the termination of employment. *In concreto*, the plaintiff's status within the organisation was not specifically addressed in that the WEU enjoyed full immunity under its constitutive instrument.[79] Also, the Canadian Supreme Court's *Amaratunga* judgment appears more defensible from the standpoint of status of the employee. The plaintiff worked in the second-highest position within NAFO's secretariat. Among various high managerial functions, he was required to assume the duties of the Executive Secretary in an acting capacity when necessary and to represent NAFO on international fora.[80] He was therefore involved in the organisation's highest managerial positions.[81]

III. Limited Standards of Diplomatic and Consular Immunity in Employment Matters

Turning now to staff disputes with diplomatic and consular agents, the construction of workable non-absolute approaches to the immunity of these officials hinges

[76] Convention on the Privileges and Immunities of the United Nations 1946, Art V, s 19.

[77] R Bandyopadhyay and T Iwata, 'Officials (Article V Sections 17–21 General Convention)' in A Reinisch and P Bachmayer (eds), *The Conventions on the Privileges and Immunities of the United Nations and its Specialized Agencies: A Commentary* (Oxford, Oxford University Press, 2016) 313, 372–73.

[78] See, eg Rome Statute of the International Criminal Court 1998, Art 48(2).

[79] Paris Court of Appeal, *Hintermann v Union de l'Europe occidentale* 10 April 1990, affirmed, Court of Cassation, *Hintermann v Union de l'Europe occidentale* 14 November 1995, No 90-43.633, (1997) 124 *Journal du droit international* 141. See Agreement on the Status of Western European Union 1955, Art 4, providing immunity from 'every form of legal process'.

[80] See the full description of the plaintiff's duties in the appellate court's *Amaratunga* judgment (n 54) para 3.

[81] Note that these conclusions are without prejudice to further possible restrictions arising from human rights challenges to immunity law, a point which will be further explored in ch 6.

on two key issues. The first one, which is discussed in section IIIA, is how to distinguish between official and non-official employment of staff. This question is crucial in that, under both the VCDR and the Vienna Convention on Consular Relations (VCCR),[82] jurisdiction may never be exercised over official acts of diplomatic and consular agents. An act's qualification as non-official is a sufficient ground for setting aside the immunity of consular agents and of diplomats at the end of their posting.[83] As regards diplomats *en poste*, the non-official act should also fall under one of the three exceptions to immunity enumerated in Article 31 VCDR. This last issue is the object of section IIIB, which discusses whether the employment of private staff may be regarded as a non-immune 'commercial activity' under Article 31(1)(c).

A. Distinguishing Official and Non-official Employment of Staff

In order to set the boundaries between official and non-official labour-related acts of diplomatic and consular agents, an initial distinction should be made according to whether an individual is formally employed by the agent's sending state or by the agent him/herself.

In the former case, as already contended in chapter three, employment-related acts of the diplomatic or consular agent that are an ordinary parcel of the process of recruitment, management or termination are *ipso facto* official, in the sense that they are carried out on the sending state's behalf: the agent is not a party to the employment relationship. An example is an ambassador's choice concerning the hiring or firing of embassy personnel.[84] In this respect, the fact that the employee may have performed part of his duties for the personal benefit of the agent is normally immaterial. In the 2020 *Bardales* case, for instance, Bardales was hired by the Consulate General of Peru to perform administrative work in its customer service. Three years after recruitment, he was assigned to work as a personal assistant to the Consul General for half of his employment time. His work as personal assistant soon outweighed his duties at the consulate: he spent most of his working hours chauffeuring the consul and running personal errands for her and her family and friends. Bardales claimed that his personal work for the Consul General was separate from his work for the consulate. He thus contended that a number of labour-related wrongful acts allegedly ascribable to the consul, including failure to provide overtime payment and retaliatory termination, did not classify as official, and attempted to sue the consul general in a personal capacity. The court

[82] Vienna Convention on Diplomatic Relations 1961 (VCDR); Vienna Convention on Consular Relations 1963 (VCCR).
[83] See ch 2, s VII.
[84] ch 3, s VA.

found all the plaintiff's duties, including personal chores, to be encompassed by his employment contract with the consulate. It found that all the alleged wrongful acts implicated the Consul General's 'consular function of managing Consulate employees' and upheld immunity *ratione materiae*.[85]

It should be stressed, however, that the above only applies to labour-related acts ordinarily connected to the management of employment relationships. There may well be acts addressed at an employee whose nature is non-official despite the employment relationship as a whole having been established in the pursuance of official functions. This point was persuasively made in *Swarna*, a lawsuit by an Indian woman working as housekeeper at the residence of a Kuwaiti diplomat to the UN. Following a common pattern in labour suits against diplomats, Swarna was forced to work in slave-like conditions and was repeatedly assaulted, abused and raped. Since the defendant had returned to Kuwait by the time of the proceedings, the court was called upon to apply the residual diplomatic immunity provision of Article 39(2) VCDR. In its words,

> assuming *arguendo* that Swarna's employment constituted an official act, it does not follow that Al-Awadi is accorded immunity for any and all acts committed against her … Al-Awadi … could not commit [common crimes directed at Swarna] and claim residual immunity merely because his initial hiring of Swarna constituted an official act. Only if the commission of such crimes could be considered an official act would residual immunity apply.[86]

Based on this test, acts that are unrelated to the ordinary management of the employment relationship – most notably tortious acts such as physical or sexual abuse – may not be considered as official acts. Of course, this would be the case a fortiori for employees hired by an agent in a personal capacity.[87] It may be noted, incidentally, that the non-official character of the agent's conduct in such cases would not preclude the attribution of the act to the employer state:[88] the agent's civil liability and the sending state's responsibility are not mutually exclusive.[89] Hence, in similar cases, a disgruntled employee would be well advised to sue both the state and the agent.[90]

[85] *Bardales v Consulate General of Peru* 1:17-cv-8897 (ALC) (SDNY 2020) 16–17. As regards Bardales's employment claims against the state of Peru, the court upheld immunity based on *Kato v Ishihara* 360 F.3d 106 (2d Cir 2004), on which see ch 4, s III.

[86] *Swarna v Al-Awadi* 622 F.3d 123 (2d Cir 2010) 139–40.

[87] ibid 138: 'If Swarna's work for the family may not be considered part of any mission-related functions, surely enduring rape would not be part of those functions either.'

[88] See Art 7 ('Excess of authority or contravention of instructions') ILC Articles on Responsibility of States for Internationally Wrongful Acts, ILC Yearbook 2001, vol II, Part 2, 31.

[89] Z Douglas, 'State Immunity for the Acts of State Officials' (2012) 82 *British Year Book of International Law* 281, 295; J Verhoeven, 'Les immunités propres aux organes ou autres agents des sujets du droit international' in J Verhoeven (ed), *Le droit international des immunités: contestation ou consolidation?* (Paris, Larcier, 2004) 61, 68.

[90] E Denza, *Diplomatic Law: Commentary on the Vienna Convention on Diplomatic Relations*, 4th edn (Oxford, Oxford University Press, 2016) 360.

The condition of individuals whose nominal employer is not the sending state but the diplomatic or consular agent raises different and more complex legal issues. In such cases, the fact that the individual is not formally in the employ of the foreign state cannot be treated as conclusive evidence that the employment is non-official. This is for two main reasons. First, a diplomatic or consular agent can contract – and thus also hire individuals – both in a private and in an official capacity, and can contract in an official capacity both expressly and impliedly.[91] Secondly, the work of an individual hired by a diplomatic or consular agent may be connected to varying degrees with the sending state's functions, possibly going as far as being carried out for the sole benefit of the state itself. Besides attending to the agent's household, these employees may perform part of their duties in the premises of the foreign state's mission, for example in the course of a gala dinner at an embassy. Other personal employees may assist the agent, more or less regularly, in performing official duties, as in the case of an interpreter or a secretary privately hired by a diplomat, or a butler attending to the reception of official guests in an ambassador's private residence.[92]

In similar cases, the prevalent legal standard in domestic case law for distinguishing between official and non-official labour-related acts is one that is well-known to state immunity law – that of the employee's functions. More specifically, courts have considered employment of staff by the agent in his or her own name to be presumptively non-official, but this presumption can be rebutted if the employee is found to have performed duties primarily for the benefit of the mission rather than the agent personally. The officiality test is thus whether the worker's duties have caused a 'direct benefit' to the foreign state.[93] This is underlain by obvious functional considerations. Because the purpose of diplomatic and consular immunity is to ensure the efficient performance of the functions of the representing state's missions,[94] courts consider that immunity *ratione materiae* can only be justified in the event of an immediate advantage to the sending state.

In *Park*, the Ninth Circuit held that Shin, Korea's Deputy Consul General, was not entitled to immunity under Article 43(1) VCCR from labour-related claims by a Chinese domestic servant. The defendant submitted that the plaintiff's functions

[91] See, eg Art 43(2)(a) VCCR: consular agents shall not be immune 'in respect of a civil action … arising out of a contract concluded by a consular officer or a consular employee in which he did not contract expressly or impliedly as an agent of the sending State'.

[92] W Spadinger, 'Private Domestic Staff: A Risk Group on the Fringe of the Convention' in P Behrens (ed), *Diplomatic Law in a New Millennium* (Oxford, Oxford University Press, 2017) 132, 142–43. cp *Baoanan v Baja et al* 627 F.Supp 2d 155 (SDNY 2009) 161: 'Functionally, not all domestic workers hired by diplomats are necessarily alike. While undoubtedly many are routinely employed and assigned to provide services related solely to the official functions of the mission … [a] diplomat could also employ and pay staff to perform personal or private tasks … that the sending State would not recognize as ordinary or necessary to the official functioning of the mission.'

[93] X Shi, 'Official Acts and Beyond: Towards an Accurate Interpretation of Diplomatic Immunity Ratione Materiae under the Vienna Convention on Diplomatic Relations' (2019) 18 *Chinese Journal of International Law* 669, 688.

[94] See the VCDR and VCCR Prambles.

were not limited to providing domestic help but also included preparing and serving food when guests were entertained at Shin's home on behalf of the Korean consulate. He thus argued that the hiring and supervision of the plaintiff were fundamental to the performance of consular functions.[95] The court dismissed this argument by noting that work at the consulate was a small fraction of her duties, thus being 'merely incidental to her regular employment as the Shin family's personal domestic servant'.[96] Subsequent decisions have conformed to *Park*'s take on consular immunity.[97]

The *Park* approach has been slightly more contentious with respect to diplomatic agents. Under the direct influence of *Tabion*, where the Fourth Circuit held that all activities incidental to a diplomat's daily life, including domestic help, were to be treated as part of official functions,[98] the 2009 *Sabbithi* judgment subscribed to the view that employment of domestic personnel is covered by residual diplomatic immunity.[99] However, from the standpoint of officiality, it is unwarranted to treat the legal status of domestic staff at diplomatic households any differently from that of workers at consular households. The two situations do not differ as to the structure of the employment relationship between the agent and the employee.[100] There is also no difference as to the benefits that the work may cause to the sending state's mission. In fact, more recent case law has disregarded *Sabbithi* and construed the standard for residual diplomatic immunity in labour matters as identical to that of consular immunity.[101]

Thus, in the aforementioned *Swarna* case, the court held that the hiring of the plaintiff was not an official act even though the plaintiff occasionally cooked and served food to official guests, in that 'these duties were incidental to her regular employment as … personal servant'.[102] In *Baoanan*, a former diplomat argued that a domestic worker's employment was official because he resided in the Philippine mission to the UN and the plaintiff's services had occurred within the premises of the mission. The court rejected this argument, holding that the physical location of the work was not dispositive.[103] The diplomat's entitlement to continuing immunity depended instead on the employee's duties, which, as the court put it, 'inur[ed] to the Bajas' personal comfort and only tangentially to the benefit of the Philippine Mission'.[104]

Swarna and *Baoanan* were followed by the English High Court of Justice in *Wokuri*, where residual diplomatic immunity was held not to prevent a housekeeper

[95] *Park v Shin* 313 F.3d 1138 (9th Cir 2002) 1142.
[96] ibid 1143.
[97] eg *Rana v Islam and Prova* 14-Cv-1993 (SHS) (SDNY 2015) 11–13.
[98] *Tabion v Mufti and Mufti* 73 F.3d 535 (4th Cir 1996).
[99] *Sabbithi et al v Al Saleh et al* 605 F.Supp 2d 122 (DDC 2009), 180 ILR 703. See also ch 3, s VA.
[100] L Rodgers, 'The Inviolability of Diplomatic Agents in the Context of Employment' in Behrens (n 92) 113, 116.
[101] In these terms, see, eg *Rana* (n 97) 11.
[102] *Swarna* (n 86) 138, affirming *Swarna v Al-Awadi* 607 F.Supp 2d 509 (SDNY 2009).
[103] *Baoanan* (n 92) 29–30.
[104] ibid 29. See also *Lipenga v Kambalame* 219 F.Supp 3d 517 (D Md 2016), affirming jurisdiction over a human trafficking civil case against a former diplomatic agent.

from suing the former Deputy Head of the Ugandan High Commission for lack of employment contract and failure to pay full salary.[105] In *Abusabib*, the respondent diplomat suggested that Article 39(2) VCDR, which does not refer to 'official functions' but only to 'functions', lent itself to a liberal construction encompassing any employment-related acts directed at domestic servants.[106] But the court held that the employment of a domestic worker performing no task outside of a diplomat's residence had too little a connection with the functions of the mission to be treated as an official function.[107] The same conclusion was reached by the German Federal Labor Court in *Pfarr*. It was contended that an individual had been forced to work for a Saudi attaché for up to 20 hours per day, fed with leftovers and given no compensation. As the defendant employer had left his post in Germany, the court held that Article 39 VCDR posed no obstacle to affirming German jurisdiction.[108]

The most authoritative restatement of this interpretation of residual diplomatic immunity in labour matters may be ascribed to the UK Supreme Court's 2017 *Reyes* judgment. The plaintiff, a Philippine national, worked for three months in a Saudi diplomat's London residence under a contract she entered into while in her home country. She alleged that her employer and his wife maltreated her, confiscated her passport and failed to pay her any salary, and sued for racial discrimination, failure to pay minimum wage and unlawful deduction of wages. Subscribing to the *Tabion* interpretation of official functions, the English Court of Appeal (CA) held that employing a domestic worker falls within a diplomats' official functions because it enables a diplomat to perform such functions.[109] The CA developed this argument with regard to the immunity of sitting diplomats, notably while assessing whether the plaintiff's employment fell within the Article 31(1)(c) VCDR exception to diplomatic immunity for 'commercial activity exercised … outside his official functions'. Because the court also found that employment was not a commercial activity,[110] the official functions prong of the analysis was not determinative. However, by the time the case reached the Supreme Court, the respondent's functions in the UK had come to an end and he could thus only claim residual immunity for official acts. The Supreme Court reversed the CA's decision and gave conclusive weight to the plaintiff's duties: it considered it 'clear' that 'the employment of domestic staff to do the cleaning, help in the kitchen and look after [the] children [was] not done for or on behalf of Saudi Arabia',[111] and concluded that the respondent could not avail himself of residual immunity.

It may be noted that the above rulings largely eschew the question of what exact duties would cause the employment of private staff to qualify as an agent's official

[105] *Wokuri v Kassam* [2012] EWHC 105 (Ch), paras 23–26.
[106] *Abusabib and Another v Taddese* [2012] UKEAT 0424_11_2012, 180 ILR 441, para 23.
[107] ibid para 31.
[108] *Pfarr v Anonymous* 22 August 2012, 5 AZR 949/11.
[109] *Reyes and Suryadi v Al-Malki and Al-Malki* [2015] EWCA Civ 32, para 29.
[110] ibid paras 11–30. For criticism of this approach see below s IIIB.
[111] *Reyes v Al-Malki and Another* [2017] UKSC 61, paras 20 and 48.

act. The test based on the plaintiff's functions only provides clear guidance in cases at the extremes of the spectrum. There is general agreement that the employment of staff who rarely, if ever, perform functions other than attending to the diplomatic or consular household should be regarded as non-official. *Baoanan* implied that the employment of private staff 'routinely employed and assigned to provide services related solely to the official functions of the mission' would, by contrast, fall within an agent's official functions.[112] But little has been said of the treatment of grey area situations. In *Reyes*, Lord Sumption stated laconically that cases where 'a private servant is employed in a diplomat's residence for purposes connected with the work of the mission' would often entail 'Difficult questions of fact'.[113] Only *Abusabib* ventured to suggest, in obiter, that an employee 'replying to correspondence, both official and personal, and managing the diary, travel arrangements and the like of the diplomat' would most likely be considered as hired in an official capacity.[114] However, in light of the broad spectrum of duties that a diplomat or consul's employee may perform, it is probably unrealistic to expect courts to devise strict criteria for determining how much these duties contribute to furthering the interests of the sending state. Inevitably, courts will be required to rule on the basis of a case-by-case analysis of the facts.

In any event, considering the employment of private staff as an agent's official act necessarily entails that the staff member in question has been hired on behalf of the sending state. This flows directly from the legal definition of official acts of diplomatic and consular agents, ie acts that are 'in law the acts of the sending State'.[115] In other words, in similar cases, the employee should be treated as a state employee. The complaint should be brought against the foreign state as the proper defendant and state immunity law should determine whether a court has jurisdiction. The fact that the sending state is not the nominal employer and that the employee is paid through private funds of the agent is immaterial in that, as seen above, an agent can also contract on behalf of the sending state impliedly. To think otherwise would have troublesome consequences. Because diplomatic and consular agents are absolutely immune for their official acts, their employees hired in an official capacity would be deprived of any legal remedy. This would introduce a dangerous disparity with individuals nominally employed by the sending state, who are entitled to sue their employer within the limits posed by restrictive state immunity.[116] A state may simply circumvent the rule of restrictive state immunity by having individuals working within diplomatic and consular missions be nominally employed by diplomatic or consular agents.

This point has often been misconceived by municipal courts. For example, in *Mohamed X v Fettouma Z*, a French appellate court found the vice-consul of

[112] *Baoanan* (n 92) 21 and 31.
[113] *Reyes* (n 111) para 48.
[114] *Abusabib* (n 106) para 31.
[115] Denza (n 90) 356–58.
[116] S Mullally and C Murphy, 'Double Jeopardy: Domestic Workers in Diplomatic Households and Jurisdictional Immunities' (2016) 64 *American Journal of Comparative Law* 677, 704.

Morocco to be immune from claims by one of his personal employees, on the grounds that the employment contract had been concluded by the vice-consul 'expressly or impliedly as an agent of the sending State'. However, while the court accepted the vice-consul's submission that the employee was 'contractually linked with the Ministry of Foreign Affairs and Cooperation of Morocco', it inconsistently refused to consider that employee as recruited by Morocco, arguing that 'All the evidence establishe[d] … that she had no mission or delegation from Morocco'.[117] Another example may be drawn from the 1982 *Goncalves* case. The plaintiff sued Portugal requesting payment for a sworn translation made at the request of a commercial attaché serving as head of the Commercial Office of Portugal's embassy in Brussels. The court dismissed the lawsuit on grounds of diplomatic immunity. It found that, because the diplomat ordered the translation on behalf of Portugal, the act at hand was 'imputable to that State' and the attaché was immune *ratione materiae*. The court, however, failed to draw the obvious consequence of its own statement – ie that the claim, which was directed against Portugal, had to be handled on the basis of state immunity.[118]

B. Employment as a Commercial Activity not Subject to Diplomatic Immunity

Unlike consular agents and former diplomatic agents, serving diplomats enjoy immunity for acts performed not only on the sending state's behalf but also in a private capacity, save for three exceptions enumerated in Article 31(1) VCDR.[119] This subsection discusses whether non-official employment of a diplomat's personal staff may be covered by the only potentially relevant exception to diplomatic immunity, ie the so-called 'commercial activity exception' of Article 31(1)(c). This exception applies to civil actions 'relating to any professional or commercial activity exercised by the diplomatic agent in the receiving State outside his official functions'.

The dominant tendency in domestic case law has been to construe the scope of 'commercial activity' narrowly, ie as not encompassing the employment of private staff.[120] This interpretation can be traced back to the leading *Tabion* case, where

[117] Court of Appeal of Montpellier (Labour Chamber), *Mohamed X and Another v Fettouma Z* 17 October 2012, Case No 11/01255, 180 ILR 416.

[118] Civil Court of Brussels (Second Chamber), *Portugal v Goncalves* 11 March 1982, 82 ILR 115, 117, considering it 'inappropriate … to refer to the jurisprudence … regarding State immunity'.

[119] Unless the serving diplomat is a national or a permanent resident of the receiving state, in which case he or she is only entitled to immunity for official acts: see Art 38(1) VCDR. See ch 2, s 6.

[120] Plaintiff employees have rarely sought – in all cases unsuccessfully – to rely on the 'professional activity' prong of the Art 31(1)(c) exception. One example is *Gonzalez Paredes v Vila and Nielsen*, 180 ILR 678, 479 F.Supp 2d 187 (DDC 2007). The plaintiff, employed jointly by the diplomat and his wife, creatively argued that, by pursuing academic studies in the US, the diplomat's wife had been engaging in a professional activity and that domestic help 'related to' said activity because it facilitated her studies. The court refused to consider academic studies as a professional activity and, in any event, held that the employment of domestic staff had too thin a connection to the pursuit of academic studies to be 'relating to' that activity (198).

a domestic worker sued a Jordanian diplomat for various violations of US labour standards and sought compensation. Besides refusing to consider the plaintiff's employment as non-official – a point discussed previously in this chapter – the Fourth Circuit also stated that labour relationships did not fall within the VCDR's notion of 'commercial activity'. In adherence to a statement of interest filed by the US State Department, the exception at hand was construed as 'relat[ing] only to trade or business activity engaged in for personal profit' and not covering 'contractual relationships for goods and services incidental to the daily life of the diplomat and family in the receiving state'.[121] This precedent has been uniformly followed in subsequent US cases,[122] and the same approach has also been dominant in other jurisdictions. In *Pfarr*, the regional labour court summarily noted that none of the Article 31(1) VCDR exceptions to immunity were applicable to the case at hand;[123] the German Federal Labor Court, which only addressed the issue of residual diplomatic immunity, considered it unnecessary to rule on the immunity of diplomat employers in post.[124] The procedural history of *Reyes* developed along the same lines. The CA was persuaded by the *Tabion* interpretation of 'commercial activity'.[125] The Supreme Court, for its part, was split on the point: three Justices expressed 'doubts' on the *Tabion* view on Article 31(1)(c),[126] while two others fully endorsed it.[127] But these views were expressed in obiter: because the respondent had already left his post, the court abstained from ruling in a binding way on the scope of the 'commercial activity exception'.[128]

It would therefore appear that no domestic court has ever delivered a binding decision construing the Article 31(1)(c) exception as encompassing employment of domestic workers. Certain courts have set aside diplomatic immunity in labour matters on different – and, at times, incorrect – grounds. For example, in *Fonseca*, the Portuguese Supreme Court affirmed jurisdiction over claims by a domestic maid at a diplomat's private residence, but did so by misconstruing the scope of diplomatic immunity as only covering official acts.[129] In *Mazengo*, a US district court rejected the immunity plea of a self-styled 'diplomat' in a claim for false

[121] *Tabion* (n 98) 537–38. In favour, see Denza (n 90) 251–52.

[122] See, eg *Gonzalez Paredes* (n 120) 193; *Sabbithi* (n 99) 127–29; *Montuya v Chedid and Another* 180 ILR 714, 779 F.Supp 2d 60 (DDC 2011) 62–65; *Fun v Pulgar and Albergrin* 180 ILR 722, 993 F.Supp 2d 470 (DNJ 2014) 474. See also *Ahmed v Hoque* WL 1964806 (SDNY 2002), considering diplomatic immunity to be absolute in labour claims but not expressly addressing the Art 31(1)(c) exception, probably because the plaintiff did not invoke it.

[123] Higher Regional Court of Berlin, *Diplomatic immunity for alleged labour exploitation case, Pfarr (on behalf of National of Indonesia) v Anonymous* 9 November 2011, 17 Sa 1468/11, 180 ILR 422, ILDC 1903 (DE 2011) para 16. The court's lack of detailed reasoning on the point might be explained by the plaintiff's failure to invoke Art 31(1)(c). Instead, she confined herself to arguing (unsuccessfully) that immunity had to be displaced because it deprived her of fundamental constitutional rights.

[124] *Pfarr* (n 108) para 3.

[125] *Reyes and Suryadi* (n 109) para 14.

[126] *Reyes* (n 111) para 57 (Lord Wilson), para 69 (Lady Hale and Lord Clarke).

[127] ibid especially paras 21–25 (Lord Sumption and Lord Neuberger).

[128] ibid para 56 (Lord Wilson). *cf* also *Wokuri* (n 105) paras 14–21, discussing *Tabion* at length but only ruling on the issue of residual immunity.

[129] *Fonseca v Larren* 30 January 1991, (1991) *Boletim do Ministério da Justiça* 403.

imprisonment, involuntary servitude and forced labour, but this was only due to the respondent's inability to prove that he actually was, as he claimed, accredited to the Tanzanian embassy.[130] In the 2014 case of *Calderon, Laporga and Villaranda*, the Irish Employment Appeals Tribunal (EAT) found that the serving ambassador of the United Arab Emirates was not immune from labour claims by three Filipino women who had worked in his private residence under what the court described as 'extreme working conditions', which included verbal and physical abuse and severe underpayment. The plaintiffs were awarded monetary compensation.[131] The key rationale for this decision was that the ambassador failed to appear before the EAT to plead diplomatic immunity.[132] This is, however, incompatible with the VCDR, which states that diplomatic immunity may only be waived by the sending state and that such waiver must be express.[133] Hence, non-appearance in court cannot qualify as a waiver of diplomatic immunity. This mistake – as well as, more generally, the fact that the EAT did not discuss Article 31 VCDR at all – was most likely due to a confusion between diplomatic and state immunity. Indeed, to further justify its approach, the court invoked a couple of state immunity cases, notably affirming that the functions performed by the appellants did not 'involve them within the exercise of public powers according to the test set out in *Mahamdia*'.[134]

Despite the pre-eminence of this interpretation of the 'commercial activity exception', there are reasons for reconsidering the dominant view. Article 31(1)(c) VCDR should be construed according to the rules of treaty interpretation enshrined in the 1969 Vienna Convention on the Law of Treaties (VCLT), which are generally held to correspond to customary international law.[135] The general rule of interpretation set forth in Article 31(1) VCLT prescribes that 'A treaty shall be interpreted in good faith in accordance with the ordinary meaning to be given to the terms of the treaty in their context and in the light of its object and purpose'. The *travaux préparatoires* may serve as supplementary means of interpretation for confirming a construction reached through the Article 31 criteria or if such criteria lead to a meaning which is ambiguous, obscure or manifestly unreasonable.[136] As will be seen below, reliance on these rules of interpretation may support a

[130] *Mazengo v Mzengi* 542 F.Supp 2d 96 (DDC 2008) 98–100.

[131] *Calderon, Laporga and Villaranda v Lootah and Alghubaisi* 25 November 2014, Cases No UD1219/2013, UD1220/2013, UD1221/2013.

[132] ibid para 1 'Preliminary matters'. According to A Kartusch, 'Domestic Workers in Diplomatic Households. Rights Violations and Access to Justice in the Context of Diplomatic Immunity' (German Institute for Human Rights, June 2011) 33, www.ilo.org/dyn/migpractice/docs/212/GIHR.pdf, there have been cases decided on similar grounds in other jurisdictions, including Belgium, France, Switzerland and the UK.

[133] Art 32(1) and (2) VCDR.

[134] *Calderon* (n 131) para 2 'Preliminary matters', referring to Case C-154/11 *Mahamdia v People's Democratic Republic of Algeria* [2013] ECR 1.

[135] See, eg *Territorial Dispute (Libyan Arab Jamahiriya/Chad)* Judgment [1994] ICJ Reports 6, para 41; *The South China Sea Arbitration (Philippines v China)* Award (12 July 2016) PCA Case No 2013-19, para 476.

[136] Art 32 VCLT.

construction of the commercial activity exception as encompassing labour claims by the private staff of diplomats in post.[137]

The interpretation of Article 31(1)(c) VCDR should start from the literal meaning of its terms. The use of the word 'activity' rather than 'act' has been prevalently interpreted as suggesting that the exception is intended to cover 'continuous acts' and not isolated transactions.[138] Thus an employment relationship certainly meets the definition of 'activity' under treaty terms. Far more contentious is whether an employment relationship falls within the ordinary meaning of 'commercial', a term which is nowhere defined in the VCDR. Courts have commonly answered this question in the negative. For example, the CA in *Reyes* affirmed that 'as a matter of ordinary language, a contract for the provision of services which are incidental to family or domestic daily life is not commercial activity'.[139] Lord Sumption of the Supreme Court agreed: 'In the ordinary meaning of the words, the "exercise" of a "professional or commercial activity" means practising the profession or carrying a business. … [The diplomat] must, so to say, set up shop.'[140]

This is not, however, the word's only natural reading. Interestingly, an argument to this effect can be drawn from the very decision in *Tabion*. The employee invoked a plain-language reading of Article 31(1)(c) whereby – as the Fourth Circuit summarised – 'Because "commerce" is simply the exchange of goods and services … "commercial activity" necessarily encompasses contracts for goods and services, including employment contracts'.[141] The court found some merit in this argument: it reasoned that 'Tabion received some pay, and she undoubtedly was active in her work for the Muftis. Looking solely at the words "commercial" and "activity", then, the phrase "commercial activity" could logically encompass the Muftis' dealings with Tabion',[142] and it went on to reject the plaintiff's reading based on context and the *travaux* (two points that will be discussed shortly below). This shows that there is no plain text obstacle to broadly interpreting the paragraph 1(c) exception as including exchanges of goods and services. In fact, employment relationships are undisputedly classified as 'commercial' in other legal settings.[143]

[137] See also Rodgers (n 100) 115–16; A Tai, 'Unlocking the Door to Justice: Protecting the Rights and Remedies of Domestic Workers in the Face of Diplomatic Immunity' (2007) 16 *American University Journal of Gender, Social Policy & the Law* 175, 192.

[138] AEF Sandström, 'Diplomatic Intercourse and Immunities – Summary of Observations Received from Governments and Conclusions of the Special Rapporteur', UN Doc A/CN.4/116 (2 May 1958) 56; J Foakes and E Denza, 'Privileges and Immunities of Diplomatic Agents' in I Roberts (ed), *Satow's Diplomatic Practice*, 7th edn (Oxford, Oxford University Press, 2016) 246, 256. But it could be argued that the literal meaning of 'activity' does not exclude isolated transactions. For example, the Foreign Sovereign Immunities Act 1976 (US FSIA), s 1603(d) defines 'commercial activity' as 'a regular course of commercial conduct or a particular commercial transaction or act'. Similarly, see also State Immunity Act 1985 (Canada SIA), s 2.

[139] *Reyes and Suryadi* (n 109) para 14.

[140] *Reyes* (n 111) para 21. See also para 51: 'There is no sense which can reasonably be given to article 31(1)(c) which would make the consumption of goods and services the exercise a commercial activity.'

[141] *Tabion* (n 98) 537.

[142] ibid.

[143] Rodgers (n 100) 115.

One relevant example is the law of state immunity. In the USA and Canada, whose state immunity instruments do not contain a provision specifically addressing contracts of employment, immunity from labour claims have been (to an extent) set aside by operation of the 'commercial activity exception' to state immunity.[144] This is because the notion of commercial activity is used in these instruments as a proxy for anything done in a private law capacity.[145] In *Reyes*, this view concerning the literal meaning of 'commercial activity' was found persuasive by Lord Wilson, who noted that, in a seminal state immunity precedent, the Canadian Supreme Court 'accepted … that a contract of employment was generally a commercial activity'.[146]

The second interpretive criterion under Article 31(1) VCLT, ie contextual interpretation, lies at the heart of the *Tabion* reading of the 'commercial' exception. It has been contended that the meaning of 'professional and commercial activity' under Article 31 VCDR should be construed as coextensive with Article 42 VCDR, pursuant to which 'A diplomatic agent shall not in the receiving State practise for personal profit any professional or commercial activity'. Article 31(1)(c) would only remove immunity for activities that are prohibited under Article 42; activities incidental to the agent's daily life, not being carried out for personal profit, would not fall within the exception.[147] The main rationale for this argument is a passage of the *travaux* where the International Law Commission (ILC), commenting on the antecedent of Article 31(1)(c) VCDR, wrote as follows:

> it was urged that activities of these kinds [ie 'professional or commercial'] are normally wholly inconsistent with the position of a diplomatic agent, and that one possible consequence of his engaging in them might be that he would be declared *persona non grata*. Nevertheless, such cases may occur and should be provided for …[148]

However, leaving aside that the language of this passage is inconclusive (at the very least, the phrase 'it was urged' betrays that this view was far from unanimous within the Commission), to assume that Article 42 prohibits all the activities that Article 31(1)(c) renders non-immune runs counter to the plain language of the treaty.[149] Article 31(1)(c) unequivocally provides for the exception to apply

[144] s 1605(a)(2) US FSIA; s 5 Canada SIA.

[145] X Yang, *State Immunity in International Law* (Cambridge, Cambridge University Press, 2012) 75.

[146] *Reyes* (n 111) para 64, citing *United States of America v The Public Service Alliance of Canada and Others (Re Canada Labour Code)* [1992] 2 SCR 50, 94 ILR 264. Against, see *Reyes and Suryadi* (n 109) para 26.

[147] *Reyes and Suryadi* (n 109) para 16; *Tabion* (n 98) 537; *Reyes* (n 111) para 38(1) (Lord Sumption). See also C-A Colliard, 'La Convention de Vienne sur les relations diplomatiques' (1961) 7 *Annuaire Français de Droit International* 3, 29, arguing that the Art 42 prohibition of commercial activities makes the Art 31(1)(c) exception effectively pointless.

[148] Draft Articles on Diplomatic Intercourse and Immunities with commentaries, ILC Yearbook 1958, vol II, 89, 98, quoted in *Reyes and Suryadi* (n 109) para 20 and *Reyes* (n 111) para 36. See also *Tabion* (n 98) 537–38. Note that Art 42 was inserted at a late stage of the VCDR drafting in order to explicitly prevent diplomats from exercising professional or commercial activity for their own profit in the receiving state under the shield of diplomatic immunity. All delegations agreed that working for profit would be incompatible with the diplomatic function: see United Nations Conference on Diplomatic Intercourse and Immunities, Vienna, 2 March–14 April 1961, Official Records, Vol 1: Summary Records of Plenary Meetings and of Meetings of the Committee of the Whole, UN Doc A/CONF.20/14, 211–13.

[149] Rodgers (n 100) 115; Tai (n 137) 194.

to all 'professional or commercial activities' of the agent, regardless of whether or not they are made for personal profit. It is indeed undisputed that the exception encompasses a whole range of commercial or professional activities that an agent does not perform for profit and that Article 42 thus does not prohibit: these include, for example, literary, artistic and academic work, or trade for charity purposes.[150]

As to the third prong of the general rule of interpretation, an examination of the object and purpose of Article 31(1)(c) does not seem able to provide conclusive guidance. The interpretation of diplomatic immunity as encompassing labour claims is underpinned – expressly or impliedly – by the assumption that exercising jurisdiction over such claims would run counter to the purpose of diplomatic immunity, which is to allow foreign state representatives to perform their functions in the receiving state effectively. For example, in *Pfarr*, the regional labour court proclaimed that 'any restrictions of immunity [would endanger] the diplomatic relations of the participating States'.[151] However, these rulings simply presuppose that adjudicating labour claims by the private staff would impair the functions of a diplomatic agent. In fact, this is far from self-evident. For instance, it is difficult to see how an action to recover back wages and other monetary benefits could affect the diplomat's ability to carry out official functions any more than a compensation lawsuit relating to a trade activity done by the agent, which by all accounts would not be immune. Moreover, a purposive reading of the 'commercial activity' exception may well lean in favour of removing immunity, in that the purpose of said exception is to provide remedies to private parties.[152] The ILC itself acknowledged that 'the persons with whom the diplomatic agent has had commercial or professional relations cannot be deprived of their ordinary remedies'.[153]

Finally, it is pertinent to refer to the VCDR's preparatory work pursuant to Article 32 VCLT. As seen above regarding the relationship between Articles 31(1)(c) and 42 VCDR, courts approving of the *Tabion* interpretation have attached great importance to the *travaux*.[154] Still, the *travaux* are quite inconclusive as regards the applicability of the exception at hand to employment. The VCDR negotiating history provides no generally agreed-upon definition of 'professional and commercial activity'.[155] The CA in *Reyes* noted that a suggestion by the Yugoslav delegate to insert a further exception to immunity for 'actions arising out of an employment agreement relating to a locally employed servant' was not adopted.[156] But this is hardly decisive, considering that this suggestion was never incorporated

[150] R van Alebeek, 'Immunity, Diplomatic' (2009) *Max Planck Encyclopedia of Public International Law*, para 36; Denza (n 90) 250–51.

[151] *Pfarr (on behalf of National of Indonesia)* (n 123) ILR 430.

[152] Rodgers (n 100) 115; Tai (n 137) 191–92.

[153] Draft Articles on Diplomatic Intercourse (n 148) 98.

[154] *Tabion* (n 98) 537: 'Accepting the broader meaning fails to take into account the treaty's background and negotiating history'; *Reyes and Suryadi* (n 109) para 20.

[155] S Duquet and J Wouters, 'Legal Duties of Diplomats Today' in Behrens (n 92) 247, 257. See also Conference Official Records (n 148) 21.

[156] *Reyes and Suryadi* (n 109) para 24, quoting from Conference Official Records (n 148) 168.

into an amendment proposal and was never further discussed at the Conference. The truth is that, while there is no univocal indication within the *travaux* that the VCDR drafters intended employment litigation to be covered by the 'commercial' exception, there is no univocal indication that they indended it not to be covered either.

In sum, as three out of five Justices of the Supreme Court put it in *Reyes*, while the *Tabion* reading of Article 31(1)(c) might appear to be the 'obvious answer' to the question whether diplomatic agents should be immune from labour proceedings, 'the more one thinks about the question, the less obviously correct does [this] answer become'.[157] No element within the letter, context or object and purpose of the Convention univocally supports this reading. Hence, the exception's interpretation encompassing employment of private staff comes across – in Lord Wilson's words – as a 'legally respectable solution'.[158]

It may be submitted that it is also the legally preferable solution. The *Tabion* approach has contributed to perpetuating a disconcerting void of legal protection for workers employed in diplomatic households.[159] It has been estimated, for instance, that one-third of cases of domestic servitude in the USA involve individuals enjoying diplomatic immunity.[160] Against this backdrop, when given the choice between two plausible constructions of the 'commercial' exception, there are compelling arguments for picking the one which better serves the protection of individual rights. First, pursuant to Article 31(3)(c) VCLT – a rule which is also reflective of general international law[161] – 'any relevant rules of international law applicable in the relations between the parties' shall be 'taken into account' when interpreting a treaty.[162] It is logical to suggest that the international norms safeguarding fundamental rights of employees, notably including those prohibiting servitude and forced labour,[163] should be considered in the construction of the exception and weigh the balance in favour of a broad reading.[164] Secondly, on a policy level, since criminal prosecution is certainly inadmissible under the VCDR in lack of waiver from the sending state,[165] civil litigation provides the best chance of curbing the distressing trend of labour exploitation in diplomatic households.

[157] *Reyes* (n 111) para 57 (Lord Wilson).
[158] ibid para 68.
[159] See *ex multis* F Staiano, 'Domestic Workers' Human Rights versus Diplomatic Immunity: Developments in International and National Jurisprudence' (2013) 22 *Italian Yearbook of International Law* 201.
[160] K Friedrich, 'Statutes of Liberty?: Seeking Justice Under United States Law When Diplomats Traffic in Persons' (2007) 72 *Brooklyn Law Review* 1139, 1160.
[161] *Oil Platforms (Islamic Republic of Iran v United States of America)* Judgment [2003] ICJ Rep 161, para 41.
[162] See C McLachlan, 'The Principle of Systemic Integration and Article 31(3)(c) of the Vienna Convention' (2005) 54 *ICLQ* 279.
[163] See, eg International Covenant on Civil and Political Rights 1966, Art 8; Convention for the Protection of Human Rights and Fundamental Freedoms 1950 (ECHR), Art 4. See also generally J Allain, *Slavery in International Law: Of Human Exploitation and Trafficking* (Leiden, Brill-Nijhoff, 2013) 143–255.
[164] *Reyes* (n 111) para 67 (Lord Wilson).
[165] Art 31 VCDR.

Again, the majority of Justices in *Reyes* perceived it as 'difficult' to forsake the broad construction of the 'commercial' exception 'and instead to favour a conclusion that [the UK legal] system cannot provide redress for an apparently serious case of domestic servitude here in our capital city'.[166]

It may be noted that, even adopting the *Tabion* reading of 'commercial activity' as participation in trade or business for personal profit,[167] an argument has been put forward that at least some work relationships would nonetheless fit into this categorisation. In particular, employees have often submitted that, even if an employment relationship were not per se commercial, the diplomat's involvement in human trafficking would make it commercial. For example, the appellant in *Reyes* had been transfered from the Philippines to the UK by means of deception for the purposes of exploitation, something that met the legal definition of 'trafficking in persons' under the 2000 Palermo Protocol.[168] The employee argued that, because human trafficking is a profitable illicit trade, an employment contract tainted by trafficking met the *Tabion* definition of 'commercial activity'.[169] The UK Supreme Court was once again split on the merits of this argument. Lord Sumption opined that human trafficking is not necessarily a commercial activity: while the activity of 'an intermediary who recruits or transports a trafficked person for money' would qualify as commercial, 'the mere employment of a domestic servant on exploitative terms' would not. He clarified, by means of analogy:

> if I knowingly buy stolen property from a professional fence for my personal use, both of us will incur criminal liability … The fence will also be engaging in a commercial activity. But it does not follow that the same is true of me.[170]

Lord Wilson, with whom two other judges concurred, found merit in the plaintiff's submission. As he put it,

> another rational view is that the relevant 'activity' is not just the so-called employment but the trafficking; that the employer of the migrant is an integral part of the chain … that the employer's exploitation of the migrant has no parallel in the purchaser's treatment of the stolen goods; and that … the employer's conduct contains a substantial commercial element of obtaining domestic assistance without paying for it properly or at all.[171]

The second view is probably more plausible. It is self-evident that there is an element of personal profit in exploiting a domestic worker.[172] Moreover, it seems

[166] *Reyes* (n 111) para 68 (Lord Wilson).

[167] *Tabion* (n 98) 538.

[168] *Reyes and Suryadi* (n 109) paras 1 and 31. See Protocol to Prevent, Suppress and Punish Trafficking in Persons Especially Women and Children, supplementing the United Nations Convention against Transnational Organized Crime 2000, Art 3.

[169] *Reyes and Suryadi* (n 109) para 33; *Reyes* (n 111) para 41.

[170] *Reyes* (n 111) para 45. See also *Reyes and Suryadi* (n 109) para 34: 'The fact that an employer derives economic benefit from paying his employee wages that are lower than the market rate does not mean that he is engaging in a commercial activity.'

[171] *Reyes* (n 111) para 62.

[172] Rodgers (n 100) 115.

too generous to analogise the diplomat employer in *Reyes* to a purchaser of stolen goods: considering that the plaintiff obtained her visa in Manila by producing a deceitful employment contract signed by the employer,[173] the diplomat's role – carrying on the analogy – looked closer in nature to that of a 'professional fence'. Still, it is important to highlight that the relevance of the 'human trafficking' challenge to diplomatic immunity is relatively limited. It would only permit jurisdiction over disputes concerning the most serious labour exploitation cases and would not cover more run-of-the-mill employment proceedings. This argument was developed as an attempt at bypassing the constraints of the *Tabion* interpretation of the 'commercial' exception.[174] However, once it is accepted that the exception should cover employment *tout court*, there is no need to treat human trafficking cases differently from any other labour claims.

It is self-evident that the above also removes the necessity of any type of consent by the sending state to jurisdiction over staff disputes against serving diplomats.[175] As a way of defeating the blanket immunity deriving from *Tabion*, it had been proposed that receiving states might require sending states to provide advance waivers of diplomatic immunity for breaches of employment contracts.[176] However, the reading of the VCDR put forward in this chapter makes waivers of immunity redundant in civil litigation over labour matters and confines their relevance to areas where no exception to diplomatic immunity applies, ie criminal or enforcement jurisdiction over diplomat employers.[177]

IV. Conclusions

This chapter sought to identify standards of limited immunity for proceedings involving IOs and diplomatic and consular agents. The main challenge of this task lies in the relative lack of relevant judicial practice, at least when compared to the wealth of cases dealing with restrictive state immunity in labour matters. It is therefore inevitable for the solutions proposed in this chapter to be only partly reflective of existing case law. This chapter's less contentious argument is that the official

[173] *Reyes* (n 111) para 1.

[174] See *Sabbithi* (n 99) 126–27.

[175] Pursuant to Art 32 VCDR, diplomatic immunity may only be waived expressly by the sending state.

[176] See American Civil Liberties Union, 'Eradicating Slavery: Preventing the Abuse, Exploitation and Trafficking of Domestic Workers by Foreign Diplomats and Ensuring Diplomat Accountability', statement before the House Foreign Affairs Committee, 18 October 2007, 2, www.aclu.org/sites/default/files/field_document/asset_upload_file359_32786.pdf: 'Congress should … requir[e] states, as a condition for their diplomats to obtain special visas for their domestic workers, to waive their diplomats' immunity for civil claims arising from a breach of the employment contract'.

[177] On criminal prosecution of persons entitled to diplomatic immunity for breach of fundamental employment rights, including instances of sending states waiving immunity, see ME Vandenberg and S Bessel, 'Diplomatic Immunity and the Abuse of Domestic Workers: Criminal and Civil Remedies in the United States' (2016) 26 *Duke Journal of Comparative & International Law* 595, 598–610.

character of employment for the purpose of diplomatic and consular immunity *ratione materiae* should depend on whether the employee's prevalent functions are performed to the benefit of the sending state. Other arguments have been put forth primarily in the form of suggestions for future judicial practice: notably, that the limited immunity of IO employers should be modelled on the restrictive state immunity standards analysed in chapter four, and that employment of private staff should fall within the scope of the Article 31(1)(c) VCDR 'commercial' exception to diplomatic immunity.

6

Reconciling Immunities and the Employees' Right of Access to Justice

I. Introduction

One of the consequences of immunity rules being procedural bars on jurisdiction is that their scope is unaffected by norms governing the merits of a claim, including substantive human rights norms.[1] Hence, although the immunities explored in the previous chapters create an obvious tension with the judicial protection of employment rights, this tension does not normally translate into a direct conflict of norms. The case is different, however, when it comes to the employees' right of access to justice, one of the basic guarantees of fair trial in civil proceedings.[2] Being itself a chiefly procedural safeguard, this human right and immunity rules impose competing obligations upon the forum state that need be reconciled.[3] And because the right of access to justice is instrumental to the protection of substantive rights,[4] addressing this conflict provides a path for indirectly reconciling employer immunities and the effectiveness of all rights of employees. There is, however, no easy way to harmonise these norms. Since *jus cogens* is not implicated, a dispositive normative hierarchy is lacking.[5] The principles of *lex specialis* and *lex posterior* are also of little avail, the norms in question covering different subject matters.[6] Against this backdrop, this conflict cannot but be accommodated by means of legal interpretation.[7]

[1] On the procedural character of immunity rules see ch 2, s II.

[2] *Golder v United Kingdom* App No 4451/70, 21 February 1975, para 36; UN Human Rights Committee (HRC), General comment 32, Article 14, UN Doc CCPR/C/GC/32 (23 August 2007) para 9. This right has acquired customary status: see D Shelton, *Remedies in International Human Rights Law*, 3rd edn (Oxford, Oxford University Press, 2015) 238.

[3] M Iovane, 'Conflicts between State-Centred and Human-Centred International Norms' in R Pisillo Mazzeschi and P De Sena (eds), *Global Justice, Human Rights and the Modernization of International Law* (Cham, Springer, 2018) 205, 218.

[4] F Francioni, 'The Rights of Access to Justice under Customary International Law' in F Francioni (ed), *Access to Justice as a Human Right* (Oxford, Oxford University Press, 2007) 1, 32.

[5] See especially ECtHR, *Al-Dulimi and Montana Management Inc v Switzerland* App No 5809/08, 21 June 2016, para 136. Against, but only re grave breaches of fundamental human rights, IACtHR, *Goiburú et al v Paraguay* 22 September 2006, Series C No 153, para 131.

[6] C Ryngaert, 'Immunities of International Organizations before Domestic Courts: Reflections on the Collective Labour Case against the European Patent Organization' (2015) 46 *Netherlands Yearbook of International Law* 393, 403.

[7] R Pavoni, 'Human Rights and the Immunities of Foreign States and International Organizations' in E de Wet and J Vidmar (eds), *Hierarchy in International Law: The Place of Human Rights* (Oxford, Oxford University Press, 2012) 71, 77.

This chapter explores the interplay of immunities and the right of access to justice of employees of foreign states, international organisations (IOs) and diplomatic and consular agents. The following two sections delve into the main judicial approaches to reconciling employer immunities and the right to a court. A first approach defers entirely to the content of international immunity law, particularly in the areas of state and diplomatic immunity (section II). A second approach, by contrast, considers restrictions on access to justice as admissible if the employee has available reasonable alternative means of redress (section III); IO immunity is frequently addressed under the latter model. Section IV argues that the coexistence of two different approaches creates the risk of discrimination among workers and remedy gaps, and puts forward that the question of what constitutes a tolerable compression of an employee's right to a court requires a consistent answer.

II. Approaches Deferring to International Obligations to Grant Immunity to Employers

The first strand of approaches regards employer immunities as admissible limitations on the right of access to justice whenever the forum state is under an international obligation to grant immunity. As will be seen, this jurisprudence has been predominantly addressed at immunities deriving from general international law. Yet, it may in principle apply – and has, on occasion, been applied – to all employer immunities regardless of their source.[8]

The main example of this approach may be found in the European Court of Human Rights' (ECtHR, the Strasbourg Court) case law on state immunity. State employees whose attempts to sue their employers were frustrated on immunity grounds have often seised the Strasbourg Court contending that the forum state's refusal to adjudicate their claims violated their right of access to a court under Article 6 ('Right to a fair trial') of the European Convention on Human Rights (ECHR).[9] According to well-established jurisprudence, the ECtHR considers limitations on this right to be admissible if they do not impair the very essence of the

[8] See, eg the early cases on IO employers' immunity, eg European Commission of Human Rights (ECommHR), *Spaans v The Netherlands* App No 12516/86, 12 December 1988: 'it is in accordance with international law that States confer immunities and privileges to international bodies … such a restriction of national sovereignty in order to facilitate the working of an international body [does not give] rise to an issue under the Convention'. The ECtHR's current approach to IO immunity in labour matters is based on the availability of alternative remedies, on which see below s III. For an overview, see S van Drooghenbroek, 'Labour Law Litigation and Fair Trial under Article 6 ECHR' in F Dorssemont et al (eds), *The European Convention on Human Rights and the Employment Relation* (Oxford, Hart Publishing, 2014) 159.

[9] Convention for the Protection of Human Rights and Fundamental Freedoms 1950 (ECHR). Art 6(1) ('In the determination of his civil rights and obligations … everyone is entitled to a fair and public hearing within a reasonable time by an independent and impartial tribunal established by law') presupposes a right of access to a court: *Golder* (n 2) para 36.

right, pursue legitimate aims and are proportionate to such aims.[10] The legitimacy aspect is unproblematic: state immunity has constantly been found to pursue the legitimate aim of 'complying with international law to promote comity and good relations between States'.[11] What is decisive is the proportionality assessment. The ECtHR considers state immunity to be a proportionate limitation if the forum state was required to grant it under 'generally recognized rules of public international law'.[12] The rationale for this approach lies in the principle of systemic interpretation: as the court has pointed out, the Convention 'should so far as possible be interpreted in harmony with other rules of international law' including the customary law of state immunity.[13]

The above principles were first applied to employment matters in *Fogarty*. The applicant worked as an administrative assistant at the US embassy in London from 1993 to her dismissal in 1995. In a first set of proceedings before English courts, whose jurisdiction was not in question because the USA waived immunity by defending on the merits, she obtained compensation for discriminatory dismissal. After two unsuccessful applications for new secretarial jobs at the embassy, Fogarty filed a fresh discrimination suit complaining that the failure to re-employ her was a consequence of her previous sex discrimination claim. At this stage, the USA claimed immunity from jurisdiction. Embassies and consulates enjoyed full immunity from labour claims under the UK legislation in force at the time.[14] Left without remedies, Fogarty applied to the ECtHR, claiming that her right to a court had been breached. The Grand Chamber ruled in favour of the respondent state. It noted that international practice was divided on whether states enjoyed immunity from claims by embassy personnel: that the UK was 'not alone in holding that immunity attaches to [these] suits' meant, in the court's view, that its practice did not 'fall … outside any currently accepted international standards'.[15] It also gave weight to the fact that the applicant's attempted lawsuit concerned her recruitment process: 'Questions relating to the recruitment of staff to missions and embassies may by their very nature involve sensitive and confidential issues', and the court was not aware of any state practice exercising jurisdiction over such claims.[16] The UK's refusal to entertain jurisdiction was thus considered a proportionate restriction on Article 6 ECHR.

[10] See, eg *Naït-Litman v Switzerland* App No 51357/07, 15 March 2018, paras 113–15. *cf* General comment 32 (n 2) para 9: distinctions regarding access to courts should be 'based on law and … justified on objective and reasonable grounds'.

[11] *McElhinney v Ireland* App No 31253/96, 21 November 2001, para 35; *Al-Adsani v United Kingdom* App No 35763/97, 21 November 2001, para 54.

[12] *Al-Adsani* (n 11) para 56.

[13] ibid para 55, referring to the Vienna Convention on the Law of Treaties 1969 (VCLT), Art 31(3)(c).

[14] UK State Immunity Act 1978 (SIA), s 16(1)(a).

[15] *Fogarty v United Kingdom* App No 37112/97, 21 November 2001, para 37.

[16] ibid para 38. See FM Palombino, 'L'immunità degli Stati stranieri dalla giurisdizione rispetto ai rapporti di lavoro e il diritto di accedere ad un tribunale: in margine al caso Fogarty' (2002) 57 *La Comunità internazionale* 79.

Fogarty betrayed a reluctance to rein in the immunity of foreign state employers, perhaps even hinting at the admissibility of blanket immunity for work at diplomatic missions.[17] It is of note that the court stopped short of affirming that immunity is only admissible when international law *requires* a state to grant it; instead, it seemed to suggest that, where there is no consensus in state practice, Article 6 could accommodate all national approaches falling 'within the area of reasonably tenable views'.[18] But this hesitancy was visibly due to the court's unwillingness to take a clear stand on the state of customary law in employment matters: without a clear picture of when international law requires immunity for state employers, the ECtHR simply lacked a legal yardstick for assessing the legitimacy of immunity grants. Starting from the more recent *Cudak* case, however, the ECtHR has adamantly affirmed that, for Article 6 not to be breached, immunity must be granted to an employer state pursuant to an obligation under general international law. Immunity exceeding this threshold has been held incompatible with the Convention.

In *Cudak*, as abundantly discussed earlier in this book, the ECtHR relied on the 2004 United Nations Convention on State Immunity (UNCSI) in order to determine the content of customary law for the purposes of the proportionality assessment.[19] Simply put, *Cudak* turned Article 11 UNCSI into a standard of compliance of state immunity in labour matters: any immunity broader than required by Article 11 was held to violate Article 6 ECHR. Because none of the Article 11 immunity grounds applied, the court ruled in favour of the applicant, a former secretary at the Polish embassy whose unfair dismissal lawsuit was barred by immunity during proceedings before the courts of Lithuania.[20] The Strasbourg Court has followed the same script in subsequent cases on the subject. In the vast majority of such cases, immunity has been held a disproportionate compression of the applicant's right to a court.[21] Only once has the ECtHR ruled otherwise on the grounds that the applicant was a national of the employer state not residing in the forum state, a situation covered by the Article 11(2)(e) UNCSI ground of immunity.[22]

The same approach was adopted by the UK Supreme Court in *Benkharbouche*. The employees challenged the legitimacy of two provisions of the UK SIA which prevented them from suing their former employers, namely section 4(1)(b),

[17] BI Bonafè, 'The ECHR and the Immunities Provided by International Law' (2010) 20 *Italian Yearbook of International Law* 55, 60.

[18] DL Jones, 'Article 6 ECHR and Immunities Arising in Public International Law' (2003) 52 *ICLQ* 463, 470.

[19] United Nations Convention on Jurisdictional Immunities of States and Their Property 2004 (UNCSI), not yet in force.

[20] *Cudak v Lithuania* App No 15869/02, 23 March 2010, paras 69–72.

[21] *Guadagnino v Italy and France* App No 2555/03, 18 January 2011; *Sabeh El Leil v France* App No 34869/05, 29 June 2011; *Wallishauser v Austria* App No 156/04, 17 July 2012, para 71 (in obiter); *Radunović and Others v Montenegro* App Nos 45197/13, 53000/13 and 73404/13, 25 October 2016; *Naku v Lithuania and Sweden* App No 26126/07, 8 November 2016.

[22] *Ndayegamiye-Mporamazina v Switzerland* App No 16874/12, 5 February 2019.

barring claims brought by foreign state employees who were neither nationals or permanent residents of the UK at the time of their hiring, and section 16(1)(a), barring claims by all embassy and consulate personnel irrespective of individual duties. The court held that these two provisions did not pass the *Fogarty/Cudak* test:

> if the legitimate purpose said to justify denying access to a court is compliance with international law, anything that goes further in that direction than international law requires is necessarily disproportionate … [U]nless international law requires the United Kingdom to treat [the respondent states] as immune as regards the claims of [their employees], the denial to them of access to the courts to adjudicate on their claim violates article 6 of the Human Rights Convention.[23]

Based on its own assessment of custom, the court concluded that section 4(1)(b) was 'not justified by any binding principle of international law'.[24] The same applied to section 16(1)(a), at least with regard to the service staff.[25]

As is clear from the above cases, this method of accommodation makes use of human rights law to set a maximum limit on the immunity of foreign state employers. This is a particularly notable aspect insofar as it brings about a paradigm shift in the relevant international law regime: the exercise of jurisdiction over claims not covered by immunity has traditionally been held to fall within the realm of sovereign freedom.[26] Yet, this approach remains highly deferential to employer immunities. It does not question the human rights legitimacy of international law obligations to grant immunity, but merely compels states to grant no more immunity than is strictly required. The scope of admissible immunity is thus entirely dependent on international immunity law.[27] This entails that a *Cudak*-like analysis can place a limit upon employer immunities only to the extent immunity law itself incorporates a limited immunity standard.[28] There is no obstacle to absolute immunity if a norm of international law requires it – or a court persuades itself that it does.

Suffice it to look at *Reyes and Suryadi*, where the English Court of Appeal (CA) interpreted Article 31 of the 1961 Vienna Convention on Diplomatic Relations (VCDR) as granting blanket immunity to sitting diplomatic agents from claims by domestic workers.[29] One of the plaintiffs' arguments was that an immunity so construed would be a disproportionate restriction upon Article 6 ECHR. While the CA accepted that the *Fogarty* test could in principle apply to diplomatic

[23] *Benkharbouche v Secretary of State for Foreign and Commonwealth Affairs and Secretary of State for Foreign and Commonwealth Affairs and Libya v Janah* [2017] UKSC 62, para 34 (Lord Sumption).

[24] ibid para 67.

[25] ibid para 69; see further ch 4, ss IIB and V.

[26] ch 2, s II.

[27] Pavoni (n 7) 72, noting that this technique denies the existence of a normative conflict as long as a court acts within the boundaries required by the applicable immunity rule.

[28] S El Sawah, 'Jurisdictional Immunity of States and Non-commercial Torts' in T Ruys and N Angelet (eds), *The Cambridge Handbook of Immunities and International Law* (Cambridge, Cambridge University Press, 2019) 142, 147, arguing that, in ECtHR case law, 'the proportionality of the restriction is entirely absorbed by the legitimacy of the purpose of State immunity'.

[29] *Reyes and Suryadi v Al-Malki and Al-Malki* [2015] EWCA Civ 32.

immunity, it nonetheless concluded that it did not call for any restriction of immunity in the case at hand. First, the court considered it 'not controversial' that 'the recognition of diplomatic immunity in civil proceedings pursues the legitimate aim of complying with a State's international law obligations to prevent hindrance to the diplomat in performing his functions'.[30] As to proportionality, it restated that 'compliance with a state's international law obligations is conclusive'.[31] The fact that absolute immunity was allegedly flowing from the VCDR, whose provisions reflected customary law, persuaded the CA that 'the international law obligations in relation to diplomatic immunity are not incompatible with article 6 of the ECHR'.[32]

A partly analogous stance was taken by the Supreme Court of Canada (SCC) in *Amaratunga* with respect to IO immunity from employment proceedings. As seen in chapter five, this judgment held the Northwest Atlantic Fisheries Organization (NAFO) immune from unfair dismissal claims by a senior employee.[33] The plaintiff challenged immunity on the basis, inter alia, of Article 14 of the 1966 International Covenant on Civil and Political Rights (ICCPR), pursuant to which, 'In the determination of … his rights and obligations in a suit at law, everyone shall be entitled to a fair and public hearing by a competent, independent and impartial tribunal established by law'. He submitted that immunity would have resulted in denial of justice by leaving him without any judicial remedy for his unlawful dismissal. The SCC quickly dismissed this challenge by noting that, in the UN Human Rights Committee jurisprudence, 'a limitation on [the right to a court] that is based on an immunity deriving from international law would not violate art. 14'.[34] What is singular about this passage is that the respondent organisation arguably did *not* derive its immunity from international law. Earlier in the judgment, the SCC had found that the legal basis of NAFO's immunity was a Canadian domestic law provision granting NAFO immunity 'to such extent as may be required for the performance of its functions'.[35] No applicable international treaty conferred immunity to NAFO. The SCC also denied that any obligation to grant immunity to IOs arose from customary law.[36] Hence, *Amaratunga* proved even more deferential to immunity than the ECtHR's *Fogarty* jurisprudence. In fact, the court brushed aside the implications of the right to a fair trial by deferring to *domestic* law obligations to grant immunity to employers.[37]

[30] ibid para 68.

[31] ibid para 70.

[32] ibid para 76. cp *Reyes v Al-Malki and Another* [2017] UKSC 61, holding that the respondent did not enjoy residual immunity and considering it 'unnecessary' to deal with the plaintiff's Art 6 ECHR challenge to diplomatic immunity (para 52).

[33] *Amaratunga v Northwest Atlantic Fisheries Organization* 2013 SCC 66. See ch 5, s II.

[34] ibid para 62, referring to General comment 32 (n 2) para 18, holding that restrictions 'based on exceptions from jurisdiction deriving from international law such, for example, as immunities' would not breach the right to a fair trial under Art 14 ICCPR.

[35] Northwest Atlantic Fisheries Organization Privileges and Immunities Order 1980 (NAFO Immunity Order), s 3(1). See *Amaratunga* (n 33) paras 32–58.

[36] ibid para 29.

[37] See also the appellate judgment, *Northwest Atlantic Fisheries Organization v Amaratunga* 2011 NSCA 73, para 73, rejecting the argument that construing the NAFO Immunity Order as granting a remedy to the employee would be more consistent with Canada's obligations under the ICCPR.

A consequence of the deference paid by the above cases to immunity – be it limited or absolute in scope – is that a similar way of accommodating conflicts with the right to a court may be de facto indistinguishable from instances where courts have conducted no human rights assessment of immunities at all. One may refer to the practice of US courts, which have traditionally refrained from addressing the compatibility of immunities with access to justice. For instance, the highly influential *Tabion* judgment, which construed the VCDR as granting diplomatic agents absolute immunity from labour claims, was not troubled by possible issues of 'unfairness' and deferred to the choices made by 'policymakers [who] have determined that apparent inequity to a private individual is outweighed by the great injury … that would arise from permitting suit'.[38] In *Brzak and Ishak*, a sex discrimination lawsuit brought by two UN employees, the plaintiffs argued that the immunity 'from every form of legal process' provided by the UN General Convention[39] would infringe upon their constitutional due process rights.[40] The Second Circuit denied the existence of conflicts between immunities of any sort and the US Constitution, generically affirming that 'legislatively and judicially crafted immunities of one sort or another have existed since well before the framing of the Constitution … and are firmly embedded in American law'.[41] In *Bisson*, a district court refused to address an ICCPR-based challenge to UN immunity because it held that treaty to be unable to create enforceable individual rights in US law.[42] However, because the *Tabion*, *Brzak* and *Bisson* courts all construed the relevant treaties as providing for blanket immunity from labour claims, their hypothetical reliance on the *Fogarty* test would not have altered their outcomes, as unequivocally proven by the CA's defence of absolute immunity in *Reyes*.

III. Approaches Requiring the Availability to Employees of Alternative Means of Redress

Primarily in the context of proceedings involving IOs, a different stance to the relationship between employer immunity and access to justice has been adopted by both the Strasbourg Court and many municipal courts. This strand of case law

[38] *Tabion v Mufti and Mufti* 73 F.3d 535 (4th Cir 1996) 539. See also *Montuya v Chedid and Another* 180 ILR 714, 779 F.Supp 2d 60 (DDC 2011) 65.

[39] Convention on the Privileges and Immunities of the United Nations 1946, Art II(2).

[40] *Brzak and Ishak v United Nations et al* 597 F.3d 107 (2d Cir 2010) 114.

[41] ibid. For a similar approach, although not in employment matters, see Italy, Constitutional Court, *Russel case* 18 June 1979, No 48, (1979) 62 *Rivista di diritto internazionale* 797, re a challenge to diplomatic immunity based on the constitutional right of access to a court, holding that diplomatic immunity was *lex specialis* vis-à-vis the Constitution inter alia because it predated the Constitution's entry into force in 1948.

[42] *Bisson v United Nations and Others* ILDC 889 (US 2008), 06 Civ 6352 (SDNY 2008) 10–11. Note that the plaintiff invoked Art 1 ICCPR (right to self-determination) instead of Art 14 on the right to a fair trial. This is, however, immaterial because the court held all ICCPR rights to be non-self-executing (11).

makes immunity's legitimacy conditional upon the employee having access to an effective means of redress other than the courts of the forum state – that is, to one of the internal remedies for settling staff disputes whose general features have been described in chapter three.[43] This section first expounds on the key features of this approach (section IIIA). It then discusses the two prongs of the 'alternative remedies test', namely the requirements that the remedy should be available to the employee (section IIIB) and that it should be effective (section IIIC).

A. The Diffusion of the 'Alternative Remedies Test' in Judicial Practice

The ECtHR developed the test analysed in this section in the two seminal judgments of *Waite and Kennedy* and *Beer and Regan*.[44] The two cases arose from similar factual circumstances and were decided on identical grounds. The applicants, formally employed by private companies, were hired out to the European Space Agency (ESA) and worked for several years at the European Space Operations Centre in Darmstadt. Invoking German employment legislation prohibiting certain forms of hiring out of workers, they initiated proceedings before German courts seeking to be recognised as ESA employees. Their legal actions, however, were dismissed pursuant to the ESA Convention's immunity provisions.[45] They thus applied to the ECtHR, contending that the German courts' refusal to examine their claims breached Article 6 ECHR.

Up to a point, the court's approach did not differ from its handling of state immunity in labour cases. Faithful to its earlier jurisprudence, the Grand Chamber recalled that admissible limitations on Article 6 should pursue a legitimate aim and be proportional to such aim.[46] Moreover, the court did not question that IO immunity pursues the legitimate aim of 'ensuring the proper functioning of such organisations free from unilateral interference by individual governments'.[47] But the distinctive element of *Waite and Kennedy* and *Beer and Regan* is that, in the proportionality assessment, the ECtHR considered whether the applicants had access to other means of redress of their employment grievances: as it famously

[43] ch 3, s IIB.

[44] *Waite and Kennedy v Germany* App No 26083/94, 18 February 1999; *Beer and Regan v Germany* App No 28934/95, 18 February 1999, on which see P Pustorino, 'Immunità giurisdizionale delle organizzazioni internazionali e tutela dei diritti fondamentali: le sentenze della Corte europea nei casi *Waite et Kennedy* e *Beer et Regan*' (2000) 83 *Rivista di diritto internazionale* 132. *cf* ECommHR, *Waite and Kennedy v Germany* App No 26083/94, 2 December 1997, para 74: 'the legal impediment to bringing litigation before the German courts … is only permissible under the Convention if there is an equivalent legal protection'.

[45] Convention for the Establishment of a European Space Agency 1975, Annex I, Art IV, providing that 'The Agency shall have immunity from jurisdiction' save for certain exceptions inapplicable to employment.

[46] *Waite* (n 44) para 59.

[47] ibid para 63.

reasoned, 'a material factor in determining whether granting ESA immunity from German jurisdiction is permissible under the Convention is whether the applicants had available to them reasonable alternative means to protect effectively their rights under the Convention'.[48] The court found such an alternative to be present in the instant cases because the ESA had set up an internal remedy – the ESA Appeals Board – to hear staff disputes.[49] It concluded that Germany did not violate Article 6: the applicants 'could and should' have filed their claims before the Appeals Board.[50]

This approach has been consistently reaffirmed in following cases. In the 2013 *Chapman* decision, the applicant was a US national who sued the North Atlantic Treaty Organization (NATO), his former employer, before Belgian courts over pension entitlements. He submitted that the existing internal remedy, the NATO Appeals Board, could not hear claims by ex-staff members and that this would deprive him of an adequate remedy. A Belgian labour court disagreed, holding that the NATO Appeals Board's jurisdiction was not limited to claims by serving staff and that its procedure complied with the *Waite and Kennedy* requirements. The ECtHR shared this view as to the availability of an alternative means of redress and declared the application manifestly ill-founded.[51] Later on, in *Klausecker*, the applicant claimed to have suffered discrimination on grounds of physical disability in the process of recruitment by the European Patent Office (EPO). As an external candidate for employment, he was found not to have standing to lodge appeals either with EPO's internal labour dispute settlement mechanism or with the International Labour Organization Administrative Tribunal (ILOAT), whose jurisdiction does not encompass claims by individuals who have not yet been recruited.[52] His attempt to bring a complaint before the German Federal Constitutional Court was also unsuccessful: the court held the EPO immune under the applicable treaty provisions and, in any event, affirmed that it lacked jurisdiction over IOs' decisions concerning recruitment.[53] In light of this, the applicant claimed that the German courts' failure to entertain jurisdiction, lacking alternative remedies at the international level, breached Article 6. However, the ECtHR found otherwise: the applicant had turned down an offer of arbitration which, in the court's view, would have provided him with 'a reasonable opportunity to have his complaint … examined on the merits'.[54]

The compatibility with Article 6 ECHR of IO internal remedies for staff disputes has also been discussed by the ECtHR in a distinct line of cases, concerning the

[48] ibid para 68; *Beer* (n 44) para 58.
[49] ESA Staff Regulations, Regulation 33.1, https://esamultimedia.esa.int/docs/LEX-L/Contracts/ESA_REG_007_EN.pdf.
[50] *Waite* (n 44) para 69.
[51] *Chapman v Belgium* App No 39619/06, 5 March 2013, paras 56–57. Similarly, also re the NATO Appeals Board, see *AL v Italy* App No 41387/98, 11 May 2000.
[52] ILOAT, *In re Klausecker* Judgment No 2657, 11 July 2007, paras 5–6.
[53] 22 June 2006, BVerfG, 2 BvR 2093/05; English summary in *Klausecker v Germany* App No 415/07, 29 January 2015, paras 13–16.
[54] *Klausecker* (n 53) para 71.

responsibility of states for IO acts. These cases were not directly concerned with IO immunity in that the applicants did not first attempt to sue their IO employers before domestic courts.[55] Instead, they submitted that the mere fact of setting up an IO possessing a deficient internal dispute settlement mechanism entailed a breach of the ECHR by the respondent states. Yet, as will be seen shortly, this line of precedents may bear relevance to the legitimacy assessment of IO immunity because the ECtHR has ruled over these applications based on a test largely coextensive with the one developed in *Waite and Kennedy*.[56]

This jurisprudence has built on the groundwork laid in *Bosphorus*, which held that states implementing binding treaty commitments arising from participation to an IO are presumed not to incur a Convention breach unless the protection of fundamental rights by the IO is found to be 'manifestly deficient'.[57] The earliest attempts to apply the *Bosphorus* test to employment matters proved unsuccessful. In *Boivin* and *Connolly*, for example, employees respectively of Eurocontrol and the European Community alleged violations of their fair trial rights during labour proceedings before the ILOAT and the European Court of Justice, and filed complaints with the ECtHR against all Members States of their employers. The ECtHR distinguished *Bosphorus*, which concerned actions made by the respondent state in its own territory, in that the applicants complained of acts adopted by organs of the employer organisation, and declared the applications inadmissible *ratione personae*.[58] A similar application was only found to be admissible in *Gasparini*, a case arising out of a labour dispute with NATO. The applicant contended that the procedure before the NATO Appeals Board, whose sessions were not held in public, violated his fair trial rights, and brought his case against the state where NATO was headquartered (Belgium) and his own state of nationality (Italy). Relying on *Bosphorus*, the ECtHR found that the NATO Appeals Board was not a 'manifestly deficient' remedy and thus ruled out any breach of the Convention by the respondent states.[59]

[55] C Ryngaert, 'The European Court of Human Rights' Approach to the Responsibility of Member States in Connection with Acts of International Organizations' (2011) 60 *ICLQ* 997, 1009.

[56] C Ryngaert, 'Belgium' in A Reinisch (ed), *The Privileges and Immunities of International Organizations in Domestic Courts* (Oxford, Oxford University Press, 2013) 55, 71.

[57] *Bosphorus Hava Yolları Turizm ve Ticaret Anonim Şirketi v Ireland* App No 4036/98, 30 June 2005, paras 155–56.

[58] *Boivin v 34 Member States of the Council of Europe* App No 73250/01, 9 September 2008, 6; *Connolly v 15 Member States of the European Union* App No 73274/01, 9 September 2008. See also *Beygo v 46 Member States of the Council of Europe* App No 36099/06, 16 June 2009; *Lopez Cifuentes v Spain* App No 18754/06, 7 July 2009, re an employee of the International Olive Council, holding that the mere fact that this IO was seated in Spain did not establish Spanish jurisdiction under Art 1 ECHR.

[59] *Gasparini v Italy and Belgium* App No 10750/03, 12 May 2009, 10. What set *Gasparini* apart from previous akin applications is unclear. Unlike *Bosphorus*, the application did not concern a specific state act: Ryngaert, 'The European Court' (n 55) 1005. *Gasparini* distinguished previous cases because the applicant complained of a 'structural lacuna' rather than a specific IO decision (7), but this may also apply eg to *Connolly* (n 58), where the applicant complained of not having been allowed to submit written observations to the Advocate General's opinion. See T Lock, 'Beyond Bosphorus: The European Court of Human Rights' Case Law on the Responsibility of Member States of International Organisations under the European Convention on Human Rights' (2010) 10 *Human Rights Law Review* 529, 539.

As mentioned above, *Gasparini* and its progeny may be relevant to the assessment of the admissible scope of IO immunity. This is because several elements in the ECtHR's case law suggest that the court adopted the same standard of review in both lines of precedents. Admittedly, *Gasparini* proclaimed that the 'non-manifest deficiency' standard was intended to be more lenient than the *Waite and Kennedy* test:

> son contrôle en vue de déterminer si la procédure devant [un] organe d'une organisation internationale … est entachée d'une insuffisance manifeste *est nécessairement moins ample* que le contrôle qu'elle exerce au regard de l'article 6 sur les procédures devant les juridictions internes …[60]

But it is hard to reconcile this statement with what the court did in practice. Far from being 'moins ample', *Gasparini*'s quality assessment of the relevant IO remedy was both longer and more detailed than the one performed in *Waite*.[61] The convergence of the two tests has become more evident in subsequent cases. In *Chapman*, the same NATO Appeals Board scrutinised in *Gasparini* passed the *Waite and Kennedy* test (although the ECtHR oddly did not refer to the quality assessment performed in *Gasparini*). In *Klausecker*, the applicant sought to hold Germany accountable for violations of both standards: besides complaining of the lack of access to domestic courts in the fashion of *Waite*, he also asserted that labour procedures within the EPO and before the ILOAT failed the test of *Bosphorus*.[62] The ECtHR relied on the two standards somewhat interchangeably. In the *Waite and Kennedy* limb, where it held the arbitration procedure to be a reasonable alternative means of redress, the court referred, '*mutatis mutandis*, to its findings in the case of *Gasparini*'.[63] As for the question whether the internal procedure was 'manifestly deficient' in *Bosphorus* terms, the court answered in the negative for no other reason than it had passed the *Waite and Kennedy* test.[64]

The de facto equivalence of the two tests puts into question the suitability of a *Bosphorus* analysis with regard to IO staff disputes. *Gasparini*'s rationale sits uneasily with the principle underlying *Waite* that, if no 'alternative remedy' is available to the employee, the state where the work is performed should provide a forum to obtain redress: this implies that, if the applicant did not attempt to sue the IO employer before municipal courts, as was the case in *Gasparini*, the application should be inadmissible for non-exhaustion of local remedies.[65] This finds confirmation in *Perez*. The applicant was a senior manager at the UN Volunteer Programme in Bonn. After being dismissed, she initiated proceedings before the UN Joint Appeals Board, an internal remedy composed of three staff members, and later before the UN Administrative Tribunal, and was granted compensation.

[60] *Gasparini* (n 59) 7 (emphasis added) ('its control to determine whether the proceedings before [a] body of an international organisation … is tainted by a manifest inadequacy is necessarily less extensive than its control under Article 6 over proceedings before internal courts').
[61] ibid 9–10. cp *Waite* (n 44) para 69. On the shortcomings of *Waite*, see further below s IIIB.
[62] *Klausecker* (n 53) para 43.
[63] ibid para 74.
[64] ibid paras 105–06.
[65] Ryngaert, 'Belgium' (n 56) 70.

Before the Strasbourg Court, she asserted that the procedures before the UN bodies were manifestly deficient in *Bosphorus* terms and that Germany, as a UN member, was responsible for such structural lacunae. The ECtHR declared the application inadmissible for failure to exhaust local remedies. It accepted Germany's defence that a complaint to the Federal Constitutional Court would have provided a remedy 'accessible and capable of providing redress' had the applicant been able to prove that the protection of her human rights in the UN framework was manifestly inferior to the standards of the German Basic Law.[66] As will be seen below, the Bundesverfassungsgericht commonly performs a *Waite*-like control over IO internal justice systems vis-à-vis constitutional access to court requirements. The failure of a *Gasparini* complaint for non-exhaustion of local remedies conclusively proves two things: first, that the *Gasparini* and *Waite and Kennedy* tests are indistinguishable; and secondly, that the *Waite* model is the preferable one for bringing issues relating to employment with IOs before the Strasbourg Court.[67]

As the above cases show, the ECtHR has so far never declared an IO internal remedy to be an inadequate alternative to domestic courts – nor, for that matter, a 'manifestly deficient' one. The court's attitude towards IO immunity has generally been deferential,[68] on the assumption that 'the test of proportionality cannot be applied in such a way as to … thwart the proper functioning of international organisations'.[69] But the fact that IO immunity has always withstood the *Waite and Kennedy* test should not overshadow the profound difference from the court's jurisprudence on state immunity in labour claims analysed in section II. Differently from *Fogarty* and *Cudak*, under *Waite* the deference towards international law immunities has never been absolute. The court's jurisprudence is unequivocal in the sense that, lacking adequate alternative remedies, a breach of Article 6 ECHR would occur notwithstanding the fact that the IO employer derives its immunity from international law. In *Perez*, for instance, the ECtHR hinted at the possibility of suing the UN before German courts to probe the adequacy of the UN internal justice system even though the UN General Convention, to which Germany is a party, entitles the organisation to full immunity from suit.[70] This approach may thus require national courts to affirm jurisdiction disregarding treaty obligations to grant immunity to IOs.[71]

[66] *Perez v Germany* App No 15521/08, 29 January 2015, para 86.

[67] In this sense, also Lock (n 59) 537. See Ryngaert, 'The European Court' (n 55) 1001, criticising *Gasparini* for attributing IO acts to Member States in defiance of the separation of legal personalities.

[68] Ryngaert, 'The European Court' (n 55) 1010.

[69] *Waite* (n 44) para 72.

[70] Art II(2).

[71] A Peters, 'Immune against Constitutionalisation?' in A Peters et al (eds), *Immunities in the Age of Global Constitutionalism* (Leiden, Brill Nijhoff, 2015) 1, 16–17; C Ryngaert, 'The Immunity of International Organizations Before Domestic Courts: Recent Trends' (2010) 7 *International Organizations Law Review* 121, 134; A Orakhelashvili, 'Jurisdictional Immunity of International Organizations: From Abstract Functionality to Absolute Immunity' in A Orakhelashvili (ed), *Research Handbook on Jurisdiction and Immunities in International Law* (Cheltenham, Edward Elgar, 2015) 497, 522–23, in the sense that the principle underlying *Waite* is not harmonious interpretation, as in *Fogarty*, but the ECHR's primacy over other international obligations.

That the 'alternative remedies test' may result in non-compliance with international treaty obligations on immunity finds abundant confirmation in domestic judicial practice. Municipal courts of many jurisdictions – primarily, but not exclusively, in ECHR state parties – have resorted to this test for assessing the legitimacy of IO employer immunity vis-à-vis Article 6 ECHR or other fair trial provisions contained in international treaties or national constitutions. The IO internal remedies' failure to meet this test has resulted in the lifting of immunity.[72] In *Siedler*, for example, a Belgian appellate court – in a decision later affirmed, in the relevant parts, by the Court of Cassation[73] – set aside the immunity of the Western European Union (WEU) in a labour dispute initiated by a former employee, and this was notwithstanding the fact that the WEU was entitled to 'immunity from every form of legal process' under the applicable treaty provision.[74] Explicitly citing from *Waite* and *Beer*, the court held that the WEU's internal procedure for staff disputes did not meet the fair trial requirements of Article 6 ECHR.[75] In *Ryabov*, the Russian Supreme Court set aside the Eurasian Development Bank's (EDB) immunity from a claim for unpaid wages and moral damages. The EDB Charter entitled the Bank to immunity for all official acts;[76] as seen in chapter three, employment relationships are normally covered by such immunity provisions.[77] Although the court oddly construed the provision as not covering employment, such a strained construction was motivated by human rights considerations. Citing *Beer and Regan*, it held that, because the EDB had not established any accessible means for protecting labour rights, granting immunity would have amounted to a breach of Article 6 ECHR and the access to court provision of the Russian Constitution.[78]

The same outcomes have been reached by courts that have assessed the legitimacy of IO immunity exclusively from the standpoint of domestic constitutional provisions. The reason for these courts' failure to explicitly cite ECtHR jurisprudence is not always straightforward, but can often be explained by the fact that the use of the 'alternative remedies test' by certain domestic courts predated *Waite*,[79]

[72] See, eg B Fassbender, 'Germany' in Reinisch (n 56) 123, 129, re the German case law discussed below in text.

[73] *Western European Union v Siedler* 21 December 2009, No S 04 0129 F, ILDC 1625 (BE 2009).

[74] Agreement on the Status of Western European Union, National Representatives and International Staff 1955, Art 4.

[75] Labor Court of Brussels, *Siedler v Western European Union* 17 September 2003, ILDC 53 (BE 2003), paras 44–63. See also Court of Cassation, *General Secretariat of the ACP Group v BD* 21 December 2009, No C 07 0407 F, ILDC 1576 (BE 2009), re immunity from execution in labour matters.

[76] Charter of the Eurasian Development Bank, Annex to the Agreement on the Establishment of the Eurasian Development Bank 2006, Art 31(1).

[77] ch 3, s VB.

[78] *Ryabov v Eurasian Development Bank* 9 July 2010, N 5-B10-49, ILDC 1559 (RU 2010), H10-H11. Pursuant to Art 46(1) of the Russian Constitution, 'Everyone shall be guaranteed protection in court of his rights and freedoms'.

[79] P Schmitt, *Access to Justice and International Organizations: The Case of Individual Victims of Human Rights Violations* (Cheltenham, Edward Elgar, 2017) 287, re Italian case law discussed below.

or more simply that the ECHR is not binding on the country of the court. Notably, for instance, the German Federal Constitutional Court has addressed the human rights legitimacy of IO employer immunity within the framework of its famous *Solange* jurisprudence,[80] according to which transfers of sovereign power to IOs should not infringe upon the fundamental rights guaranteed by the German Basic Law.[81] In the seminal 1981 *Eurocontrol II* judgment, the court enquired whether the system of judicial protection of labour rights established by Eurocontrol met the Basic Law's minimum requirements on access to justice, and was satisfied that the employees could find adequate protection by recourse to the ILOAT.[82] The same jurisprudence has been restated more recently in a complaint brought by three French employees of the EPO. The complainants challenged the constitutionality of the EPO President's disciplinary decision concerning the illegitimate use of internal email systems for union purposes, which was later upheld by the ILOAT.[83] The court dismissed the complaint on other procedural grounds, but affirmed in obiter that it would have declared it admissible had the complainants proved the existence of 'structural deficits' within the legal protection afforded by the ILOAT.[84]

Other pioneering uses of this test may be drawn from the case law of Argentina and Italy. In the 1983 *Cabrera* case, the Argentine Supreme Court dealt with a labour claim against the Comisión Técnica Mixta de Salto Grande, a bilateral Argentine–Uruguayan organisation that enjoyed full immunity under its headquarters agreement. Noting that the Comisión did not provide for any internal remedy available to employees, the court held that barring employees from bringing suit would have been unconstitutional for breach of the right to court.[85] The *Cabrera* test was reiterated in *Duhalde*, where the Supreme Court deferred to the World Health Organization's absolute immunity because its adherence to the ILOAT provided employees with adequate alternative remedies.[86]

Italian judges, for their part, recognised the unfairness of depriving IO employees of judicial remedies as early as in the 1931 *Profili* case, an employment dispute against the International Institute of Agriculture. The only internal remedy available to the employee was an appeal to the same organ that sanctioned his dismissal. While the Court of Cassation refused to draw consequences on the plane of its

[80] Fassbender (n 72) 127.

[81] *Solange I* Order of the Second Senate of 29 May 1974, BverfGE 37, 291; *Solange II* Order of the Second Senate of 22 October 1986, BverfGE 73, 339, both re the European Communities.

[82] *Eurocontrol II* Order of 10 November 1981, BverfGE 58, 1, 2 BvR 1058/79. As seen in ch 3, s IIB, this ruling was based on a supposed lack of subject-matter jurisdiction and not on immunity. But all that matters for the present analysis is that the court verified the compatibility of the lack of German jurisdiction (whatever its rationale) with the constitutional right to a remedy.

[83] ILOAT, Judgment No 2228, 16 July 2003.

[84] *B and Others* Order of the Second Senate of 3 July 2006, 2 BvR 1458/03, ILDC 1751 (DE 2006) paras 22–24. See also *S* Order of the Second Senate of 4 April 2001, 2 BvR 2368/99, ILDC 133 (DE 2001), re a patent attorney's challenge to an EPO Board of Appeal decision.

[85] *Cabrera v Comisión Técnica Mixta de Salto Grande* 5 December 1983, CSJN Fallos 305:2150.

[86] *Duhalde v Organización Panamericana de la Salud – Organización Mondial de la Salud Oficina Sanitaria Panamericana* 31 August 1999, CSJN Fallos 322:1905.

adjudicative powers – the case was dismissed for lack of subject-matter jurisdiction – it nonetheless speculated that 'a more progressive system' of judicial protection was evidently needed.[87] In more recent times, the Corte di Cassazione has not hesitated to remove IO immunity where it has excessively limited the employees' right to bring their cases to court under Article 24 of the Italian Constitution.[88] The rationale for this jurisprudence lies in the Italian analogue of the *Solange* reservation – the *controlimiti* doctrine.[89] As the court explained in *Colagrossi*, where a Food and Agriculture Organization (FAO) employee alleged that the ILOAT's exclusive jurisdiction infringed Article 24, limitations of national sovereignty by international commitments 'are legitimate even when they interfere with the rights of citizens in domestic law, provided that, as in the present case, the interference does not violate constitutional guarantees'.[90]

The most notable instance where this doctrine has led to the repudiation of an IO's treaty-based immunity is the 2007 *Drago* judgment, where an individual employed by International Plant Genetic Resources Institute (IPGRI) under a temporary contract complained about the legality of termination of employment. Based on a headquarters agreement clause providing full immunity,[91] both the first instance and the appellate courts declined jurisdiction. On final appeal, Drago challenged the constitutionality of the IPGRI's absolute immunity on the grounds that no effective internal remedy existed. The Court of Cassation ruled that the existing internal remedy for staff disputes did not meet basic due process requirements and entailed a breach of Article 24.[92] It only refrained from referring the matter to the Constitutional Court – the only court empowered to strike down international treaties for conflicting with the Constitution[93] – by means of a legal artifice: it construed Article 5 of the IPGRI's Headquarters Agreement, providing a duty for the IPGRI to 'establish suitable procedures for resolving disputes with its employees', as a prerequisite for immunity, thus holding that the Agreement itself did not require immunity in the case at hand. This strained construction, criticised earlier in this book,[94] was justified by the need to interpret the Agreement in conformity with Article 24.[95]

[87] *Istituto Internazionale di Agricoltura v Profili* 26 February 1931, 5 ILR 413, on which see also ch 3, s IIA.

[88] R Pisillo Mazzeschi, 'Immunità giurisdizionale delle organizzazioni internazionali e Costituzione italiana' (1976) 59 *Rivista di diritto internazionale* 489; P Pustorino, 'The Immunity of International Organizations from Civil Jurisdiction in the Recent Italian Case Law' (2009) 19 *Italian Yearbook of International Law* 57, 65–69.

[89] On which see D Amoroso, 'Italy' in FM Palombino (ed), *Duelling for Supremacy: International Law vs National Fundamental Principles* (Cambridge, Cambridge University Press, 2019) 184.

[90] *Colagrossi v FAO* 18 May 1992, No 5942, 101 ILR 386, 394. But see Court of Cassation, *Paradiso v ICAMAS* 13 February 1991, No 1513, (1992) 28 *Rivista di diritto internazionale privato e processuale* 603, finding no conflict between IO immunity and Art 24.

[91] Agreement between the Italian Republic and the International Plant Genetic Resources Institute (IPGRI) regarding the headquarters seat of IPGRI 1991, Art V(1).

[92] *Drago v International Plant Genetic Resources Institute (IPGRI)* 19 February 2007, No 3718, ILDC 827 (IT 2007) paras 6.5–6.6.

[93] Amoroso (n 89) 192–94.

[94] ch 3, s VI.

[95] *Drago* (n 92) para 6.7.

The 'alternative remedies test' can also be encountered in the judicial practice of, inter alia, Switzerland, the Netherlands, Austria, the UK and France.[96] The approach of the French Court of Cassation stands out for grounding the use of this test not on international human rights instruments nor on the Constitution, but instead on the concept of international *ordre public*. This feature may appear baffling, as it relies on a concept peculiar to conflict of laws for assessing the domestic applicability of international legal sources.[97] In practice, however, the relevant French case law conforms to the same scheme as other jurisdictions. In a 2005 case, the Court of Cassation disregarded the African Development Bank's full immunity:[98] the Bank's failure to set up an internal justice system for dismissed employees constituted 'un déni de justice fondant la compétence de la juridiction française'.[99] In *Illemassene*, by contrast, the immunity of the Organisation for Economic Co-operation and Development (OECD) passed the *ordre public* test. The court found that the plaintiff, a former consultant, was entitled to bring claims to the OECD Administrative Tribunal and that this remedy met the necessary fair trial requirements.[100]

Notwithstanding the external differences between the above approaches, all courts balancing the immunity of IO employers with right to a court provisions may be regarded as relying on essentially the same judicial standard as a result of extensive (although often tacit) judicial dialogue and cross-pollination.[101] The German and Italian courts, for example, have substantiated their scrutiny of IO remedies through constitutional clauses 'substantively equivalent' to Article 6 ECHR.[102] The German *Solange* jurisprudence likely influenced the ECtHR's early development of the *Waite and Kennedy* doctrine,[103] and *Waite*, in turn, has been referenced in the Bundesverfassungsgericht's more recent decisions on the subject.[104] The French Court of Cassation's unorthodox reliance on denial of justice as a component of *ordre public* was also certainly influenced by *Waite*.[105] Even the Argentine Supreme Court in *Cabrera* correlated the Constitution's fair trial

[96] For case law, see below in this section.

[97] A de Nanteuil, 'L'application en France des règles internationales relatives aux immunités' (2010) 56 *Annuaire Français de Droit International* 807, 836.

[98] Agreement Establishing the African Development Bank 1963, Art 52(1).

[99] *African Development Bank v X* 25 January 2005, No 04-41012, ILDC 778 (FR 2005) para 3 ('a denial of justice establishing the jurisdiction of the French courts').

[100] *Illemassene v Organisation for Economic Co-operation and Development* 29 September 2010, No 09-41030, ILDC 1749 (FR 2010) para 5.

[101] A Reinisch, 'Transnational Judicial Conversations on the Personality, Privileges, and Immunities of International Organizations – An Introduction' in Reinisch (n 56) 11.

[102] A Reinisch and G Novak, 'International Organizations' in A Nollkaemper and A Reinisch (eds), *International Law in Domestic Courts: A Casebook* (Oxford, Oxford University Press, 2018) 170, 183. See also R Pavoni, 'Italy' in Reinisch (n 56) 155, 166–67, in the sense that the Court of Cassation should have expressly taken into account relevant ECtHR case law.

[103] Fassbender (n 72) 130.

[104] *B and Others* (n 84) para 22.

[105] S El Boudouhi and G Dannenberg, 'France' in S Kadelbach et al (eds), *Judging International Human Rights: Courts of General Jurisdiction as Human Rights Courts* (Cham, Springer, 2019) 453, 465. Moreover, in non-labour cases the Court of Cassation has expressly grounded the 'alternative remedies test' on Art 6 ECHR: *SATRE and CSR v League of Arab States* 14 October 2009, No 08–14.978.

provision with international standards through citation of Articles 8 and 10 of the 1948 Universal Declaration of Human Rights.[106] In sum, the domestic law provisions on which the 'alternative remedies test' has been based may be regarded as proxies for the equivalent international norm safeguarding the right to a court.[107] This entails that all national courts applying the 'alternative remedies test', even in the framework of a *Solange*-like refusal to comply with treaty obligations, should properly be regarded as addressing not just a conflict between domestic and international law, but also one between two international norms, namely jurisdictional immunity and fair trial.[108]

B. The Requirement of Availability of the Alternative Remedy

Following the ECtHR's dicta in *Waite* and *Beer* – which enquired 'whether the applicants had available to them reasonable alternative means to protect effectively their rights' – the classic rendition of the 'alternative remedies test' breaks down into a two-pronged test of availability and effectiveness. This subsection focuses on the first prong, while the remedy's qualitative requirements will be addressed in the following subsection.

The first, and arguably most crucial, issue is whether the availability of an alternative means of redress should be regarded in all cases as a *conditio sine qua non*. This point has been kept somewhat ambiguous in ECtHR jurisprudence. In *Waite* and *Beer*, the court refrained from describing the availability of a remedy as an imperative prerequisite for immunity, but only described it as 'a material factor' in the proportionality assessment.[109] It thus seemed to imply that there might be cases where IO immunity can be compatible with a fair trial even though alternative remedies are not guaranteed.[110] This suspicion materialised in *Mothers of Srebrenica*, where the Dutch courts' grant of immunity to the UN from claims relating to its failure to prevent the Srebrenica genocide was found not to violate Article 6 ECHR even though no alternative means of redress were available to the aggrieved parties. The ECtHR affirmed that its judgments in *Waite* and *Beer* 'cannot be interpreted [in the sense] that in the absence of an alternative remedy

[106] RE Vinuesa, 'Argentina' in Reinisch (n 56) 17, 21.

[107] G Novak and A Reinisch, 'Desirable Standards for the Design of Administrative Tribunals from the Perspective of Domestic Courts' in O Elias (ed), *The Development and Effectiveness of International Administrative Law* (Leiden, Brill Nijhoff, 2012) 273, 299.

[108] FM Palombino, 'Introduction' in Palombino (ed) (n 89) 1, 3: in 'cases where national decisions refraining from giving effect in domestic legal orders to international law are based on rules of domestic law that conform to, or give effect to, another rule of international law [the real issue] is not the clash between distinct legal orders, but the coordination of different international norms'.

[109] A Reinisch, 'The Immunity of International Organizations and the Jurisdiction of Their Administrative Tribunals' (2008) 7 *Chinese Journal of International Law* 285, 292.

[110] N Angelet and A Weerts, 'Les immunités des organisations internationales face à l'article 6 de la Convention européenne des droits de l'homme' (2007) 134 *Journal du droit international* 3, 10.

the recognition of immunity is *ipso facto* constitutive of a violation of the right of access to a court'.[111] But the *Srebrenica* limitation on the 'alternative remedies test' should arguably not be extrapolated to staff disputes. In fact, the court distinguished its previous jurisprudence on IO immunity precisely because, up to that moment, it had only concerned staff claims.[112] For the same reason, it also distinguished its *Bosphorus/Gasparini* jurisprudence on equivalent protection.[113] The decision in *Srebrenica* came down to the fact that the dispute concerned the Security Council's powers under Chapter VII UN Charter and its role in maintaining international peace and security.[114] In the context of staff disputes, by contrast, the ECtHR has never suggested that the availability of an alternative remedy may be dispensed of.

Municipal case law largely supports the view that the availability requirement admits no exception in labour matters, even though a more lenient standard may be followed in other domains.[115] In a 2012 case concerning the International Committee of the Red Cross's immunity from enforcement proceedings initiated by an employee, the Swiss Federal Tribunal unequivocally endorsed such a strict interpretation of *Waite* by holding that Article 6 ECHR 'n'est respecté que si le justiciable dispose d'autres voies raisonnables pour protéger efficacement [ses] droits'.[116] This decision may be contrasted to the earlier judgment in *NML Capital*, where the same court, again in the context of immunity from execution, held that the Bank for International Settlements was immune from claims brought by two investment funds even though the claimants had no alternative means of redress. The court treated the availability of alternative remedies as only one factor within a broader proportionality test, and gave decisive relevance to the necessity to protect the Bank's international payment operations, which – it argued – would have been jeopardised by the lifting of immunity.[117] This seeming inconsistency has been

[111] *Stichting Mothers of Srebrenica and Others v the Netherlands* App No 65542/12, 11 June 2013, para 164.

[112] ibid para 149.

[113] ibid para 150.

[114] MI Papa, 'The *Mothers of Srebrenica* Case before the European Court of Human Rights: United Nations Immunity versus Right of Access to a Court' (2016) 14 *Journal of International Criminal Justice* 893, 902–03. See also *Mothers of Srebrenica* (n 111) para 154.

[115] BI Bonafè, 'Italian Courts and the Immunity of International Organizations' (2013) 10 *International Organizations Law Review* 505, 535, re Italian case law. See also Ryngaert, 'The Immunity' (n 71) 135, generally arguing that 'it is not so much a question of *whether* a "reasonable alternative means" test ought to be performed, but rather of *how* this test should actually be conducted' (emphases in the original). But see The Hague Court of Appeal, *Vakbondsunie van het Europees Octrooibureau (VEOB) and Staff Union of the European Patent Office (SUEPO) v European Patent Organisation* 17 February 2015, ECLI:NL:GHDHA:2015:255, para 3.10, holding the lack of available remedies to trade unions as not determinative and also considering the seriousness of the alleged breach of social rights involved. For a criticism of this passage, which confused procedural and substantive aspects, see Ryngaert, 'Immunities' (n 6) 401–03.

[116] *X v Comité international de la Croix-Rouge and Office des poursuites de Genève* 20 September 2012, No 5A_106/2012, para 7.2.1 (internal quotations omitted) ('is respected only if the litigant has other reasonable avenues to effectively protect [his] rights').

[117] *NML Capital Ltd and EM Limited v Bank for International Settlements and Debt Enforcement Office Basel-Stadt* 12 July 2010, No 5A 360/2010, ILDC 1547 (CH 2010) para 4.5.

persuasively explained by the fact that the Federal Tribunal '[attaches] different degrees of importance to the (non-)availability of an alternative means, depending on the context and categorization of the case', and considers that only staff cases warrant 'the automatism of an article 6 violation' in default of alternative means.[118]

As for what makes a remedy unavailable, the easiest scenario is where an IO has not established any remedy whatsoever for settling staff disputes. While this is infrequent for medium-sized or large organisations, it is much more prevalent in smaller or bilateral ones. For instance, in *Amaratunga*, the SCC acknowledged that the 'absence of a dispute resolution mechanism or of an internal review process' for NAFO employees was such that 'the appellant ha[d] no forum in which to air his grievances'.[119] As seen in section II, the court deferred to immunity despite the lack of internal remedies, confining itself to describing the outcome as 'unfortunate'.[120] It is noteworthy that the first instance court had instead set aside NAFO's immunity on the grounds that leaving the employee without redress 'would be inconsistent with [the] basic right [to a fair hearing] as enshrined in the ICCPR'.[121]

Where no internal mechanism of dispute resolution exists, employees whose claims are barred by immunity could only put their hope in a waiver of immunity from the respondent IOs. Because treaties frequently stipulate a duty upon organisations to waive immunity where it 'would impede the course of justice', it has been suggested that waivers may constitute a sufficient guarantee against denial of justice.[122] But this guarantee is purely illusory. Most instruments only apply this duty to the immunity of IO officials and not to the immunity of the IO itself.[123] Moreover, because this duty is commonly conditioned upon the waiver not being prejudicial to the organisation's interests, these treaty clauses do not alter the nature of waiver as an act 'operat[ing] only as a matter of grace'.[124]

More commonly, an availability issue arises where an IO is equipped with an internal justice system which cannot be accessed by an individual employee, either because it discriminates among employees as regards *jus standi* or because it does

[118] T Neumann and A Peters, 'Switzerland' in Reinisch (n 56) 241, 265–66. *cf* also *Jananyagam v Commonwealth Secretariat* 12 March 2007, Appeal No UKEAT/0443/06/DM, ILDC 1763 (UK 2007), applying the *Waite* test to a staff dispute, with England and Wales High Court, *Entico Corporation Ltd v United Nations Educational Scientific and Cultural Association (UNESCO)* 18 March 2008, [2008] 1 CLC 524, paras 24–27, re a commercial claim, awkwardly ruling out conflicts with fair trial because UNESCO predated the ECHR, but also justifying deferring to immunity by invoking, for some reason, the *Fogarty* criteria on state immunity. For criticism, see D Sarooshi and A Tzanakopoulos, 'United Kingdom' in Reinisch (n 56) 275, 294–96. As for *Entico*'s intertemporal argument, it can be objected that the ECtHR has regularly applied the *Waite* test to NATO, which also predated the ECHR: see, eg *Chapman* (n 51).

[119] *Amaratunga* (n 33) paras 60 and 63.

[120] ibid para 63.

[121] *Amaratunga v Northwest Atlantic Fisheries Organization* 2010 NSSC 346, paras 75–76.

[122] CH Brower, 'International Immunities: Some Dissident Views on the Role of Municipal Courts' (2001) 41 *Virginia Journal of International Law* 1, 27.

[123] See, eg Convention on the Privileges and Immunities of the United Nations 1946, Art 5, s 20, only referring to immunity of UN officials. But see Convention for the Establishment of a European Space Agency 1975, Annex I, Art IV(a), where the duty of waiver covers the immunity of the organisation.

[124] Orakhelashvili (n 71) 506.

not allow for review of certain acts or decisions. While international administrative tribunals have sometimes construed their jurisdiction broadly in order to avoid denials of justice,[125] avenues of recourse that are not envisaged by the letter of their statutes may not be created through judicial interpretation.[126] Thus, the jurisdiction of IO internal remedies may incur gaps *ratione temporis*, *materiae* or *personae*.[127] For example, claims by job applicants normally fall outside the jurisdiction of administrative tribunals and other internal remedies.[128] In *In re Klausecker*, the ILOAT acknowledged that the applicant's claims fell into a 'legal vacuum', and considered it 'highly desirable that the Organisation should seek a solution affording the complainant access to a court'.[129] The ECtHR later found that the possibility of arbitration offered to the applicant constituted a sufficient remedy,[130] but it should be stressed that the applicant would have had no remedy in the absence of the employer's willingness to arbitrate. This was the case in *Sevens*, where a Belgian court set aside NATO's immunity from a claim by a failed job applicant because NATO's internal remedies were not competent to review decisions concerning the hiring of applicants.[131] *Drago* is a further example in point. The ILOAT lacked competence over the plaintiff's claims because the IPGRI had only recognised its jurisdiction after the dispute arose. Moreover, the staff rules expressly removed any 'action based on expiration of an appointment by its own terms', as Drago's claim likely was, from the purview of the IPGRI Appeals Committee, an internal remedy for staff members.[132] The Cassazione concluded that the IPGRI had 'preclud[ed] recourse to any form of jurisdictional protection'.[133]

These cases highlight that the availability of an alternative remedy cannot be assessed *in abstracto* but depends on the specific conditions of an individual employee. Such a customised analysis was startingly lacking from the seminal judgments in *Waite* and *Beer*. In reproaching the applicants for failure to bring their complaints before the ESA Appeals Board,[134] the ECtHR cited the provision

[125] See, eg UN Administrative Tribunal, *Zafari v the Commissioner-General of the United Nations Relief and Works Agency for Palestine Refugees in the Near East* Judgment No 461, 10 November 1990, affirming jurisdiction over claims by local UN staff not covered by other internal remedies.

[126] CF Amerasinghe, 'International Administrative Tribunals' in C Romano, K Alter and Y Shany (eds), *The Oxford Handbook of International Adjudication* (Oxford, Oxford University Press, 2013) 316, 326–27. See, eg UN Dispute Tribunal, *Mirella et al v Secretary-General of the United Nations* 29 December 2017, No UNDT/2017/099, para 55.

[127] See, eg UN Dispute Tribunal, *Kimungui v Secretary-General of the United Nations* 22 December 2014, No UNDT/2014/147, denying jurisdiction *ratione personae* over claims by a contractor; Commonwealth Secretariat Arbitral Tribunal, *Saroha v Regional Director, Commonwealth Youth Programme (CYP Asia)* 14 July 2000, CSAT/2, denying jurisdiction over claims by a staff member locally recruited in India.

[128] See, eg ILOAT, *In re Liaci* Judgment No 1964, 12 July 2000, para 4.

[129] *In re Klausecker* (n 52) para 6.

[130] *Klausecker* (n 53).

[131] Brussels Tribunal of First Instance, *Sevens v NATO and Belgium* 12 March 2013, Case No 12/1586/C.

[132] *Drago* (n 92) para 6.6.

[133] ibid para 6.8.

[134] *Waite* (n 44) para 69.

of the ESA Staff Regulations giving the Appeals Board competence 'to hear disputes relating to any explicit or implicit decision taken by the Agency and arising between it and a staff member'.[135] However, it did nothing to make sure that the applicants could be qualified as 'staff members'. Because they had been supplied to ESA by private companies, it is dubious at best that the Appeals Board had jurisdiction *ratione personae*.[136] Even more astonishingly, the ECtHR was aware that the Board's competence over the applicants' claims was problematic, but opined that 'it would have been for the ESA Appeals Board … to settle the question of its jurisdiction'.[137] The court was therefore content with the mere existence of the Appeals Board,[138] and seemed to imply that the requirements of Article 6 ECHR would be met by the applicants' right to appeal to the Board 'only to be refused the status of agents'.[139] Finally, the ECtHR suggested that an adequate alternative means could have been provided by the possibility for the applicants to sue their formal employers (that is, the private companies that hired them out to ESA) before domestic courts.[140] But this was an incongruous remark, insofar as it referred to a different legal relationship.[141] As Ryngaert has rightly pointed out, 'a claimant should be allowed to bring a case … against the international organization itself for the alternative means test to be satisfied'.[142]

An alternative and more sensible course of action is provided by the Swiss courts' approach to the issue of availability in *ZM*. In this case, which predated *Waite* and *Beer*, the Arab League was sued by a Syrian individual employed at the League's Office of the Permanent Observer to the UN in Geneva. Having concluded that a norm of customary international law entitled the League to full immunity from labour lawsuits,[143] the first instance court was troubled by the possibility of a denial of justice and suggested that absolute immunity could incur

[135] ESA Staff Regulations (n 49) Regulation 33.1.

[136] A Reinisch, 'Waite and Kennedy v. Germany, Application No 26083/94; Beer and Regan v. Germany, Application No 28934/95' (1999) 93 *American Journal of International Law* 933, 936.

[137] *Waite* (n 44) para 69.

[138] M Kloth, *Immunities and the Right of Access to Court under Article 6 of the European Convention on Human Rights* (Leiden, Brill Nijhoff, 2010) 142–43.

[139] E Gaillard and I Pingel-Lenuzza, 'International Organisations and Immunity from Jurisdiction: To Restrict or to Bypass' (2002) 51 *ICLQ* 1, 7.

[140] *Waite* (n 44) para 70: 'it is in principle open to temporary workers to seek redress from the firms that have employed them and hired them out'. See also *Jananyagam* (n 118) para 52, re a contractor recruited through an external agency, upholding immunity despite the employee not having access to the Commonwealth Secretariat Administrative Tribunal and holding that arbitration proceedings previously instituted between the external agency and the Secretariat could have provided the plaintiff with a forum to air her grievance. But the plaintiff was not a party to the legal relationship that had been submitted to the arbitral panel.

[141] ECommHR, *Waite* (n 44) Dissenting Opinion of G Ress, para 2: 'such action against a company seated abroad does not appear a practical solution to the applicants' problems. Above all, they could not, in such proceedings, have secured the right asserted by them, namely an employment contract with the European Space Agency as borrowing employer. Accordingly, these proceedings cannot be regarded as a substitute [of] the requirement of access to court.'

[142] Ryngaert, 'Belgium' (n 56) 68.

[143] An unconvincing view for reasons exposed in ch 2, s VIA.

limitation based on the lack of equivalent protection.[144] But the application of the 'alternative remedies test' raised problems similar to *Waite*: while the League did operate an administrative tribunal in Cairo, it was unclear from the staff regulations and existing academic literature whether the tribunal had jurisdiction over claims by local employees. In order to 'be certain that the applicant would at least have the real possibility of recourse',[145] the Geneva court chose to suspend the proceedings and to give the applicant a period of time in which to attempt to bring his case to the tribunal in Cairo.[146] On appeal, the Federal Tribunal rejected the plaintiff's human rights challenge to the League's immunity because he had failed to lodge his complaint with the administrative tribunal within the time limit given by the first instance court. This rendered the unavailability of the remedy in question merely 'hypothetical'.[147] This indicates that suspending domestic proceedings without prejudice to the issue of immunity may be a prudent way of handling misgivings about the concrete accessibility of an IO's internal remedy. A similar solution relieves domestic courts of the need to render a purely speculative prognosis on the way the internal remedy will construe its jurisdiction.[148]

The risks inherent in assessing the availability of a remedy *in abstracto* are even greater if one considers that, in exceptional circumstances, an individual may be unjustly prevented from accessing a remedy which is endowed with jurisdiction on paper. An example may be drawn from *Trempe*. The plaintiff worked for three years for the International Civil Aviation Organization (ICAO) in Montreal as a distribution clerk under a series of temporary contracts. When he was informed by the Chief of the Personnel Branch of the ICAO that his contract would not be renewed as a consequence of the elimination of his position, he did not appeal. Two months later, though, he found out that his position had not been abolished, a new distribution clerk had been temporarily hired and a vacancy notice had been issued for his former post. He thus filed an appeal to the ICAO's Secretary General (SG) arguing that his contract's non-renewal amounted to disguised dismissal, but the SG declined to consider the appeal because the ICAO's Staff Rules required requests for reconsideration to be filed within one month from notification of the decision. The SG also declined a subsequent request from Trempe to be granted

[144] Geneva Labor Court, *ZM v Permanent Delegation of the League of Arab States to the UN* 17 November 1993, 116 ILR 643, para 33: 'immunities … cease to apply at the moment when an abuse of law starts'.

[145] ibid para 32.

[146] ibid para 34.

[147] *ZM v Arab League* 25 January 1999, No 4C.518/1996, (2000) 10 *Revue suisse de droit international et européen* 642.

[148] Neumann and Peters (n 118) 257 and 261–62, noting that this is especially true where a respondent IO does not provide the domestic court sufficient information on the alternative means of redress. See also A Reinisch, *International Organizations before National Courts* (Cambridge, Cambridge University Press, 2000) 368, noting that domestic courts usually assess the availability and effectiveness of an alternative remedy 'on the basis of an *ex ante* evaluation of what standard of procedural fairness they expect the alternative forum to provide. There is usually no possibility of resuming jurisdiction where that expectation has been disappointed. Exactly this kind of fall-back guarantee, however, would be of crucial importance for individual litigants.'

the right to appeal to the UN Administrative Tribunal (UNAT), and rejected a recommendation from an Appeal Commission to allow the appeal despite his non-compliance with the limitation period. Trempe eventually appealed to the UNAT anyway, but it declined jurisdiction. It held that the SG had full discretion as to whether to waive the limitation period, irrespective of whether Trempe had been prevented from filing a timely application by reason of false information given by a representative of the organisation.[149] After these unsuccessful attempts, Trempe turned to the Canadian courts. The Quebec Superior Court recognised an element of unfairness in the way the ICAO and the UNAT had handled his case and found it 'disputable and ambiguous' whether he was in a position to lodge a complaint within the time limit.[150] However, foreshadowing the deferential attitude towards IO employer immunity later espoused by the SCC in *Amaratunga*,[151] it deferred to the ICAO's supposedly absolute immunity from jurisdiction.[152]

A final issue concerning availability is whether access to justice should be guaranteed to persons other than individual employees – notably, trade unions. This issue was addressed by the Dutch courts in a collective labour rights case against the EPO. Two unions challenged a provision of newly adopted service regulations which introduced an obligation to notify in advance any strikes to the EPO President and endowed the President with the power to requisition employees to ensure the IO's minimum functioning and to set a maximum duration for the strikes. The unions complained that these measures constituted an undue restriction on trade union rights as recognised by multiple international instruments.[153] In an attempt to overcome the EPO's treaty-based immunity on the basis of the *Waite and Kennedy* doctrine, the claimants contended that, because neither the ILOAT nor other internal remedies had competence over collective labour disputes, they had been absolutely deprived of remedies to protect the collective right to strike. EPO's defence, for its part, hinged on the argument that the ILOAT was competent to hear individual complaints against internal regulations, including those concerning strikes. Hence, the case boiled down to whether an individual right to appeal constituted a reasonable alternative, in *Waite* terms, to the unions' right to bring collective claims.

[149] UNAT, *Trempe v The Secretary General of the International Civil Aviation Organization* Judgment No 728, 21 November 1995, para V.

[150] *Trempe v Staff Association of the International Civil Aviation Organization and ors* 20 November 2003, ILDC 1748 (CA 2003) para 105.

[151] Above n 33; on which see above s II.

[152] *Trempe* (2003) (n 150) para 88. Note that Trempe only claimed infringement on his right to life, liberty and security under s 7 of the Canadian Charter of Rights and Freedoms 1982 – an admittedly strained argument that was found to be at odds with existing Canadian case law on the Charter (para 93). This strategy may perhaps be explained by the lack of a provision equivalent to Art 6 ECHR within the Canadian Charter (see G MacNeil's ILDC analysis of *Trempe*, para A7), but Trempe could have invoked the substantially equivalent Art 14 ICCPR.

[153] eg Art 6 of the European Social Charter (Revised) 1996 (right to bargain collectively); Art 11 ECHR (freedom of assembly and association).

This question was answered differently at the various stages of the proceedings. The Hague Court of Appeal struck down immunity, reasoning that an individual complaint could not be seen as an effective remedy for the enforcement of collective rights.[154] The Supreme Court reversed, on the grounds that Article 11 ECHR, guaranteeing the right to form and join trade unions, did not give unions a right of access to court,[155] and that, in any event, the power of union members to individually challenge EPO decisions affecting unions, 'although inferior to [remedies] under national law, constitute[d] a sufficiently reasonable alternative for effectively protecting the right to collective action'.[156] Several aspects of this second decision do not appear entirely persuasive. First, its reliance on Article 11 to infer non-existence of a right to a court for trade unions was misplaced. This right derives from Article 6 ECHR,[157] whose guarantees, according to ECtHR jurisprudence, also apply to legal persons seeking recognition of a right of their members or of their own.[158] It is therefore unclear why trade unions should not qualify for protection under this provision. Secondly, the argument that individual remedies could adequately compensate for the lack of collective ones appears questionable, considering that EPO employees could only appeal against measures taken against them individually (eg a dismissal for illegal strike).[159] The appellate court thus had a point in affirming that collective rights would in principle require collective remedies.[160]

It is nevertheless likely that the Supreme Court's reticence to set aside immunity was also informed by other considerations – namely, a perception that the appellate court's decision had resulted in an excessive encroachment upon the EPO's ability to perform its functions. This is because, having moved on to the merits, the court had upheld all claims by the unions and adopted remedies which arguably violated the EPO's immunity from enforcement proceedings. Such remedies included an order to allow unimpeded access to internal email systems, an order to allow collective bargaining and a prohibition to apply the provisions of internal regulations infringing the right to strike.[161] The execution of this judgment was blocked by the Dutch government in order to safeguard the organisation's immunity from enforcement measures.[162] But while it is certainly resonable to take into account an organisation's functional needs also in the course of a *Waite* assessment of alternative remedies, this preoccupation cannot result in denying the obvious

[154] *VEOB and SUEPO* (n 115) paras 3.8–3.9.

[155] *European Patent Organisation and the Netherlands v Vakbondsunie van het Europees Octrooibureau (VEOB) and Staff Union of the European Patent Office (SUEPO)* 20 January 2017, Case No 15/02186, paras 5.5–5.6.

[156] ibid para 5.8.

[157] *Golder* (n 2) para 36.

[158] See *Collectif national d'information et d'opposition à l'usine Melox – Collectif Stop Melox and Mox v France* App No 75218/01, 28 March 2006, En droit, para 4.

[159] C Ryngaert and F Pennings, 'Jurisdictional Immunity and Infringement of Fundamental Labor Rights' (2017) 3 *International Labor Rights Case Law* 327, 331–32.

[160] *VEOB and SUEPO* (n 115) para 3.8.

[161] ibid Decision in the principal appeal.

[162] Ryngaert, 'Immunities' (n 6) 404–05.

fact that no redress was available to the complainants in the *EPO* case. Based on the *Waite* jurisprudence, this finding should have naturally resulted in them being given access to domestic courts. A more pertinent way of addressing functional concerns is to seek ways for domestic courts to safeguard an organisation's functional needs *while* exercising jurisdiction.

A reasonable balance, which can avoid excessive interference without emasculating the test of equivalent protection, may perhaps be struck by differentiating according to the claim's subject matter.[163] It may be recalled from previous chapters that this approach is widely used by domestic courts with respect to the immunity of state employers.[164] Italian case law has consistently applied this same approach to the construction of IO immunity standards, including in trade union claims,[165] and this book has submitted that this solution lends itself to being generalised.[166] Now, it would make little sense if, as a consequence of an internal justice system's failure to pass the *Waite and Kennedy* test, national courts were allowed to affirm jurisdiction over claims that may not be adjudicated under any limited standard of IO immunity – particularly where such limited standards would presumably pass the *Waite* test themselves. Going back to the *EPO* case, this approach would have prevented the Dutch courts from affirming jurisdiction over requests for injunctions or orders for specific performance. Italian courts, for example, have refused to adjudicate collective claims aimed at challenging an IO's alleged 'anti-union behaviour', a conduct also encompassing illegal limitations on the right to strike.[167] Conversely, jurisdiction may have been entertained over collective claims relating to the economic conditions of employment, conceivably including claims for compensation for violation of the right to strike.

C. The Requirement of Effectiveness of the Alternative Remedy

The second prong of the 'alternative remedies test' concerns effectiveness: in order to ensure a meaningful protection of the right to a court, it is imperative not to settle for the mere existence of a remedy but to conduct an assessment of its quality.[168]

[163] See A Reinisch, 'To What Extent Can and Should National Courts Fill the Accountability Gap?' (2013) 10 *International Organizations Law Review* 572, 581–82: 'it is … apparent that not all domestic litigation will imply the same degree of interference with the functioning of international organizations … If litigants seek to force an international organization to adopt or to refrain from adopting a specific resolution determining its core functions, this is clearly different from a mere civil liability judgment'.

[164] ch 4, s VIB.

[165] Court of Cassation, *Sindacato UIL (Bari Branch) v Bari Institute of the ICAMAS* 4 June 1986, No 3732, 87 ILR 37, (1987) 70 *Rivista di diritto internazionale* 184; *Camera Confederale del Lavoro CGIL and Another v Bari Institute of the ICAMAS* 27 April 1979, No 2425, 78 ILR 86.

[166] ch 5, s II.

[167] Art 28 Law No 300 (1970) (Italy). See, eg *Sindacato UIL* (n 165) 190.

[168] Reinisch, *International Organizations* (n 148) 368; Ryngaert, 'Belgium' (n 56) 62. See also JH Gerards and LR Glas, 'Access to Justice in the European Convention on Human Rights System' (2017) 35 *Netherlands Quarterly of Human Rights* 11, 13–14, in the sense that the right of access to justice is both procedural and substantive because it requires a remedy to meet certain quality requirements.

Although *Waite* failed to perform a similar scrutiny,[169] in more recent case law the ECtHR has not shied away from performing a more meticulous enquiry into the features of the alternative means of redress.[170] However, it has been argued that the procedural safeguards looked at by the ECtHR in the progenies of both *Waite* and *Gasparini* are manifold and make it problematic to discern a coherent pattern.[171] Differing views as to what characteristics an effective remedy should possess have also been expressed in domestic case law.[172]

A first possible approach to effectiveness consists in scrutinising the compatibility of the alternative remedy with the full range of fair trial guarantees that are normally expected from domestic judiciaries.[173] An example of a similar approach may be found in the Brussels Labour Court of Appeal's judgment in *Siedler*. The court noted that the WEU Appeals Commission, ie the internal remedy made available to the plaintiff, had a properly jurisdictional nature, was competent to order payment of damages and reimbursement of costs, and guaranteed adversarial procedure.[174] However, it also held that this mechanism had a number of decisive shortcomings which prevented it from passing the *Waite and Kennedy* test:

> the public character of the debates is not guaranteed … nor is the publication of the decisions guaranteed. The designation of members is assigned to an intergovernmental Council, which appoints members of the Commission for a period of two years. The method of designation and the short period of the mandate carry the risk of linking the members of the commission too closely with the organization. … There is no provision for the eventuality of challenging impartiality. The recourse provided by the WEU personnel stature does not offer *all the guarantees inherent in the notion of due process* …[175]

Yet, such a strict control may be criticised for failing to appreciate the peculiarities of IO internal remedies.[176] It is logical not to expect these mechanisms of dispute settlement to replicate *in toto* the features of domestic labour courts, if only because due process guarantees vary significantly among legal orders. Furthermore, it should be recalled that the *Waite* doctrine itself mandates respect

[169] The ECtHR was content with the ESA Appeals Board being qualified as 'independent of the Agency' by the ESA Staff Regulations: see *Waite* (n 44) para 69.

[170] C Treichl, 'The Denial of Oral Hearings by International Administrative Tribunals as a Factor for Lifting Organizational Immunity before European Courts: A(nother) Critical View' (2019) 16 *International Organizations Law Review* 407, 425.

[171] ibid 427.

[172] C Focarelli, *International Law as Social Construct: The Struggle for Global Justice* (Oxford, Oxford University Press, 2012) 440, noting that 'different assessments [have been] provided by different courts (and even by the same court in different cases) as to the equivalence of the procedural guarantees offered by the alternative forums'.

[173] In favour, see A-M Thévenot-Werner, 'The Right of Staff Members to a Tribunal as a Limit to the Jurisdictional Immunity of International Organisations in Europe' in A Peters et al (eds), *Les acteurs à l'ère du constitutionnalisme global – Actors in the age of global constitutionalism* (Paris, Société de legislation comparée, 2014) 111, 131–32.

[174] *Siedler* (n 75) para 59.

[175] ibid paras 60–62 (emphasis added; internal references omitted).

[176] Reinisch, 'The Immunity' (n 109) 302, terming *Siedler* 'overly zealous'.

for IO functional needs to the extent possible,[177] and that the consequence of a ruling of non-effectiveness may be to require the forum state to disregard treaty obligations to grant immunity.[178] The German *Solange* doctrine articulates around the idea that requiring a protection identical to the German Basic Law would run counter to the 'openness' towards international cooperation, a principle which is equally enshrined in the Basic Law.[179] These aspects suggest that an alternative remedy should not be subject to overly stringent review.

Most courts and commentators only posit that an alternative remedy should meet basic requirements of independence and fairness.[180] Again, the Bundesverfassungsgericht in *Eurocontrol II* considered the ILOAT to be an adequate remedy because it 'conformed to an international minimum standard of basic procedural fairness as it is derived from developed legal orders following the rule of law and from the procedural law of international courts'.[181] The Strasbourg Court, for its part, has predictably relied on the Article 6 ECHR fair trial requirements, but it appears to have applied them with some flexibility.[182] For example, in *AL v Italy*, it analysed the key procedural guarantees of the NATO Appeals Board and concluded that this remedy 'remplit *essentiellement* les conditions prévues par l'article 6 de la Convention'.[183] Overall, the requirements around which a consensus has emerged broadly correspond to the minimum standards of fair trial in civil proceedings as laid out in international human rights instruments and jurisprudence.[184] Independence and impartiality certainly lie at the core of these guarantees.[185] Other fundamental requirements include – at a minimum – the equality of parties, which should be given a reasonable opportunity to present their case; the procedure's expeditiousness; and the power to render binding decisions and to grant effective remedies, including compensation.[186] Additionally, it has been argued that effectiveness should also be measured against the applicable

[177] Above s IIIB.

[178] Above s IIIA.

[179] K Hailbronner, 'Immunity of International Organizations from German National Jurisdiction' (2004) 42 *Archiv des Völkerrechts* 329, 334; Fassbender (n 72) 126–27.

[180] Reinisch and Novak, 'International Organizations' (n 102) 183.

[181] *Eurocontrol II* (n 82) 91.

[182] See C Ryngaert's ILDC analysis of *Western European Union* (n 73) A5: 'in respect of … dispute settlement mechanisms of international organizations, the Article 6 fair trial standards may be applied in a somewhat relaxed manner'.

[183] *AL v Italy* (n 51) En droit (emphasis added) ('essentially meets the requirements of Article 6 of the Convention').

[184] See *ex multis* WA Schabas, *The European Convention on Human Rights: A Commentary* (Oxford, Oxford University Press, 2015) 264–97.

[185] EC Okeke, 'The Tension between the Jurisdictional Immunity of International Organizations and the Right of Access to Court' in P Quayle (ed), *The Role of Administrative Law at International Organizations* (Leiden, Brill Nijhoff, 2021) 25, 41.

[186] In similar terms, see Novak and Reinisch, 'Desirable Standards' (n 107) 301–02. See also Parliamentary Assembly of the Council of Europe, Resolution 2206 (2018), 'Jurisdictional immunity of international organisations and rights of their staff', para 6.4, recommending Member States and IOs to 'ensure that internal redress mechanisms at all levels are independent and impartial, respect the principle of equality of arms and issue reasoned decisions, … so that decisions are fair and taken within a reasonable time'.

substantive law, which should be clearly identifiable and provide rights that are not 'theoretical or illusory'.[187]

These core due process requirements do not encompass the full range of fair trial guarantees that a domestic legal system may require from its own judiciary. For example, international human rights law does not recognise a right to a second instance in civil matters,[188] and accordingly human rights challenges to IO internal justice systems based on the lack of appellate review have invariably failed.[189] This does not mean that more ample guarantees are not to be hoped for: on the contrary, as Novak and Reinisch have put it, 'arguments of legitimacy … militate in favour of a particularly high standard of due process when it comes to employment disputes involving international organizations'.[190] Thus, the UN's choice to reform its internal justice by setting up a two-tier system can certainly be lauded, and it may be suggested that it should set an example for other IOs.[191] The question here, however, is not which standards may be desirable *tout court*, but which deficiencies should justify the adoption of a measure of last resort, such as the lifting of immunities deriving from international treaty obligations.

From this viewpoint, reliance on internationally accepted standards reinforces the legitimacy of the 'alternative remedies test'. Critics of the *Waite* approach usually point to the risk of unilateral interference by national courts on IO internal justice systems. In a typical expression of this sentiment, den Dekker has written:

> National courts cannot be the ultimate authority assessing what type, quality or (future) effectiveness of dispute settlement mechanisms 'ought to be achieved' by international organisations in order for them to 'earn' respect for their immunity … When national courts adopt such practice … international organisations stand to lose their independence …[192]

Arguments of this sort simply echo the functionalist policy-based rationales for absolute IO immunity criticised earlier in this book.[193] With specific regard to the present discussion, one may further object that there is nothing unilateral in reviewing the effectiveness of internal justice systems vis-à-vis the minimum standards of fair trial, insofar as all such systems should be expected to meet these

[187] A Reinisch and UA Weber, 'In the Shadow of Waite and Kennedy: The Jurisdictional Immunity of International Organizations, the Individual's Right of Access to the Courts and Administrative Tribunals as Alternative Means of Dispute Settlement' (2004) 1 *International Organizations Law Review* 59, 98.

[188] *Andrejeva v Latvia* App No 55707/00, 18 February 2009, para 97.

[189] See, eg *Illemassene* (n 100) re the OECD Administrative Tribunal.

[190] Novak and Reinisch, 'Desirable Standards' (n 107) 279.

[191] D Gallo, 'The Right of Access to Justice for the Staff of International Organizations: The Need for a Reform in the Light of the ICJ Advisory Opinion of 1 Feb. 2012' in R Virzo and I Ingravallo (eds), *Evolutions in the Law of International Organizations* (Leiden, Brill Nijhoff, 2015) 509, 530–32. On this reform, see ch 3, s IIB.

[192] G den Dekker, 'The HCCH and Functional Immunity: On Origins, Scope, and Access to Court' in T John et al (eds), *The Elgar Companion to the Hague Conference on Private International Law* (Cheltenham, Edward Elgar, 2020) 11, 20–21.

[193] ch 3, s III.

standards according to the international legal framework under which they operate. IOs are bound by human rights norms forming part of customary international law,[194] and this also applies to the right of access to justice.[195] Furthermore, basic standards of due process and human rights are incorporated into the corpus of general principles of civil service law developed by international administrative tribunals.[196] The 'alternative remedies test' therefore finds a strong policy justification in its capacity to incentivise IOs to live up to the standards set by international human rights law.[197]

The great variety of existing mechanisms of internal justice would make it impossible for this book to attempt a comprehensive evaluation of their quality vis-à-vis minimum fair trial requirements.[198] This may often require a complex legal and factual assessment: because, as argued above, the analysis should not stop at the remedies' de jure features but should take into account any de facto impairment of the right to a fair trial, it cannot but be performed on a case-by-case basis.[199] The remainder of this section will thus be limited to a selective analysis of relevant alternative remedies.

International administrative tribunals have generally been found to be adequate alternatives to national courts, primarily in light of their independence from the core institutional structure of an IO and their ability to grant remedies to the employees in a binding way. For instance, the Italian Court of Cassation held in *Colagrossi* that, the ILOAT being authoritative, impartial and fully competent to adjudicate over the employee's claims, there were no 'unreasonable obstacles' to the protection of the plaintiff's rights.[200] The Bundesverfassungsgericht similarly held that:

> The proceedings before the ILOAT are independent of the internal appeal proceedings. On the basis of its legally defined powers and under the rules of due process, the Tribunal decides on the subject matter of the proceedings submitted to it only in

[194] Shelton (n 2) 46.

[195] Final Report on Accountability of International Organisations (2004) 71 ILA Reports of Conferences – Report of the Seventy-First Conference held in Berlin, 16–21 August 2004, 164, 207–09; Schmitt (n 79) 118: 'a customary law to establish administrative dispute settlement mechanisms is progressively emerging for international organizations'.

[196] See, eg ILOAT, *In re Chadsey* Judgment No 122, 15 October 1968, 2; ILOAT, *In re Rubio* Judgment No 1644, 10 July 1997, para 12, considering 'valid' the principle that 'an employee of an [IO] is entitled to the safeguard of an impartial ruling by an international tribunal on any dispute with the employer'. See G Ullrich, *The Law of the International Civil Service: Institutional Law and Practice in International Organisations* (Berlin, Duncker & Humblot, 2018) 100–51, especially 142–44 (on the right to a fair trial).

[197] Reinisch, 'To What Extent' (n 163) 581.

[198] See extensively A-M Thévenot-Werner, *Le droit des agents internationaux à un recours effectif. Vers un droit commun de la procédure administrative internationale* (Leiden, Brill Nijhoff, 2016).

[199] For a de jure assessment, see International Administrative Law Centre of Excellence, 'Internal Justice Systems of International Organisations Legitimacy Index 2018', https://rm.coe.int/internal-justice-systems-of-international-organisations-legitimacy-ind/1680952638, taking into account inter alia a mechanism's overall structure, the content and clarity of the applicable law, and the main procedural features of first and second instances of litigation.

[200] *Colagrossi* (n 90) 394. See also Court of Cassation, *Carretti v FAO* 23 January 2004, No 180.

> accordance with legal rules and principles. Its judges are obliged to be independent and impartial pursuant to Article III of the ILOAT Statute. Accordingly … ILOAT's status and its procedural rules satisfy … the international minimum standards for basic procedural justice …[201]

This shows that, according to most domestic courts, the key de jure features of administrative tribunals suffice to establish a presumption of compatibility with fair trial guarantees.[202] The presumption should, however, be rebuttable in light of the specific circumstances of a case. In a 2013 decision, a Dutch court set aside the immunity of EPO because, although the ILOAT provided an independent and impartial remedy available to the employee, the ILOAT Registrar had informed the applicant that the procedure would have taken up to 15 years.[203] This decision is defensible because the right to have one's cause heard within a reasonable time is one of the key requirements of fair trial in international human rights law.[204]

Various reasons may call into question the adequacy of administrative tribunals in concrete cases. For example, a tribunal's uncritical deference to legal and factual assessments performed by internal appeals committees not independent from the organisation's management may be problematic from the standpoint of the tribunal's independence.[205] Further issues arise with regard to the entitlement to a 'public hearing', as expressly provided for by Article 6(1) ECHR. Under the reformed UN internal justice system, oral hearings are regularly held at first instance and the public may be excluded only under 'exceptional circumstances'.[206] The ILOAT, by contrast, enjoys broad discretion as to whether to allow oral hearings and whether or not to conduct them in public.[207] For decades, the Tribunal's standard practice has been to disallow applications for oral proceedings and to rule exclusively based on written submissions.[208] The view has been expressed that 'there are no grounds for concluding that obligatory oral hearings result in fairer and better judgments'.[209] But this view only holds up to the extent that written

[201] *B and Others* (n 84) para 23. See also Austria, Supreme Court, *Manfred B v European Patent Organization* 30 March 1998, 8 Ob A78/98y, re the ILOAT; *Illemassene* (n 100) para 4, re the OECD Administrative Tribunal.

[202] Novak and Reinisch, 'Desirable Standards' (n 107) 291–92. But see Treichl (n 170) 426, arguing that this presumption imposes an exceedingly heavy burden of proof upon the employee.

[203] The Hague District Court, *European Patent Organization v X* 16 July 2013, ECLI:NL:RBDHA:2013:10282.

[204] Art 6(1) ECHR; General comment 32 (n 2) para 27.

[205] Reinisch and Weber (n 187) 102. See, eg ILOAT, *In re Micheal* Judgment No 736, 17 March 1986, para 4: 'the Tribunal must attach great importance to the findings of the internal Appeals Committee … the members of the Committee will have the background knowledge necessary to evaluate the evidence properly'.

[206] Rules of Procedure of the United Nations Dispute Tribunal, UN General Assembly Resolution 64/119 (16 December 2009), Art 16.

[207] Art V ILOAT Statute.

[208] A Talvik, 'The ILO Administrative Tribunal: Shaping the Internal Review Process' in A Talvik (ed), *Best Practices in Resolving Employment Disputes in International Organizations* (Geneva, International Labour Office, 2015) 63, 66, note 24, noting that 'The last oral hearing held by the Tribunal dates back to its 67th Session in 1989'.

[209] CF Amerasinghe, 'Reflections on the Internal Judicial Systems of International Organizations' in Elias (n 107) 33, 51–52. See Dutch Supreme Court, *X v European Patent Organisation* 23 October 2009,

statements from the parties suffice to make a fair assessment of the factual and legal issues:[210] the lack of hearings should not prevent the parties from presenting their case, including their evidence, and contesting the other side's arguments in accordance with the principle of equality of arms.[211]

It is questionable whether the ILOAT's practice always meets similar standards.[212] It has been noted that oral hearings may be indispensable for a proper assessment of an employment case, particularly when sensitive information (eg concerning abuse or harassment) is implicated.[213] Moreover, and perhaps more worryingly, the Tribunal's constant refusal to hold hearings has on occasion been accompanied by an express reluctance to gather evidence from the plaintiff employees.[214] A confirmation of the problematic character of these shortcomings from the standpoint of *Waite* may be drawn from *Perez*. The applicant challenged the compatibility with Article 6 ECHR of the UN justice system in force at the time, which resembled the ILOAT in many respects. Although the ECtHR declared the application inadmissible for non-exhaustion of local remedies, it did note in obiter that the procedural flaws alleged by the applicant, 'if proven to be true, raise[d] an issue under Article 6'.[215] This applied, inter alia, to

> the fact that she did not have an oral hearing at any stage of the proceedings regarding her dismissal, despite the fact that in her case there were issues of both credibility and contested facts. Moreover, she claimed that she had not had access to all documents submitted by the [UN], in breach of her right to equality of arms.[216]

Indications that a blanket denial of oral hearings may be problematic from the standpoint of human rights can also be drawn *a contrario* from *Gasparini*. The ECtHR considered the NATO Appeals Board to be an adequate alternative remedy, notwithstanding that its hearings could only be held in private.[217] The court did, however, specifically discuss whether the non-publicity of the procedure prevented a meaningful participation of all parties, and noted that the ban on public hearings was highly nuanced by the possibility for the parties to participate in the hearings and develop oral arguments in support of their written statements.[218]

No 08/00118, ILDC 1464 (NL 2009) para 3.5, upholding immunity because the applicant failed to prove that the ILOAT's systematic failure to hold oral hearings affected the fairness of the final ruling.

[210] *Döry v Sweden* App No 28394/95, 12 November 2002, para 37.

[211] *Dombo Beheer BV v Netherlands* App No 14448/88, 27 October 1993, para 33.

[212] Treichl (n 170) 431–35.

[213] A Reinisch and C Knahr, 'From the United Nations Administrative Tribunal to the United Nations Appeals Tribunal – Reform of the Administration of Justice System within the United Nations' (2008) 12 *Max Planck Yearbook of United Nations Law* 447, 479.

[214] Reinisch and Weber (n 187) 108. See, eg ILOAT, *In re Kern (No 11)* Judgment No 2101, 30 January 2002, para 6: 'it is in vain that the complainant seeks to introduce evidence and even to call witnesses, to explain the meaning of the Agreement entered into between Germany and the EPO … The interpretation of contracts is not normally a matter of evidence but a question of law.'

[215] *Perez* (n 66) para 65.

[216] ibid.

[217] *Gasparini* (n 59) 8–9.

[218] ibid 9–10. See also *Chapman* (n 51) para 27; *AL v Italy* (n 51) En droit. Note that the NATO Administrative Tribunal, which succeeded to the NATO Appeals Board in 2013, conducts hearings

Other factual scenarios would be less difficult to appraise. It is unquestionable, for instance, that an internal appeal to an administrative organ, such as the possibility to lodge a request for reconsideration to the Secretariat, or to a deliberative organ not empowered to take binding decisions, would not meet the most elementary requirements of independence and procedural fairness.[219] This principle was reaffirmed by the French Court of Cassation in 2014. A wrongful termination claim was brought against the Pacific Community, an IO headquartered in New Caledonia which, pursuant to its headquarters agreement with France, enjoys jurisdictional immunity for its official acts.[220] The court upheld a judgment of the Noumea Court of Appeal setting aside immunity. It observed that the Pacific Community Staff Rules established a mechanism of staff dispute resolution whereby either the standing committee of the IO's governing body or the director-general had the ultimate say. The fact that the staff were not provided with 'un recours de nature juridictionnelle comportant des garanties d'impartialité et d'équité' ('a judicial remedy with guarantees of impartiality and fairness') was found to be contrary to the French conception of *ordre public*.[221]

In other circumstances, irrespective of their denomination, internal appeal mechanisms may not be qualitatively inferior to full-fledged administrative tribunals: the NATO Appeals Board discussed in *Gasparini* provides a clear example.[222] But a conclusion as to whether a remedy can be considered as a proper judicial body should only be reached through a sufficiently detailed analysis of its due process guarantees. Regrettably, many courts have proved reluctant to perform a stringent assessment of such remedies.[223] In 2009, for example, the Geneva Court of Appeal reversed a first instance judgment which, on the basis of *Waite*, had lifted the immunity of an unnamed organisation on the grounds that employees could only access an internal appeals commission empowered to address non-binding recommendations to that organisation's Secretary-General. The appellate court satisfied itself of a formal assurance from the organisation that the recommendation would be treated as binding.[224] In the 2005 *Pistelli* case, the Italian Court of Cassation dismissed the plaintiff's argument that the European University Institute's internal remedies in force at the time did not comply with constitutional

in public unless 'exceptional circumstances' require in camera proceedings: NATO Civilian Personnel Regulations, Annex IX, Regulations Governing Administrative Review, Mediation, Complaint and Appeal, Art 6.7.1.

[219] Reinisch and Weber (n 187) 101.

[220] Accord de siège entre le Gouvernement de la République française et la Communauté du Pacifique 2003, Art 6.

[221] *Secrétaire général de la communauté du Pacifique v X* 13 May 2014, No 12-23805.

[222] See also M Vidal's ILDC analysis of *Siedler* (n 75) A4, re the WEU Appeals Commission.

[223] Reinisch and Novak, 'International Organizations' (n 102) 183.

[224] Juridiction des prud'hommes, *E v T* 25 March 2009, No C/18260/2005-4, 10–11, on which see Neumann and Peters (n 118) 260–62. See also Cyprus, Supreme Court, *Stavrinou v United Nations and Commander of the United Nations Force in Cyprus* 17 July 1992, ILDC 929 (CY 1992) para 66, rejecting a constitutional right to court challenge to UN immunity on the grounds that the UN Force in Cyprus provided for a settlement mechanism with local personnel. The mechanism in question was a merely administrative recourse to the Commander of the Force: see A Constantinides' ILDC analysis, A6.

fair trial guarantees. The court quickly referred to the procedure for selection of the Appeals Board members – who were chosen from a list to be compiled by an international juridical body – and found the procedure to constitute a sufficient guarantee of impartiality and independence.[225] However, it failed to assess the Board's composition, the qualification of its members, and the fairness of its procedural rules and of the applicable substantive law.[226]

Yet other issues arise with regard to arbitration, which is normally the only remedy available to the so-called 'non-staff personnel', such as contractors.[227] Despite the lack of a formal employment relationship, such individuals often make up a portion (often substantial) of an IO's workforce.[228] Hence, there seems to be no reason why the means of redress available to these individuals should be held to lower standards than those available to staff members.[229]

The issue came to the fore in *Klausecker*. After unsuccessfully attempting to bring his claim before the ILOAT, which lacked jurisdiction *ratione personae*, the applicant turned down an EPO's offer to conclude a contract of arbitration. The ECtHR employed a comparatively strict standard in reviewing the compatibility of the offer to arbitrate with the *Waite and Kennedy* doctrine, and only upheld its adequacy after scrutinising a number of key procedural features of the proposed arbitration – namely, the procedure for the selection of the arbitrators, the fact that the dispute would have been adjudicated according to the same substantive law applicable by the ILOAT and the possibility of oral (albeit private) hearings with the assistance of counsel.[230] The procedure's quality did not look substantively inferior to remedies scrutinised by the ECtHR in cases not relating to arbitration, such as *Gasparini* or *Perez*.[231]

[225] *Pistelli v European University Institute* 28 October 2005, No 20995, ILDC 297 (IT 2005) paras 14.2–14.3.

[226] ibid M Iovane's ILDC analysis, A3. See also Germany, Higher Administrative Court of Hesse, *A v European Organisation for the Exploitation of Meteorological Satellites (EUMETSAT)* 17 February 2010, ILDC 2247 (DE 2010), para 19, re the EUMETSAT Appeals Board; Germany, Federal Administrative Court, *European School Employee Bonus Case* 20 October 1992, Case No 2 C 2.90, 108 ILR 664, re the European Schools Appeals Chamber, even though it did not comprise any professional judge; Italy, Court of Cassation, *Nacci v Bari Institute of the ICAMAS* 8 June 1994, No 5565, 114 ILR 540, (1994) 77 *Rivista di diritto internazionale* 838, holding an internal appeals mechanism compliant with fair trial guarantees based on a minimal analysis of its composition. cp *Drago* (n 92) para 6.6, considering a similar mechanism as 'an internal remedy, which does not provide jurisdictional protection'.

[227] See, eg the template of a UN individual contractor agreement (https://content.unops.org/HR-Documents/ICA_contract/ContractAnnex-English.pdf) providing for arbitration under UNCITRAL rules (s 17.2).

[228] MC Herrera, 'Is the UN Violating International Labour Standards?' (*European Journal of International Law: Talk!*, 29 October 2019), www.ejiltalk.org/is-the-un-violating-international-labour-standards/, noting that non-staff personnel make up 40% of the current UN workforce.

[229] *Kimungui* (n 127) para 34: 'It is a disturbing state of affairs that individual contractors cannot have access to a justice system as staff members considering that the functions they perform are generally no different from those performed by staff members.' See also the report by the Joint Inspection Unit, 'Review of Individual Consultancies in the United Nations System' (2012) UN Doc JIU/REP/2012/5, 20–22.

[230] *Klausecker* (n 53) paras 70–74.

[231] But see R Gulati and T John, 'Arbitrating Employment Disputes Involving International Organizations' in Quayle (n 185) 141, 148, considering the offer to arbitrate 'belated'. The offer for

Of course, not all arbitral proceedings meet these standards. An early case in point is the 1955 *Maida* judgment of the Italian Court of Cassation. At issue here was the lawfulness of the arbitration clause contained in the Staff Regulations of the International Refugee Organization, a now-dissolved specialised agency of the UN which enjoyed full immunity under the UN Specialized Agencies Convention.[232] The court found that the clause in question was unenforceable because it did not comply with mandatory requirements for the validity of arbitration clauses in Italian law – namely, it failed to stipulate the number of arbitrators and a procedure for their appointment. Reasoning that, in default of arbitration, the dispute would have been deprived of a judge, it affirmed Italian jurisdiction.[233] In so doing, it channelled a *Solange*-like analysis of the alternative remedy through application of domestic norms regulating recourse to arbitration in labour disputes.[234] Another example of a likely deficient arbitral procedure in labour matters may be drawn from the French *De Beaugrenier* case.[235] Unlike *Maida*, here the Cour de cassation did not find any violation of French international *ordre public*. Still, it is remarkable that the only arbitrator, who had been nominated in advance by the organisation, was under no obligation to motivate the final decision.[236] That decisions should be sufficiently reasoned is one of the core guarantees of a fair trial.[237]

IV. The Risk of Remedy Gaps and the Need for a Consistent Approach

As seen so far in this chapter, international and domestic jurisprudence has worked out two alternative approaches for reconciling employer immunities and the employees' right to a court. The case law of the ECtHR – by far the most influential court in this matter – shows that the choice between the two approaches invariably depends, with very occasional exceptions, on the identity of the employer.

an arbitration contract was received around 8 months after the ILOAT's decision on jurisdiction: see *Klausecker* (n 53) para 24.

232 Convention on the Privileges and Immunities of the Specialized Agencies 1947, Annex X.

233 *Maida v Administration for International Assistance* 27 May 1955, 23 ILR 510, (1956) 39 *Rivista di diritto internazionale* 546, 548–49.

234 *cf* Reinisch, *International Organizations* (n 148) 225, in the sense that the *Maida* court might have based its decision on an implied waiver of jurisdiction. For a decision expressly relying on implied waiver, see Paris Court of Appeal, *UNESCO v Boulois* 19 June 1998, 1999 *Revue de l'arbitrage* 343, on which see Gaillard and Pingel-Lenuzza (n 139) 13, lifting immunity following UNESCO's refusal to appoint an arbitrator despite a binding arbitration agreement, but expressly citing the ECHR and stating that leaving the employee without an arbitral remedy would have breached French *ordre public*. For decisions upholding the arbitrability of labour disputes with IOs, see Uruguay, Supreme Court of Justice, *Comisión Técnica Mixta de Salto Grande v Amado Campos* 21 July 2006, No 106/2006, 3–5; *Villa v United Nations Development Program* 5 March 2010, No 38/2010.

235 *De Beaugrenier v UNESCO* 11 February 2009, No 07-44240.

236 Thévenot-Werner, 'The Right' (n 173) 130.

237 *H v Belgium* App No 8950/80, 30 November 1987, para 53; HRC, *Verlinden v The Netherlands* Comm No 1187/2003, 31 October 2006, para 7.7.

Notably, the 'alternative remedies test' has only been applied to staff disputes with IOs. Courts have not been open to making the immunities of other employers conditional upon the availability to their employees of alternative means of obtaining redress: the human rights scrutiny of these other immunities has been limited to verifying that they stemmed from, and remained within the bounds of, international immunity law obligations. Overall, the immunities of state and diplomat employers have thus received more deferential treatment than IO employers' immunities.

Case law rarely expounds on the rationale for this divide: for the most part, the two approaches appear to have simply developed along parallel but distinct tracks. Nonetheless, obiter comments provide a glimpse into one of the likely main reasons why courts have not performed an assessment of alternative remedies outside of labour cases against IOs. These courts have proceeded under the assumption that employees of foreign states or of their agents may always sue their employers before the courts of the foreign states themselves. Hence, in cases involving state, diplomatic and consular immunity, the 'alternative remedies test' would be satisfied *in re ipsa* because there would always be another competent national forum. The same view was voiced by the International Law Commission (ILC) in its commentary to the 1991 Draft Articles on state immunity.[238] Commenting on the provision of Draft Article 11 immunising a state if 'the employee is a national of the employer State at the time when the proceeding is instituted',[239] the ILC wrote that, for employees covered by this clause, 'Remedies and access to courts exist in the employer State'.[240]

There is no doubt that this rationale had a decisive influence on the early development of the 'alternative remedies test' by municipal courts. For example, in the 1983 *Cabrera* judgment, the Argentine Supreme Court opined that a fundamental difference between state immunity and IO immunity was that recourse against the state would always be possible before its own domestic courts. In the absence of internal alternative remedies, by contrast, IO immunity would result in impunity and 'claimants would be deprived of the elemental right to have access to a court'.[241] Substantially identical arguments were developed by the Italian Court of Cassation in the 1994 *Nacci* judgment[242] and by a German regional labour court's decision in *Pfarr*. In barring claims by an Indonesian woman who suffered egregious labour

[238] Draft Articles on Jurisdictional Immunities of States and Their Property, with commentaries, ILC Yearbook 1991, vol II, Part 2, 13.

[239] Draft Art 11(2)(d), the antecedent of Art 11(2)(e) UNCSI (which, however, removes immunity if the employee 'has the permanent residence in the State of the forum').

[240] 1991 Draft Articles (n 238) 44, para 12. See also H Fox and P Webb, *The Law of State Immunity*, 3rd edn (Oxford, Oxford University Press, 2013) 585: 'even where a claim against a State arises out of the exercise of sovereign authority, an alternative forum is available in the courts of the defendant State; no such alternative forum is available in respect of a dispute arising with an international organization'.

[241] Vinuesa (n 106) 21–22, commenting on *Cabrera* (n 85).

[242] *Nacci* (n 226) 847: 'con riferimento agli Stati esteri, … se non è possibile invocare la tutela giurisdizionale del giudice italiano, è sempre aperta la possibilità di far ricorso agli organi della giurisdizione interna dei predetti Stati'.

law violations while working at the residence of a Saudi attaché, the German court brushed off concerns that the worker could not enforce her rights by stating, inter alia, that it could not be excluded that she could sue her employer before Saudi courts.[243]

An attempted challenge to state immunity brought on grounds of lack of alternative remedies was recently dismissed by the Strasbourg Court for essentially the same reasons.[244] The case in question is the 2019 *Ndayegamiye* judgment. As may be recalled from chapter four, the applicant, a Burundian national residing in France, was a senior employee at the Permanent Mission of Burundi to the UN in Geneva. After her attempts to sue Burundi before Swiss courts were frustrated by state immunity, she filed a case against Switzerland before the ECtHR. The Strasbourg Court found no breach of the Convention because her claim fell within the immunity ground of Article 11(2)(e) UNCSI (nationals of the employer state not residing in the state of the forum).[245] One of the points raised by the applicant was that, by declaring Burundi immune from suit, the Swiss courts had left her without judicial means of obtaining redress. She acknowledged that in the past she had brought an employment-related complaint before Burundian authorities, but submitted, first, that such remedy was only administrative in nature, and secondly, that it was not available to her anymore due to changes in Burundi's political leadership.[246] With respect to this argument, the ECtHR commenced by restating its official position whereby 'la compatibilité de l'octroi de l'immunité de juridiction à un État avec l'article 6 § 1 de la Convention ne dépend pas de l'existence d'alternatives raisonnables pour la résolution du litige'.[247] But the court did not stop there and also felt it necessary to add that the employee had access to courts in her state of nationality. In particular, it satisfied itself that, during the proceedings before the Swiss courts, Burundi had given 'reassurances' that the Bujumbura Administrative Court was competent over the dispute and that the applicant's claims were not time-barred according to the law of Burundi.[248]

These obiter statements indicate a reticence on the part of courts (and the ILC) to accept that certain employees may be left utterly remediless. This is an understandable concern: a similar outcome would be intuitively unfair. Unfortunately, the belief that the foreign state's courts may always provide a fallback runs the risk of being no more than a comforting delusion. This view neglects that, in certain

[243] Higher Regional Court of Berlin, *Diplomatic immunity for alleged labour exploitation case, Pfarr (on behalf of National of Indonesia) v Anonymous* 9 November 2011, 17 Sa 1468/11, 180 ILR 422, ILDC 1903 (DE 2011) para 29.

[244] See also Reinisch and Weber (n 187) 85–86, noting that this rationale probably underpinned early ECtHR cases on state immunity, including *Al-Adsani* (n 11).

[245] *Ndayegamiye* (n 22) on which see further ch 4, ss IVC and V.

[246] ibid para 43.

[247] ibid para 64 ('the compatibility of the granting of jurisdictional immunity to a State with Article 6(1) of the Convention does not depend on the existence of reasonable alternatives for the resolution of the dispute').

[248] ibid.

countries, the government may never be sued either de jure or de facto,[249] or that various procedural or factual obstacles may prevent an employee from going to court – not least the high costs of litigating the case in a country other than the one of performance of the work.[250] This assumption is even more astonishing when applied to employees of foreign state agents. These workers are often third-country nationals who may have never worked or even set foot in their employer's sending state. It is doubtful at best that the sending state's courts would consider the mere nationality of the employer as a sufficient link for establishing jurisdiction – unless, at least, the employment contract contains a choice of forum in favour of the sending state's courts. However, the validity of part of such forum selection clauses may be doubtful in most legal orders if one applies – as seems reasonable to do – the same limitations on party autonomy that apply to employment contracts with foreign states.[251]

Moreover, even assuming that the foreign state's courts do have jurisdiction (or that an employer state's generic 'reassurances', as in *Ndayegamiye*, suffice to prove that they do), the problem remains that the proceedings before such courts may not necessarily meet the basic requirements of a fair trial – the same requirements that, when IO immunity is at stake, the ECtHR and municipal courts expect from an 'effective' alternative remedy.[252] For example, municipal courts may not be sufficiently independent from the government to rule impartially over disputes between state employees and the state, or between high-ranking officials such as diplomats and consuls and their own employees.[253] In this respect, the *Pfarr* court's suggestion that in 2011 an Indonesian woman with limited economic means could have litigated a labour exploitation case against a Saudi diplomat before Saudi courts seems quixotic at best.[254] Also, the foreign state's courts may not be able to grant effective remedies, such as an adequate amount of compensation. While employment at foreign state establishments or diplomatic and consular households is normally subject to local employment laws, the foreign state's courts may not be empowered to apply foreign employment law, or the law of the state where the work is performed may not be applicable extraterritorially.[255]

[249] J Foakes and R O'Keefe, 'Article 11' in R O'Keefe and CJ Tams (eds), *The United Nations Convention on Jurisdictional Immunities of States and Their Property: A Commentary* (Oxford, Oxford University Press, 2013) 183, 206.

[250] Excessive costs may impair the right to court by deterring parties from seeking remedies: see HRC, *Äärelä and Näkkäläjärvi v Finland* Comm No 779/97, 24 October 2001, para 7.2; ECtHR, *Kreuz v Poland* App No 28249/95, 19 June 2001, paras 60–67.

[251] See ch 4, s VII.

[252] Above s IIIC.

[253] See *mutatis mutandis* R Nigro, 'Immunità degli Stati esteri e diritto di accesso al giudice: un nuovo approccio nel diritto internazionale?' (2013) 96 *Rivista di diritto internazionale* 812, 828, re disputes over grave violations of human rights.

[254] See J Drohla's ILDC analysis of *Pfarr* (n 243) A9. Note that, in most cases of labour exploitation in diplomatic households, bringing a case before the courts of the agent's sending state would likely compromise the employee's immigration status in the receiving state, which normally depends on their employment situation and thus on the will of the (possibly abusive) employer: see W Spadinger, 'Private Domestic Staff. A Risk Group on the Fringe of the Convention' in P Behrens (ed), *Diplomatic Law in a New Millennium* (Oxford, Oxford University Press, 2017) 132, 140–41.

[255] Foakes and O'Keefe (n 249) 205–06.

Remarkably, in other cases regarding state immunity in employment matters, the Strasbourg Court has been far from insensible to these issues. In *Cudak*, the respondent government argued that the applicant, a Lithuanian national, could have brought her claims before the courts of her employer state Poland, and that for this reason the Lithuanian courts' refusal to adjudicate her claims did not disproportionately restrict her right to a court. The Polish courts had jurisdiction and would have applied Lithuanian law pursuant to a contract choice-of-law clause. Lithuania also took care to demonstrate that the applicant's claim was not time-barred under Lithuanian law.[256] But the ECtHR dismissed this argument:

> such a remedy, even supposing that it was theoretically available, was not a particularly realistic one in the circumstances of the case. If the applicant had been required to use such a remedy she would have encountered serious practical difficulties which would have been incompatible with her right of access to a court, which, like all other rights in the Convention, must be interpreted so as to make it practical and effective, not theoretical or illusory.[257]

It defies logic that, while Polish courts were not considered to be a reasonable alternative to the courts of Lithuania, Burundian courts were treated in *Ndayegamiye* as a reasonable alternative to those of Switzerland, or the Saudi courts in *Pfarr* to those of Germany.

To summarise, pursuant to the current case law of the ECtHR and the many municipal courts that have followed its lead, individuals working for employers other than IOs may be left de jure or de facto without effective means of redress. This is highly problematic on several counts. First, it makes one of the tenets of the Strasbourg Court's jurisprudence on the right of access to justice, ie that limitations are admissible as long as they 'do not restrict or reduce the access left to the individual in such a way … that the very essence of the right is impaired',[258] sound like empty words. Secondly, with more specific regard to employment cases, it is in striking contrast with the attention paid by these courts to making sure that all IO employees have access to effective means of obtaining redress.[259] This raises a troubling question: if IO employees, then why not employees of foreign states or diplomatic agents?

An appropriate way of approaching this question is to inquire whether there exist any special circumstances justifying more deferential treatment of the immunities of state and diplomat employers as compared to IO immunity. Or – rephrasing the question in the language of the ECHR – whether there are valid reasons why the proportionality assessment of limitations on the employees' right to a court should work differently for state and diplomatic immunity than it does for IO immunity.

[256] *Cudak* (n 20) para 34.

[257] ibid para 36.

[258] See, eg *Fogarty* (n 15) para 33; *Cudak* (n 20) para 55; *Ndayegamiye* (n 22) para 51.

[259] See E Voyiakis, 'Access to Court v State Immunity' (2003) 52 *ICLQ* 297, 312, note 63, describing the contrast between *Fogarty* and *Waite* as regards the proportionality assessment as 'startling to say the least'.

Arguably the strongest argument against making state employers' immunity contingent on the availability of alternative remedies may be drawn from a passage of the International Court of Justice's (ICJ) judgment in *Jurisdictional Immunities*, which held as follows:

> The Court can find no basis in the State practice from which customary international law is derived that international law makes the entitlement of a State to immunity dependent upon the existence of effective alternative means of securing redress. Neither in the national legislation on the subject, nor in the jurisprudence of the national courts which have been faced with objections based on immunity, is there any evidence that entitlement to immunity is subjected to such a precondition. States also did not include any such condition in either the European Convention or the United Nations Convention.[260]

This passage was referenced in *Ndayegamiye* in support of the statement that the proportionality of limitations on the right to a court deriving from state immunity 'ne dépend pas de l'existence d'alternatives raisonnables pour la résolution du litige'.[261] The court also cited its own judgment in *Mothers of Srebrenica*, which, as seen earlier in this chapter, affirmed that a lack of alternative remedies in the context of IO immunity was not '*ipso facto* constitutive of a violation of the right of access to a court'.[262]

There are two main reasons why invoking *Jurisdictional Immunities* and *Srebrenica*, as the ECtHR did in *Ndayegamiye*, seems misplaced in this context. First, the point here is not whether state practice treats human rights violations as non-immune acts in the same fashion as, say, *acta jure gestionis*, or whether the law of state immunity recognises a 'last resort' exception. What is at issue, instead, is how state immunity obligations interact with the human right of access to court. We are discussing, in other words, possible *extrinsic* limitations on immunity law based on its interplay with human rights law, not the scope of immunity obligations per se.[263] Hence, such limitations are not subject to the evidentiary standard for the ascertainment of customary norms. As Pavoni has well argued, 'the search for a further, tie-breaking rule is unnecessary and misconceived … these two obligations express competing rules and values whose reconciliation is a matter well within the power of interpretation of courts'.[264] Secondly, the ICJ's assertion that no state practice supports withholding immunity for lack of alternative remedies,

[260] *Jurisdictional Immunities of the State (Germany v Italy: Greece intervening)* Judgment [2012] ICJ Rep 99, para 101, re Italy's argument that the courts of the forum state may provide a forum of last resort to victims who had no access to other means of redress.

[261] Above n 247.

[262] *Mothers of Srebrenica* (n 111) para 164, cited in *Ndayegamiye* (n 22) para 64, and itself citing para 101 of *Jurisdictional Immunities* (n 260).

[263] See *Jurisdictional Immunities* (n 260) Dissenting Opinion of Judge Yusuf, paras 28–30, citing *Waite* and *Beer*.

[264] Pavoni, 'Human Rights' (n 7) 86. See also A Bianchi, 'L'immunité des Etats et les violations graves des droits de l'homme: la fonction de l'interprète dans la détermination du droit international' (2004) 108 *Revue générale de droit international public* 63.

however correct it might be in the specific context of that case,[265] has no foundation when applied to employment, where *Solange* limitations on IO immunity have prospered in municipal case law.

In this respect, it is important to stress that both *Jurisdictional Immunities* and *Srebrenica* were concerned with very different issues than employment matters. The former judgment discussed immunity for *jus cogens* violations committed during World War II. The ICJ's staunch refusal to inject human rights considerations into its reasoning was very likely affected by a comprehensible systemic concern – ie that permitting jurisdiction over individual reparation claims 'would have opened the door to a flow of litigation before municipal courts that might have disrupted the whole system'.[266] There is obviously no similarity with individual claims for breach of employment contracts or labour legislation, all the more when considering that a large portion of such claims are already amenable to local jurisdiction based on the existing standards of limited immunity discussed earlier in this book. *Srebrenica*, for its part, concerned claims by victims of alleged wrongdoings by UN peacekeepers. As seen above, the ECtHR distinguished this case from *Waite* precisely because it did not have to do with employment.[267] It is therefore inexplicable that *Ndayegamiye* cited *Srebrenica* in employment matters and neglected to cite its employment-specific precedents which have consistently sanctioned limiting immunity based on a lack of alternative remedies.

The ECtHR has also rationalised its differential treatment of employer immunities on the grounds that different legal bases would warrant different degrees of deference. Notably, it has justified deferring to state immunity obligations out of respect for customary international law. An oft-cited passage of *Fogarty* averred that 'measures … which reflect generally recognised rules of public international law on State immunity cannot in principle be regarded as imposing a disproportionate restriction on the right of access to court'.[268] By contrast, when it comes to immunities that find their legal bases in treaty or municipal law – as is the case with IO immunity – the court has seemingly been induced to perform a more thorough scrutiny by a concern that states would otherwise be able to bypass their ECHR obligations by voluntarily undertaking contrary commitments. For instance, it

[265] For critical comments on the ICJ's treatment of Italy's 'last resort' argument, see, *ex multis*, Dissenting Opinion of Judge Yusuf (n 263); B Conforti, 'The Judgment of the International Court of Justice on the Immunity of Foreign States: A Missed Opportunity' (2011) 21 *Italian Yearbook of International Law* 133: 'It is not true that there is no practice supporting the last resort argument.' *cf* also Italy, Constitutional Court, *Simoncioni and ors v Germany and President of the Council of Ministers of the Italian Republic (intervening)* 22 October 2014, No 238, ILDC 2237 (IT 2014), in the sense that leaving victims of international crimes without remedies, as required by *Jurisdictional Immunities* (n 260), would be unconstitutional.

[266] A Bianchi, 'On Certainty' (*European Journal of International Law: Talk!*, 16 February 2012), www.ejiltalk.org/on-certainty/. See *Jurisdictional Immunities* (n 260) para 102: 'the Court cannot fail to observe that the application of any such condition [ie of alternative remedies], if it indeed existed, would be exceptionally difficult in practice, particularly in a context such as that of the present case'.

[267] Above s IIIB.

[268] *Fogarty* (n 15) para 36; reproduced in *Cudak* (n 20) para 57; *Sabeh El Leil* (n 21) para 49; *Radunović* (n 21) para 64.

held in *Chapman* that it would be 'incompatible with the purpose and object of the Convention if the States, by transferring powers to international organisations, were thereby absolved from their responsibility under the Convention'.[269] This logic is closely reminiscent of the German *Solange* reservation to transfers of sovereign powers. The Italian Court of Cassation has expressed the same concern in even clearer terms. In *Pistelli*, it justified its use of the 'alternative remedies test' by affirming that the constitutional right to a court could only be overridden by 'a universal rule recognised by the international community … But this prevalence is no longer justified when the sacrifice of the cardinal principle of the Constitution arises … from a commitment freely undertaken by our Republic'.[270]

However, the differences in the legal sources of immunity cannot conclusively justify a differential treatment of employees. The above-quoted passages make a valid argument for not deferring uncritically to treaty-based employer immunities, but do not provide any explanation as to why the deference towards custom-based immunities should be absolute. Being generally accepted does not make such norms underogable, nor does it imply that conflicts with the right of access to justice should always be resolved in favour of immunity. Even from a purely normative perspective it appears arbitrary to play favourites among different immunities. All immunities share the same rationale of facilitating the performance of sovereign or organisational functions.[271] Hence they may all be said to 'occup[y] an important place in international law and international relations',[272] and indeed both the ECtHR and municipal courts have shown significant deference towards IO immunities as well, treating the lifting of immunity as a last-resort measure for cases where the right to court is nullified. It can be agreed that custom-based immunities should receive the same amount of deference, but it is questionable that they should deserve more.

V. Conclusions

This chapter has submitted that, in order to reconcile employer immunities and the employees' right to a court, the test of equivalent protection should not be limited to litigation involving IOs but should be extended to all employment-related cases. However, because the withholding of immunity for lack of alternative remedies constitutes a last-resort measure, it is important to stress that the primary pathway for ensuring broader access to court for employees is and should remain the

[269] *Chapman* (n 51) para 50. Similarly, see *Waite* (n 44) para 67; ECommHR, *Waite* (n 44) Dissenting Opinion of G Ress and 14 others, para 1: 'Immunities of international organisations, created by subsequent treaties, cannot be considered as a kind of general unwritten exception to the scope of application of the ECHR.'

[270] *Pistelli* (n 225) para 14. In identical terms, *Drago* (n 92) para 6.5.

[271] ch 2, s III.

[272] *Jurisdictional Immunities* (n 260) para 57, re state immunity.

application of limited immunity standards, in accordance with what was said in the previous chapters of this book. If courts rejected unduly extensive constructions of employer immunities, most employees would end up having access to the forum state's courts by operation not of international human rights law, but of immunity law itself. An illustrative example may again be drawn from *Ndayegamiye*, where the ECtHR's finding that Switzerland had not breached Article 6 ECHR hinged on the assumption that, by upholding immunity, Swiss courts had acted within the boundaries of customary law as embodied by Article 11 UNCSI. This is because the applicant was a national of the employer state not residing in the state of the forum, a situation covered by the immunity ground of Article 11(2)(e).[273] However, as was demonstrated in chapter four, it is strongly disputable that customary law actually required immunity in the factual circumstances of said case. Had the court performed even a cursory examination of state practice, it would have likely ruled in favour of the applicant.[274] Hence, any discussion of the availability of alternative remedies was ultimately unnecessary: the grant of immunity in this case was disproportionate under both the *Fogarty/Cudak* and the *Waite and Kennedy* doctrines. This suggests that an adequate protection of the rights of employees should be attained by courts by combining both limited immunity standards and doctrines developed in human rights jurisprudence.

[273] *Ndayegamiye* (n 22) paras 62–63.
[274] ch 4, s VIII.

7

Conclusions

The complexities of the international law regime of jurisdictional immunities in employment matters boil down to one fundamental normative question – how to reconcile the functional needs of employers, that immunities are meant to safeguard, with the employees' need for legal redress. This seemingly straightforward question has received a staggering array of answers in international and judicial practice. Of course, many factors may explain the cacophony of legal and policy approaches to immunities in labour cases, the most obvious being the variety of relevant legal sources, the differences among categories of employers and employees, and the influence of domestic law conceptions over municipal courts confronted with immunity issues. Yet no such factor makes inconsistencies any less troubling, let alone suggests that uncertainty in the law or differential treatment of workers should be accepted with resignation. This book has attempted to shed light over the international law governing immunities in employment disputes. It has done so with the goal in mind of furthering consistency – as much consistency, that is, as allowed by the existing legal framework. Overall, it has sought to demonstrate that bringing coherence to this notoriously intricate area of international law is not just a lofty policy objective, but also the most legally sound course of action, and that the existing international law regime can afford a reasonable balance between the needs of employers and employees.

I. Argument No 1: Absolute Employer Immunity Is an Unfounded Legal Myth

A first step in this process has been to tear down the myth of absolute immunity in employment litigation. Although particularly strong in labour disputes with international organisations and foreign state agents, support for blanket immunity has proven surprisingly durable even in areas like state immunity, where it is generally considered to be a thing of the past. This view betrays a somewhat mystical reverence for the functional needs of employers which arguably has no sound basis either in law or in policy. Chapter three of the book sought to prove that in labour matters, not unlike civil adjudicative jurisdiction at large, limited rather than absolute immunity is the norm. Thus, international law obligations to grant blanket immunity to employers truly exist only where set forth by unequivocal treaty provisions, as is notably the case with instruments granting immunity from every form of legal process to international organisations (IOs). And even in such cases, as seen in chapter six, absolute immunity may be subject to challenges based on human righs law where the employee has no access to alternative means of redress, or where the available remedies do not meet basic due process requirements.

II. Argument No 2: Well-Defined Standards of Limited Employer Immunity Can Be Identified

A second argument advanced by this book has been that relinquishing absolute immunity does not entail yielding to legal uncertainty. The alleged lack of precise standards of limited immunity for labour disputes has been another long-running theme in legal scholarship, particularly with respect to the law of state immunity. It is not hard to explain why: because employment relationships with foreign states straddle the divide between private and public acts, the classic formulation of the restrictive immunity doctrine – ie the distinction between *acta jure imperii* and *acta jure gestionis* – is not readily applicable to labour, and this difficulty has been reflected in a great variety of approaches by domestic courts. Still, as chapter four has tried to demonstrate, it is mostly an anachronism to affirm that state immunity has not developed clear standards for labour matters. Special Rapporteur Sucharitkul voiced this view during the early phases of the codification process of state immunity, at a time when reported instances of application of the restrictive doctrine to employment cases were limited to a handful of European states and the solutions reached by courts were largely tentative and experimental.[1] Now, almost 40 years later, extensive judicial and legislative practice, as well as the codification itself, have ensured that the law of state immunity in employment matters has developed into a reasonably well-defined sector of immunity law. For example, it is settled that the application to labour of the restrictive doctrine takes place through a limited range of employment-specific immunity tests – nature of the workplace, functions and status, nationality and residence, or subject matter. Reliance on such tests renders the conceptual difficulties of applying the public/private divide to labour of limited practical relevance. And while domestic practice does remain highly diverse, the rules of treaty construction and of custom ascertainment allow the content of existing international law obligations in this domain to be established with sufficient clarity. In fact, it is precisely in light of this diversity in state practice that the customary law of state immunity comes across as quite permissive in labour matters. It is broadly accepted that jurisdiction may not be exercised where the employee has diplomatic, consular or military status, or

[1] S Sucharitkul, 'Fifth Report on Jurisdictional Immunities of States and Their Property', ILC Yearbook 1983, vol II, Part 1, 34.

where the claim's subject matter is not limited to monetary aspects, but it is arguable that no other obligation to uphold immunity can plainly be said to exist under general international law.

As for IOs and diplomatic and consular agents, the domestic courts' long-lasting inclination towards blanket immunity has complicated the emergence of employment-specific immunity standards, and at the same time has swept the need for such standards under the rug. However, once it is established that absolute immunity is generally as unsustainable for IOs, diplomats and consuls as it is with respect to states, a need for viable standards of non-absolute immunity arises for claims involving these employers. Chapter five submitted that the relative scarcity of pertinent case law – at least compared to state immunity – does not prevent this need from being met. In the case of IOs, it was suggested that employment-specific immunity tests may be drawn from the customary law of state immunity. In the case of foreign state agents, non-absolute immunity standards derive from the interpretation of the relevant provisions of the Vienna Convention on Diplomatic Relations and the Vienna Convention on Consular Relations. So far, domestic courts have only affirmed jurisdiction over consular agents and former diplomatic agents, on the assumption that hiring personal staff does not fall within these agents' official functions. But the preferable construction of these instruments is that the receiving state's jurisdiction may encompass all such agents, including serving diplomats: this is because the hiring of private staff can fall within the scope of the exception to diplomatic immunity for commercial activity performed by the agent outside of official functions.

III. Argument No 3: The Equivalent Protection Test Should Apply to All Employer Immunities

This book has strived to demonstrate that the existing international law regime can allow adequate judicial protection of employees. This conclusion flows, first and foremost, from this book's defence of non-absolute standards of immunity in labour litigation – something which in itself broadens the avenues of legal redress by envisioning a greater role for the courts of countries where the work is performed. More saliently, though, whether jurisdiction may be affirmed over employers entitled to immunity is not just a question of immunity law, but also one of human rights law, in the sense that immunity rules need to be reconciled with the employees' right of access to justice. This issue has been the subject of an ever-increasing body of case law which has contributed to providing employees with broader access to court. Nevertheless, as highlighted in chapter six, a striking and oft-neglected aspect of this jurisprudence is that courts have failed to come up with a consistent answer to the question of what constitutes a tolerable compression of an employee's right to a court. The European Court of Human Rights has treated customary state immunity obligations with unconditional deference, and domestic case law following its lead has gone so far as sanctioning blanket employer immunities where it considered them – wrongly – to be required by custom. By contrast, the prevalent approach to the immunity of IOs has also been deferential, but not unconditionally so: here, the human rights legitimacy of employer immunities has been made dependent on the availability to employees of effective means of obtaining redress other than the forum state's courts. Chapter six made the argument that the coexistence of two disparate approaches creates remedy gaps and unreasonable discrimination among workers. Once it is accepted that IO employees should always have access to effective means of redress, there is no valid reason why the same doctrine of equivalent protection should not be extended across the board.

IV. The Way Forward: Human Rights Law as an Agent of Coherence

It may be wondered, in conclusion, if the above three arguments suffice to quench the need for consistency in the immunity law regime for labour claims. The answer is – mostly, but perhaps not entirely. This is because reasons inherent to international immunity law make fragmentation deeply ingrained in this legal regime.

First of all, it is clear that the fact of being developed and applied primarily within domestic legal orders multiplies risks of conflicting interpretations of the same norms and of differing attitudes towards the relationship between different branches of international law – eg between state immunity and international organisation immunity, or between immunity and human rights. The involvement of domestic legal orders has long been recognised as one, possibly the earliest, source of fragmentation of international law: as the International Law Commission pointedly noted in its works on the subject, 'international law was always relatively "fragmented" due to the diversity of national legal systems that participated in it'.[2] But another, more peculiar reason of fragmentation originates in the very legal structure of immunity rules. As was further elaborated at the outset of chapter two, it is in the nature of such norms not to prevent states from granting broader immunity unilaterally – that is, from declining jurisdiction in cases where no obligation to grant immunity exists. Hence inconsistencies are, to an extent, physiological features of immunity law. Insofar as diverging views may be tenable from the standpoint of international law itself, clarifying the scope of international obligations on employer immunities may not be quite enough to incentivise judicial approaches to converge.

[2] Report of the Study Group of the International Law Commission, 'Fragmentation of International Law: Difficulties Arising from the Diversification and Expansion of International Law', finalised by M Koskenniemi, 13 April 2006, UN Doc A/CN.4/L.682, para 16.

Yet, there is a way by which this difficulty too may be resolved. The solution again involves human rights law. Unlike immunity law, international human rights obligations have the capacity to set a limit to the amount of immunity that courts can grant to employers, thus overcoming the hoary legal adage that states are free to grant broader immunities than international law requires. This process is best demonstrated by the case law of the Strasbourg Court concerning state immunity. As was seen in chapter six, the court considers the immunity of state employers to be compatible with the employees' right of access to justice only to the extent that the immunity grant is compelled by international law, which has the conspicuous effect of barring unilateral grants of state immunity under the European Convention on Human Rights and thus promoting greater coherence among domestic approaches. This shows that human rights law may play a broader systemic role in this field as the agent of coherence. A sound combination of limited immunity standards and principles developed in human rights jurisprudence holds the key not only to ensuring adequate protection of labour rights, but also to blunting the inconsistencies of employer immunities and providing greater legal certainty to all parties to employment proceedings.

BIBLIOGRAPHY

Books

Ahluwalia, K, *The Legal Status, Privileges and Immunities of the Specialized Agencies of the United Nations and Certain Other International Organizations* (The Hague, Nijhoff, 1964).

Akehurst, MB, *The Law Governing Employment in International Organizations* (Cambridge, Cambridge University Press, 1967).

Allain, J, *Slavery in International Law: Of Human Exploitation and Trafficking* (Leiden, Brill-Nijhoff, 2013).

Amerasinghe, CF, *Principles of the Institutional Law of International Organizations*, 2nd edn (Cambridge, Cambridge University Press, 2005).

Amerasinghe, CF, *The Law of the International Civil Service: As Applied by International Administrative Tribunals*, 2nd edn (Oxford, Oxford University Press, 1994).

Badr, GM, *State Immunity: An Analytical and Prognostic View* (The Hague, Nijhoff, 1984).

Bankas, EK, *The State Immunity Controversy in International Law. Private Suits Against Sovereign States in Domestic Courts* (Berlin, Springer, 2005).

Bordin, FL, *The Analogy between States and International Organizations* (Cambridge, Cambridge University Press, 2019).

Buscemi, M, *Illeciti delle Nazioni Unite e tutela dell'individuo* (Naples, Editoriale Scientifica, 2020).

Casolari, F, *L'incorporazione del diritto internazionale nell'ordinamento dell'Unione europea* (Milan, Giuffrè, 2008).

Cassese, A (Frulli, M, ed), *Diritto internazionale*, 3rd edn (Bologna, il Mulino, 2017).

Conforti, B and Iovane, M, *Diritto internazionale*, 12th edn (Naples, Editoriale scientifica, 2021).

Countouris, N, *The Changing Law of the Employment Relationship. Comparative Analyses in the European Context* (London, Routledge, 2007).

Crawford, J, *Brownlie's Principles of International Law*, 9th edn (Oxford, Oxford University Press, 2019).

De Bellis, S, *L'immunità delle organizzazioni internazionali dalla giurisdizione* (Bari, Cacucci, 1992).

De Sena, P, *Diritto internazionale e immunità funzionale degli organi statali* (Milan, Giuffrè, 1996).

Denza, E, *Diplomatic Law: Commentary on the Vienna Convention on Diplomatic Relations*, 4th edn (Oxford, Oxford University Press, 2016).

El Sawah, S, *Les immunités des États et des organisations internationales – Immunités et procès équitable* (Brussels, Larcier, 2012).

Fick, BJ (ed), *International Labour Law* (Cheltenham, Edward Elgar, 2015).

Focarelli, C, *International Law as Social Construct: The Struggle for Global Justice* (Oxford, Oxford University Press, 2012).

Fox, H and Webb, P, *The Law of State Immunity*, 3rd edn (Oxford, Oxford University Press, 2013).

Giuttari, TR, *The American Law of Sovereign Immunity: An Analysis of Legal Interpretation* (New York, Praeger Publishers, 1970).

Jenks, CW, *The Proper Law of International Organisations* (London, Stevens & Sons, 1962).

Jennings, R and Watts, A, *Oppenheim's International Law*, 9th edn (Oxford, Oxford University Press, 1992).

Kelsen, H, *The Law of the United Nations. A Critical Analysis of Its Fundamental Problems* (New York, Praeger, 1950).

Klabbers, J, *An Introduction to International Institutional Law*, 3rd edn (Cambridge, Cambridge University Press, 2015).

Kloth, M, *Immunities and the Right of Access to Court under Article 6 of the European Convention on Human Rights* (Leiden, Brill Nijhoff, 2010).
Lorimer, J, *The Institutes of the Law of Nations*, vol 1 (Edinburgh, Blackwood, 1883).
Muller, AS, *International Organizations and Their Host States: Aspects of their Legal Relationship* (The Hague, Kluwer, 1995).
Okeke, EC, *Jurisdictional Immunities of States and International Organizations* (Oxford, Oxford University Press, 2018).
Pellet, A, *Les voies de recours ouvertes aux fonctionnaires internationaux* (Paris, Pedone, 1982).
Quadri, R, *La giurisdizione sugli Stati stranieri* (Milan, Giuffrè, 1941).
Reinisch, A, *International Organizations before National Courts* (Cambridge, Cambridge University Press, 2000).
Salerno, F, *Diritto internazionale. Principi e norme*, 5th edn (Padua, Cedam, 2019).
Sbolci, L, *Controversie di lavoro con Stati stranieri e diritto internazionale* (Milan, Giuffrè, 1987).
Schabas, WA, *The European Convention on Human Rights: A Commentary* (Oxford, Oxford University Press, 2015).
Schermers, HG and Blokker, NM, *International Institutional Law*, 6th edn (Leiden, Brill Nijhoff, 2018).
Schmitt, P, *Access to Justice and International Organizations: The Case of Individual Victims of Human Rights Violations* (Cheltenham, Edward Elgar, 2017) 287.
Schreuer, CH, *State Immunity: Some Recent Developments* (Cambridge, Grotius, 1988).
Seyersted, F, *Common Law of International Organizations* (Leiden, Nijhoff, 2008).
Shany, Y, *Regulating Jurisdictional Interactions between National and International Courts* (Oxford, Oxford University Press, 2007).
Shelton, D, *Remedies in International Human Rights Law*, 3rd edn (Oxford, Oxford University Press, 2015).
Spence, D and Bátora, J (eds), *The European External Action Service: European Diplomacy Post-Westphalia* (Basingstoke, Palgrave Macmillan, 2015).
Tanzi, A, *L'immunità dalla giurisdizione degli agenti diplomatici* (Padua, CEDAM, 1991).
Thévenot-Werner, A-M, *Le droit des agents internationaux à un recours effectif. Vers un droit commun de la procédure administrative internationale* (Leiden, Brill Nijhoff, 2016).
Ullrich, G, *The Law of the International Civil Service: Institutional Law and Practice in International Organisations* (Berlin, Duncker & Humblot, 2018).
van Alebeek, R, *The Immunity of States and Their Officials in International Criminal Law and International Human Rights Law* (Oxford, Oxford University Press, 2008).
Wellens, K, *Remedies against International Organisations* (Cambridge, Cambridge University Press, 2002).
Yang, X, *State Immunity in International Law* (Cambridge, Cambridge University Press, 2012).
Zarra, G, *Parallel Proceedings in Investment Arbitration* (Turin/The Hague, Giappichelli/Eleven, 2017).

Articles

Adatci, M and de Visscher, C, 'Rapport sur l'art. 7, al. 4: Privilèges et Immunités diplomatiques des Agents de la S.D.N.' (1924) *Annuaire de l'Institut de droit international* 1.
Adinolfi, G, 'L'immunità delle organizzazioni internazionali dalla giurisdizione civile nella giurisprudenza italiana' (2007) 23 *Comunicazioni e studi* 233.
Angelet, N and Weerts, A, 'Les immunités des organisations internationales face à l'article 6 de la Convention européenne des droits de l'homme' (2007) 134 *Journal du droit international* 3.
Anzilotti, D, 'Gli organi comuni nelle società di Stati' (1914) 9 *Rivista di diritto internazionale* 156.
Anzilotti, D, 'L'esenzione degli Stati stranieri dalla giurisdizione' (1910) 5 *Rivista di diritto internazionale* 471.

Arsanjani, M, 'Claims Against International Organizations: *Quis Custodiet Ipsos Custodes?*' (1980-81) 7 *Yale Journal of World Public Order* 131.
Atteritano, A, 'Immunity of States and Their Organs: The Contribution of the Italian Jurisprudence in the Past Ten Years' (2009) 19 *Italian Yearbook of International Law* 31.
Bianchi, A, 'L'immunité des Etats et les violations graves des droits de l'homme: la fonction de l'interprète dans la détermination du droit international' (2004) 108 *Revue générale de droit international public* 63.
Bonafè, BI, 'Italian Courts and the Immunity of International Organizations' (2013) 10 *International Organizations Law Review* 505.
Bonafè, BI, 'The ECHR and the Immunities Provided by International Law' (2010) 20 *Italian Yearbook of International Law* 55.
Bordin, FL, 'Reflections of Customary International Law: The Authority of Codification Conventions and ILC Draft Articles in International Law' (2014) 63 *ICLQ* 535.
Bouchez, LJ, 'The Nature and Scope of State Immunity from Jurisdiction and Execution' (1979) 10 *Netherlands Yearbook of International Law* 3.
Brower, CH, 'International Immunities: Some Dissident Views on the Role of Municipal Courts' (2001) 41 *Virginia Journal of International Law* 1.
Brownlie, I, 'Contemporary Problems Concerning the Jurisdictional Immunity of States, Preliminary Report' (1987) 62 *Annuaire de l'Institut de droit international* 13.
Caplan, LM, 'State Immunity, Human Rights, and Jus Cogens: A Critique of the Normative Hierarchy Theory' (2003) 97 *American Journal of International Law* 741.
Castro, AM, 'Abuse of Diplomatic Immunity in Family Courts: There's Nothing Diplomatic about Domestic Immunity' (2014) 47 *Suffolk University Law Review* 353.
Cataldi, G, 'I recenti sviluppi della giurisprudenza italiana in materia di controversie di lavoro con Stati stranieri' (1991) 27 *Rivista di diritto internazionale privato e processuale* 691.
Colliard, C-A, 'La Convention de Vienne sur les relations diplomatiques" (1961) 7 *Annuaire Français de Droit International* 3.
Conforti, B, 'The Judgment of the International Court of Justice on the Immunity of Foreign States: A Missed Opportunity' (2011) 21 *Italian Yearbook of International Law* 133.
Conforti, B, 'Ancora sull'atteggiamento della Corte di cassazione in tema di immunità degli Stati stranieri dalla giurisdizione italiana' (1990) 73 *Rivista di diritto internazionale* 911.
Crawford, J, 'International Law and Foreign Sovereigns: Distinguishing Immune Transactions' (1983) 54 *British Year Book of International Law* 75.
Cully, K, 'Jurisdictional Immunities of Intergovernmental Organizations' (1982) 91 *Yale Law Journal* 1167.
Damrosch, L, 'Changing the International Law of Sovereign Immunity through National Decisions' (2011) 44 *Vanderbilt Journal of Transnational Law* 1185.
de Nanteuil, A, 'L'application en France des règles internationales relatives aux immunités' (2010) 56 *Annuaire Français de Droit International* 807.
Dickinson, A, 'Status of Forces under the UN Convention on State Immunity' (2006) 55 *ICLQ* 427.
Dominicé, C, 'L'immunité de juridiction et d'exécution des organisations internationales' (1984) 187 *Recueil des cours* 145.
do Nascimento e Silva, GE, 'The Vienna Conference on Consular Relations' (1964) 13 *ICLQ* 1214.
Douglas, Z, 'State Immunity for the Acts of State Officials' (2012) 82 *British Year Book of International Law* 281.
Dumberry, P, 'Incoherent and Ineffective: The Concept of Persistent Objector Revisited' (2010) 59 *ICLQ* 779.
Ehrenfeld, A, 'United Nations Immunity Distinguished from Sovereign Immunity' (1958) 52 *American Society of International Law Proceedings* 88.
Ferrari Bravo, L, 'Le controversie in materia d'impiego presso enti internazionali e la giurisdizione italiana' (1956) 39 *Rivista di diritto internazionale* 550.
Finke, J, 'Sovereign Immunity: Rule, Comity or Something Else?' (2011) 21 *European Journal of International Law* 853.

Fox, H, 'Employment Contracts as an Exception to State Immunity: Is All Public Service Immune?' (1995) 66 *British Year Book of International Law* 97.
Franzina, P, 'L'immunità giurisdizionale degli Stati rispetto alle controversie di lavoro, fra equo processo e diritto internazionale generale: il caso Guadagnino' (2011) 10 *Int'l Lis: supplemento di documentazione e discussione sul diritto giudiziario transnazionale* 81.
Friedrich, K, 'Statutes of Liberty?: Seeking Justice under United States Law When Diplomats Traffic in Persons' (2007) 72 *Brooklyn Law Review* 1139.
Gaillard, E and Pingel-Lenuzza, I, 'International Organisations and Immunity from Jurisdiction: To Restrict or to Bypass' (2002) 51 *ICLQ* 1.
Gaja, G, 'Quale immunità degli Stati esteri per le controversie di lavoro?' (1991) 74 *Rivista di diritto internazionale* 920.
Gaja, G, 'Immunity from Jurisdiction of the International Centre for Advanced Mediterranean Agronomic Studies' (1977) 3 *Italian Yearbook of International Law* 310.
Gargiulo, P, 'Croce rossa internazionale' in *Digesto delle discipline pubblicistiche*, IV vol (Turin, UTET, 1989) 488.
Garnett, R, 'The Rights of Diplomatic and Consular Employees in Australia' (2018) *University of Melbourne Law School Research Series* 5.
Garnett, R, 'State and Diplomatic Immunity and Employment Rights: European Law to the Rescue?' (2015) 64 *ICLQ* 783.
Garnett, R, 'State Immunity and Employment Relations in Canada' (2015) 18 *Canadian Labour and Employment Law Journal* 643.
Garnett, R, 'The Precarious Position of Embassy and Consular Employees in the United Kingdom' (2005) 54 *ICLQ* 705.
Garnett, R, 'The Perils of Working for a Foreign Government: Foreign Sovereign Immunity and Employment' (1998) 29 *California Western International Law Journal* 133.
Garnett, R, 'State Immunity in Employment Matters' (1997) 46 *ICLQ* 81.
Gerards, JH and Glas, LR, 'Access to Justice in the European Convention on Human Rights System' (2017) 35 *Netherlands Quarterly of Human Rights* 11.
Hafner, G, 'United Nations Convention on Jurisdictional Immunities of States and Their Property (2004)' (2010) *Max Planck Encyclopedia of Public International Law*.
Hafner, G and Lange, L, 'La convention des Nations Unies sur les immunités juridictionnelles des États et de leurs biens' (2004) 50 *Annuaire Français de Droit International* 45.
Hailbronner, K, 'Immunity of International Organizations from German National Jurisdiction' (2004) 42 *Archiv des Völkerrechts* 329.
Hammerschlag, D, 'Morgan v. International Bank for Reconstruction and Development' (1992) 16 *Maryland Journal of International Law* 279.
Henquet, T, 'The Jurisdictional Immunity of International Organizations in the Netherlands and the View from Strasbourg' (2013) 10 *International Organizations Law Review* 538.
Higgins, R, 'Certain Unresolved Aspects of the Law of State Immunity' (1982) 29 *Netherlands International Law Review* 265.
Iovane, M, 'L'influence de la multiplication des juridictions internationales sur l'application du droit international' (2017) 383 *Recueil des cours* 233.
Jones, DL, 'Article 6 ECHR and Immunities Arising in Public International Law' (2003) 52 *ICLQ* 463.
Karagiannakis, M, 'State Immunity and Fundamental Human Rights' (1998) 11 *Leiden Journal of International Law* 9.
Köhler, U, 'Contracts of Employment under the UN Convention on Jurisdictional Immunities of States and Their Property' (2004) 9 *Austrian Review of International and European Law* 191.
Kowalski, M, 'Consuls' (2013) *Max Planck Encyclopedia of Public International Law*.
Krieger, H, 'Between Evolution and Stagnation – Immunities in a Globalized World' (2014) 6 *Göttingen Journal of International Law* 177.
Kunz, JL, 'Privileges and Immunities of International Organizations' (1947) 41 *American Journal of International Law* 828.

Lalive, J-F, 'L'immunité de juridiction des États et des organisations internationales' (1953) 84 *Recueil des cours* 205.
Lammers, JG, 'Immunity of International Organizations: The Work of the International Law Commission' (2013) 10 *International Organizations Law Review* 276.
Lauterpacht, H, 'The Problem of Jurisdictional Immunities of Foreign States' (1951) 28 *British Year Book of International Law* 220.
Ling, Y-L, 'A Comparative Study of the Privileges and Immunities of United Nations Member Representatives and Officials with the Traditional Privileges and Immunities of Diplomatic Agents' (1976) 33 *Washington and Lee Law Review* 91.
Lock, T, 'Beyond Bosphorus: The European Court of Human Rights' Case Law on the Responsibility of Member States of International Organisations under the European Convention on Human Rights' (2010) 10 *Human Rights Law Review* 529.
Lowe, V, '*Res Judicata* and the Rule of Law in International Arbitration' (1996) 8 *African Journal of International and Comparative Law* 38.
Martha, RSJ, 'International Financial Institutions and Claims of Private Parties: Immunity Obliges' (2011) 3 *The World Bank Law Review* 93.
McGuinness, ME, 'Medellín v. Texas, 128 S.Ct. 1346 (2008)' (2008) 102 *American Journal of International Law* 622.
McLachlan, C, 'The Principle of Systemic Integration and Article 31(3)(c) of the Vienna Convention' (2005) 54 *ICLQ* 279.
Migliorini, S, 'Immunità dalla giurisdizione e Regolamento (CE) 44/2001: riflessioni a partire dalla sentenza *Mahamdia*' (2012) 95 *Rivista di diritto internazionale* 1089.
Milhaupt, CJ, 'The Scope of Consular Immunity under the Vienna Convention on Consular Relations: Towards a Principled Interpretation' (1988) 88 *Columbia Law Review* 841.
Miller, AJ, 'Privileges and Immunities of United Nations Officials' (2007) 4 *International Organizations Law Review* 169.
Morelli, G, 'L'istituto internazionale di agricoltura e la giurisdizione italiana' (1931) 56 *Il Foro Italiano* 1424.
Mullally, S and Murphy, C, 'Double Jeopardy: Domestic Workers in Diplomatic Households and Jurisdictional Immunities' (2016) 64 *American Journal of Comparative Law* 677.
Nigro, R, 'Immunità degli Stati esteri e diritto di accesso al giudice: un nuovo approccio nel diritto internazionale?' (2013) 96 *Rivista di diritto internazionale* 812.
Nino, M, 'State Immunity from Civil Jurisdiction in Labor Disputes: Evolution in International and National Law and Practice' (2014) 50 *Rivista di diritto internazionale privato e processuale* 819.
Orakhelashvili, A, 'State Immunity and Hierarchy of Norms: Why the House of Lords Got It Wrong' (2008) 18 *European Journal of International Law* 955.
Palombino, FM, 'Judicial Economy and Limitation of the Scope of the Decision in International Adjudication' (2010) 23 *Leiden Journal of International Law* 909.
Palombino, FM, 'L'immunità degli Stati stranieri dalla giurisdizione rispetto ai rapporti di lavoro e il diritto di accedere ad un tribunale: in margine al caso Fogarty' (2002) 57 *La Comunità internazionale* 79.
Papa, MI, 'The *Mothers of Srebrenica* Case before the European Court of Human Rights: United Nations Immunity versus Right of Access to a Court' (2016) 14 *Journal of International Criminal Justice* 893.
Pavoni, R, 'La jurisprudence italienne sur l'immunité des États dans les différends en matière de travail: tendances récentes à la lumière de la Convention des Nations Unies' (2007) 53 *Annuaire Français de Droit International* 211.
Pisillo Mazzeschi, R, 'Immunità giurisdizionale delle organizzazioni internazionali e Costituzione italiana' (1976) 59 *Rivista di diritto internazionale* 489.
Pustorino, P, 'The Immunity of International Organizations from Civil Jurisdiction in the Recent Italian Case Law' (2009) 19 *Italian Yearbook of International Law* 57.
Pustorino, P, 'Immunità giurisdizionale delle organizzazioni internazionali e tutela dei diritti fondamentali: le sentenze della Corte europea nei casi *Waite et Kennedy* e *Beer et Regan*' (2000) 83 *Rivista di diritto internazionale* 132.

Quaglino, A, 'In tema di immunità del CIME dalla giurisdizione italiana nelle controversie in materia di lavoro' (1974) 10 *Rivista di diritto internazionale privato e processuale* 487.

Reinisch, A, 'To What Extent Can and Should National Courts Fill the Accountability Gap?' (2013) 10 *International Organizations Law Review* 572.

Reinisch, A, 'The Immunity of International Organizations and the Jurisdiction of Their Administrative Tribunals' (2008) 7 *Chinese Journal of International Law* 285.

Reinisch, A, 'Accountability of International Organizations According to National Courts' (2005) 36 *Netherlands Yearbook of International Law* 119.

Reinisch, A, 'The Use and Limits of *Res Judicata* and *Lis Pendens* as Procedural Tools to Avoid Conflicting Dispute Settlement Outcomes' (2004) 3 *The Law and Practice of International Courts and Tribunals* 37.

Reinisch, A, 'Waite and Kennedy v. Germany, Application No. 26083/94; Beer and Regan v. Germany, Application No. 28934/95' (1999) 93 *American Journal of International Law* 933.

Reinisch, A and Knahr, C, 'From the United Nations Administrative Tribunal to the United Nations Appeals Tribunal – Reform of the Administration of Justice System within the United Nations' (2008) 12 *Max Planck Yearbook of United Nations Law* 447.

Reinisch, A and Weber, UA, 'In the Shadow of Waite and Kennedy: The Jurisdictional Immunity of International Organizations, the Individual's Right of Access to the Courts and Administrative Tribunals as Alternative Means of Dispute Settlement' (2004) 1 *International Organizations Law Review* 59.

Riddell, A, 'Administrative Boards, Commissions and Tribunals in International Organizations' (2012) *Max Planck Encyclopedia of Public International Law*.

Ronzitti, N, 'Rapporti di lavoro con Stati membri dell'Alleanza atlantica ed esenzione dalla giurisdizione' (1972-IV) *Giurisprudenza di merito* 25.

Rossi, P, 'Controversie di lavoro e immunità degli Stati esteri: tra codificazione e sviluppo del diritto consuetudinario' (2019) 102 *Rivista di diritto internazionale* 5.

Rossi, P, 'The International Law Significance of *Jam v. IFC*: Some Implications for the Immunity of International Organizations' (2019) 13 *Diritti umani e diritto internazionale* 305.

Rossi, P, 'Conflicting Approaches of the Court of Cassation to State Immunity in Employment Disputes' (2017) 27 *Italian Yearbook of International Law* 431.

Ryngaert, C, 'Immunities of International Organizations Before Domestic Courts: Reflections on the Collective Labour Case Against the European Patent Organization' (2015) 46 *Netherlands Yearbook of International Law* 393.

Ryngaert, C, 'The European Court of Human Rights' Approach to the Responsibility of Member States in Connection with Acts of International Organizations' (2011) 60 *ICLQ* 997.

Ryngaert, C, 'The Immunity of International Organizations Before Domestic Courts: Recent Trends' (2010) 7 *International Organizations Law Review* 121.

Ryngaert, C and Pennings, F, 'Jurisdictional Immunity and Infringement of Fundamental Labor Rights' (2017) 3 *International Labor Rights Case Law* 327.

Schröer, F, 'De l'application de l'immunité juridictionnelle des Etats étrangers aux organisations internationales' (1971) 75 *Revue générale de droit international public* 712.

Schwenk, EH, 'Jurisdiction of the Receiving State over Forces of the Sending State under the NATO Status of Forces Agreement' (1972) 6 *International Lawyer* 525.

Seyersted, F, 'Jurisdiction over Organs and Officials of States, the Holy See and Governmental Organisations (2)' (1965) 14 *ICLQ* 493.

Shi, X, 'Official Acts and Beyond: Towards an Accurate Interpretation of Diplomatic Immunity Ratione Materiae under the Vienna Convention on Diplomatic Relations' (2019) 18 *Chinese Journal of International Law* 669.

Silverstein, R, 'Revisiting the Legal Basis to Deny International Civil Servants Access to a Fundamental Human Right' (2017) 25 *Michigan State International Law Review* 375.

Sinclair, I, 'The Law of Sovereign Immunity: Recent Developments' (1980) 176 *Recueil des cours* 113.

Singer, M, 'Jurisdictional Immunity of International Organizations: Human Rights and Functional Necessity Concerns' (1995) 36 *Virginia Journal of International Law* 53.

Staiano, F, 'Domestic Workers' Human Rights versus Diplomatic Immunity: Developments in International and National Jurisprudence' (2013) 22 *Italian Yearbook of International Law* 201.
Stewart, DP, 'The UN Convention on Jurisdictional Immunities of States and Their Property' (2005) 99 *American Journal of International Law* 194.
Sucharitkul, S, 'Developments and Prospects of the Doctrine of State Immunity: Some Aspects of Codification and Progressive Development' (1982) 29 *Netherlands International Law Review* 252.
Tai, A, 'Unlocking the Door to Justice: Protecting the Rights and Remedies of Domestic Workers in the Face of Diplomatic Immunity' (2007) 16 *American University Journal of Gender, Social Policy & the Law* 175.
Talmon, S, 'Jus Cogens After Germany v. Italy: Substantive and Procedural Rules Distinguished' (2012) 25 *Leiden Journal of International Law* 979.
Treichl, C, 'The Denial of Oral Hearings by International Administrative Tribunals as a Factor for Lifting Organizational Immunity before European Courts: A(nother) Critical View' (2019) 16 *International Organizations Law Review* 407.
van Alebeek, R, 'Immunity, Diplomatic' (2009) *Max Planck Encyclopedia of Public International Law.*
Vandenberg, ME and Bessel, S, 'Diplomatic Immunity and the Abuse of Domestic Workers: Criminal and Civil Remedies in the United States' (2016) 26 *Duke Journal of Comparative & International Law* 595.
Viterbo, A, 'Immunità dalla giurisdizione della Banca mondiale e diritto di accesso al giudice' (2018) 12 *Diritti umani e diritto internazionale* 397.
Voyiakis, E, 'Access to Court v State Immunity' (2003) 52 *ICLQ* 297.
Webb, P, 'The Immunity of States, Diplomats and International Organizations in Employment Disputes: The New Human Rights Dilemma?' (2016) 27 *European Journal of International Law* 745.
Webb, P, 'Should the 2004 UN State Immunity Convention Serve as a Model/Starting Point for a Future UN Convention on the Immunity of International Organizations?' (2013) 10 *International Organizations Law Review* 319.
Weiss, A, 'Compétence et incompétence des tribunaux à l'égard des états étrangers' (1923) 1 *Recueil des cours* 521.
Wen, AH, 'Suing the Sovereign's Servant: The Implications of Privatization for the Scope of Foreign Sovereign Immunities' (2003) 103 *Columbia Law Review* 1538.
Whytock, CA, 'Foreign State Immunity and the Right to Court Access' (2013) 93 *Boston University Law Review* 2033.
Wickremasinghe, C, 'International Organizations or Institutions, Immunities before National Courts' (2009) *Max Planck Encyclopedia of Public International Law.*
Wood, M, 'Do International Organizations Enjoy Immunity under Customary International Law?' (2013) 10 *International Organizations Law Review* 287.
Wouters, J, Ryngaert, C and Schmitt, P, 'Western European Union v. Siedler, General Secretariat of the ACP Group v. Lutchmaya, General Secretariat of the ACP Group v. B.D.' (2011) 105 *American Journal of International Law* 560.
Young, E, 'The Development of the Law of Diplomatic Relations' (1964) 40 *British Year Book of International Law* 141.

Chapters from Edited Collections

Amerasinghe, CF, 'International Administrative Tribunals' in C Romano, K Alter and Y Shany (eds), *The Oxford Handbook of International Adjudication* (Oxford, Oxford University Press, 2013) 316.
Amerasinghe, CF, 'Reflections on the Internal Judicial Systems of International Organizations' in O Elias (ed), *The Development and Effectiveness of International Administrative Law* (Leiden, Brill Nijhoff, 2012) 33.
Amirfar, C, 'Waivers of Jurisdictional Immunity' in T Ruys and N Angelet (eds), *The Cambridge Handbook of Immunities and International Law* (Cambridge, Cambridge University Press, 2019) 167.

Amoroso, D, 'Italy' in FM Palombino (ed), *Duelling for Supremacy: International Law vs. National Fundamental Principles* (Cambridge, Cambridge University Press, 2019) 184.

Bandyopadhyay, R and Iwata, T, 'Officials (Article V Sections 17–21 General Convention)' in A Reinisch (ed), *The Conventions on the Privileges and Immunities of the United Nations and its Specialized Agencies: A Commentary* (Oxford, Oxford University Press, 2016) 313.

Banifatemi, Y, 'Jurisdictional Immunity of States – Commercial Transactions' in T Ruys and N Angelet (eds), *The Cambridge Handbook of Immunities and International Law* (Cambridge, Cambridge University Press, 2019) 125.

Boon, KE, 'Immunities of the United Nations and Specialised Agencies' in T Ruys and N Angelet (eds), *The Cambridge Handbook of Immunities and International Law* (Cambridge, Cambridge University Press, 2019) 201.

Bothe, M, 'Remedies of Victims of War Crimes and Crimes against Humanities: Some Critical Remarks on the ICJ's Judgment on the Jurisdictional Immunity of States' in A Peters et al (eds), *Immunities in the Age of Global Constitutionalism* (Leiden, Brill, 2015) 99.

Bruns, K, 'On the Road to Vienna: The Role of the International Law Commission in the Codification of Diplomatic Privileges and Immunities' in P Behrens (ed), *Diplomatic Law in a New Millennium* (Oxford, Oxford University Press, 2017) 54.

Burci, GL, 'Immunity of Property, Funds, and Assets (Article III Section 4 Specialized Agencies Convention)' in A Reinisch (ed), *The Conventions on the Privileges and Immunities of the United Nations and its Specialized Agencies: A Commentary* (Oxford, Oxford University Press, 2016) 99.

Cannizzaro, E, 'A Higher Law for Treaties?' in E Cannizzaro (ed), *The Law of Treaties Beyond the Vienna Convention* (Oxford, Oxford University Press, 2011) 425.

Cannizzaro, E and Palchetti, P, '*Ultra Vires* Acts of International Organizations' in J Klabbers and Å Wallendahl (eds), *Research Handbook on the Law of International Organizations* (Cheltenham, Edward Elgar, 2011) 365.

den Dekker, G, 'The HCCH and Functional Immunity: On Origins, Scope, and Access to Court' in T John et al (eds), *The Elgar Companion to the Hague Conference on Private International Law* (Cheltenham, Edward Elgar, 2020) 11.

de Visscher P and Verhoeven, J, 'L'immunité de juridiction de l'État étranger dans la jurisprudence belge et le projet de convention du Conseil de l'Europe' in *Immunité de juridiction et d'exécution des États* (Brussels, Institut de sociologie, 1971) 35.

Duquet, S and Wouters, J, 'Legal Duties of Diplomats Today' in P Behrens (ed), *Diplomatic Law in a New Millennium* (Oxford, Oxford University Press, 2017) 247.

El Boudouhi, S and Dannenberg, G, 'France' in S Kadelbach et al (eds), *Judging International Human Rights: Courts of General Jurisdiction as Human Rights Courts* (Cham, Springer, 2019) 453.

Elias, O and Thomas, M, 'Administrative Tribunals of International Organizations' in C Giorgetti (ed), *The Rules, Practice, and Jurisprudence of International Courts and Tribunals* (Leiden, Nijhoff, 2012) 159.

El Sawah, S, 'Jurisdictional Immunity of States and Non-Commercial Torts' in T Ruys and N Angelet (eds), *The Cambridge Handbook of Immunities and International Law* (Cambridge, Cambridge University Press, 2019) 142.

Fassbender, B, 'Germany' in A Reinisch (ed), *The Privileges and Immunities of International Organizations in Domestic Courts* (Oxford, Oxford University Press, 2013) 123.

Foakes, J and Denza, E, 'Privileges and Immunities of Diplomatic Agents' in I Roberts (ed), *Satow's Diplomatic Practice*, 7th edn (Oxford, Oxford University Press, 2016) 246.

Foakes, J and O'Keefe, R, 'Article 11' in R O'Keefe and CJ Tams (eds), *The United Nations Convention on Jurisdictional Immunities of States and Their Property: A Commentary* (Oxford, Oxford University Press, 2013) 183.

Fox, H, 'The Restrictive Rule of State Immunity – The 1970s Enactment and Its Contemporary Status' in T Ruys and N Angelet (eds), *The Cambridge Handbook of Immunities and International Law* (Cambridge, Cambridge University Press, 2019) 21.

Francioni, F, 'The Rights of Access to Justice under Customary International Law' in F Francioni (ed), *Access to Justice as a Human Right* (Oxford, Oxford University Press, 2007) 1.

Gallo, D, 'The Right of Access to Justice for the Staff of International Organizations: The Need for a Reform in the Light of the ICJ Advisory Opinion of 1 Feb. 2012' in R Virzo and I Ingravallo (eds), *Evolutions in the Law of International Organizations* (Leiden, Brill Nijhoff, 2015) 509.

Gazzini, T, 'The Relationship between International Legal Personality and the Autonomy of International Organizations' in R Collins and ND White (eds), *International Organizations and the Idea of Autonomy: Institutional Independence in the International Legal Order* (London, Routledge, 2011) 196.

Grant, T, 'Article 2(1)(a)' in R O'Keefe and CJ Tams (eds), *The United Nations Convention on Jurisdictional Immunities of States and Their Property: A Commentary* (Oxford, Oxford University Press, 2013) 40.

Grant, T, 'Article 6' in R O'Keefe and CJ Tams (eds), *The United Nations Convention on Jurisdictional Immunities of States and Their Property: A Commentary* (Oxford, Oxford University Press, 2013) 105.

Gulati, R and John, T, 'Arbitrating Employment Disputes Involving International Organizations' in P Quayle (ed), *The Role of Administrative Law at International Organizations* (Leiden, Brill Nijhoff, 2021).

Iovane, M, 'Conflicts between State-Centred and Human-Centred International Norms' in R Pisillo Mazzeschi and P De Sena (eds), *Global Justice, Human Rights and the Modernization of International Law* (Cham, Springer, 2018) 205.

Neumann, T and Peters, A, 'Switzerland' in A Reinisch (ed), *The Privileges and Immunities of International Organizations in Domestic Courts* (Oxford, Oxford University Press, 2013) 241.

Novak, G and Reinisch, A, 'Desirable Standards for the Design of Administrative Tribunals from the Perspective of Domestic Courts' in O Elias (ed), *The Development and Effectiveness of International Administrative Law* (Leiden, Brill Nijhoff, 2012) 273.

Okeke, EC, 'The Tension between the Jurisdictional Immunity of International Organizations and the Right of Access to Court' in P Quayle (ed), *The Role of Administrative Law at International Organizations* (Leiden, Brill Nijhoff, 2021) 25.

Orakhelashvili, A, 'Jurisdictional Immunity of States and General International Law – Explaining the *Jus Gestionis* v. *Jus Imperii* Divide' in T Ruys and N Angelet (eds), *The Cambridge Handbook of Immunities and International Law* (Cambridge, Cambridge University Press, 2019) 105.

Orakhelashvili, A, 'Jurisdictional Immunity of International Organizations: From Abstract Functionality to Absolute Immunity' in A Orakhelashvili (ed), *Research Handbook on Jurisdiction and Immunities in International Law* (Cheltenham, Edward Elgar, 2015) 497.

Orzan, MF, 'International Organizations and Immunity from Legal Process: An Uncertain Evolution' in R Virzo and I Ingravallo (eds), *Evolutions in the Law of International Organizations* (Leiden, Brill Nijhoff, 2015) 364.

Palombino, FM, 'Introduction' in FM Palombino (ed), *Duelling for Supremacy: International Law vs. National Fundamental Principles* (Cambridge, Cambridge University Press, 2019) 1.

Pavoni, R, 'The Myth of the Customary Nature of the United Nations Convention on State Immunity: Does the End Justify the Means?' in A van Aaken and I Motoc (eds), *European Convention on Human Rights and General International Law* (Oxford, Oxford University Press, 2018).

Pavoni, R, 'Italy' in A Reinisch (ed), *The Privileges and Immunities of International Organizations in Domestic Courts* (Oxford, Oxford University Press, 2013) 155.

Pavoni, R, 'Human Rights and the Immunities of Foreign States and International Organizations' in E de Wet and J Vidmar (eds), *Hierarchy in International Law: The Place of Human Rights* (Oxford, Oxford University Press, 2012) 71.

Peters, A, 'Immune against Constitutionalisation?' in A Peters et al (eds), *Immunities in the Age of Global Constitutionalism* (Leiden, Brill Nijhoff, 2015) 1.

Reinisch, A, 'Immunity of Property, Funds, and Assets (Article II Section 2 General Convention)' in A Reinisch (ed), *The Conventions on the Privileges and Immunities of the United Nations and its Specialized Agencies: A Commentary* (Oxford, Oxford University Press, 2016) 63.

Reinisch, A, 'Privileges and Immunities' in JK Cogan et al (eds), *The Oxford Handbook of International Organizations* (Oxford, Oxford University Press, 2016) 1048.

Reinisch, A, 'Transnational Judicial Conversations on the Personality, Privileges, and Immunities of International Organizations – An Introduction' in A Reinisch (ed), *The Privileges and Immunities of International Organizations in Domestic Courts* (Oxford, Oxford University Press, 2013) 11.

Reinisch, A and Novak, G, 'International Organizations' in A Nollkaemper and A Reinisch (eds), *International Law in Domestic Courts: A Casebook* (Oxford, Oxford University Press, 2018) 170.

Reinisch, A and Wurm, J, 'International Finance Institutions before National Courts' in DD Bradlow and DB Hunter (eds), *International Finance Institutions and International Law* (Alphen aan den Rijn, Wolters Kluwer, 2010) 103.

Rodgers, L, 'The Inviolability of Diplomatic Agents in the Context of Employment' in P Behrens (ed), *Diplomatic Law in a New Millennium* (Oxford, Oxford University Press, 2017) 113.

Ryngaert, C, 'Belgium' in A Reinisch (ed), *The Privileges and Immunities of International Organizations in Domestic Courts* (Oxford, Oxford University Press, 2013) 55.

Sari, A, 'The Immunities of Visiting Forces' in T Ruys and N Angelet (eds), *The Cambridge Handbook of Immunities and International Law* (Cambridge, Cambridge University Press, 2019) 559.

Sarooshi, D and Tzanakopoulos, A, 'United Kingdom' in A Reinisch (ed), *The Privileges and Immunities of International Organizations in Domestic Courts* (Oxford, Oxford University Press, 2013) 275.

Saunders, PM, 'Canada' in A Reinisch (ed), *The Privileges and Immunities of International Organizations in Domestic Courts* (Oxford, Oxford University Press, 2013) 73.

Schmalenbach, K, 'Dispute Settlement (Article VIII Sections 29–30 General Convention)' in A Reinisch (ed), *The Conventions on the Privileges and Immunities of the United Nations and its Specialized Agencies: A Commentary* (Oxford, Oxford University Press, 2016) 529.

Sorel, J-M and Boré Eveno, V, 'Article 31 – General Rule of Interpretation' in O Corten and P Klein (eds), *The Vienna Conventions on the Law of Treaties: A Commentary* (Oxford, Oxford University Press, 2011) 804.

Spadinger, W, 'Private Domestic Staff: A Risk Group on the Fringe of the Convention' in P Behrens (ed), *Diplomatic Law in a New Millennium* (Oxford, Oxford University Press, 2017) 132.

Talvik, A, 'The ILO Administrative Tribunal: Shaping the Internal Review Process' in A Talvik (ed), *Best Practices in Resolving Employment Disputes in International Organizations* (Geneva, International Labour Office, 2015) 63.

Thévenot-Werner, A-M, 'The Right of Staff Members to a Tribunal as a Limit to the Jurisdictional Immunity of International Organisations in Europe' in A Peters et al (eds), *Les acteurs à l'ère du constitutionnalisme global – Actors in the age of global constitutionalism* (Paris, Société de legislation comparée, 2014) 111.

van Alebeek, R, 'Part III: Proceedings in Which State Immunity Cannot Be Invoked' in R O'Keefe and CJ Tams (eds), *The United Nations Convention on Jurisdictional Immunities of States and Their Property: A Commentary* (Oxford, Oxford University Press, 2013) 153.

van Alebeek, R and Pavoni, R, 'Immunities of States and their Officials' in A Nollkaemper and A Reinisch (eds), *International Law in Domestic Courts: A Casebook* (Oxford, Oxford University Press, 2018) 100.

van Drooghenbroek, S, 'Labour Law Litigation and Fair Trial under Article 6 ECHR' in F Dorssemont et al (eds), *The European Convention on Human Rights and the Employment Relation* (Oxford, Hart Publishing, 2014) 159.

Verhoeven, J, 'Les immunités propres aux organes ou autres agents des sujets du droit international' in J Verhoeven (ed), *Le droit international des immunités: contestation ou consolidation?* (Paris, Larcier, 2004) 61.

Villalpando, S, 'The Law of the International Civil Service' in JK Cogan et al (eds), *The Oxford Handbook of International Organizations* (Oxford, Oxford University Press, 2016) 1069.

Vinuesa, RE, 'Argentina' in A Reinisch (ed), *The Privileges and Immunities of International Organizations in Domestic Courts* (Oxford, Oxford University Press, 2013) 17.

Walter, C and Preger, F, 'Immunities of Civil Servants of International Organisations' in T Ruys and N Angelet (eds), *The Cambridge Handbook of Immunities and International Law* (Cambridge, Cambridge University Press, 2019) 542.

Wouters, J, Duquet, S and Meuwissen, K, 'The Vienna Conventions on Diplomatic and Consular Relations' in AF Cooper et al (eds), *The Oxford Handbook of Modern Diplomacy* (Oxford, Oxford University Press, 2013) 510.

INDEX

Introductory Note

References such as '178–79' indicate (not necessarily continuous) discussion of a topic across a range of pages. Wherever possible in the case of topics with many references, these have either been divided into sub-topics or only the most significant discussions of the topic are listed. Because the entire work is about the 'immunities' and 'employment law', the use of these terms (and certain others which occur constantly throughout the book) as entry points has been minimized. Information will be found under the corresponding detailed topics.

www.ingramcontent.com/pod-product-compliance
Lightning Source LLC
Chambersburg PA
CBHW071352220926
51613CB00008B/95
9781509952977